LAND SPECULATION

Also by Brigadier General Oppenheimer and available from The Interstate:

COWBOY ARITHMETIC

"Cattle as an Investment"

COWBOY ECONOMICS

"Rural Land as an Investment"

COWBOY LITIGATION

"Cattle and the Income Tax"

(with James D. Keast)

MARCH TO THE SOUND OF THE DRUMS

LAND SPECULATION

An Evaluation and Analysis

by

Harold L. Oppenheimer

THE INTERSTATE
Printers & Publishers, Inc.
Danville, Illinois

Library of Congress catalog card number: 72-83481

Preface

In a newspaper dated September 24, 1972, there was an announcement that the federal government was planning to take 3,200,000 additional agricultural acres out of private ownership or use to expand the national park system. On the financial page it was indicated that short yearling steers hit 44¢ per pound, steer calves 52¢ per pound, and culled slaughter cows 27¢ per pound. Gold on the international market was at $65 per ounce.

If any agricultural economist had predicted these situations in 1970, he would have been recommended for the booby hatch. The essence of the above is that the agricultural and rural land industry is in a state of violent transition.

The prices noted have caused the rentals on large ranches to go up 50% in the last six months. The 80% de facto devaluation of the dollar is causing a vigorous revival of European interest in U. S. rural land. The Russian grain purchase has jumped futures by 30%, throwing all feedlot operations out of kilter. The dramatic effect of the 7% investment credit on breeding stock and its possible removal in 1973 could swing cow prices 20% in either direction. Nobody dares to predict the effect of a bill establishing a $2.20 per hour minimum wage for agricultural workers which would be applied to all farms and ranches engaged in interstate commerce.

At the risk of the booby hatch treatment, I shall make a prediction:

If, by the year 1976, the following are true—

1. 400-pound steer calves are selling at 56¢ per pound.
2. Culled cows are at 30¢ per pound.
3. Because of the new minimum wage bill, labor costs per cow on a 2,000-head ranch are at 30% of a 400-cow ranch.
4. Rents are at $85 per cow on a 2,000-head ranch.
5. Corn is at $1.65 per bushel.
6. Gold is at $75 per ounce.
7. 6% of our range land has been absorbed for non-livestock purposes.

Then: A 2,000-cow ranch in a single land assemblage with reasonable handling facilities will be selling for double its 1972 price.

H. L. Oppenheimer

September 1972

Table of Contents

PART I

BACKGROUND AND POLITICAL HISTORY

Chapter I

The Long-Range Play in Land Speculation

The United States, including Alaska and Hawaii, has approximately 3,550,000 square miles of land and had a 1960 population of around 180,000,000 people. Of the land area about 590,000 square miles are in Alaska with very limited agricultural use. Based on 640 acres (one section) to the square mile and excluding Alaska, we find approximately 2,000,000,000 acres in the United States. About half of this area could be called agriculturally productive.

"By the middle of the 20th century there were more than 4,775,000 farms in the United States covering more than 1,150,000,000 acres of which about 330,000,000 were under cultivation."[1]

Between 1920 and 1960 approximately 60,000,000 acres of crop land used to produce feed for horses and mules were released for other purposes by the switch to tractors. Because of mechanization, fertilizers, new hybrid seeds, and irrigation, farm output increased 36% between 1940 and 1956 with very little addition in acreage.

"The number of persons on farms declined steadily after 1910, with the decline accelerating after 1940. In 1956 only 13.3% of the nation's population was on farms, compared with nearly 35% in 1910. Farm employment showed a similar decline from 13,555,000 in 1910 to 7,869,000 in 1956."[2]

In general, the productivity per man hour in agriculture during the last 20 years has increased more rapidly than in the rest of the American economy. However, this general statement hides the fact that in many areas it has stayed constant but in areas where large land assemblages have taken place, permitting the use of modern techniques and equipment, the increase has been phenomenal, hitting figures like 300% and 400%.

At first glance it looks as if this increased productivity rate will go on forever and our great-grandchildren are still going to be trying to get rid of food surpluses. However, let us take a second glance at the picture:

---

[1] *Encylopaedia Britannica*, Vol. 22, 1962, p. 848B.
[2] *Idem.*

1. We have seen 60,000,000 acres of top crop land that used to feed horses and mules go "kerchunk" into human food production. This is about 20% of the land suitable for cultivation.

2. We have seen in the arid states almost every drop of run-off water allocated for irrigation and municipalities, with half of the western states now in the courts fighting over the water. There are *no* big western streams flowing into the sea with unused water. Water tables, artesian wells, etc., are rapidly deteriorating and it is highly questionable whether new lands going into irrigation will match the lands going out because of water consumption in these states for non-agricultural use.

3. Only large assembled tracts of land can use the new equipment. You can't use a $50,000 self-propelled hay conditioner and pelletizer in an area of 100-acre alfalfa fields. It is easier to talk about a 2,000-acre field than it is to assemble it from multiple ownerships. Land is now moving into strong hands, as it has done in Europe. Further assemblage into the large economically productive units is going to be a slow and expensive process.

4. Only a really cataclysmic event, such as the desalinization of sea water at such a cheap rate that it could be pumped inland to compete with run-off water for crop irrigation, could reverse this trend. However, even the strongest enthusiasts of this program do not think it will be cheap enough to be used for more than industrial and municipal use, at least in this century.

Now, on the other hand, we are facing some Malthusian facts:

1. Our population is increasing at 2½% per year on a geometric progression. The World War II babies are now having babies of their own. In 1982, there will be 80,000,000 more Americans.

2. Most of the original American cities started in areas of good crop land and fertile soil along the river bottoms. They started as agricultural communities or as trade centers for agricultural areas. As they grew they took in surrounding land. Most of this is our best agricultural land.

3. Every year, for roads, housing developments, parks, water reservoirs, military bases, airports, and factories, approximately 1% of the total American land is being taken up. This amounts to over 2,000,000 acres. Because of the historical background mentioned in the preceeding paragraph, two-thirds of this comes out of our most productive agricultural land. In 20 years, this will amount to 40,000,000 acres!

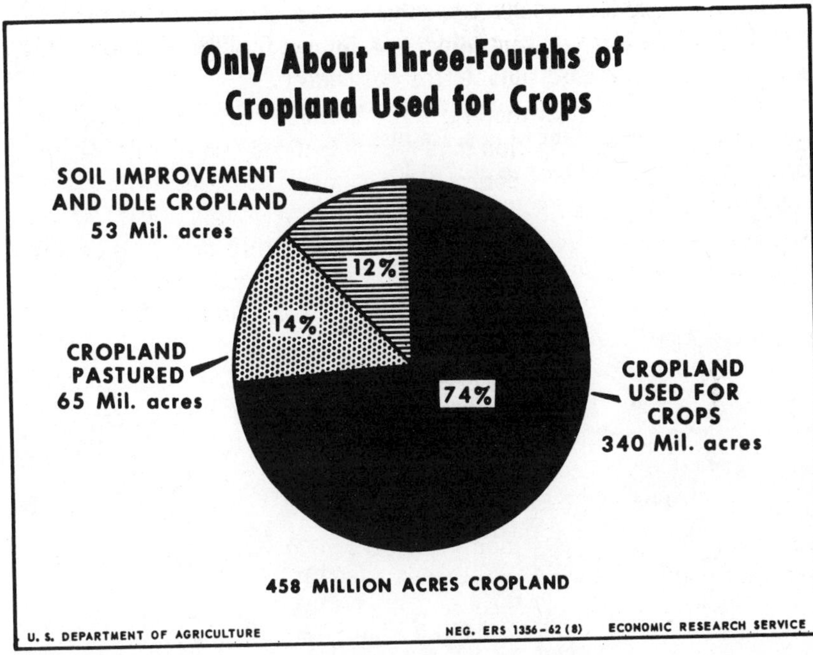

Of the approximate 2 billion acres in the United States (excluding Alaska), about 70% of this land is under private ownership and the balance is Federal or state land. Of the former, about one-third is suitable for cultivation. The distribution of these 458 million acres is in accordance with the above chart. (Courtesy, U.S. Department of Agriculture)

4. Land is the only commodity of which there is only so much on the earth's surface. It can't be overproduced in a factory or floated in a new stock issue.

Conclusion: Unless someone repeals the law of supply and demand, productive agricultural land is one of the best long-range investments on the market.

Over the years in Western Europe and Latin America there has been an element of social prestige connected with the ownership of large tracts of rural land that made most of this land unavailable at any price and put a totally non-economic premium on what little hit the market. Even in this country enough of this factor exists that the present prices are so high that on net leases it is difficult to get more than 3% or 4%.

However, apart from the special growth and demand patterns which seem to indicate a steady increase in value *and* a steady increase in rent, we have an element of security and stability matched by few other investments.

Quoting from Bernard Baruch's autobiography:

"I have heard, for example, that one of the Rothschilds, who certainly were among the wisest financiers of their day, set out to make secure the fortune of a loved one. He decided to invest this fortune in Austrian and German government bonds, English consols above par, and French rentes above par. When the story was told me many years later, this estate had shrunk to only a fifth of its original worth. The Austrian and German securities were completely valueless, of course, while the others had depreciated considerably.

"One cannot, in other words, make an investment and take for granted that its worth will remain unchanged. New sources of supply coming from hitherto untapped areas of the world may transform the competitive position of a company, as will changes in people's habits or technological innovations. Often something will shrink in value because of one discovery, as coal did in relation to oil and electricity, only to be given new economic life by another development such as the new chemical uses being made of coal.

"Actually one can point to only a few things whose value has resisted the change of time down through the centuries – and even then not without fluctuations. Among these I would list some minerals like gold, silver, and copper; precious stones; works of art; and crop-bearing lands.

"Even with these things one must add the qualification 'at least so far.' The development of cultured pearls, for example, has nearly destroyed the old value of pearls. As for gold, some governments, including our own, have passed laws making its possession illegal."[3]

In connection with "crop-producing land," Mr. Baruch may have been including pastures producing grass crops that could be consumed by livestock. In connection with "works of art" he must also have been aware that paintings of Rosa Bonheur were going for $200,000 a half century ago and today can be bought for $10,000. However, in common with works of art, tracts of land cannot be manufactured and no two are alike.

However, when Mr. Baruch referred to income-producing agricultural land, he must have implied three additional qualifications: (1) The land had to have sufficient water to produce its crops. (2) It had to be in a marketing area or near transportation so that its crops could be sold. (3) It had to be of sufficient size that there would be enough produce to support a man and his family.

[3]*My Own Story*, Bernard Baruch, Henry Holt & Co., Inc., 1957, p. 255.

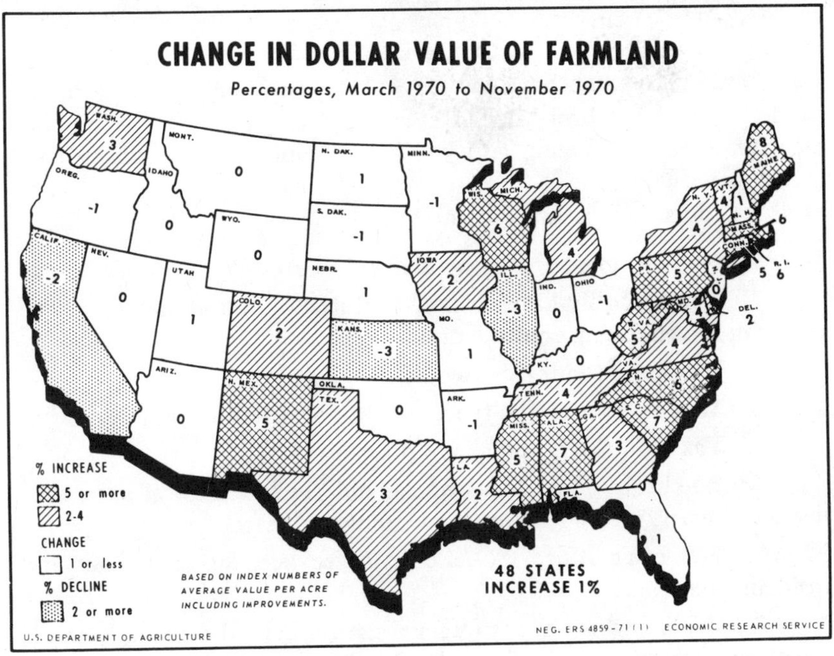

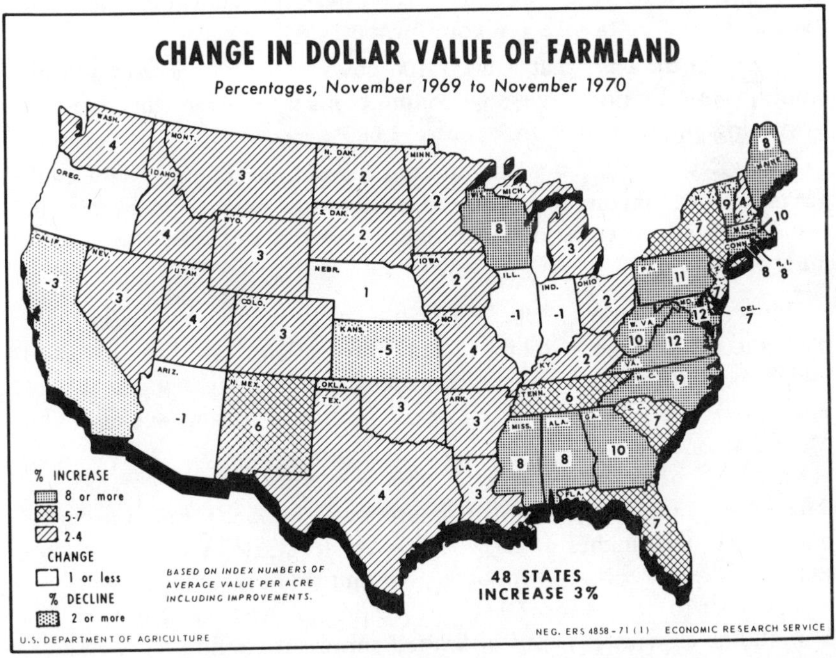

Despite the disastrous drop in the stock market, land prices still increased 3% in 1970. Variations in states ran from 12 to —1. Historically, 6% per year has been the average west of the Mississippi.

For example, if you own 640 acres that you bought from a homesteader, who went broke, in an area of Wyoming that can support only 20 cows to a section and you are surrounded by a strong land owner who will not sell or lease any more land to you, you do not have "productive agricultural land."

1. Nobody can support himself on 20 cows.

2. You probably have no stock water and can't afford the $2,000 to put in a well, pump, and windmill.

3. Fencing on four sides would cost $3,200.

4. Maintenance on the fence would cost $100 per year.

5. Taxes on the property are probably $30 per year.

6. You have had it! This land can only be leased to the surrounding land owner, who might pay you enough for taxes.

7. You can't afford to build fence to keep his cattle out and maintain the fence.

8. Wyoming is an open range state where the small operator must *fence out* his neighbor's cattle. You have no claim for damages if the neighbor's cattle are on your property.

9. On the basis that it takes 100 cows to support a man and his family, you do not have an economic investment in this part of Wyoming unless you own or lease 3,000 acres.

10. Besides the fence and water problem, on 20 cows you can't get any rent from anybody but the contiguous owner because no one could even afford to send a man over to watch and feed this small a number.

We will now repeat that the previous references to the speculative play and long-range stability of agricultural land refer to that land which has sufficient size, water, and access to a market that it can produce a salable product at a profit or can be rented to someone else who can do so.

Recently there has arisen a phenomenon known in the trade as a "medicine show." A group of promoters and publicity men purchases one of the old ranches of 30,000 acres in, let's say, Arizona. On this ranch it takes 60 acres to support a cow and there is sufficient water in a good year to handle just 500 head. Additional well water is mostly a 1 in 100 shot, with it being in limited supply if found.

Twenty modern homes will just about consume as much water as 500 cows, without allowing anything for lawns and gardens.

This group then proceeds to divide the 30,000 acres into 3,000 "ranch sites" of 10 acres each and sells them at $1,000 apiece with $50 down and $5 per month for the rest of your life.

One-third of the cash received goes to advertising in the New York and Chicago papers, one-third goes to the attorneys preparing the deeds and abstracts, one-sixth represents the cost of the promoters, and one-sixth is the promoters' profit. As operational ranch land the property was worth $15 per acre. The Chicago bus driver who buys this "Arizona ranch" at $100 per acre to "retire on" or as an "inflation hedge" is in for a disappointment.

The term "medicine show," incidentally, results from the brass bands, circus barkers, chorus girls, free beer, etc., that are occasionally used at a highly advertised "big land sale." Sometimes the promoters actually recreate the frenzy of the Oklahoma Land Rush.

At first these types of deals were looked on with great amusement by the local people in many of the western states. However, they suddenly realized that an increasing number of the old integrated ranches that formed a major part of their states' productive income were being broken up. Enough of the new buyers would retain ownership, even if 60% defaulted on their notes, ever to permit these ranches to be legally put back together again as economic units.

While no known Federal law is apparently being violated, the state legislatures are becoming alarmed and are passing laws to make these "developers" furnish proof that they can produce the roads, water, and utilities they advertise. It looks as if these laws will put about 90% of such developers out of business.

However, I personally know of about 3,000,000 acres of productive grazing land that have been taken out of economic use in the last few years by this gimmick. To my knowledge less than 3% of this land has ever seen a road put in or a house built. This land has to be added to the acreage that has legitimately been taken out of production by non-agricultural use.

Despite the temporary aggravations of crop surpluses and grain storage costs, every administration, Republican or Democratic, has instinctively felt that the preservation and improvement of our American soil constituted the single most important element in our long-range national prosperity and survival.

The Federal Government has attempted to promote this objective by numerous programs, some of which involve:

1. Making large-scale grants to the states and state universities to maintain agricultural research stations as well as the nationwide county

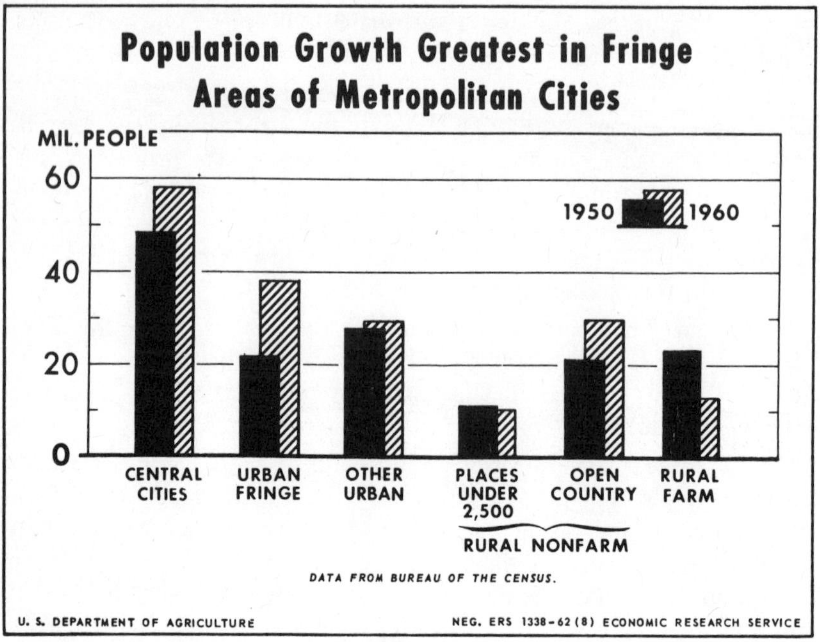

In the ten-year period 1950 to 1960 suburban areas doubled in population, "open country" substantially increased, small towns lost slightly, and "strictly rural" areas lost 40%. (Courtesy U.S. Department of Agriculture)

agents system providing advisory services for farmers and ranchers at every local level.

2. Constructing, sponsoring, and participating in massive soil reclamation, water, and irrigation systems over the nation.

3. Participating directly with the individual farmer and rancher by cash contributions through the ASC program in brush clearance, dam and pond construction, insect and weed eradication, etc. Tied in with this program has been a rigid control and supervisory system set up through the Bureau of Land Management, Forest Service, and other government agencies to prevent the abuse of Federal and state lands from overcultivation, overgrazing, and lack of weed and erosion control. In many areas where ranchers are tied in with attached government leases or with government cash contributions, the various Federal agencies have been able to use these factors as leverage to get the land owners to engage in the proper soil conservation and improvement programs on adjacent land of their own not directly involved in the government program.

4. Attempting through indirect participation to further this objective by granting substantial tax subsidies to encourage large ranchers as well as wealthy absentee owners to continue in these directions.

Many of the following points are common to all real estate, but some are unique to agricultural real estate.

1. There has been very little objection to being able to deduct at the time of purchase the current year plus 12 months' interest in advance at the legal maximum rate in the state concerned.

2. On brand new fencing, the government permits a ten-year longevity for depreciation purposes. On most older ranches, the fencing can easily be demonstrated to have had an average previous life of five years, which gives you five years remaining longevity, for a depreciation rate of 20% per year. On the large western ranches with major tracts of Taylor grazing land or state land attached to the deeded land, recent decisions of the Bureau of Land Management have acknowledged in most cases that the fencing on the government land belongs to the lessee. In the more arid sections of the country, on a given ranch purchase, an extremely high proportion of fence value can be established relative to land value, particularly when a high proportion of the cost can be allocated to the acquisition of a government lease. This usually results in a situation in which, at least during the first five years, while this depreciation lasts, it matches or exceeds the amortization payments of the mortgage.

3. While not unique to rural real estate, older improvements here are also entitled to the 150% declining balance depreciation rate.

While the preceding is attractive, it is in the liberality of the maintenance and improvement treatment that the government demonstrates its policy of using tax subsidies for encouraging actions furthering the public welfare.

1. The current costs of maintenance, repairs, reseeding, fertilizing, clearing of irrigation ditches, etc., are immediately deductible.

2. Where it can be demonstrated that certain tracts of land were at one time used for cultivation and grazing but, through poor soil practices, lack of fertilizer, and carelessness, the land gradually deteriorated in value, brush encroached on former pastures, the irrigation ditches grew over, and wind and water erosion decreased the productive value — in these cases you can "restore the land to its original use." In other words, you can deduct the cost of clearing off the encroaching brush, cleaning up the old irrigation ditches, bulldozing out the erosion ditches, and putting in fertilizer to restore the original soil nutrients.

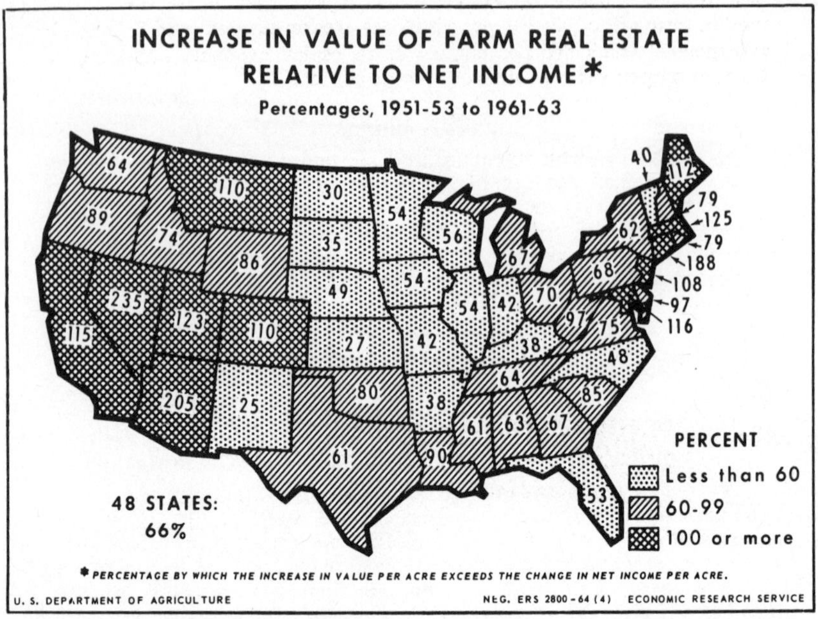

Agricultural productivity or net rental income bears very little relationship to land value. A 3% net return on market value is realistic; 5% is fantastic; 8%, and somebody is lying. (Courtesy, U.S. Department of Agriculture)

This is all currently deductible and does not have to be capitalized and depreciated.

3. Going further, in the 1954 Tax Bill, Congress passed Section 175. In essence, the unique "Soil and Water Conservation Expenditures" section permits rural land owners to get a tax subsidy in a field that has never been permitted before. This particular section of the law has the promise of being the most controversial and litigated area with which the Internal Revenue Department has been connected in a long while. The test cases are only now beginning to come down the pike and form a general pattern. The depreciation recapture provision of the 1969 Act also includes the recapture on sale of these deductions, but, while you retain ownership, you get them. This is such an important part of the rural real estate investment field that the first three subsections are quoted here in their entirety:

SEC. 175. SOIL AND WATER CONSERVATION EXPENDITURES

(Sec. 175 (a))

(a) In General—A taxpayer engaged in the business of farming may treat expenditures which are paid or incurred by him during the taxable year for the purpose of soil or water conservation in respect of land used in farming, or for the prevention of erosion of land used in farming, as expenses which are not chargeable to capital account. The expenditures so treated shall be allowed as a deduction.

(Sec. 175(b))

(b) Limitation—The amount deductible under subsection (a) for any taxable year shall not exceed 25 percent of the gross income derived from farming during the taxable year. If for any taxable year the total of the expenditures treated as expenses which are not chargeable to capital account exceeds 25 percent of the gross income derived from farming during the taxable year, such excess shall be deductible for succeeding taxable years in order of time; but the amount deductible under this section for any one such succeeding taxable year (including the expenditures actually paid or incurred during the taxable year) shall not exceed 25 percent of the gross income derived from farming during the taxable year.

(Sec. 175 (c))

(c) Definitions.—For purposes of subsection (a) —

(1) The term "expenditures which are paid or incurred by him during the taxable year for the purpose of soil or water conservation in respect of land used in farming, or for the prevention of erosion of land used in farming" means expenditures paid or incurred for the treatment or moving of earth, including (but not limited to) leveling, grading and terracing, contour furrowing, the construction, control, and protection of diversion channels, drainage ditches, earthen dams, watercourses, outlets, and ponds, the eradication of brush, and the planting of windbreaks. Such term does not include —

(A) the purchase, construction, installation, or improvement of structures, appliances, or facilities which are of a character which is subject to the allowance for depreciation provided in section 167, or

(B) any amount paid or incurred which is allowable as a deduction without regard to this section.

Notwithstanding the preceding sentences, such term also includes any amount, not otherwise allowable as a deduction, paid or incurred to satisfy any part of an assessment levied by a soil or water conservation or drainage district to defray expenditures made by such district which if paid or incurred by the taxpayer, would without regard to this sentence constitute expenditures deductible under this section.

(2) The term "land used in farming" means land used (before or simultaneously with the expenditures described in paragraph (1)) by the taxpayer or his tenant for the production of crops, fruits, or other agricultural products or for the sustenance of livestock.[4]

What are some of the bad points about rural land investment?

1. To be economically productive and to take advantage of modern techniques and equipment, the land areas have to be large. If they are large, they are expensive, and when great sums of money are

[4]Sec. 175 (a), (b), (c), *Internal Revenue Code*, Commerce Clearing House, Inc., 1960, pp. 4075-4076.

involved, it is not easy to find a quick sale when you want to get your capital out. You do not have liquidity.

2. Because of the crop surplus situation and the general depression of agriculture (which, however, I believe is only temporary), you have to be satisfied at this time with a 3% or 4% net return if you are going to put the property out to rent with a financially responsible tenant.

3. An incompetent tenant or poor management practices can substantially deteriorate the worth of your investment in a short period of time, just as a competent tenant or good practices can substantially increase its value. This is the type of investment that you have to watch personally or you have to hire somebody competent to watch for you.

4. The income, in addition to being small, is not steady either. It is subject to violent fluctuations if you are operating the property yourself, with a bonanza one year and no income for several years thereafter. No investment in the United States is so subject to weather conditions. If your principal crop is wheat, a 30-minute hailstorm before

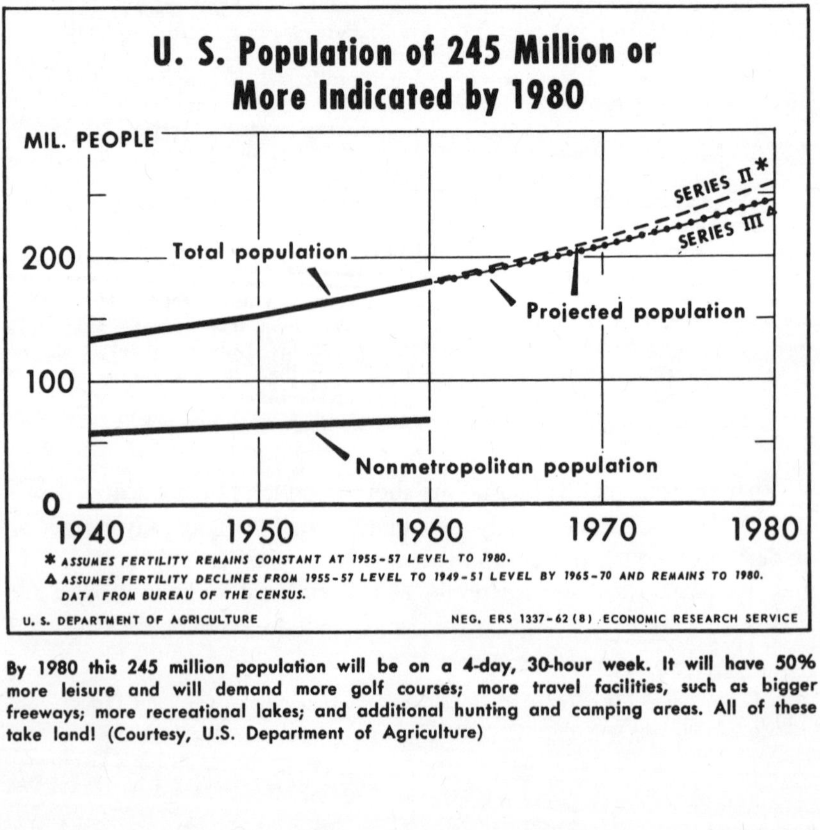

By 1980 this 245 million population will be on a 4-day, 30-hour week. It will have 50% more leisure and will demand more golf courses; more travel facilities, such as bigger freeways; more recreational lakes; and additional hunting and camping areas. All of these take land! (Courtesy, U.S. Department of Agriculture)

harvest can completely wipe out a year's work and investment. The operational end of farming is no game for people with weak nerves. Contrary to the popular supposition that most farmers and ranchers are of a steady, conservative, "play it safe" temperament, the opposite is the general case. Most of us are wild speculators and gamblers, quite the equal of anything found at Monte Carlo. This has been especially true in recent years as most forms of agriculture have become specialized. In the old days, a farmer had a garden patch, three or four crops, a couple of milk cows, some chickens, some hogs, and a variety of other livestock. The collapse of a given market, a sudden storm, or a bit of an epidemic couldn't hurt him too much and he always had enough to eat. Today, on the half dozen Kansas ranches with which I am familiar, each running over 1,000 head of cattle, I do not believe that a single one of these ranchers maintains a milk cow, and all of the family food comes from the local grocery store. As a matter of fact, I don't believe that any of these particular ranchers ever slaughters any of his own beef, and his wife gets that in the grocery store too.

If someone has an hour to spare, he can more productively use it in patching a fence or repairing a tractor than in milking a cow. Things have come a long way from the "old family farm."

Here is our summary of the whole field of rural land investment.

1. Operationally and income-wise, it is highly speculative, but on the long pull for intrinsic worth it has no equal for stability and security within the investment field.

2. Because of the permanent value of our land to the American economy, the government has granted tax subsidies matched in few other fields.

3. On a narrow equity land purchase with prepaid interest, high depreciation, and the deductibility of both current and long-range capital improvements on soil and water conservation, there is no easier way for converting income dollars into a permanent, ever-improving capital asset.

4. With an annual population increase of 2% on a geometric progression and an annual removal of 2,000,000 acres of agricultural land for non-agricultural use, there is no area in the investment field that promises a surer and more spectacular play in a 20-year period.

Chapter II

The Big Spreads

This chapter is going to be a thumbnail historical sketch of the big cattle empires which rose and fell on our western range. We are not going to try to cover all of them and we will limit ourselves to those which have at one time or another directly or indirectly operated over tracts of ground in excess of 600,000 acres.

Because of the almost complete impossibility of ever assembling this size tract from groups of small holdings once the land has been split up into little farms and ranches, you will find that almost all of the big spreads originated early in the 1800's or just after the Civil War and usually before or just after the territory became a state.

The general pattern involves a strong character with capital acquired by inheritance or from some other enterprise moving into an area which consists largely of open range, government lands, and Indian territory. He proceeded to acquire choice tracts of land around the water holes and established his headquarters. In some areas he acquired the watered districts by recorded deed; in other areas he held them by force-of-arms. His cattle ranged in common with other large ranches as far as they could graze from water. The amount of land they occupied was generally limited only by the amount of capital he had available to buy cattle and hire gunmen.

Naturally, when the range was unlimited and the only competition for grass was with wild game, there was no problem except for Indian forays. However, when the cattle population expanded sufficiently that a drought put a squeeze on pasture, then the strong survived and the weak went under. As things became more civilized, various states, territories and districts developed a law of "customary range." This was a mutual agreement among the ranchers that apart from the deeded homesteads and water holes, the use of certain general areas of range land belonged to the person who got there first and who had been grazing it for a number of years. This was not usually limited to a single person but to groups of five or six ranchers in the general area and their immediate relatives. Boundaries of "customary range" were usually large rivers, generally insurmountable mountain crests, and other natural obstacles that cattle would not usually cross.

After the Civil War, fences and barbed wire came into common use and land rights were more clearly delineated. Formal title was taken from the government in many areas with regular deeds being recorded.

About this time in the more settled and congested areas it became customary to record water rights. On given streams the men who first recorded had certain priorities and various use rights which could not be infringed by late comers even if they moved upstream to the original settler.

In the very complex system of laws and customs that developed, range rights, range leases, and water rights could be bought and sold as well as deeded land. Most of the "big spreads" that existed in the late 19th Century and continued on into the early 20th Century or are still in existence, have possibly 30% or 40% deeded land, controlling all of the water and good meadows. This land is "checkerboarded" with the various tracts of federal or state grazing land controlled by lease permits from one or another bureau of the government or state involved.

"In 1906, Theodore Roosevelt enlarged the forest reserves and began the active policy of conserving, improving and enlarging the public lands. Now 405,595,899 acres are federally owned in the eleven "Public Lands" states of the West. The proportion controlled by the government varies from 35% in Montana to 87% in Nevada with an average of 54% for all eleven.

Supervision of this mighty slice of America is divided among the Departments of the Interior, National Defense, and Agriculture with eight major bureaus (National Forests, Grazing Districts, Indian Reservations, National Parks, Soil Conservation, Navy, Army, Fish and Wildlife) handling the actual administration through even more numerous subdivisions."[1]

Generally speaking, anyone who was strong enough and capable enough to assemble and hold a tract of American land in excess of 400,000 acres had a dramatic impact on the history of his State and in many cases moved on to the national scene, either financially or politically.

We shall start off with the King Ranch which is probably the most famous although it is not the largest as often believed. Also it is not typical of most of the "big spreads" for the following reasons:

1. It was mostly on deeded land.
2. It started over 100 years ago and is still going strong.

---

[1]*Cowboys and Cattle Kings*, Sonnichsen, University of Oklahoma Press, 1950, p. 223.

3. The original King, Kennedy, and Kleberg families have consistently produced leaders every generation and have stayed firmly in control.
4. From the very beginning members of the family have not only been pioneers in ranch administration but all have been of a scientific bent and have been one of the most constructive forces within the entire industry.

THE KING RANCH

Richard King was born July 10, 1824 in New York City of Irish immigrant parents. Almost nothing further is known of his background or lineage. At the age of 11, after being apprenticed to a jeweler, he ran away to sea as a stowaway and subsequent cabin boy on the Desdemona. Over the next ten years he worked himself up to be a pilot and subsequently a captain on the riverboats that plied the coastal ports and rivers along the Gulf of Mexico.

In 1843 he started a long association with another riverboat captain named Mifflin Kennedy who came from a devout Quaker family in Chester County, Pennsylvania. During the period 1846 to 1848 both King and Kennedy were instrumental in supplying the forces of Zachary Taylor along the Rio Grande and subsequent operations into Matamoros and Monterrey.

On March 1, 1850 the firm of M. Kennedy & Company of Brownsville, Texas was organized with four equal partners: King, Kennedy, Charles Stillman, and James O'Donnell. Within a few years this firm had almost a complete monopoly of all trade along the Rio Grande and to all the ports of Northeastern Mexico. It was estimated that the firm consistently averaged out a profit of $40,000 per year on an original capital investment of $80,000. Besides that, the partners participated individually in joint ventures with others on speculations with the cargoes.[2] There is no question but that the purchasing power of the dollar was ten times during that period what it is today so this became one of the principal businesses of the area.

In 1852, Kennedy married Petra Vela de Vidal, the 26 year old widow of a colonel in the Mexican Army, and the mother of five. The bridegroom accepted the faith of his Catholic bride. The bride came from a major landowning family with connections all along the border. Both King and Kennedy spoke Spanish and had numerous close friends with the top land grant families in both Mexico and Texas. This may have been one of the explanations of their phenomenal success in both trade and their later land purchase programs.

[2] *The King Ranch*, Tom Lea, Little, Brown & Co., 1957, Vol. I, pp. 1-94.

In 1852, King became interested in land speculation and with a party rode into an area 125 miles north of the Rio Grande near the Santa Gertrudis Creek. He later said to Kennedy, "Land and Livestock have a way of increasing in value. Cattle and horses, sheep and goats, will reproduce themselves into value. But boats—they have a way of wrecking, decaying, falling apart, decreasing in value, and increasing in cost of operation."[3]

In February of 1852 an act of the Texas Legislature had confirmed the ownership of original Spanish and Mexican land grants to rightful heirs and succeeding purchasers. However, the owners had all been driven off by Indians, mustangers (gatherers of wild horses), and assorted border outlaws. King set himself to start purchasing these lands from the heirs and owners who had been driven off and who considered them to be economically worthless without an army of guns to hold them.

His initial purchase was the 15,500 acres of the Rincon de Santa Gertrudis from the widow and heirs of Juan Mendiola on July 25, 1853 for the sum of $300, coming to about 2c per acre.[4] At this time he was a partner with Legs Lewis, a captain in the Texas Rangers, who was able to furnish military support to hold this and subsequent acquisitions. The two built a fortified camp on the Santa Gertrudis which was the beginning of the ranching industry between the Nueces and the Rio Grande.

The drought conditions of 1854 and 1855 enabled King and Lewis to pick up cattle at $5 per head to stock the ranch. To all ranch operations King applied his detailed and meticulous bookkeeping and records that he had used in the steamboat business. Shortly afterwards King's steamboat partner Kennedy started buying lands in the area.

In December of 1854 King married Henrietta Chamberlain, the daughter of a Presbyterian minister from New England. Her father had founded one of the first Protestant churches in the Rio Grande area.

In December of 1860 the firm of R. King & Company was formed for the pooling of all land and livestock interests. King had a three-eighths interest, Kennedy a three-eighths interest, and James Walworth two-eighths. Walworth was another steamboat skipper who had worked for M. Kennedy & Company.

During the war M. Kennedy & Company put many of their boats under Mexican Registry and made huge profits smuggling cotton and

---

[3]*Idem*, p. 100.
[4]*Idem*, p. 105-110.

supplies through the Union blockade. Substantial amounts of King beef went to New Orleans for the Confederacy. After Brownsville was captured by Union troops, King fled his ranch one jump ahead of a Federal cavalry patrol. While the Civil War caused considerable loss, their trading profits, stuck in gold in Matamoros, salvaged both the ranch and the shipping companies after the war.

In 1866 partner Charles Stillman withdrew from the shipping company and retired to New York. There his money from the border developed the National City Bank of New York. Walworth died and King and Kennedy bought his interest from the estate for $50,000. In 1867 and 1868, King and Kennedy divided their holdings and started the stupendous job of fencing with heavy posts and three planks. Barbed wire didn't come in till 1874. With the division King started using the new brand, the Running W. By 1870, they had liquidated most of the shipping company and were putting their full time in ranching.

With the Texas Rangers prohibited by order of the Reconstruction regime, the next ten years were devoted to repelling marauders from across the border. Texas ranchmen estimated that about 200,000 head were being stolen annually. In 1870, The Stock Raisers Association of Western Texas was formed with Mifflin Kennedy as President. In 1874, the Texas Rangers were reconstituted and, under their famous Captain L. H. McNelly, the situation was rapidly brought under control. King, however, had managed to hold his own with his armed retainers, fortified relay stations, and a shotgun loaded with buckshot which he carried instead of the traditional six shooter. Both McNelly and King had their paid informers across the border. As much by this as any other means they were able to be at the right place at the right time.

On June 12, 1875, the Ranger captain caught 12 bandits on the Palo Alto prairie and dumped their bodies in the main square of Brownsville for relatives to identify and claim. The advent of the telegraph line and the ability to alert and assemble both the Rangers and the U. S. Army broke the back of the rustler movement.

Richard King's motto was: "Buy land and never sell." He ultimately acquired title to more than 600,000 acres. "Every land acquisition King ever made was done through lawyers. They transacted the business. They advised King when he had rights to possession. King bought every piece of land he came to own. He sometimes bought one piece again and again to satisfy multiple claimants."[8]

---

[8] *Idem*, p. 300.

Richard King died in 1885. Under the management of his widow and Robert Kleberg, Sr., his son-in-law, the ranch was increased to over 1,200,000 acres. At the death of Mrs. King in 1925, her will provided for some division of the property ten years after her death. However, some parts of it were put back together again. The present King Ranch Corporation has about 735,000 acres.[6]

Aside from their ranch acquisitions and operations, the King, Kennedy and Kleberg families had an astonishing record as experimenters and innovators:

1. They developed the Santa Gertrudis breed, a stabilized cross between the Shorthorn and the Brahma, for tropical countries, which has become one of the principal breeds of the southern U.S. and Latin America.
2. They were one of the principal developers and popularizers of the Quarter Horse, and the King Ranch Quarter Horses have become so famous as to almost be considered a separate sub-breed.
3. They did not oppose the advent of settlers but encouraged them and practically founded and developed the town of Kingsville with the Kleberg Town and Improvement Company.
4. In conjunction with the Bureau of Animal Husbandry and with experiments actually conducted at the ranch, Robert Kleberg was one of the principal leaders in the study and elimination of Texas Cattle Tick Fever. He sponsored the organization of the Texas Livestock Sanitary Commission and was its first head.
5. Robert J. Kleberg, Jr. has been one of the Southwest's leaders in scientific brush eradication and has personally invented much of the equipment generally used.
6. They have currently expanded their integrated operations into Pennsylvania, Australia, Cuba, and Brazil. (The Cuban operations were recently confiscated by Fidel Castro.)

THE BAY STATE LAND AND CATTLE COMPANY

This company was started in the 1870's with Massachusetts and Maine capital in addition to Scottish and English money. Its founders started in western Nebraska with the Half Circle Block. By the spring of 1883, they were expanding fast and bought out the Circle Arrow Ranch for $700,000. The next year they bought out "Coad's Kingdom" stretching from Chimney Rock to Scotts Bluff. In addition, they leased Union Pacific Railroad lands all the way into Wyoming and the Big Horn Basin. Under their new manager, John A. McShane, they built

[6] *The Big Ranch Country*, J. W. Williams, Terry Brothers, 1954, pp. 251-255.

up to a herd of 150,000 head.[7]

Very little of the land was deeded, but by the law of "customary range" enforced by the power of top hired guns and domination of the local state legislatures, they controlled over 3,000,000 acres.

The blizzards of 1886 and 1887 reputedly caused the Bay State a loss of 100,000 head. "The carcasses formed an almost solid covering between Pumpkin Creek and the roughly parallel Wild Cat Mountains; the deep creek bed choked with the dead stock for ten miles. It broke the great power of the Bay State, with all its eastern and British backing, and opened a vast new region to settlers, and to rival cattle empires."[8]

THE FRENCH-GLENN CATTLE COMPANY

At the age of 23, Pete French left the Sacramento Valley in California May 13, 1872 for southeastern Oregon with 1,200 two-year-old Shorthorn heifers, 40 bulls, and 50 picked horses. The cattle and a good supply of ready cash were being supplied by his future father-in-law, the famous Dr. Hugh Glenn of the Jacinto Land Grant and at that time the biggest wheat producer in the U.S.

Over a period of a quarter of a century, until he was shot by a settler he was trying to drive out, he amassed control of over a million acres on a 60,000 head operation running along the Blitzen Valley east of the Steens Mountains. His operation differs from many of the others in that he moved into an area of existing operations and had to assemble his position by purchase and maneuver as well as the customary force. While there were fertile river valleys which permitted the operation of small farms, he had the advantage in this later period of being almost 300 miles from the nearest railhead at Winnemucca, Nevada over very difficult terrain. This put smaller ranchers who did not have the proper staff for a big trail drive at an economic disadvantage.

The growth of his empire was accomplished by both traditional and novel means:

1. He had a large and constant supply of gold and cash through his family connections and his own astute business dealings, to use to buy out his neighbors on various fluctuations of the cattle cycle.
2. He initially purchased strategic tracts of government land at $1 per acre with federal scrip that he had bought at a discount.

---

[7] *The Cattlemen*, Mari Sandoz, Hastings House, 1958, p. 241.
[8] *Idem*, p. 261.

3. He used his purchases in strung out 40 acre strips to tie up the perimeter of each of his ranches on natural mountain boundaries which he immediately blocked with fences along the gaps.
4. He was one of the first men in Oregon to use a surveyor and record deeded water rights for irrigating his low meadows and effectively squeezing out any new settlers.

The following conversations from Elizabeth Lambert Wood's excellent fictionalized biography, "Pete French, Cattle King" may not have taken place but they are typical of the period:

> "Pete," added Rye, his voice again slow and deliberate, "in time you'll change your mind. You'll grow to have a better understanding of events taking place in Harney Valley. The old days of free land and free everything are gone forever. Let's both bless today and let the old times go. The little fellows have come in. There's land enough for all."
>
> "Rye, you know I won't do any of them any harm if they will let me alone. Most of them settled around the edge of P Ranch to fatten off my cattle. They don't call it rustling but they live off me."
>
> "Take it easy, Pete. Why don't you let them do it?"
>
> "Let them do it! Do you know that I tried hiring some and caught them putting their own brands on my calves while I was paying them wages?"[9]
>
> . . . .
>
> Oliver turned white, and, clearly frightened, coughed and sputtered, "I'll have the law on you Pete French. I'm holding out to get this pasture. . . . The land hasn't been surveyed. My rights are just as good as yours, and maybe a whole lot better."
>
> "The only difference," Pete answered, "is that I happened to get here first. Oliver, let me buy you out lock, stock and barrel. I'll pay you a good price, bigger than anyone else will offer."[10]

After Pete French was shot, the empire gradually disintegrated. Part was acquired by Handley's Double O to the north and part by the Swift Packing Company. Subsequently the federal government took over most of the valley for one of our major wildlife sanctuaries.[11]

THE XIT

This ranch is unique in that it was assembled entirely out of deeded land and more or less at one fell swoop rather than over a period of generations like the King Ranch. In 1882 the State of Texas had set aside approximately 3,500,000 acres of land west of the Panhandle to be deeded to the firm that would build a new capitol at Austin. The

---

[9] *Pete French, Cattle King*, Elizabeth Lambert Wood, Binfords and Mort, 1951, p. 207.

[10] *Idem*, p. 215.

[11] *Idem*, p. 229.

contract was awarded to Taylor, Babcock, and Company of Chicago. The deeds were to be accomplished at the completion of the capitol building which was estimated to cost $3,000,000.

To develop, fence, and stock the property, they formed the Capitol Freehold Land and Investment Company, Limited, with principally British capital and acquired $15,000,000. The English officials included such men as the Earl of Aberdeen and the Marquis of Tweeddale, a Scotch banker, who was Chairman of the Board.

B. H. Campbell, the first manager, was one of the first to make extensive use of the new barbed wire and constructed almost 750 miles of fence. Campbell was one of the original founders of the American Shorthorn Breeders' Association and constantly brought in a top quality of Shorthorn and Hereford bulls. By the fall of 1887 the herds totaled nearly 120,000.

A general dissatisfaction of the British stockholders with the operating profits caused them to have Campbell fired, and Abner Taylor and A. G. Boyce were put in charge in 1888.

Early in 1890 Boyce leased 2,000,000 acres between the Yellowstone and the Missouri rivers in Montana—bringing the XIT range to 5,000,000, the giant of them all.[12]

By 1901 the XIT began to sell off its land. By 1906, 2,000,000 acres had been sold. Some of the sales were to the Matador Land and Cattle Company of Dundee, Scotland which now began to move up to first place in Texas.

BEN SNIPES

Ben Snipes was born in 1835 in North Carolina. His family moved to Tennessee when he was two and on to Iowa when he was twelve.

"School was held three months during the winter, when kids could be spared from the farm. I had to walk three miles to school, most of the time through deep snow. After every snow storm, we'd have new trails to break. But we always got to school. I had to know everything our teacher could tell me. I went to that school until I was sixteen and had passed all the grades taught there. I even went back the last year to see if I had missed anything."[13]

In 1854 he arrived in eastern Washington's Yakima Valley with nothing but a horse. Like many another large operator he got his start by supplying beef from a few head of cattle to the various mining strikes after 1849. The following conversation would have been typical

[12] *The Cattlemen*, Mari Sandoz, Hastings House, 1958, pp. 296-325.
[13] *Ben Snipes, Northwest Cattle King*, Roscoe Sheller, Binfords and Mort, 1959.

on a strike in the Canadian Cariboo country on the Fraser River where he really got rolling: "What do you have to pay for beef?" Ben wondered if he might find a way to supply it, as he had done in California.

"BEEF! Man, there ain't no beef! A man came in here a couple of weeks ago with three or four pack mules loaded with meat that was so rotten you couldn't tell what it was. He called it beef but it was mostly bone and gristle. He got a dollar on up to two or three a pound."[14]

In addition to catching a hungry market, Snipes made three other favorable and traditional moves for a future Cattle King: One, he was the first white man to move effectively in on a new public range. Two, he was able to win the confidence and support of the local Indians. Three, he was able to get the equity support and financial backing of a couple of "silent partners."

In 1861, at the age of 26, Ben Snipes was the largest single cattle operator in the Northwest. The winter of 1862, however, wiped out 70% of his herds and he determined never again not to have reserves of hay and winter feed. The winter had been just as hard on all the other neighboring ranchers but they did not have his stamina and he was able to buy out their herds and range rights at distress prices the next spring.

"You've just bought me out, Ben. I'm sick of the whole business. I'll take your twelve hundred now. The whole deal is yours and so is the risk." Once more Ben Snipes had the entire Valley to himself.[15]

From a personal standpoint he was noteworthy for dressing unobtrusively, never drinking, never smoking, and seldom swearing. He upbred the livestock of the entire area by bringing in Durham bulls and Hambletonian horses to cross with the native animals.

With his hay reserves and large supplies of cash he survived the disastrous winter of 1871-72 and bought out his neighbors in volume the following spring. Cows were going at $6 per head that had been selling at $100 three years before.

By 1874 he may have owned over 125,000 head grazing on a land empire the size of England.

The drought of 1880 on overgrazed pastures and the severe winter of 1881 without adequate hay reserves caught him short. His losses were over 50,000 head but for the third time he started on the way back.

---

[14] *Idem*, p. 16.
[15] *Idem*, p. 124.

Around 1886 he started to put his money into Seattle real estate and into a private bank at Ellensburg, Benjamin E. Snipes and Company. A second branch bank was opened at Roslyn. The panic of 1893 caught his banks, the cattle herds, and his Seattle real estate and forced him into bankruptcy. In the meanwhile the settlers had taken over the open range.

In 1904, at the age of 69, he again was on his way back with a small ranch but in 1906 he died.

SWAN LAND AND CATTLE COMPANY, LIMITED

The original assemblage was made by Alexander Hamilton Swan who also formed the Wyoming Hereford Association which was probably historically the most important single entity in importing Herefords and popularizing the breed through the range country. From 1921 on to the present day it has been operating as the Wyoming Hereford Ranch.[16]

A Scotch group formed the Swan Land and Cattle Company, Limited in 1883 and bought out the Swan holdings in Wyoming and Nebraska. The land claimed was centered on the Laramie River, a range 130 miles long east and west, and from 42 to 100 miles north and south, mostly public domain. The next year the company bought railroad lands, which were checkerboarded in alternate sections with the public domain and open only to regular settler entry.[17]

John Clay, a Scotsman who had been put in charge by the overseas interest, was the principal leader of the Wyoming Stock Growers Association which completely dominated the legislature and political officials of Wyoming for many years and extended its influence into Colorado, Nebraska, and even to the Capitol in Washington.

They were able to prevent any round-up being held by anyone without a foreman appointed by the Association to conduct it. No brands were recognized but those of the big ranchers. In addition, a $3,000 bond was required to be posted which eliminated any small rancher. They brought in hired gunmen as range detectives and kept inspectors at all stockyards and railheads.

"There was no denying that the British cattle interests and their employees were determined to have the Wyoming range regulated and orderly. Perhaps they looked upon the American public domain as something like their own early backlands, to be gifted by the king to

[16] *The Hereford in America*, Ornduff, p. 53.

[17] *The Cattlemen*, Mari Sandoz, Hastings House, 1958, p. 247.

his favorites or appropriated by any aggressive chieftain with the long bows to hold it."[18]

The blizzards of '86 and the subsequent collapse of the cattle market rocked the Swan holdings badly and they were forced to give up part of their empire. The steady influx of settlers and their votes put in sheriffs and legislators hostile to the big cattle companies and their political power was broken. When President Cleveland threatened to call out the cavalry to remove cattle from the Indian lands and forced the removal of 130 miles of Swan fencing on the public lands, it was the beginning of the end.

The final breakup of the big empires on the public domain came with the advent of Theodore Roosevelt and his appointment of the famous Confederate Cavalry leader, Colonel Mosby, as his range inspector. In June 1904, the Kinkaid Act went into effect permitting every bona fide homesteader to take up to 640 acres of land. If the settler had received a 160-acre homestead in the past, he could enter 480 now, the new homestead requiring five year residence and $800 in improvements.[19]

The large cattlemen tried to take advantage of this with false filings from eastern pensioners, whose names they used, and numerous other devices. The President cracked down and in the "Roosevelt Roundup" dozens of the large ranchers were hauled into court. When most were acquitted or fined lightly Roosevelt brought in the Secret Service to protect surveyors, fired a U.S. Marshal, and cleaned house on the local judiciary. In 1911 Bartlett Richards, the brother of a Governor of Wyoming, whose holdings in Nebraska and Wyoming were second only to the former Swan empire, was sent to prison, where he died. An era had come to an end.[20]

THE MATADOR

About 1879, H. H. Campbell in conjunction with A. M. Brittain, a Fort Worth banker, began to assemble land around Ballard Springs, Texas and gave their company the name of Matador. In 1883, A. M. Brittain went abroad and joined forces with some Scotch financiers from Dundee, Scotland, and raised $1,250,000 for expansion. In 1891, Campbell resigned to go into business for himself, but when he quit they were branding 20,000 calves per year.

In 1902, the Matador Land and Cattle Company bought another 200,000 acres in Oldham County along the Canadian River west of

[18] *Idem*, p. 335.
[19] *Idem*, p. 447.
[20] *Idem*, p. 448-455.

Amarillo. This was purchased from the XIT, which was now starting to liquidate. In 1904, they secured a government lease of 500,000 acres on the Cheyenne Reservation in South Dakota. They also picked up another lease along the Saskatchewan River in Canada. By 1906 they were well above 1,000,000 acres in controlled land. In 1913, they picked up another 550,000 acre lease on the Belknap Indian Reservation near Harlem, Montana.

Back in Texas they continued to assemble deeded land and shortly were close to the 1,000,000 acre mark with possibly an equal amount of lease and controlled range in other sections, making a total of 2,000,000 acres.

In 1891, A. J. Lingertwood became local manager and Murdo MacKenzie, superintendent. Following Lingertwood, J. M. Jackson was manager from 1909 until 1924. In later years, M. J. Reilly was manager until his death in 1946.[21]

The famous "V" of the Matador brand became associated with possibly the most outstanding group of Hereford commercial breeding stock in the country. Generally the brand alone was worth a 2c per pound premium at all of the big auctions and stockyards. Murdo MacKenzie, for a number of years, bought carloads of the top registered bulls from the internationally known Robert H. Hazlett herds of El Dorado, Kansas. "In 1931 and again in 1935, the Matador company bought the top-price bull of the National Western sale at Denver, the latter being also the champion bull of the show there."[22]

In 1951, the famous Lazard Freres & Co. of 44 Wall Street bought out the company and put Mr. Albert K. Mitchell in charge. He had formerly been twice president of the American Hereford Association and was one of the top cattlemen in the U.S. Over the course of the next nine years, lands and cattle were sold off, principally to smaller ranchers on the fringe of this vast empire. A major portion of the female breeding stock was purchased by syndicates headed by Mr. Buster Wheat of Allen, Kansas and Oppenheimer Industries, Inc., Kansas City, Missouri.

THE WAGGONER ESTATE

This included 510,000 acres south of Vernon, Texas and, until recently, 176,000 acres east of Las Vegas, New Mexico. By including oil rights, this might be the most valuable ranch holding in the U.S.

Dan Waggoner was in northwestern Wichita County as early as 1879 and on the lower Pease by 1881. He had a grass lease on the

[21] *The Big Ranch Country*, J. W. Williams, 1954, pp. 120-125, pp. 216-218.
[22] *The Hereford in America*, Ornduff, 1957, p. 144.

Kiowa-Comanche Reservation in Oklahoma of around 500,000 acres that was put under fence and held past 1900.

The famous Indian Chief, Quanah Parker, was actually employed by Waggoner as an extra ranch hand. During this period his famous 3-D brand shared the Indian ranges with Burnett's Four Sixes, and Sugg's O H Triangle.

Where he differed from his neighbors and other lease operators was that he saw the coming end of the open range and started to assemble deeded lands by purchase from 1900 on.[23]

One famous story of the early range was the time a rustler stole 144 steers of Waggoner's and put a Box around the 3-D with a bar iron. "No Box 3-D was registered so Dan recorded the new brand in his own name and went to reclaim the steers from the brand burner, with the weight of the guns on his side, of course."[24]

An example of how the owners and managers of the Big Spreads have moved on to the national scene is the case of the manager of the Waggoner Estate from 1941 to 1953, Mr. R. B. Anderson. He was first Deputy Secretary of Defense and was Secretary of the Treasury in President Eisenhower's Cabinet.

THE FOUR SIXES

Burk Burnett started operating on government leases east of the Waggoners at about the same time. By 1905, he was forced out and moved to King County, 125 miles southwest of Wichita Falls, and Carson County, 30 miles northeast of Amarillo. His son, Tom Burnett, started his own Triangle Brand and began assembling his own deeded lands. In 1918, the oil boom hit the area and both groups of lands were on their way to becoming very valuable.

One of the interesting features of this family was the rigid will of Burk Burnett, who died in 1922, which will keep the over $6,000,000 estate intact until the death of his granddaughter, Anne. This could preserve the oil-heavy ranch into the next century and be one of the great fortunes of the country.[25]

The present holdings of the Burnett estate and family are about 450,000 acres.

GRANVILLE STUART

Stuart was a Virginian of Scotch descent and may have been the first to start in the beef business in Montana. In 1860, he started

[23] *The Big Ranch Country*, Williams, 1954, pp. 139-141.
[24] *The Cattlemen*, Sandoz, 1958, p. 221.
[25] *The Big Ranch Country*, Williams, 1954, pp. 202-206.

fattening lame oxen from settlers on the Oregon Trail in Idaho Territory and sold them as food to the mining camps. In 1866, Nelson Story drove in the first group of 600 Texas longhorns from the Bozeman Trail. By 1880, range overcrowding already existed in western Montana and Granville Stuart brought the first herd over the divide into central Montana. This area became one of the great open range sections of the country. Stuart had married an Indian girl and was still able to maintain his range rights even after the government started to kick off the other white ranchers.

The shift in the period 1880 to 1883 was phenomenal. In a three year period the country shifted from vast herds of buffalo and no cattle to no buffalo and over 600,000 head of cattle. "The great herds on this last stand of the open range grazed upon millions of acres to which the herds' owners had no right other than the fact that they got there first, a 'squatter's right' which was given recognition of sorts in 1877 in the curious law of 'customary range.' In many instances, owners of 30,000 or 40,000 head of cattle owned not one square foot of the land they used, nor even the land upon which their ranch buildings stood."[26]

The branding of "mavericks" became an extremely profitable business. To quote Stuart himself, "Near our home ranch we discoverd one rancher whose cows invariably had twin calves and frequently triplets, while the range cows in that vicinity were nearly all barren and would persist in hanging around this man's corral, envying his cows, their numerous children and bawling and lamenting their own childless state. This state of affairs continued until we were obliged to call around that way and threaten to hang the man if his cows had any more twins."[27]

COLONEL GOODNIGHT

In 1856, at the age of 20, Charlie Goodnight formed a partnership with his stepbrother, Wes Sheek, to run cattle to Palo Pinto County, in the Comanche country. The next ten years were spent alternating in service with the Rangers and constant skirmishes with the Indians.

In 1866, in company with Oliver Loving, he started a major drive into New Mexico. For the next few years the two men pioneered constant trail drives to Fort Sumner, Denver, and Santa Fe and made a considerable fortune, mostly on government contract sales. After Loving died from wounds in an Indian raid, Goodnight established the

---

[26] *Montana: High, Wide, and Handsome*, J. K. Howard, Yale University Press, 1959, pp. 107, 108.
[27] *Idem.*

first major ranch in southern Colorado near the Apishapa River in 1867.[28]

In 1876, after having formed a partnership with the Irish nobleman, John Adair, they moved from their headquarters at Trinidad, Colorado, into the Palo Duro Canyon of the Texas Panhandle. This was the beginning of the famous JA brand taken from the initials of John Adair. At its height, in both deeded and leased land, the partnership controlled over 1,300,000 acres. On Adair's death the range was split up but Mrs. Cornelia Adair, the widow, kept much of her portion intact and the present Cornelia Adair Estate is one of the principal landowners in the country (319,000 acres).[29]

Goodnight was also one of the principal owners of the Interstate Land and Cattle Company which at one time controlled almost 3,000,000 acres of New Mexico public range. Here a major battle ensued with Teddy Roosevelt in his program of making private ranchers remove all their fencing from the public lands. Roosevelt won.[30]

C. C. SLAUGHTER

C. C. Slaughter was the first native cattle king of Texas. His father, who had dealt in early wild Spanish cattle, had been Sam Houston's right hand man and the first man to be married in the Republic, C. C. being the first child born of the marriage.[31]

He started on his own in the cattle business when he was seventeen years old with $520 he had made by hauling and trading lumber and wheat along the Trinity River. He invested the money in a herd of cattle which he moved 300 miles northwest where he started the Long S Ranch on Dillingham Prairie.[32] Although there is some argument about it, he is supposed to have trailed the first Texas herd into Abilene and shipped it out by rail.

He shortly went into banking and became president of the First National Bank at Dallas. By 1879, he was supposed to have made over $1,500,000 from cattle and was buying up state lands in Texas almost by the county. In addition, he leased an empire of a ranch in Montana and was trailing steers up there to finish on the hearty northern grasses.[33]

At his height in 1905, he is credited with 100,000 cattle on 1,500,000

[28]*The Cattlemen*, Sandoz, 1958, pp. 83-85.
[29]*The Big Ranch Country*, Williams, 1954, pp. 213-215.
[30]*The Cattlemen*, Sandoz, 1958, p. 443.
[31]*Idem*, p. 58.
[32]*Great Roundup*, L. Nordyke, William Morrow & Co., 1955, p. 19.
[33]*The Cattlemen*, Sandoz, 1958, pp. 238, 239.

acres of both deeded and leased land.[34] Substantial subdivision and sale of the lands continued by the estate until 1937 when the discovery of oil in Hockley County made wealthy the remaining heirs who still held part of the old ranch.[35]

SMS[36] OF STAMFORD, TEXAS

S. M. Swenson came over from Sweden in the early 1830's and made his first trip to Texas in 1838. He became one of the biggest merchants in Austin when the capital was moved there and was a close personal friend of Sam Houston. When the Civil War broke out he wasn't in favor of secession and ran off to New Mexico. He reputedly got most of his assets converted into gold and buried under a chimney in his home. When the war ended, he was established in New York and became an investment banker associated with such men as Frank Vanderlip and Mortimer Schiff. In 1888 he brought back his nephew A. J. Swenson from Sweden, whose family has been managing the ranch ever since.

However, the ranch does not belong to them but is the property of the corporation started by S. M. Swenson before he left Texas. "He bought scrip covering railroad lands, purchased additional land and eventually had three enormous blocks of real estate he called the Ellerslie, Flat Top, and Throckmorton Ranches."[37]

In 1906, they organized a corporation which bought the huge Spur Ranch on the plains at the base of the Texas Panhandle. The stockholders were Vanderlip, Schiff, Emery and Swenson. Emery owned three-fifths of the stock. The group developed a town in the middle of their holdings and sold off thousands of acres of farm land between 1910 and 1915. They combined the sturdy traditions of the Old West with the grim business methods of Wall Street.

About the time World War II began, the corporation was dissolved. The owners divided the property and the Swenson Land and Cattle Company bought all but Emery's share. The Emery heirs wanted $5 an acre, but old E. P. Swenson wouldn't pay it. He said he would not give money like that for land he was used to getting for $2 an acre. Now that same land is going for as high as $20 but nobody anticipated the land boom that followed the war and the Emery holdings were allowed to remain in the possession of the heirs. AJ's son, Eric Swenson, is now in charge of the Emery acreage. Although the grouped holdings

---

[34] *Idem*, p. 120.
[35] *The Big Ranch Country*, 1954, p. 230.
[36] *Cowboys and Cattle Kings*, Sonnichsen, University of Oklahoma Press, 1950, p. 141.
[37] *Idem*, p. 143.

are probably less than one-third of what they were at the zenith, they still involve over 300,000 acres. The "SMS" brand is still known as one of the outstanding "name" brands in the country.

RAILROAD AND UNIVERSITY LANDS

During the 19th Century when the railroads were crossing the country, both the Federal Government and the States deeded them public lands as compensation to encourage their more rapid construction. The Federal Government characteristically gave them alternate sections on either side of the right-of-way. Texas had a deal with Jay Gould's Texas and Pacific to give them 16 to 20 sections for every mile of construction. Gould put in 900 miles but the State did not have the necessary 12,000,000 acres of public land left and settled with 5,000,000 acres which was the greatest quantity ever transferred to a single private establishment.

This generally ran across West Texas in the vicinity of Midland and Odessa. Most of this was disbursed but Fraser, Burr and McAlpin acquired a good portion of it and the firm still owns 1,700,000 acres and is the largest private landowner in the state of Texas. They do not operate it as a ranch but lease it to others.[38]

The University of Texas owns over 2,000,000 acres granted by the state near the Pecos River which has considerable oil revenue. They lease to private ranchers at substantially less than market rents and with many of the characteristics of the old Taylor right leases.

The Union Pacific has retained tremendous land holdings which make up sections of some of the finest ranches in the country. The St. Louis-San Francisco Railway Company has large holdings, including 50% of the stock of the New Mexico and Arizona Land Company, which at one time had over 750,000 acres of deeded lands with most of the minerals intact.

NEW MEXICO AND ARIZONA LAND COMPANY

The stock for this company is traded on the American Stock Exchange. There are 1,000,000 shares authorized, issued and outstanding, of which, as just mentioned, over 50% are controlled by the St. Louis-San Francisco Railway Company in St. Louis. The headquarters of both companies are in St. Louis.

The landholdings lie generally along U. S. Highway #66 running from Kingman, Arizona to Albuquerque, New Mexico. The principal holdings lie very close to the Arizona-New Mexico border. There are 589,977 acres owned in fee and 762,992 additional mineral right acres.

---

[38] *The Big Ranch Country,* Williams, 1954, pp. 230-232.

The company customarily leases out its lands rather than attempting to physically operate them.

During the 1960-70 period, the stock wildly fluctuated generally in the range from 9 to 25. This was caused principally by various rumors relating to oil and uranium possibilities.

Because many of the deeded acres are checkerboarded with state leases, Indian leases, and other land owned in fee by private lessees, the grazing lands of this particular company are an integral part of ranch operations that might total as much as 3,000,000 acres.

CAP MOSSMAN

This section has been titled after the manager rather than after outfits he ran or their owners because in his case the man was more significant than the ranches. In the last part of the 19th century and the beginning of the 20th, we saw appearing on the horizon of the cattle industry professional managers representing the interests of giant corporations and the assemblages of capital from the East and Europe. These were men like John Clay of the Swan and Murdo Mackenzie of the Matador.

Usually they did not possess any great personal wealth, were not related to anyone of importance, and arrived on the scene after most of the free lands of the open range had been taken up. Most of the properties were in the hands of estates, stockholders, and widows, and these managers arrived as hatchet men or salvagers of the estates and correctors of the incompetencies of some of their more flamboyant predecessors. Using other people's capital and other people's land and representing the interests of absentee owners, they moved to the front, not only by qualities of toughness, leadership, and brains, but principally by complete integrity and loyalty to the business interests of the people they represented. The greatest of this new breed was Burton C. Mossman.

He was born on a farm near Aurora, Illinois, in 1867 and his family moved to Lake City, Minnesota, about six years later. His father entered the 36th Illinois volunteers as a private at the beginning of the Civil War and was mustered out as a major with four battle wounds. In 1882 the family moved to the territory of New Mexico.

When the foreman of the Bar A Bar near Hot Springs, New Mexico, was killed by lightning, Burt Mossman was made temporary foreman at the age of twenty-one, running an 8,000 head spread. His outstanding performance in cleaning up an unsatisfactory operation caused the Lankfords of Pueblo, Colorado, the principal owners, to retain him permanently as manager. The droughts of the early 1890's and the

Cleveland "panic" of 1893 put the Lankfords under such financial pressure that they directed Mossman to liquidate.

His reputation as a tough, hardnosed, efficient operator came to the ears of Mr. Frank C. Bloom, a banker at Trinidad, Colorado, who had a big loan together with the Thatchers of Pueblo on 12,000 head at the Bar OO Ranch, an enormous outfit in the Bloody Basin area north of Phoenix, Arizona. This ranch had over 12,000 head of principally wild cattle in some of the roughest country in the United States. There was a high proportion of ten-year-old steers and bulls that the owners had never been able to gather and work, much less ship to market. Mossman developed some new techniques in gathering and in building holding pastures and hired Mexican *vaqueros*. He was shortly gathering and shipping the cattle out at a 2,000 head clip. After a couple of years he had secured enough collateral to pay off the mortgages and all of the back interest for his banker employers.

His next big job was to straighten out the vast two million acre spread of the Aztec Land and Cattle Company along the Santa Fe Railroad in the general vicinity of Holbrook and Flagstaff. This operation could run 60,000 head and historically was the second largest in the United States, running behind only the giant XIT.

The Aztec Land and Cattle Company, controlled by Seligman Bros. in New York, had purchased a little over one million acres from the Santa Fe Railroad. The sections were alternate sections with federal land in between. By having the land checkerboarded in this manner the company for all practical purposes controlled two million acres of the range. Various officials and directors of the railroad were also tied into the outfit and its management. For fourteen years the company had paid no dividends on either stock or bonds and had won the unsavory reputation of harboring more outlaw cowboys, more thieving hands, and more murderous neighbors than any ranch in the country. "Rustlers and horse thieves were as thick as fleas on a dog's back." At that time it had around 50,000 head of cattle and a couple of thousand horses. "It not only offered a great chance for a new manager to make a killing, but to get well killed on the side. All in all it was the toughest, biggest, deadliest, and the most grueling job in America–if a man had nerve enough to take it. Burt Mossman had plenty of this nerve so he took it. He signed a contract in late December in 1897."[39]

In a period of about ten days Mossman had fired half of the staff personnel, personally brought into jail at the point of a rifle three

[39]*Cap Mossman, Last of the Great Cowmen*, Frazier Hunt, Hastings House, New York, 1951, p. 84.

neighbors whom he caught butchering cattle, and generally put the fear of God into all of the operators lining his borders who had been living off the ranch for years. He was able, by cooperation with the various sheriffs in the area and with civic leaders, to get juries selected who started convicting people that his hired hands brought in. Over the next few years he sent about twenty rustlers to the territorial prison at Yuma.

In 1901 Governor Murphy of the Arizona Territory asked Mossman to lay out a plan for the formation of the Arizona Rangers and to take over their direction in order to get the entire territory cleaned up. On March 21, 1901, the law was passed establishing the Rangers, with a captain whose salary was to be $120 per month, one sergeant at $75 per month, and not more than twelve privates at $55 per month. As captain his career over the next few years made him one of the legends of the West.

In 1905 when Theodore Roosevelt appointed a governor who wanted his own staff, Mossman resigned as head of the Rangers and was hired by Mr. James Coburn of Kansas City, who was general manager of the Hansford Land and Cattle Company, a Scotch outfit that ran the famous Turkey Track brand, with headquarters at Lakewood on the Pecos River in New Mexico. Again, it was a situation of managerial trouble, drought, and no profits. The Scotch directors gave Mossman authority to expand the operation with relatively drought-proof grazing leases in South Dakota and authorized him to bid on the Cheyenne Reservation near Evarts on the Missouri River. This lease involved over a million acres and the directors thought it was too much to tackle alone so a joint venture was arranged with Mr. Murdo Mackenzie of the Matadors. They were successful in obtaining the bid on the lease on May 1, 1905. Mackenzie and Mossman then split the lease and a 40-mile fence was constructed across the lease. By fall Mossman was ready to receive Turkey Track cattle from the South.

Again there was rustler trouble and problems with unauthorized herds using his grass, and again he straightened out the situation in his usual forthright manner. The following year two more leases of 330,000 and 390,000 acres were made available and again he was the successful bidder. This, added to what he already had, brought the South Dakota operation up to over one million acres. The total cost of this grass came to $53,000 per year.

As evidence of the tremendous reputation he had acquired as manager, a British syndicate headed by Kuhn, Loeb of New York which acquired seven million acres of grazing land in the state of Sao Paulo,

Brazil, attempted to hire him. The salary offered was $50,000 per year, which in the early 1900's was a tremendous amount for an executive in any line of activity, much less ranching, which has always been notoriously poor paying for top management. He declined the offer and recommended his friend Murdo Mackenzie, who took it.

In 1914 the government took a major part of the Dakota lease from him and opened it up to settlers so he moved a large part of his cattle to the Crow Agency land in Montana, which was being leased by Mat Tshirgi, who was taking tenant cattle.

In 1925 Mossman was instrumental in forming the Diamond A Company, which included much of the Turkey Track, a good part of the Bloom and Thatcher operations on the Hondo, and the Wagon Mound, plus his Dakota lease and some interests in Montana. Outside of being one of the major cattle operations in the country, the company had shares in as many as 50,000 sheep on its New Mexico ranges.[40]

In the Franklin Roosevelt administration Mossman was instrumental in designing much of the legislation and many of the regulations connected with the Taylor Grazing Act and was often called upon as a consultant by Secretary Ickes of the Department of Interior. In 1944 the Diamond A was liquidated and Cap Mossman, who was then being severely troubled by arthritis, was able to retire with a comfortable portion from his share of the corporation. "He had stuck with range cattle for sixty years—since that day in 1884 when he had to work for the little Hat Ranch as a kid cowboy, and made his first dream come true. He had seen it all and done it all. He had twisted the monkey's tail and seen the elephant, as they used to say. He had handled more than a million head of cattle. Throughout all his life he had battled uncompromisingly the eternal enemies of all cowmen—the Elements and Hard Times."[41]

KERN COUNTY LAND COMPANY

Although now controlled by Tenneco, Inc., The Kern County Land Company is one of the largest farming, ranching and landowning companies in the U. S. today and possibly only one American in 50 has ever heard of it. The assets of the company undoubtedly have a market net worth in excess of $200,000,000.

Despite the company's reputation for its oil operations, its VVV Ranch around Seligman, Arizona, and the San Juan Boquillas Ranch

[40] *Idem*, p. 272.
[41] *Idem*, p. 276.

in southern Arizona, together with its Gray Ranch in New Mexico, make it the principal landowner in both states. Formerly, its holdings in southern Oregon made it the chief operator in that state.

Kern County itself is in California and the headquarters of the company are in San Francisco. It may directly or indirectly control more irrigated farm land in California than any other single entity. (109,586 net acres are devoted to irrigated farm lands, of which Kern operates 18,556 acres and the balance of which is farmed by independent farmers under lease.[42])

"The company, incorporated in San Francisco in 1890, had its beginnings in the 1870s. It was started by James Ben Ali Haggin and Lloyd Tevis, two businessmen who had been very successful in the West since coming here from Kentucky.

"Among their ventures was the launching of the great Homestake Mine in the Black Hills of South Dakota in 1877, a project in which they were associated with Senator George Hearst.

"Haggin and Tevis foresaw that the railroads would open up the San Joaquin Valley and began to acquire land along the Kern River for cattle ranching. Apparently the first purchase was made in 1873. Parcels in the Carrissa area were acquired in 1874, and the San Emidio Grant—the site of the present San Emidio Ranch in Kern County—was acquired in 1878.

"The Victorio Land and Cattle Company, a KCL subsidiary with headquarters at Deming, New Mexico, was incorporated by Haggin and Tevis in 1899. It was transferred to the Kern County Land Company by Haggin in 1910 to assure continuity of management. There are two major areas included—the Animas in Grant and Hidalgo counties, and the Armendaris in Sierra and Socorro counties, the latter area recently acquired by the Armendaris Land Development Corporation.

"In Arizona, the subsidiary Boquillas Cattle Company operates the VVV Ranch that runs from Seligman north to the Grand Canyon. It was acquired in 1948.

"The so-called San Juan Boquillas Ranch, now running about 7,000 stocker steers, is in southern Arizona in Cochise County and includes the old Spanish Grants of San Rafael de Valle and San Juan de los Boquillas y Nogales, and was acquired in the period from 1901 to 1912.

"The VVV and Gray Ranches are run as cow-calf operations. The San Emidio Ranch in Kern County and the Carrissa area in San Luis

---

[42] *Moody's Industrial Manual*, July, 1969, p. 1,005.

Obispo County, California, are stocker ranches. The company has recently discontinued operation of its Gosford Feed Yard in Kern County."[43]

The following is quoted from Moody's Industrial Manual:

"In 1957 merged Chewacan Land & Cattle Co., a subsidiary.

"In December 1958 company sold Oregon Ranch and escrow opened covering ZX Ranch in southern Oregon to Sinter & Brown Co. Transaction included 171,000 acres of fee land and related grazing leases totaling over 1,000,000 acres, all ranch equipment, operating inventories, and over 18,000 head of cattle.

"As part of transaction company acquired Santa Rita Ranch, a 6,000 acre cattle property and Alliance Ranch, a 500 acre farm both near Paso Robles, California.

"In 1958 company, with others formed Marin Oak Development Co. a residential development project.

"Company owns and operates agricultural and cattle properties in California. Subsidiaries operate desert ranches for breeding of calves in Arizona, New Mexico and Oregon. Extensive acreage is leased for farming and company also operates canal system for irrigation purposes in Kern County Land is leased for oil development to the major oil companies operating in California.[44]

"In 1967 Tenneco Corporation acquired all outstanding stock of The Kern County Land Company,[45] and continues to operate it as a subsidiary. Tenneco's consolidated land use revenues were $82.7 million in 1969.[46]

ARMENDARIS LAND DEVELOPMENT CORPORATION

In contrast to almost all the other big spreads, Armendaris Land Development Corporation is strictly a 20th Century phenomenon. Formed in 1969 primarily through the consolidation of a number of existing cattle operations, Armendaris holds over a million acres in the West and Midwest.

Foremost among its holdings is the Armendaris Ranch, from which the company's name is derived. Located in southwestern New Mexico, about 100 miles northwest of El Paso, Texas, the ranch is the company's largest single property. In fact, the company's ownership of the Armendaris, and the Border Ranch, located on the Mexican border makes it a principal private landowner in New Mexico.

In California, too, Armendaris Land Development Corporation has compiled major holdings. In addition to several smaller properties

[43] Letter 26 March 1970, Jack L. Tindall, Manager Cattle Operations, The Kern County Land Company.

[44] *Moody's Industrial Manual*, 1959, p. 2,900.

[45] *Idem*, 1969, p. 1,005.

[46] 1969 Annual Report, Tenneco, Inc., p. 19.

throughout the state, the company has assembled either through purchase or through options it expects to exercise, slightly less than a quarter of a million acres in the Carrizo Plains, in San Luis Obispo County. Much of this land is currently in cultivation to wheat or used for winter grazing, essentially in stocker operations.

Armendaris has plans for expansion into Nevada, too. It anticipates exercising an option to purchase the Winecup Ranch, a large, 604-square-mile portion of northeastern Nevado's Elko County. Originally founded in 1886 by a former Nevada governor, the Winecup has had a colorful history. It too is presently a cattle ranch.

Parts of Colorado, Kansas, Missouri, Montana, and Wyoming have also felt the Armendaris "brand": most of the holdings in these states consist of rural lands, and like the ranch and farm properties in California and New Mexico, are presently leased on a short-term basis to local ranchers and farmers.

But as one of the major landowning entities in the country today, the company realizes that the solely agricultural ways of its predecessors of the 19th Century are somewhat anachronistic, that the cost squeezes of today necessitate a diversified use of existing resources. In this light, as its name implies, the company plans to emphasize development, along both agricultural and non-agricultural lines. The Armendaris Ranch offers a good example.

The Armendaris Ranch has about thirty miles of frontage on the Elephant Butte Reservoir, a 50,000-acre lake which is a major southwestern recreational area featuring facilities for water sports, camping and fishing, with hunting and mineral springs nearby. In addition, the Rio Grande, which flows through the ranch for approximately 47 miles, and other topographical characteristics also present many similar opportunities for development along recreational lines. Complementing this is the company's continued improvement of agricultural facilities on the ranch.

Other rural properties also have locations suitable for recreational development or near to areas already so developed. Still other holdings, more closely situated to urban areas, may be more suitable for commercial or residential development.

The location of other Armendaris land lends itself to other unique operations. The Border Ranch, for example, adjacent to one of the limited number of United States government cattle crossing stations between Mexico and the United States, seems to be ideal for use in the company's program of Mexican cattle importation. Under this modern agricultural undertaking, Mexican cattle of mixed grades are purchased, imported, grazed and fattened, for subsequent sale to feed lot operators, packers or ranchers in the Southwest and Midwest. In this, as in other areas, the company's financing the purchases of cattle is but another way toward agricultural profit unknown to the cowmen of Matt Dillon's time.

But few of the big spreads today can afford to maintain interests in only rural land; Armendaris is no exception. The company owns over half a million square feet of land in downtown Kansas City, Missouri, land containing blighted apartment buildings, warehouses, and parking facilities, in short, property well suited for urban development consisting of high rise apartments, office buildings, hotels and stores.

Thus Armendaris Land Development Corporation, as a modern and forward-looking "big spread," illustrates well the look of land-holding giants of the future—the simultaneous use of the land for both agricultural and non-agricultural purposes. Perhaps only in this way can the "big spread," as we have seen it develop, continue to survive.

The largest stockholder of Armendaris is Oppenheimer Industries, Inc., of Kansas City, Missouri, holding a 19% interest. Oppenheimer Industries is traded over-the-counter and has 900 public stockholders.

Chapter III

The Battle of 1963

In the President's tax message to the Congress of January 24, 1963, certain recommendations were advanced to change the tax treatment of farmers and ranchers. These recommendations covered such areas as capital gains at time of death, depreciation recapture, and income averaging. Spokesmen for agriculture generally opposed the first two and supported the latter.

Another area covered by the tax message was the proposed nullification of many capital gains benefits through a device called the "Excess Deductions Account." This device, which came to be known as "EDA," proposed discriminatory tax measures against all owners of ranches and cattle who possessed outside incomes in excess of $15,000 per year.

Those in agriculture who sensed an opportunity to bar the flow of competing outside investment capital into the industry either supported EDA or gave tacit approval through reserving judgment. Small ranchers, farm management groups, country bankers, purebred associations, and others who appreciated the part played by outside risk capital were almost unanimous in their opposition.

The testimony which follows describes the fight against EDA, ending in ultimate victory as the proposal went down to defeat when committee hearings came to a close.

STATEMENT OF HON. PETER H. DOMINICK,

A U.S. Senator from the State of Colorado

The Chairman. Mr. Mitchell and Mr. Hart.

The Chair understands our very distinguished colleague from the State of Colorado, the Honorable Peter H. Dominick, would like to present the next two witnesses, Mr. Mitchell and Mr. Hart.

Senator Dominick. Mr. Chairman, I appreciate this privilege you have given to me to appear before this committee. I do not think I have had the opportunity of doing it before; we have been so busy in the other body.

It is a real privilege to introduce to you Stephen Hart, who will be giving testimony on behalf of the National Livestock Association. He is a former partner of mine, a knowledgeable man in the tax field, and I am sure the information he gives to you will be of much value to the committee in its deliberations, and I know that he will enjoy giving answers to whatever questions you may have in connection with this.

The Chairman. Thank you, Senator, we appreciate your coming back to the House side of the Capitol.

It is my understanding, Mr. Mitchell, you would like to be first of the two?

Mr. Mitchell. Yes.

The Chairman. Please identify yourself for the record by giving your name and address and capacity in which you appear.

Mr. Mitchell. I am Albert K. Mitchell, of Albert, N. Mex., chairman of the National Livestock Tax Committee.

The Chairman. We are glad to have you with us and you are recognized.

Do you want to identify the others with you at this time?

Mr. Mitchell. Mr. Stephen Hart, general counsel, and Mr. Claude Maier, who is also with the firm, and Mr. W. W. Brainard, who is a producer of livestock.

The Chairman. We are glad to have all of you with us.

STATEMENT OF ALBERT K. MITCHELL,

Chairman, National Livestock Tax Committee

Mr. Mitchell. I am chairman of the National Livestock Tax Committee, which is nationwide in scope and represents the great majority of the National, regional, State, and breed livestock associations, numbering more than 50 such associations, with several hundred thousand individual members throughout the United States. The names of these associations are listed below. Almost every phase of the livestock industry is represented by our committee through these organizations, including producers of beef and dairy-type cattle, sheep, and horses, and feeders of cattle and sheep.

Here with me to testify is Mr. Stephen H. Hart of the law firm of Holland & Hart, Denver, Colorado, who has been counsel to the committee since its organization approximately 20 years ago. As the members of your committee will recall, we have had occasion to appear before the Ways and Means Committee several times during the past few years to discuss proposals and amendments to the income tax laws which have particular and specific effect upon the livestock industry.

We appreciate the very friendly and cooperative reception which we have received and hope that our comments and the written material which we propose to file will be of assistance to the committee in its deliberations.

General Policy

First, we would like to state what we conceive to be the general policy of the livestock industry. We favor a tax cut. Present tax rates are discouraging to the livestock industry and undoubtedly hamper its economic growth. We, as an industry, are willing to pay our share of such a tax cut through the adoption of any reasonable tax reform; however, we feel quite strong that each reform proposal should be carefully examined to determine if it is a true reform or merely an additional complication or inequity in the present tax structure. We feel equally strongly that the Government should pay its way in support of a tax cut by reducing its expenditures. We are of the firm opinion that a government can only be as sound as its fiscal policies, and operating at a deficit is anything but sound.

There are six proposals contained in the President's tax message and elaborated on in the statement and explanation submitted by Secretary of the Treasury Douglas Dillon, which are of direct and particular concern to the livestock industry. I will summarize our views.

Capital Gains on Death or Gift

The proposal which causes us the deepest concern is that subjecting to income tax the appreciation in value of property transferred as a gift or included in a decedent's estate at the time of his death. We fear that the enactment of such a law would force the sale in their entirety of thousands of family-owned ranches throughout the country, because livestock operations are not liquid, they do not produce a cash return on their value sufficient to pay such a tax (in addition to estate and inheritance taxes) out of profits, and ranches are so constituted that they cannot be sold in part like securities. Ranches must be maintained as a unit and lose a substantial part of their value if broken up into smaller uneconomic pieces.

Averaging of Income

We believe that the averaging of income proposal will be of benefit to the livestock industry because of the extreme fluctuations in income of farmers and ranchers resulting, among other causes, from changes in climatic conditions and market fluctuations. We have long urged the adoption of an averaging concept and are very gratified that this proposal is included in the administration's 1963 tax program. We want to urge certain changes in the proposal, however, in order that the device will better accomplish its purpose.

Depreciation Recapture, Investment Credit, and Capital Asset Holding Period

Mr. Hart will offer our comments on the proposed inclusion of livestock in the depreciation recapture provisions and the allowance of an investment credit for livestock. We have no objection to extending the holding period for capital assets to 1 year.

Excess Deductions Account

We note with interest the proposal to eliminate possible abuses by high-bracket taxpayers investing in the livestock business, by the creation of an "excess deductions account" which would eliminate or reduce capital gains on the sale of farm properties or livestock to the extent of farm losses used as deductions against nonfarm income. We feel that we must reserve judgment on this proposal until we know how it will actually be drafted and what will be its specific provisions. It could have a deleterious effect upon a substantial segment of the livestock industry. It might be possible, however, to limit its provisions so that it would accomplish its intended purpose of eliminating abuses without actually interfering with traditional and legitimate livestock operators, including those with outside incomes and those newcomers entering the livestock business in good faith.

Now I would like to introduce Mr. Stephen H. Hart, our counsel, who will comment in detail on some of the technicalities involved in these specific proposals.

STATEMENT OF STEPHEN H. HART,

Attorney for the National Livestock Tax Committee

Mr. Hart. Before elaborating on Mr. Mitchell's testimony, I would like to emphasize his qualifications, for the information of this honorable committee. This is a portion of my statement that he had not read in advance.

Mr. Mitchell is a past president of the American National Cattlemen's Association, the New Mexico Cattle Growers' Association, the American Hereford Association, and the American Quarter Horse Association. He is a past chairman of the National Livestock & Meat Board and of the advisory committee on livestock to the Secretary of Agriculture.

He is presently chairman of the board of the International Stock Show at Chicago, and vice-chairman of the board of the National Western Stock Show in Denver. He is a trustee of Cornell University. He has probably had a broader experience in the tax, scientific, economic, practical and governmental problems of livestock than anyone in the industry, and I think he is the most universally respected livestock man in the United States.

I. Capital Gains on Death or Gift

We are very concerned about the effect on the livestock industry of the proposal to tax appreciation in the value of property transferred by gift or on death. Due to a combination of factors this proposal is especially burdensome to ranchers.

LACK OF LIQUIDITY

In the first place, the estate of a deceased rancher will not ordinarily contain liquid assets. The typical working rancher has the bulk of his capital invested in land. The rest is tied up in his animals and equipment. Even if these assets are not mortgaged, they cannot be sold off to raise cash without affecting the ability of the ranch to carry on as a working unit and more often than not, either the land or the animals, or both, are mortgaged. Any measure which contributes to this lack of liquidity problem increases the chances that a ranch will have to be sold on the death of its owner instead of passing to his heirs. Ironically, while death is treated as a sale under this proposal, unlike the ordinary sale, no cash is generated to pay the resulting taxes, and the liquidity problem is thereby compounded.

INTEGRATED ECONOMIC UNIT

The typical ranch is an integrated economic unit. It has its water, its range, and its facilities for handling a given number of livestock units efficiently. It cannot ordinarily be sold off in parcels without lowering the value of both the part that is sold and the part that remains. It is not like a portfolio of stocks which can be sold in parcels without loss in value. Therefore, if problems of raising cash to pay expenses and taxes cannot be worked out on the death of the owner, economics will dictate that the decedent's family sell off the entire ranch and leave the livestock business entirely. We think this is unhealthy, and that any tax measure contributing to such a result is unwise.

Coupled with this lack of liquidity is the fact that the rancher's principal asset is land. By a conservative estimate, 75 percent of the average rancher's principal asset is land. By a conservative estimate, 75 percent of the average rancher's capital investment is in his land.[1] The immense appreciation in land values in the last 20 years is common knowledge. As a result, the cards are stacked against the average rancher under this proposal because he is more likely to die with the kind of appreciated asset which this proposal will tax.

LOW RETURN ON INVESTMENT

Nor is the rancher in a position to gain the liquidity necessary to meet these added taxes during his lifetime. In this business, capital investment must be large and return is low. It has been estimated in one Department of Agriculture publication that an investment of $200,000 is required before expenses can be met in the typical cattle operation.[2] After a reasonable amount of the rancher's return has been allocated to his labor, the ranch may show no return on its capital investment. For instance, one Government survey of the economics of ranching in our Southwestern States specified, and I quote:

> From 1952-57, net ranch income was so low that little return was available for either capital charges or returns to the operator and his family for their labor and management.[3]

Another extensive survey by the Government of representative cattle operations found only two with returns on capital of over 4 percent and concludes:

---

[1] *Cattle Ranches, Organization, Costs, and Returns, Southwestern Nonmigratory Grazing Area, 1940-59*, Farm Economics Division, Economic Research Service, U.S. Department of Agriculture, in cooperation with Agricultural Experiment Station, New Mexico State University, p. 10.

[2] *Economic Relationship of Grazing Fees and Permitted Use of Public Rangelands to Net Income of Western Livestock Ranches: A Regional Analysis*, U.S. Department of Agriculture, Economic Research Service, Farm Economics Division, p. 1.

[3] Cattle Ranches, supra, p. 30.

> Returns of 2 to 3 percent were quite common in each ranching area for ranchers with more than 400 animal units.[4]

We submit that returns of this magnitude will not permit the rancher to lay aside during life the cash to meet any additional tax burden at his death, nor will they permit his estate to earn enough to pay these taxes after his death.

As a result of this combination of factors—lack of liquidity, a low return, and appreciation in land values—this measure will operate oppressively on ranchers as a group, and will, if passed, only accelerate the process whereby thousands of family-owned ranches will be broken up on the deaths of the present owners.

POLICY NOT APPLICABLE

Nor does the policy behind this measure apply to the livestock industry. As we understand it, this policy is to free capital that is "locked in" by the threat of capital gains tax. However, a ranch is not an investment in stock, to be turned over by the investor routinely. The ranch is acquired to be retained and developed for raising livestock, and its owner traditionally passes it on intact to his family for generations. If this proposal is passed, its effect will be exactly opposite to that desired for a stable and healthy livestock industry.

The Technical Explanation of the proposal by the Treasury terms it "moderate as a practical matter." If it were, we seriously wonder whether it is worth the addition of another complicated provision to our Revenue Code. The truth of the matter is, however, at least with respect to ranchers, that it would be not at all moderate as a practical matter. It would be disastrous.

II. Averaging of Income

In his 1963 tax message, the President proposed an income-averaging provision which is intended to afford equitable tax treatment for taxpayers with widely fluctuating annual incomes. Those of us who have observed the tax penalty borne by such taxpayers welcome this proposal. Livestock raisers are particularly subject to large fluctuations in annual incomes. These fluctuations reflect the hazards and uncertainties of their business. Growth and development of their herds and their sales volume are profoundly affected by extremes of climate and weather. Prices in their market shift abruptly, depending upon such factors as weather, supply and demand, and foreign competition.

[4] "Economic Relationship of Grazing Fees, etc.," supra, p. 46.

Epidemics of disease can suddenly decimate their herds. I extensively documented the fact of these fluctuations and illustrated the inequity which exists under present laws in a statement I made to this committee in March 1959.

III. Excess Deductions Account

The next item is excess deductions account. On the other items I have discussed up to this point, I am sure there would be universal agreement within the livestock industry. The excess deductions account, on the other hand, may create a difference of opinion. I am sure it has created a difference of opinion and we have not, in the time available, been able to poll all of the individual associations among the 50 which we represent, and I am quite sure that most of them don't yet understand exactly the effect of this provision. As a matter of fact, it hasn't been drafted yet, so we don't know its exact effect.

TECHNICAL PROBLEMS

The excess deductions account (EDA) proposal necessarily poses a number of technical problems. The legitimate livestock industry has no quarrel with the expressed intention of the administration to eliminate abuses by high-bracket taxpayers with large nonfarm income who secure tax advantages by investing in farm activities which tend to produce losses deductible against ordinary income in the early years, but which subsequently give rise to capital gains. It is stated by the Treasury that such practices

> tend to create unfair competition for farmers who may be competitors and who do not pay costs and other expenses out of tax dollars but who must make an effective economic profit in order to carry on their farming activities.

Certainly the legitimate farmer or rancher does not condone such practices, but it is difficult to draw the line between the legitimate operator who from time to time realizes losses on his farming or ranching operation and the high-bracket "tax-gimmick" taxpayer against whom the proposal is aimed.

LEGITIMATE FARMERS SHOULD NOT BE PENALIZED

In the first place, a legitimate farmer should not be penalized because he happens to have outside nonfarm income. As a matter of fact, it is often impossible for a farmer to get his farm operation started unless he does have resources over and above his investment in the farm or ranch, because of the customary losses during the early years of the venture.

The livestock industry, depending as it does on climatic conditions, is subject to wide fluctuations in sales and prices (and thus income) over which the stockman has no control. More particularly, in the so-called purebred or registered livestock operation, it customarily takes a number of years before the herd numbers and the reputation and worth of its breeding stock are established so that a profitable operation is possible.

A successful livestock industry is premised upon improvement in breeding lines which comes about chiefly from the activities of the purebred operators. Without outside income to fill in the gaps of loss years, many purebred operators would be forced out of business and the expansion and growth of the industry thereby impaired for lack of improved blood lines.

INDUSTRY NOT BENEFITED

On the other hand, we do not feel that the livestock industry as a whole is benefited by the "tax gimmick" investment of large sums of money in livestock raising schemes, which are not intended to produce an economic profit but are designed solely to create a tax profit by virtue of operating losses coupled with capital gains. Such practices artificially inflate the cost of land out of all proportion to its true economic worth and endanger the entire tax structure of the livestock industry. Artificially raised prices of land make it more difficult or impossible for traditional farmers and ranchers to continue and expand their operations and in recent years have produced a tendency toward the forced breaking up of established ranch units.

SUGGESTED DEFINITIONS

Where should the line be drawn? First of all, we believe that if an excess deductions account proposal is to be enacted, a broad and clear definition of income from farming should be set forth in the statute. Farm income should include not only the actual return from the sale of crops, livestock, produce, and other typical farm commodities but also include all returns from the farmland itself.

It is not uncommon that land which is temporarily not being used by a farmer is rented out for pasturing or put out on crop shares. Often natural deposits such as gravel, minerals, and oil and gas are discovered on the ranch. Income from all of these should be treated as farm income (though of course, such income from outside sources should not).

Farm real estate itself is occasionally sold, and we believe that this should be included in farm income.

A more complex problem results from farms which are operated in corporate form. Certainly income from a farm partnership should be treated as farm income. By the same token the income from a subchapter S corporation engaged in the farming business should be treated as farm income. We think that the same should apply to dividends from a corporation engaged in farming, which does not so elect.

The definition of nonfarm income should be clearly restricted so that the proposal actually affects only those investors not truly interested in farming or ranching at an economic profit against whom the excess deductions account proposal is aimed. It seems only fair that capital gains should be excluded from nonfarm income, unless such capital gains are of a recurring nature, such as from the sale of timber, coal, patents, and the like.

Conclusion

The Chairman. We thank both of you for your very fine statements, and we appreciate you other two gentlemen accompanying Mr. Mitchell and Mr. Hart to the witness stand.

Any questions?

Mr. Curtis. I was impressed by the statement and some things you point out in criticism of the proposed estate tax treatment. This could be avoided, I imagine, if the ranching industry became involved in a corporate form of business, but even there it would not help if the corporation were closely held in a family group; am I right in that observation?

Mr. Hart. That is right.

I think if this provision were adopted it would force the gradual disappearance from the industry of not only ranches owned individually and by partnerships and families but also those owned by corporations closely held, and I think the eventual result would be huge publicly owned corporations in control of the farming and ranching lands.

Mr. Curtis. It would be my observations that that can result. Certainly up to date we have been trying to encourage the family farm, and I am very pleased, I might add, in spite of general statements to the contrary, that farming and ranches still are largely held by the family, and, although they have grown into larger units, they are still the family farm; is that correct?

Mr. Hart. That is right.

Mr. Curtis. The second point I want to dwell on a bit is averaging income, and I was very happy about your statement on this. The difficulty has been to set this up mechanically. I think most people are in favor of income averaging. I do believe that possibly your recommendations of change is one that always worried me as regards the proposal of the President.

It follows to some degree along the lines of bills I have put in. Those bills do not take into account unused standard deductions and unused exemptions. This has always worried me because our lower income groups are the ones, as you point out, are the ones most affected.

If we could figure out the proper language and mechanics, I think this would be very desirable to put in.

Mr. Watts. Now, with reference to the excess deductions account, I am very glad that you made it clear there was not unanimity of thought on that subject.

I have read your statement twice, and as I get it, overall, you do not object to a man being in some other kind of business and owning a farm?

Mr. Hart. Not at all.

Mr. Watts. You do not want to penalize him?

Mr. Hart. Not at all.

Mr. Watts. He is a legitimate farmer and farming for farming's sake, whether it is in livestock, grain, or the horse business, and is losing money, and you do not want people punished?

Mr. Hart. No.

Mr. Watts. The fellow who went into farming solely for the capital gains?

Mr. Hart. That is right but we are not after anybody.

Mr. Watts. Well, I mean, if there is a legitimate profit, it is in that area?

Mr. Hart. It is the area of a man who goes into a farming operation purposely to lose money or not caring whether he loses money, because he has a tax gimmick that will bring him out with a profit.

Mr. Watts. That is a better way of saying what I said, that the fellow that is causing the trouble, if there is any trouble, and I assume there is, is the fellow who is in the farming business not for the farming business but solely for the purpose of gaining a capital gains treatment on something that he may have lost some money on and deducted from ordinary income?

But I know you have no designs on anybody to affect the legitimate operation where a fellow is natural farming or whatever kind of farming there is, even though he does not lose money?

Mr. Hart. Right.

Mr. Watts. The problem, as I see it, is separating the goats from the sheep?

Mr. Hart. That is the problem. This EDA approach is something novel and something new, and it has not been defined. We cannot say whether it would work or would not, but it is the most modest approach that has come to our attention. Other approaches would be much more severe and would harm the industry much worse.

Mr. Watts. You are assuming that something has to be done. Of course, I do not know of a single field of taxation in this Nation today that there are not some gimmicks or shortcuts; and they are always used by someone big; and the question that arises in my mind is as to whether the abuses are big enough to take a shotgun blast at a single industry and say that if you are a businessman or lawyer or doctor or whatever you might be or you own some stocks or bonds that you can own a part of a building and depreciate that and spend a lot of money and lose money on it and still deduct that from your income. But the farming business is the only one picked out where if any money is lost in it you suffer the consequences. That is another problem.

Mr. Hart. The solution should be nondiscriminatory, that is for sure, and it should not affect, if it is possible to draft it in that way, the legitimate person who is in the business of farming, ranching, raising horses, whatever it may be, for the customary motives and not just for a tax gimmick.

Mr. Watts. Irrespective of what his income might be on the outside?

Mr. Hart. That is right. We have no quarrel with people of high income. We welcome them in our business.

Mr. Watts. It is a fact, is it not, at least I have been told this in my part of the country, that many of these farmers who have outside income have done a tremendous job in spending lots of money in developing better bloodlines of stock and new types of stock that probably could not have been developed with the actual cash income off the farm itself?

Mr. Hart. That is right. True. In the purebred line you almost have to have outside income before you can develop an operation, but our point would be that the aim of the taxpayer should be to develop a going, self-sufficient, profitable unit and not just to produce a loss and then sell out at a capital gain.

Mr. Watts. A lot of these gimmick fellows are just feedlot fellows, are they not?

Mr. Hart. I do not think there is so much of that in the feedlot business because there is no capital gain in the feedlot business. That is all ordinary income.

Mr. Watts. That is right.

Let me ask you this question: In attempting to reach some kind of remedy, would it be of any benefit to prolong the time that livestock must be held before it would be subject to capital gains?

Mr. Hart. That would be adopting a solution which would hurt all the cattlemen, again, to solve a problem which is limited in its scope.

Mr. Watts. With cattle, they are held usually a year?

Mr. Hart. That is right.

Capital-gain animals are held for more than a year, and ordinarily they are held for their full productive life, but where there is a sellout or there is a drought and one has to sell drastically, one can be forced to sell young animals just the same as old.

It often happens that quite legitimately a person will claim capital gain on livestock held between a year, 2 years, or 3 years.

Mr. Watts. That can happen, too, in the dairy business if a man loses a cow or for some reason or another the cow becomes unproductive for a certain period of time, and I wanted to explore that, but time is short. I thank you, sir.

Mr. Alger. I do not think you can answer the question that I would like to ask and that would be, why we are getting these tax reforms, but I would like to ask you about what you said in page 4 of your statement. You said:

> As a result of this combination of factors, lack of liquidity, a low return, and appreciation in land values, this measure will operate oppressively on ranchers as a group, and will, if passed, only accelerate the process where-

by thousands of family-owned ranches will be broken up on the deaths of the present owners.

Do you know we are subsidizing progress where it tends to break up family farms and estates? Does it strike you there might be something coincidental there, or not?

Mr. Hart. I really do not think ranchers were thought of when this provision was suggested.

Mr. Alger. I do not jump to that conclusion but in trying to grope for a reason, why would a knowledgeable President and knowledgeable advisers come here with a recommendation like this. The kindest thing I can say is ignorance, economically.

I am not trying to put you on the spot. I asked this yesterday. I asked, "Do you think it is possible the President lacks a basic knowledge of economics in the private market?"

Allow me to rephrase the question, "Do you suppose it is possible that our President does not understand ranching and your business?"

That is the kindest implication you are seeking?

Mr. Hart. I do not think I should be asked to answer that.

Mr. Alger. Thank you.

The Chairman. Mr. Keogh.

Mr. Keogh. Do I summarize your position correctly or incorrectly when I say that you advocate this, that a rancher might have outside income up to $50,000, as you have proposed, but that one who has no outside income should not become a rancher?

Mr. Hart. No. I am not advocating anything.

This EDA proposal has not yet been defined. It has only been stated in the most vague and general terms, and all I am saying is that on behalf of the industry that we represent we want to take a look at it; we want to see what it provides before we take a position for or against. We recognize that there is this situation.

Mr. Keogh. You want to be sure that those who are in the business of ranching are not adversely affected, is that not your position?

Mr. Hart. That is right.

Mr. Keogh. But you are relatively disinterested as to how it may affect those who are not now in the ranching business but might want in the future to go into it?

Mr. Hart. No. We feel that the ranching business should be kept open for anybody who wants to go in. There should be no barriers established.

We feel there should be no discrimination against anybody just because he has outside income.

Mr. Keogh. Well, how do you translate your high-sounding phrase of "legitimate rancher" into legislative language and how do you define your tax gimmick when it admittedly is done in accordance with existing law?

Mr. Hart. There is nothing fraudulent or illegal about it. The laws with respect to this area are presently drafted in such a way that a man can make a tax profit out of an economic loss and we feel that that is unhealthy.

Mr. Keogh. But the impact of those existing provisions of the code fall evenly on the rancher, too, do they not, as on the legitimate rancher?

Does he not have access to existing law?

Mr. Hart. He certainly does, but it is the interplay of these things.

Mr. Keogh. You have no objection to that, do you?

Mr. Hart. None whatsoever, because the legitimate rancher is in the business to make money. He is trying to produce an economic profit, and if he does not he is going to go broke.

Mr. Keogh. And if he sells his ranch he wants to take capital gains on the difference between the sales price and his basis?

Mr. Hart. He certainly does.

Mr. Keogh. But you are here speaking for that industry and you are, in effect, recommending that that same treatment not be accorded people who are not now in the ranching business?

Mr. Hart. I make no differential between those who are now in the ranching business and those who are not.

Mr. Keogh. Would you agree or disagree with this statement, that the outside capital that has gone into your industry has served an economic purpose?

Mr. Hart. A great majority of my industry I think would feel that money which is purely tax motivated has done harm.

Mr. Keogh. Why and how?

Mr. Hart. Because it has artificially inflated values and artificially inflated prices to where the return on the investment is reduced, to where the ability to continue in the business has decreased.

Mr. Keogh. Well, I suspect we will have testimony that will be at variance with that statement.

STATEMENT OF FLOYD L. MADDEN,

President of American Society of Farm Managers and Rural Appraisers, Dayton, Ohio

The Chairman. Mr. Madden, will you please identify yourself for the record by giving us your name, your address, and the capacity in which you appear?

Mr. Madden. I am Floyd L. Madden, 3223 Allendale Drive, Dayton, Ohio. I am here representing the American Society of Farm Managers and Rural Appraisers as their president.

The Chairman. You are recognized, Mr. Madden, proceed.

Mr. Madden. The American Society of Farm Managers and Rural Appraisers has over 1,400 members in 45 states. As president of the society, I have been authorized by its executive committee to represent the society before this committee.

The society strongly feels that taxpayers with an adjusted gross income from nonfarm sources in excess of $15,000 should not be denied the same tax treatment as other suppliers of capital in farm activities, because of the element of differentiation. It is one thing to differentiate as to what capital should be invested in, but quite another thing to differentiate as to the source of capital.

It may be argued the former is economic guidance, done for the best interests of the Nation, but no such argument could defend the latter.

It simply denies equal freedom or privilege to people furnishing capital in farm activities. It is certainly unfair, if not legally indefensible.

Let us examine briefly some practical and typical farm activities with reference to this differentiation as to the source of capital.

For example, an 80-cow dairy herd is developed on a farm. The landowner and tenant farmer each own an individual one-half interest. For good and sufficient reasons, the herd should be sold. Imagine the complications if the proceeds to each owner from the sale were to receive different tax treatment. The tenant farmer may want to dispose of the entire herd by one liquidation sale. This would be a sound decision as it would be uneconomical to operate the dairy unit on a basis substantially less than full capacity. It may be advantageous for the landowner to string out the sale of the herd over a period of years, if he is denied capital gains tax.

Let us imagine the case of two brothers who each inherited a one-half interest in the family farm. The older one had stayed on the farm to help his father. The younger was a practicing physician by the time both parents died. The younger brother purchased the farm chattels in the estate. The farm activities continued uninterrupted. Should there be a differentiation in tax treatment on the sale of depreciable farm chattel property or on the sale of all or a part of the real estate farm property just because the younger brother has an adjusted gross income in excess of $15,000? It certainly doesn't seem fair.

Besides denying equal freedom or privilege to people furnishing capital in farm activities, differentiation in tax treatment definitely interferes with sound decision making, the backbone of successful management.

Now let us turn to differentiation as regards the economic activity into which capital should be invested. As previously suggested, guidance by differentiation may be defended on the grounds that it is best for the country to give preferential treatment to one economic activity over another.

Surely it is not the intent of the proposed change in the income tax laws to discourage the flow of capital into farm activities, but it will be the result. This should not happen. Why? Simply because it has been mainly the supply of capital available for use in farm activities that has made possible the use of new technology and improvement in our land resources.

Of the three factors of production: land, labor, and capital, farmers are relying more and more on capital for several reasons. Land and labor costs are increasing. The application of capital to land to improve drainage with the use of tile, open ditches, or other means and to improve fertility through the use of more lime and insecticides have also contributed to increased production. Power machinery and mechanical equipment have reduced labor requirements. This trend will continue. Even though our population is sure to increase, we will be eating more of the food we want and paying less for it, provided the flow of capital into farming is not restricted.

In addition, while this efficiency and productiveness was being developed, land, our basic economic resource, was improved and depressed areas uplifted. Whether cutover timberland, low-fertility cotton land, wet and uncleared land, eroded land of the Corn Belt formerly devoted to row crops, or similar land elsewhere, venture capital has come to the rescue in improving and restoring this land to its highest and best agricultural use.

A high percentage of the rolling and hilly land that was once devoted to excessive production of row crops has been converted to ranching operations. Timber now is growing on much of the wornout cotton land of the southeast. This land that has been improved and restored with the assistance of venture capital is today's best evidence that Congress made a wise decision, when in writing the present tax laws, it gave a capital gains advantage to those investors who were willing to invest capital in these lands and bring them back to their highest and best use. The job is not finished. At this time I would like to add there is another effect and that is the effect of the cattle here when venture capital moves into a depressed area the people in the area can also improve their own area.

Our members could furnish many examples of the restoration of wornout farmland. Here is one that comes to me from Nebraska:

> Pawnee County, Nebr., in the southeast part of the State, was one of the first counties settled more than a hundred years ago. This area is rolling country where the original topsoil was not very deep and not of especially good quality. After a hundred years of farming, much of the land in the area would be classed semi or marginal land from the standpoint of crop production. This area had a very heavy loss of farm population with many, many sets of improvements unoccupied. The only answer to the rehabilitation of this land was to put it back to grass and utilize it for livestock production. Capital in the immediate community was not available for this purpose.
>
> We have a well-to-do client for whom we have put together some 3,800 acres of this type of land which has been reestablished into native grass pastures at a very substantial cost for seed and fertilizer. Soil erosion has been brought under control. The rehabilitation of this 3,800 acres of land will, in the long run, contribute much to the local community. We are now running 800 to 1,000 head of cattle annually on this area which would not have supported half that many 5 years ago.

The following came from one of our members in Georgia. The South has been called "land poor," and justly so. And I forgot to mention this, it comes from a letter from one of our members in Georgia:

> After World War II, we were still farming with mules down here. People owned tremendous acreages, but had no money to farm them except on sharecropper basis. These large tracts of land attracted northern capital because they were sizeable, which automatically made them poten-

> tially efficient. After risk capital came in here, southerners themselves became confident of the area and began to invest. Between the two, tremendous changes have taken place. The capital that has been put in this area has created wealth, jobs, security, taxes, and all the things that the chamber of commerce talks about. Agriculture has done more for southwest Georgia than any other single industry in the last 15 years, and it is because money has come into it to improve it, develop it, and make it produce.

We believe that denying equal income tax treatment to investors in farm activities is unfair and that such a denial would discourage capital flow into agriculture, which would seriously interfere with efficiency and further improvement in our agricultural lands. In our opinion, the differentiation should be between those who are merely running a hobby farm for tax deduction purposes and those who are really in the farming business.

Mr. Chairman, I thank you for the opportunity to appear before the committee.

The Chairman. We appreciate you coming before the committee and expressing your views.

Are there any questions?

Mr. Byrnes. You did not mention it specifically, but I gather your testimony is directed primarily at the proposal related to the excess deduction account?

Mr. Madden. Well, if nonfarm capital and farm capital were both going to be subject to the excess deduction account, we would take no stand.

Mr. Byrnes. I think you made a very valuable contribution. I just wanted to pinpoint the area of recommendation in which your testimony was directed.

I think you made a valuable contribution. I think this is an attempt to control where capital comes from and I think it is rather preposterous we should do that. I think you made a very good point.

The Chairman. Mr. Keogh.

Mr. Keogh. Mr. Madden, are you, in effect, saying that if punitive provisions are enacted that would make it less attractive or increasingly impossible for outside capital to go into the agricultural industry generally, and that industry will suffer?

Mr. Madden. Yes, sir; that is what we are saying.

Mr. Keogh. Thank you.

The Chairman. Mr. Watts.

Mr. Watts. Mr. Madden, I think this is a very fine statement. It coincides with my thinking on the subject entirely.

Of course, we have been able to outdo the world in many fields, but if there is a single field that I know of where we have gone way ahead of anybody else in the world it is in the field of agriculture, and I do not think it was ever intended by the Constitution, or that it should be done by any law enacted by Congress, to draw a line as to who may get into the farming business and what kind of treatment he could get if he got into it. And even though there might be some few abuses in some instances, people might go into the farming business for a certain specific reason. I believe you will agree with me that to take a shotgun approach to the thing such as is being attempted here would have a very serious effect on the part of industry.

Mr. Madden. Yes, sir; I agree.

Mr. Watts. Certainly, there is no way in the world to judge why a man goes into the farming business.

Generally, it is a very nonlucrative business; is it not, sir?

Mr. Madden. That is correct.

Mr. Watts. And Congress, heretofore, has been trying to aid the ailing agricultural industry; and to turn around and deny capital, awfully badly needed in the farming industry, would be a serious mistake; would it not?

Mr. Madden. I think so.

Mr. Watts. Could there be such a motive behind this as to lessen competition to certain people?

Mr. Madden. I would hope not.

Mr. Watts. I would, too.

But we have always labored under the delusion that anybody who wanted to go into the farming business in the United States had the right to?

Mr. Madden. Yes.

Mr. Watts. And certainly this would limit some people from going into the farming business?

Mr. Madden. I think it would discourage them.

Mr. Watts. I thank you.

The Chairman. Mr. Jennings.

Mr. Jennings. I certainly agree with your statement. I think it is a very, very fine one.

I would like to make this one observation. The very people putting this capital into the farming area are perhaps carrying on some of the best conservation of our lands to pass on to future generations than anyone that we know of. There is one question I have here and that is on the last sentence of your statement, where you say:

> In our opinion the differentiation should be between those who are merely running a hobby farm for tax reduction purposes and those who are really in the farming business.

Who is going to determine that, and how?

Mr. Madden. That is the most difficult thing to determine.

Even farmers in it to make money actually show losses and I would not know what the figure is, and I would presume that there are farmers in our country today that if it was not for the fact they could deduct their depreciation from their earnings, would be in pretty bad shape.

Mr. Jennings. I am satisfied of that.

But, from a practical standpoint, I just do not know how you are going to determine who is in this business for hobby farming and who is in the business for the purpose of farming, I suppose you would say, because that is what it boils down to.

The Chairman. Any further questions?

We thank you for your statement and for answering our questions.

Without objection, the committee will recess until 2 p.m. this afternoon.

(Whereupon, the committee recessed at 12:30 p.m. to reconvene at 2 p.m. the same day.)

After Recess

(The committee reconvened at 2 p.m., Hon. Wilbur D. Mills, chairman of the committee, presiding.)

The Chairman. The committee will please be in order.

Colonel Oppenheimer, Mr. Greenough, Mr. Puckett, Mr. Trimble, Mr. Furlong, and Mr. Bierman.

Colonel Oppenheimer, it is my understanding that you and these gentlemen would like to present your testimony as a group or a team and perhaps it would be better in view of that fact that we let each of you make your statement before any of you are interrogated.

Colonel Oppenheimer. Yes, sir, that will be fine.

The Chairman. All right, we will proceed on that basis, then. You be the captain of the team, if you will, and lead off and then present the witness you want to hear next.

Colonel Oppenheimer. Thank you, sir.

The Chairman. Colonel, will you identify yourself and then each of you as you are recognized?

STATEMENT OF COL. HAROLD L. OPPENHEIMER,

Chairman of the Board, Oppenheimer Industries,
Kansas City, Missouri

Colonel Oppenheimer. My name is Harold L. Oppenheimer. I am the head of a farm management firm representing approximately 350 farm and ranch livestock owners with agricultural operations covering 14 States, principally in the Great Plains area. I was raised on a Missouri farm, spent 22 years on active duty and in the Reserve of the United States Marine Corps, and presently hold the rank of colonel. Directly and indirectly, our group employs over 1,500 people within the agricultural field.

Mr. Chairman, before I get going I would like to make a correction in some of the written testimony that you have. Mr. L. C. Carpenter, on the front page, was formerly commissioner of agriculture in the state of Missouri. The State of New Mexico is in error.

Mr. Floyd Madden, who preceded us, wants to ask that his testimony be considered completely independent of our group. Finally, in the body of the material we have a recommendation for an alternate plan of taxation. We would like to withdraw that. We will submit a modification of that at a later date.

The Chairman. All right, sir.

Colonel Oppenheimer. Incidentally, in that particular regard, the main point was that we had put in the recovery of depreciation as ordinary income. We now decide that that would be harmful to the industry.

The Chairman. All right.

Colonel Oppenheimer. I am here to introduce a group of people of varied interests within the agricultural field who by personal appearance or written testimony are opposing Secretary Dillon's proposed change in the tax law regarding capital gains on farms and livestock in which people with nonfarm incomes over $15,000 per year are going to be discriminated against.

Before we start, we wish to state that we are in agreement with Secretary Dillon in opposing the gimmick-type transaction described in his exhibit 15. This type of thing is characterized by fictitious purchase prices unrelated to market conditions to create a false depreciation allowance, guaranteed repurchase agreements or guaranteed calf crop percentages to eliminate normal market risks in return for excess deductible charges in some other form, and maintenance costs so high that any possibility of economic profit is removed.

Our group is planning to demonstrate:

That the Secretary's method of eliminating these sham transactions is going to seriously damage a number of legitimate operators as well as the industry.

An alternative plan, which is by no means satisfactory, and which still fails to eliminate this new and unique method of discriminating against a specific industry, but still accomplishes the Treasury's main objective of eliminating a sham transaction and secures more tax revenue than the original proposal. It is only moderately damaging to a legitimate investor and a legitimate operator provided that the operation is reasonably efficient and well organized. This alternative proposal has by no means been approved by the organizations appearing with us but is only submitted for study.

We tried, in selecting the people here as well as the making of their statements, to get a complete range of the farming and ranching industry. We have small ranchers from out West. We have feed lot operators. We have wealthy people from the East. We have people in the management field. We have tried to cover the whole works.

The first gentleman who is going to talk is Mr. William Greenough, formerly manager of the Antler Land and Cattle Co. in Montana who is now operating his own spread near Bridger, Mont. His subject will be that this proposal will cut off a much needed source of risk capital from small farmers and ranchers trying to stabilize their operations by acquiring additional land on lease or additional cattle on shares.

Mr. Greenough.

STATEMENT OF WILLIAM GREENOUGH,

Bridger, Montana

Mr. Greenough. My family and I have been in the ranching business for over three generations. My father was one time a mountain guide for President Theodore Roosevelt in Montana, and my brother is in the Cowboy Hall of Fame. I myself for a long number of years was the general manager of the Antler Land and Cattle Co., which had over 600,000 acres, along the Montana-Wyoming border and was the largest ranch in Montana. I am presently owner and operator of a ranch near Bridger, Mont.

I never expect to have $15,000 in nonfarm income but me and guys like me throughout the Montana-Wyoming area have always, since the very first days of the cattle business out there, going back to Civil War times, have had outside capital come in from England or the East, and in recent years from people who are attracted by the tax advantages.

In our country you need a minimum of five or six men to gather cattle and handle them and you need a certain minimum amount of trucks and hay equipment. You need this whether you are running 500 head or 5,000 head. That's the reason why it is a very tough deal for a man to make it in this country if he can't get up to over 1,000 head because his operating costs won't be much more than a man with 300 head and his calf crop and revenue will be 3 times greater. That is the main reason that half of the smaller ranchers in Wyoming and Montana like myself are going to be put out of business if we can't get cattle on shares or maintenance contracts from people with outside capital, and we know we won't get them if this proposed law goes through.

The other reason we need these people is that it is the only way I can think of that you can hedge against a falling market. Back in 1953 I had built up a herd of my own and I got caught in the big market drop that year and got forced out. I told myself that never again if I ever got on my feet again would I ever have all of my eggs in one basket and I would try to get other people to partially stock my ranch so that they could share some of the market risks with me. There are a lot of people all through the West who have lots of money but who feel the same way I do that they would like to have partners in this deal so that they wouldn't have to take all the chances of a market drop by themselves.

A number of years ago one of the bankers told me, "Bill, as long as you can ride a horse and have got a saddle, I will finance you on any cattle or ranch you want to go into." Well, after this market drop wiped me out in 1953, I went to see this banker and said, "I can ride a horse and I've got a saddle and I would like to have you start me up again." However, all I got out of the banker was some pleasant conversation. Shortly after that I was able to start back in with the help of some of these people that you are trying to pass this law against.

There is an old saying that the only way to get started in the cattle business is to inherit money or marry it. I think I have let both of them go by. There is some feeling among the big ranchers that if the smaller rancher and farmer are forced into bankruptcy and put out of business that production will go down and prices will go up, and in the meantime they can buy my land cheap and take over my leases because there won't be any small ranchers to compete with them. They are probably right in this about getting our land cheap, but I don't think it is necessarily going to cut down production as the same land is going to be used for running cattle for one of the big ranchers and it just means that us little ranchers are going to be forced out. It is my opinion that the Senators and Representatives from Montana, Wyoming and Idaho are just not going to let this happen, at least if they are the same kind of people they used to be.

Colonel Oppenheimer. Thank you, Mr. Greenough.

The Chairman. Thank you, Mr. Greenough, for a very interesting statement.

Colonel Oppenheimer. This is Mr. Earl Puckett, chairman of the board of Allied Stores, member of the Board of Governors of the Federal Reserve Bank of New York, and owner and developer of two famous breeding herds in Illinois and Tennessee.

He is going to cover the point that the change in the law is going to stop the flow of investment capital to the improvement of wornout farms and raising the level of distressed agricultural communities and the implementing of policies in this direction that the Department of Agriculture has been attempting to carry out for a 30-year period, and second, that the development of outstanding breeding herds has been encouraged by the present tax structure and such development has been of major benefit to many local areas as well as the entire country.

The Chairman. Mr. Puckett.

STATEMENT OF B. EARL PUCKETT,

Chairman of the Board, Allied Stores, Inc.; Member of Board of Governors, Federal Reserve Bank of New York

Mr. Puckett. My name is B. Earl Puckett. I have been chief executive officer of Allied Stores Corp. for the past 30 years and director of other corporations, including New York Federal Reserve. I grew up on a small and very poor farm in southern Illinois. I have owned and operated this and other farms for over 40 years and now own and operate 1,200 acres in Illinois and a similar amount in mid-Tennessee.

I might say although I am appearing with Colonel Oppenheimer I do not retain his services. I operate these farms myself. I specialize in high quality, registered Hereford cattle, polled and horned, for breeding purposes. Just last week I sold 42 such females to 34 individual farmers as additions to their herd.

The objective of such a breeding program is herd improvement. Accomplishments in this respect require a very extended period of time—several years to a few decades. I started my Hereford program in 1952. I sold less than 10 females for breeding in the first decade. I am now in a position to sell 100 a year.

The hazards of such a program are great. As an example, I started my pedigree Hereford operation with 100 females and three good bulls, with a capital outlay for the herd of approximately $100,000. Two or three years later it was discovered that certain cow families have a genetic problem known as dwarfism. I owned those cow families and my fine breeding herd had to be marketed for slaughter at near a complete loss. Only a long-range program scientifically operated and adequately financed has a chance in this breed improvement field.

On the other hand, breed improvement must go on at an accelerated pace in order to assure a low-cost future food supply. Public welfare demands it. The average farmer cannot either finance it or assume the hazardous risks inherent therein. It is now being done on a free enterprise basis, effectively and efficiently, by a relatively few farmers with a keen interest in their work and who are so fortunate as to be able to assume risk.

The question is, Will this committee and Congress permit them to continue? If not, the Department of Agriculture will have to take over as the job must be done. I doubt that the bureaucrats can do it. I know they cannot do it well. I know they cannot do it for the many costs that are now being incurred, including tax costs to the Government, if any.

The cattleman is a strong individualist by nature. Traditionally, we ask for no price subsidies. Consequently, beef price trends are most favorable for the consumer, relatively, and the consumption trend is ever upward. The only economical answer to grain surpluses is more and better grass farming and beef production. This transition is occurring. Breed improvement accelerates this trend.

Every developer of quality breeding stock employs from 3 to 4 times the help that would be required to operate his farm on a traditional basis. Also, such a breeder actually operates a demonstration farm of great educational value to his community.

In my own case, as in many others, this education takes on extension course aspects. I regularly loan bulls to neighbors, motivated somewhat by self-interest. By doing so I get an economical test on the bull's breeding attributes and I protect my own cow herd from the hazard of an inferior bull breaking through a dividing fence and doing irreparable harm. The neighbor benefits greatly and eventually becomes a customer.

In closing, our present structure is working effectively, efficiently, and economically. The cattleman has not been a problem for the Government. My plea, think before you make one of him. He will help you solve your grain problems if you not only permit but encourage him. Discouragement can lead only to additional farm calamities. How can you be sure that any modification of existing tax laws will be helpful or more subject to equitable administration?

Thank you. I would like to make one more comment, if I may. Listening to some testimony and questioning this morning I was very greatly impressed to find out that some people thought that certain sections of the cattle industry can operate without outside capital. I have been in the banking business, directly and indirectly, for a good part of it, and that is contrary to everything that I know anything about.

As far as I know, the cattle business must have outside capital in one form or another. It has had it traditionally, and will have to have it continuously. I can understand why such a statement might be made by certain people because I know many ranchmen in Texas, New Mexico, Colorado, and Oklahoma, with big oil interests and if they happen to have enough oil income and if they choose to define that as being ranching, then they might not have to have outside help.

But the ranchmen I know have to have outside cash or outside income even though it may be from their own ranch or they have some oil. Again, outside capital has been in the past at times largely obtained by borrowing. With fluctuations in the market, the ranchmen have been swept aside.

Today the trend is much more to do it by capital equity participation. It is much safer. It is better for the country.

Thank you.

The Chairman. Very well.

Colonel Oppenheimer. Mr. James Trimble, majority leader of the Missouri Legislature, farmowner, and executive secretary of the National Cattlemen's Cooperative. He is going to talk on the special problem of the farmer on the edge of a metropolitan area who is being forced out because of high taxes and other reasons and must have a secondary profession in order to survive.

Second, he will talk about the necessity for subsidized outside risk capital coming into agriculture to alleviate its distress during its current transition period.

We are going to eliminate the statement from Armour & Co.

The Chairman. Mr. Trimble.

STATEMENT OF HON. JAMES TRIMBLE

My name is James Trimble. I live at Route 1, Kearney, Mo. I am the majority leader of the Missouri House of Representatives. My family has been in the cattle business in Kearney for four generations. When I retired from the Marine Corps in 1952, I intended to actively work the farm which I presently own, but because of a physical disability suffered during the war, I was advised to engage in a less strenuous activity.

I am speaking to you today on behalf of a substantial segment of our population that will be adversely affected by the proposed change in the tax law aimed at preventing outside risk capital from coming into the farm and livestock business. It occurs to me that the type of legislation intended by the Treasury Department is aimed at removing from the cattle industry the kind of "gentleman-farmer" who has no expectation of economic profit and who invests in cattle and other agricultural endeavors solely for the purpose of saving tax dollars. I concur in the Treasury's objective, but I feel that this particular proposal is certain to eliminate from the cattle business a large number of legitimate operators and would work a severe hardship upon a group of people supporting and being supported by the industry through many related activities.

The area that I represent in the Missouri Legislature is a suburban community which has nearly doubled in population during the past 10 years. Taxes have spiraled, creating unusual pressures on farm owners in our county. These unusual expenses have left only two alternatives to landowners in this area. They must either sell to real estate investors or operate their farms in conjunction with a supplementary source of income. It is important to note that 95 percent of the farmers in my county presently derive outside income because of the inability to maintain their property as an agricultural entity due to the encroaching suburban development. Without this supplementary income, most of this land would find its way into the hands of developers. All of us are greatly concerned that this will cause premature and disorderly development creating the kind of rural slum which is so detrimental to areas such as this throughout the United States.

In other communities, such as Kansas City, Wichita, St. Joseph, Topeka, and Springfield, for instance, there live a substantial number of people who derive their principal income from nonfarm sources of whose agricultural interests are as real and important to them as any other phase of their livelihood. There is the Kansas City merchant, for instance, who owns a small farm near Liberty, Mo.; the banker in Springfield who has a herd of breeding cattle on the outskirts of town; and the owner of an automobile agency in St. Joseph who has a spread nearby leased to a neighboring farmer. There is also the widow living in Wichita, whose husband died leaving her the ownership of a 1,000-acre farm and a sizeable breeding herd. These are not people of great wealth or means. Nor are they the hobbyists whose interests in agricultural endeavors are purely recreational. These are all people who themselves or through family have been brought up to the land. Because of one circumstance or another, they cannot make this their principal source of income. These are the people who are going to be seriously affected by the proposed legislation.

In moderate-sized urban areas such as the ones I have described, the interest and ownership maintained by local residents in rural communities is an important two-way street with benefits derived both by the rural community and the city dweller. As most of you know, a farmer's commerce depends to a large extent on the relationships he has established in neighboring communities.

Today many of the people who derive their livelihood from this industry consist of a group that is gradually encroached upon by the suburbs. Their real estate taxes have gone up so high that it is no longer possible for them to consider the farm an economically possible agricultural investment. In many cases they are just far enough beyond the housing developments yet they cannot get an equitable price for their land. In many instances they have been forced to take city jobs to supplement their income or even to go into other professions. Many of these properties are today owned by widows, minors, and older people. They do not have any "nonfarm income" but the only market for them during this transition period are people who are interested in purchasing, operating, and maintaining the farm, but who are in a group now singled out for discrimination by the proposed changes in the tax law. Without this group being available as a market, or at least to hold prices up to a reasonable level, the present ownership is going to be gradually squeezed out of business and forced to liquidate under unfavorable circumstances. We cannot permit this to happen.

Even the large ranchers in and about these communities do not profit from the distress of their smaller associates in the business. While the large rancher himself may not require outside capital, he is still far better off when more orderly markets are created, distressed selling is eliminated, and operations are in the hands of those who can maintain a decent standard of living.

In this connection, the words of Mr. Herbert Pike during his keynote speech before the 25th annual meeting of the National Farm Institute in Des Moines last year, stresses the particular importance of the owner-operator relationship. Mr. Pike states, and I quote:

> The coming 10-year pattern will be the part-owner-operator. He will own his own headquarters farm with the buildings and rent additional unimproved land from a landlord. This is a better deal for both parties. It is encouraging to see that an increasing number of farmers are securing capital, organizing efficiently, and employing both men and machines to an advantage. They have the ability and the time to pursue the intangibles in farming, to keep adequate records, and to make sound decisions. They can afford to educate their sons and offer them a career at home worthy of their ability.

Another area of vital interest that will be affected by the proposed legislation are various commercial endeavors located throughout the United States that are engaged in extensive programs of research and development supported largely by the kinds of funds which will be eliminated by this bill. Take, for example, the efforts of Armour & Co., the large packinghouse that is presently engaged in a research program expected to result in a substantial improvement in the quality of beef throughout the United States. I would like to review a brief statement from M. W. M. Elder, the director of trade relations and general manager of the beef cattle improvement research program of Armour & Co., in this connection.

> Armour & Co. is presently engaged in a research program which is expected to result in a substantial improvement in the quality of beef. Essentially, this is a breeding program premised on (1) the knowledge that certain desirable beef characteristics, such as flavor, tenderness, leanness, and color, are of a heritable nature, and (2) the belief that through the use of the semen of those bulls that have shown the capability of imparting these desirable characteristics to their offspring a beef supply can be produced to meet the quality demand of the consuming public.
>
> When proved bulls are found, their semen is offered at low cost to ranchers for artificial insemination use. The program has aroused great interest, but its progress depends to a large extent on the ability of the rancher to retain the heifers from the controlled breeding and add them to the cow herd, thereby upgrading the herd and establishing a source of future better beef. Historically, cattle raising has been a marginal type operation, frequently requiring the sale of heifers for slaughter to meet current operating expenses. Obviously, this condition retards the growth of quality herds, and it would appear that if progress toward the desired objective is to be made, reliance must be placed on those whose income permits and/or incentive warrants the retention and raising of their heifer calves each year.
>
> We believe that enactment of the President's proposal on the taxation of farm property (including cattle) would further limit the number of available participants in the beef cattle improvement research program and thereby further impede its progress. Since the program will assist the rancher in producing a better product at no increase in cost, help the feeder on faster turnover and better feed conversion, help the retailer by natural elimination of excess waste fat loss, and provide the consumer the quality product wanted, any impediment to the program will have a detrimental effect on a large segment of the economy.

In summary, then, I have endeavored to point out the kinds of individuals, interests, and commercial endeavors located in communities throughout the United States that will be seriously affected by the proposed legislation. I believe that the implications of this bill have not yet been fully appreciated by its proponents in terms of the tremendous number of individuals to be affected. The flow of risk capital in all the areas surrounding our communities must not be cut off. Cattle raising and farming have been a vital prop of our economy since the earliest days of our Nation. We must not jeopardize their interests.

The Chairman. Thank you, Mr. Trimble.

Colonel Oppenheimer. Mr. James Furlong, president of the Green City, Mo., Chamber of Commerce, vice president of Green City Feedlots, president of the Green City Grain Corp. This is the effect on the town of Green City by capital coming in that was stimulated by the present tax law.

STATEMENT OF JAMES FURLONG,

President, Green City, Mo., Chamber of Commerce; Vice President of Green City Feedlots, Inc.

Mr. Furlong. I am 28 years of age, attended Kansas State University, am married, and have two children. I come from a family with a long history of cattle grazing and feeding. My grandfather, Dan Casement, was one of the original cattlemen in Kansas, starting at the time of the cattle drives up from Texas in 1880. He was one of the original members of the National Cattlemen's Association.

I am now the vice-president of the Green City Feedlots, Inc., and president of the Green City Chamber of Commerce.

Green City, Mo., is typical of the small rural farm community not only in Missouri but throughout the entire United States, has declined from a prosperous thriving community to an area of depressed economy and ever-decreasing population. Small farms can no longer support family units and the youth of Green City has migrated to larger communities upon graduation from high school. Green City lost its railroad and was bypassed by the through highway. The community had been reduced to small grain farms with farmers marketing their grain by feeding out cattle and hogs. With the advent of large commercial feedlots, he has had an increasing economic disadvantage in the purchasing and marketing of livestock for feeding.

About 4 years ago, a farm management agency interested outside investors in purchasing worn out abandoned farmland that had grown up in brush and converting it into livestock operations. The introduction of outside risk capital into the area has revitalized the economy. Local people were hired to manage the operation, and local farmers were able to supplement their income, assisting in building fences, reseeding pastures, and so forth. Local merchants benefited from the purchases of building materials, fertilizers, seed, and so forth.

The grain farmer suddenly found that he had local sources to purchase high-quality feeder calves. Farmers who did not have the capital to stock their pastures are realizing income through leasing grazing rights to their new neighbors.

With the increasing availability of good quality cattle, the local citizens were able to obtain outside financing to establish a feedlot corporation. As the main activity of the feedlot is in the fall and winter, it provides employment to farmhands during their slack season. It also provides farmers with a local market for grain, hay, and silage.

The availability of good quality cattle has attracted buyers from the neighboring Corn Belt States. Green City now has a large weekly livestock auction which brings additional outside dollars into the local economy.

A real indicator for the increasing vitality of the economy is that bank deposits in the last 3 years have increased by 47 percent. Time savings deposits have increased 78 percent.

The entire outlook of the citizens has changed. Green City has installed a city water and sewage system, has paved the town square, and again is assuming the role of a thriving community. The citizens have formed a non-profit cooperative with the aim of attracting new industry which is associated with agriculture.

Outside risk capital has literally saved this community from extinction. Land which has declined in price for several decades now has a ready market.

All of the stimuli outlined above would be abolished if the current tax incentives were removed. A community of this type could not attract heavy industry as it is not blessed with an abundance of natural resources, has already lost the primary transportation means, and has no attraction to industry other than agricultural.

The Chairman. Thank you, Mr. Furlong.

Colonel Oppenheimer. Mr. Jacquin D. Bierman, senior partner of J. K. Lasser & Co., a nationally known firm of tax accountants, a well-known writer on tax law, with 12 years' service in the Treasury Department is going to discuss technical defects in the proposed change in the law.

STATEMENT OF JACQUIN D. BIERMAN,

Partner, J. K. Lasser & Co., New York, New York

Mr. Bierman. My name is Jacquin D. Bierman. I am a partner in the accounting firm of J. K. Lasser & Co., whose principal office is in New York City. I speak for Oppenheimer Industries, Inc. of Kansas City, Mo., as well as for various livestock and farmowners.

If it would be agreeable, and in the interest of saving time, instead of reading my complete statement I should like to skim over the highlights of it. I should like to make amendment to one or two proposals contained on one of the pages, for the record.

The Chairman. Without objection your entire statement will appear in the record.

Mr. Bierman. Thank you, sir.

Secretary Dillon has explained in the hearings before the committee that the proposals as to livestock, citrus groves and other farm properties are carefully limited to abuse cases of persons with large amounts of nonfarm income. Now, this statement appears to equate tax abuse with legitimate risk investment taken by persons who happen to have large amounts of nonfarm income and who put their money to work on the farms. This is obviously incorrect.

There may be abuse cases; and we recognize that there are some. We deplore them and we would propose that legislation, if necessary, be written to strike them down. But there are certainly bona fide and legitimate cases of persons with high income who invest in the farm and livestock areas and not all of these persons who make such investments can be charged with tax abuse.

I take it, then, that the Treasury's basic approach is to cover farm investments geared to abuse cases. A type of approach to that, for example, would be something like the present section 269 which eliminates certain tax advantages in corporate areas where there are acquisitions whose principal purpose is tax avoidance. Some general section such as that could certainly be written.

Also, in terms of analyzing the situations in which we find there to be no economic validity, we think specific statutes could be written, and we would be prepared to submit for your recommendation, if you desired, language along those lines. We all recognize that cases with no economic justification should be given no standing.

But what about persons with large amounts of nonfarm income who legitimately invest their money at the risk of the market? Should they be penalized? Should they be given different treatment, for example, from a cattleman who has large amounts of income from wholly unrelated farm sources?

Why should there be any distinction between income from one unrelated source and from another unrelated source? If the Treasury is interested in seeing there is no conversion of ordinary deductions into capital gain, this problem goes much, much further than just the farm area. Practically every phase of investment activity or business life involves deductions, with the creation of values which at some time may be sold at capital gain.

To take a perfectly obvious and possibly little-thought-of example: if a person invests in low dividend securities and pays interest on loans necessary to buy those securities, pays fees to investment counsel, pays custodian fees to hold the securities, those are deducted and legitimately so. But the Treasury would not even suggest that those deductions be used to convert capital gain on the sale of securities into ordinary income.

Basically, this problem goes much deeper than the farm area. But the farm has been singled out for what we regard to be highly inconsistent and discriminatory treatment.

In the so-called interaction of ordinary deductions and capital gain situations, the Treasury has taken four different types of positions in four different types of cases.

In the recapture of depreciation on personal property it has taken one position. In the proposals it now makes for depreciation recapture in the case of real estate, it would only convert capital gain on sale into ordinary income to extent of depreciation. In the case of mineral properties, it takes a third position and in the case of the farm area it has taken a wholly different and fourth position.

But in none of these, except in the farm area, has the Treasury taken the position that ordinary everyday operating and maintenance expense should be utilized to convert capital gain into ordinary income. It has done this in the farm area.

Now, it appears to me that the so-called reform—I dislike the use of the word "reform" because "reform" only means "change," and unless there is a valid reason for reform we should not talk about it as reform, we should talk about it as change—but the changes which the Treasury would make I think are essentially discriminatory in three ways.

In the first place, they would treat capital gains from farm sources completely different from any other situation. In the second place, this is the first example I know of where the Treasury has proposed legislation where the type or the character of the income, capital gain or ordinary income, is geared to the source of the investment in the activity. In the third place, the characterization of the income as capital gain or ordinary income according to the Treasury would depend on the tax bracket of the taxpayer, how much additional nonfarm adjusted gross income the person would have.

Although constitutional questions have been rather rare in the tax field for a long time, I suggest to you that these proposals so approach the area of direct taxation geared to an individual rather than to an activity that constitutional questions could potentially be involved.

It is my feeling that the essential approach of the Treasury in the farm area case is basically fallacious through the creation and attempt to distinguish between types of income. Because of this fallacious underpinning of the proposal, we run across all kinds of complications which we should not have to be concerned with in the tax area.

For example, if we are concerned with distinguishing between types of income, what is farm income and what is nonfarm income? And why should it make a difference whether income is derived from the property which is handled as a ranch or from some other property which may be next door and produces exactly the same kind of income?

If I get gravel from my ranch, under one suggestion that would be farming income. If I get gravel from a pit next door to my ranch, that would be nonfarm income. The bases for these distinctions just do not exist. To be concerned with such distinctions in a tax fashion indicates that the fundamental approach to the law is just wrong. What logic is there in distinguishing between different kinds of unrelated farm income and unrelated nonfarm income?

This is another distinction which we should not have to consider: The Treasury proposal would set a cutoff point of $15,000 of nonfarm income. That cutoff point could be any cutoff point. But the point is that if an individual had less than the cutoff point income none of his farm loss could be converted into ordinary income when property was sold. But if he had more than the cutoff point income, all of the losses would be converted into ordinary income. So that because of the swing of $1 below or above the cutoff point, we might have several of tens of thousands of dollars of capital gain converted into ordinary income.

Will mandatory joint returns or consolidated returns be required for the sake of aggregating all these elements of income and loss, and in the case of related groups, how far will attribution rules have to be carried?

Supposing operating deductions and operating loss carryovers absorb nonfarm adjusted gross income? To what extent would those be used first to wipe out the nonfarm income and to what extent would the farm losses be used to wipe it out?

For how many years would this excess deductions account be carried over?

What would happen in the event of death? Would the current case of disposition of farm property under various tax free exchanges or nontaxable transfers be recognized under the law?

What kind of farm expenses would be included in computing the excess deductions account? Would interest, taxes, casualty losses from drought be included? In the "hobby loss" provision, which is section 270 of the law, none of those expenses are determined in computing the $50,000 amount which would strike down deductions. Yet the Treasury does not apparently propose to eliminate them from EDA.

We suggest that the "hobby loss" provision, plus legislation, if required, to eliminate the sham, the gimmick-type of case, is all that the Treasury really needs.

Mr. Keogh. Excuse me, I didn't hear the last phrase—the $50,000 hobby—what did you say?

Mr. Bierman. I said that section 270 relating to the hobby loss situation plus legislation if required to eliminate the sham or the abuse case is all that the Treasury really is interested in at this time. We believe that there is certainly adequate precedent under the decisions, decisions going up to the Supreme Court, for the Treasury to strike down sham cases.

But if additional statutes are needed, those statutes we feel could be drafted to strike down the types of abuses that exist.

The Treasury proposal, the present Treasury proposal, is not the first time that this ordinary income capital gain dichotomy has been presented to the Congress. This happened in 1951 and this situation was specifically directed to the Congress in 1952 by correspondence between the Secretary of the Treasury and the various tax committees of the Congress. And the Congress specifically decided to leave the tax rules as they stand today. There has been nothing that has happened in the last 10 or 12 years which should in any way cause these basic rules to be revised.

If there are problems involved with hobby farms, there is a long line of cases by which certain tests have been laid down to strike out the hobby cases. But we believe it is wrong for the Treasury to attempt to take an abuse situation and then to write a general statute geared to an abuse situation. General statutes should be written in general terms and not in terms of abuses.

While I have been concerned basically with the technical approach to the Treasury proposal, there are certain positive considerations I should like to just point out very briefly.

The capital gain provisions have been a deliberate encouragement to risk capital to invest in livestock and farming operations. Obviously, risk capital comes from nonfarm as well as farm sources. If these incentives for which there has been no showing of lack of continued need, if these incentives are taken away by Treasury proposals, then this risk capital is going to dry up, producing some of the conditions you have heard today.

We question whether this really represents national policy. Obviously, any funds invested become income to someone else. If cattle are bought or repaired or seed put in the ground, or feed is supplied to cattle, the expense becomes income to the recipient. If these sources of investment are dried up by the Treasury proposal, these sources of income, too, will no longer be available for taxation by the Treasury Department.

Capital invested in livestock and farming has furnished additional sources of income to distressed farms and farm areas, has provided markets for existing farms, has sparked rehabilitation of rundown farms, has made farm opportunities available to young technically trained men who don't have the capital to start in business themselves and has encouraged the maintenance of breeding herds which otherwise would not have existed.

The Treasury, we think, has viewed this so-called problem from the very narrow viewpoint of the so-called loophole. The loophole can't be very large because it estimates that only $5 million is involved in the whole problem. We wonder whether the Treasury has considered the basic economic policy determinations that have led to the present tax rules and the economic ramifications that will result if there is any change.

Certainly, we believe that a more complete study is indicated before the drastic provisions proposed by the Treasury Department should be accepted.

Thank you very much.

The Chairman. Thank you, Mr. Bierman.

Colonel Oppenheimer. May I call on a man not listed to read a proposed piece of legislation that would eliminate the so-called gimmick hobby-type deal, we think. Mr. Levitt.

The Chairman. Identify yourself, if you will, because you are not listed here in this agenda.

Colonel Oppenheimer. Mr. Levitt is vice-president of my management firm. He resides in New York.

Mr. Keogh. I would like the committee to know that the young man is a bearer of a distinguished name and is the son of the very able comptroller of the State of New York.

The Chairman. We are glad to have you with us.

STATEMENT OF ARTHUR LEVITT,

Vice President, Oppenheimer Industries,
Kansas City, Mo.

Mr. Levitt. I am Arthur Levitt, Jr. I live in New York. I am in charge of the eastern operations of Oppenheimer Industries.

The suggested legislation is intended to eliminate the tax abuses from certain livestock and farm cases. I will briefly outline its provisions. It pertains to section 275, disallowance of certain farm expenses and losses:

> (a) Expenses and losses otherwise deductible under sections 162(a) and 165(c) incurred by an individual in the trade or business of farming shall be considered as personal expenses under section 262 if any of the following has occurred:
>
> (1) Any property, including livestock (as defined in section 1231(b)(3)), is purchased or sold by the individual during any taxable year of such trade or business at a price other than the fair market value of such property within the market area of such purchase or sale, or
>
> (2) The individual has received a guarantee in respect of property used in such trade or business of (A) the life or lives of any livestock, or (B) the increment of any livestock over its lifetime, or (C) the sales price of any property, including livestock, or (D) the sale of any number of livestock, or
>
> (3) The individual has an option, or is subject to a call, to sell any property used in such trade or business, other than the normal future delivery contract common to the trade or business of farming.
>
> This section should be applicable only with respect to events occurring after December 31, 1963.

Finally, section 1231(b) is to be amended by adding at the end thereof the following new subparagraph (5):

> (5) Exception. Such item shall not include any farm property, including livestock, if any of the events specified in section 275(a) has occurred.

Thank you.

The Chairman. Thank you, Mr. Levitt.

Colonel Oppenheimer. It is our contention that the redoing of the existing law as so designed would completely eliminate the abuse that was cited by Secretary Dillon without upsetting the whole industry.

We do not have enough time to read any of our statements. I would like to list who have given us statements, which you have copies of, to indicate widespread support of our position in totally opposing excess deductions account:

Mr. Jay B. Dillingham, president of the Kansas City Stockyards and former president of the Kansas City Chamber of Commerce; his statement which you have copies of is in regard to the disruption of the entire Kansas City economy that will be caused by the proposed change in the law.

Mr. Harold Humphreys, senior vice-president of the First National Bank of Kansas City, the detrimental effect on country banks and extension of credit through the Midwest.

Mr. L. C. Carpenter, director of public affairs, Missouri Farmers Association, the necessity of outside capital during transition phase of agriculture.

Mr. W. D. Davis, president of Farm Management Associates, former president of American Society of Farm Managers and Rural Appraisers, former president of National Institute of Farm Brokers, the scope of farm management industry as an integral part of agricultural economy.

Mr. Winthrop Rockefeller, financier, philanthropist, one of the primary developers of Santa Gertrudis breed and owner and operator of Winrock Farms at Morrilton, Ark., the contribution of present tax laws in creating and developing markets for registered herds as well as stimulation of depressed agricultural areas.

These particular statements and people were merely selected to illustrate the wide range of opposition to this proposed change in the law.

In summary, as I have stated at the outset, we and our associated ranch and herd owners as well as the group that are with us today are in entire agreement with the Secretary in his opposition to the so-called tax gimmicks and tax loopholes. But, we firmly believe that items of this nature must be clearly differentiated from a tax subsidy, which is not an accident of the law, but was purposely set forth by Congress to accomplish a specific purpose for the public good.

Thank you.

The Chairman. Without objection, the material appended to the statement that Colonel Oppenheimer has submitted will be included in the record, including the additional statements of those listed to whom you have referred.

Colonel Oppenheimer. There are some missing, sir.

The Chairman. Yes; you will get them in to us rather promptly, will you?

Colonel Oppenheimer. Yes.

The Chairman. Fine.

(The documents referred to follow:)

Example I

HOW THE PRESENT LAW SALVAGED A SMALL MISSOURI AGRICULTURAL COMMUNITY

Mr. "A" and his son are Missouri farmers who own 300 acres of rolling pasture and 100 acres of bottom land, 15 acres of which are in supported wheat and the balance, alfalfa. The land is valued at $200 per acre, or $80,000. They have $20,000 in trucks, cars, and machinery and are attempting to make a living off of a 100-cow breeding herd, surplus hay, and the revenue gained from the Government on their supported wheat.

They produce 90 calves per year worth $110 each for a total gross of $9,900. Fifty tons of alfalfa not needed in the operation bring a sale price of $20 a ton or a gross of $1,000 and they average $1,100 from the Government on their wheat. The total gross income is $12,000. The property is 50 percent mortgaged.

Gasoline, utilities, taxes, supplies, supplementary feed, veterinary bills, and other direct costs of the farm come to $3,000 per year. Interest on $50,000 in mortgages comes to $3,000 per year. Minimum necessary maintenance repairs, depreciation, etc., on machinery, improvements, replacement of aged cows comes to $3,000 per year.

After money is taken out for supporting the families of the father and son, nothing is left for amortization and mortgage; the property is gradually going downhill; no return is being made on equity in the investment; and the standard of living is just above a subsistence level.

Mr. "B" to the north owns 200 acres of cultivated land in extremely poor condition, 15 acres of which is under wheat allotment, 20 acres under corn allotment, and the balance in free grains, on which he gets a very poor price as there is no market locally and they have to be transported to a central terminal 200 miles away. He grosses approximately $2,000 per year from the Government on his supported crops and about $3,000 per year on his unsupported crops. He nets approximately $3,000 per year for his labor, gets no return on his capital investment, and is barely able to make it.

Mr. "C" to the west is an elderly man who has 400 acres—350 in rough pasture which has gradually been encroached upon by the brush, some exhausted cultivated land which has been corn-farmed for years with no additional fertilizer put on, and a 15-acre wheat allotment. He nets approximately $2,000 per year, one-half of which comes from Government price supports and he and his wife are living under extremely severe conditions trying to pay their taxes and support themselves on this amount. He recognizes that his farm is worth $100 per acre, but it has gone so far downhill that there is no local market because no one in that area has sufficient capital to purchase it and to put the necessary fertilizer and improvements back in order to make it productive. Local people also recognize that if it is put back into production it would make no better a situation than the farm owned by Mr. "A" and the amount of possible net return on capital would just not justify the risk.

The small town 10 miles away has been steadily going downhill in population on every census since 1890, most of the storekeepers would like to sell out but there are no buyers, and the bank is considering paying off their depositors and stockholders and liquidating.

At this time, the local farm management firm is able to secure the interest of Mr. "D" who is a sophisticated investor that is attracted to the situation by the fact that by investing in land and cattle in this area he can expense out a certain amount of money which is deductible to him in his high tax bracket from other sources of income and has a reasonable chance of making a small profit on a future sale which will recover most of his previous expenses with the entire gain taxable at capital gain rates. He now purchases Mr. "C's" farm for $40,000, which permits Mr. "C" to retire to town and live out his remaining years in relative comfort. He purchases this land with Mr. "C" taking back a 7-percent purchase money mortgage. The 7 percent is deductible to Mr. "D" and is only taxable to Mr. "C" at a very small tax bracket, but the interest and the amortization assure Mr. "C" and his wife of an adequate retirement income.

Next, Mr. "D" proceeds to spend $50 per acre, or an additional $20,000 over a 4-year improvement program designed to convert the entire farm into improved permanent pasture. He hires Mr. "B" to do the work and he purchases all of his supplies and fertilizer, etc., in the local town.

He now purchases 100 cows which he places with Mr. "A" on a maintenance contract at $80 per cow per year. The cows cost him $250 per head and the Government permits him to depreciate them over a 7-year period. He further plans to retain all of his heifer calves for replacement and let his herd grow to the maximum to fill out his improved pasture as the improvement program being conducted by Mr. "B" proceeds over the 4-year period.

Because of the herd growth and retention of most of his calf crop, together with the depreciation that he is getting on his purchase, he is now picking up an additional annual loss that he is writing off against his high outside income. For the purposes of this example, let us assume that his total losses from the operation of his cattle herd, depreciation on his cattle herd, improvement program on the farm, interest on the farm mortgage, depreciation on existing improvements on the farm, has now come to $20,000 per year. He is in a 70-percent tax bracket. If one subtracts the eventual 25-percent capital gains tax from this we arrive at 45 percent. Forty-five percent of $20,000 is $9,000 per year which the Government is losing in tax revenue from Mr. "D."

What is happening in the neighborhood? Mr. "A" with no increase in labor is picking up an additional $8,000 per year from Mr. "D's" herd, which he is running in conjunction with his own. This will increase as Mr. "D's" herd increases. Out of the $8,000 maintenance, he is paying Mr. "D" $2,000 in rent, purchasing $2,000 in feed from Mr. "B" who now has a local market for some of his produce and he is making more efficient use of his machinery with only a $500 increase in expense.

Both Mr. "A" and Mr. "B" have decided that they can drop their 15-acre wheat allotments and convert the land to alfalfa as they now have a market for it. The additional cattle for Mr. "A" and the improvement program that Mr. "B" is conducting take too much of their time to be bothered with the small wheat acreage. Mr. "D" has also authorized Mr. "A" to drop Mr. "C's" former allotments as he wants the additional permanent pasture and they were too small to mess with.

The net taxable take-home pay of Mr. "A" and Mr. "B" has been increased $3,000 per year each. This has placed them both in a 30-percent bracket and the Government pockets $1,800 in taxes. The balance of the approximate $16,000 per year cash that Mr. "D" is spending in the neighborhood are high velocity dollars and they generally pass through three hands before leaving the community. On the assumption that everyone's hands that they pass through are in a 25-percent bracket, the Government is making approximately $8,000 in taxes from this activity. The wheat and corn allotments of farmers "A," "B," and "C" have all been dropped and the Government is saving $4,000 on the price support program.

The general activity of Mr. "D" in improving his farm, painting his barns, fixing his perimeter fences has had a traditionally contagious effect, and the farmers on his borders are fixing their fences in cooperation with him, putting fertilizer in their land, and generally upgrading the situation. More important than the money has been the correction of a situation of neighborhood demoralization and despair.

The adjoining town has a population of 300. The interest paid by Mr. "D" to "C," the improvement and farm repair work going to Mr. "B" and suppliers in the town, and the cow maintenance going to Mr. "A" have had a dramatic effect in revitalizing a distressed community, completely disproportionate to what the effect would be in a larger city.

Mr. "D" is not a philanthropist but a hard-headed businessman. He has every expectation of getting every dollar that he has expensed out in a 70-percent bracket back plus a small profit and pay no more than 25 percent on the total.

However, he would not have engaged in these activities if it were not for the present tax structure. He will not engage in these activities if the proposed change is passed by Congress.

If the proposed change in the law is reviewed not in the light of trying to punish Mr. "D" and discriminate against him, but in the light of whether the net return to the Government in savings on price supports plus increased tax revenue gained from the recipients of Mr. "D's" expense money is reviewed, the Government makes a profit. Apart from this consideration, the small agricultural community is salvaged.

In summary, this type of change in the tax law should not be analyzed only as to the moral value of Mr. "D's" motives, but what the net cost to the Government is and what the benefits to the country are from these dollars that Mr. "D" has spent.

Example II

NECESSITY OF OUTSIDE RISK CAPITAL TO PREVENT FORCED LIQUIDATION ON LARGE WESTERN RANCHES

The western cattle industry historically has had to rely on outside capital for support. In the late 1880's and early 1900's the cattle industry in New Mexico, Colorado, Wyoming, Montana, western Kansas, and Nebraska was developed by money supplied by corporate sources in England and Scotland. Even in those days, millions of dollars were required to acquire sufficient land and stock to insure an economic operation. During recent years the industry has relied on individual eastern investors for their capital.

To illustrate this point, the following actual example is provided:

A large ranch in the Panhandle of Texas was founded over 100 years ago in the early 1850's by a pioneer family. Descendants of the original pioneers have through the years continued to expand the operation, acquiring additional land and eventually developing a 1,000-head unit.

At today's prices the entire holdings are worth nearly a million dollars with ranch land worth $600 per cow unit, nearly $250,000 in cattle and $100,000 in equipment. The direct descendants of the founders are a grandmother and two young granddaughters. At the time her son was killed in an automobile accident in the early 1950's, the grandmother was reluctant to sell the ranch as she would like to hold it in the family until the granddaughters were married, and in fact would have had difficulty in finding a buyer during this period of drought years.

At this same time a young local rancher who was running 200 head of cattle on leased land decided that he would have to abandon the cattle business as his small operation was not economically feasible. As he had a good reputation in the area for honesty and ability, the grandmother offered to sell the cattle and lease her land to him. With his limited capital, he would not have been able to accept her offer if he had not found an eastern banker who was attracted to cattle as an investment because of the current tax laws.

Today the grandmother is living in Dallas, sending her granddaughters to good schools on the $32,000 per year she collects from leasing her ranch. The young man is prospering in the ranching business as his 200 head of cattle and his share of the calves from the 800 head owned by the eastern banker provide him with a good economic unit.

The continued operation of this ranch and the holding together of the high-quality cattle developed for over 100 years has a more far-reaching economic impact than just the three families concerned with the present ownership and lease rights. The ranch is a major source of the high-quality cattle for a large livestock auction in a neighboring town. A local feedlot finds that it is able to compete with feedlots in the grain States because of the availability of good feeder cattle in the immediate vicinity.

With the many hazards of drought, blizzards, epidemics and fluctuating markets which are common to the livestock industry, the banker would not want to remain in the cattle business under the proposed revisions to the tax laws pertaining to livestock. Without the capital the rancher could not continue and the ranch would have to be sold. This same circumstance would be repeated several hundred times throughout the West.

STATEMENT OF JAY B. DILLINGHAM,

President, The Kansas City Stockyards Co.

I am president of the Kansas City Stockyards Co. and a former president of the Kansas City Chamber of Commerce, and have been active in farming and breeding herds in the Clay County, Mo., area. I am extremely sorry that a previous business commitment prevents me from giving testimony at the hearings on March 6, but I am writing this statement to be read by any of the groups associated with Oppenheimer Industries or the Missouri Farmers Association.

1. A major portion of the Kansas-Missouri economy and a substantial portion of the cattle coming into the Kansas City stockyards for

over half a century have been owned by individuals with substantial nonfarm income or have been grazed on land such as the Kansas Bluestem or Oklahoma Osage, which is owned by individuals of wide and varied financial interests.

The protection and security of being able to offset drought or catastrophe losses in a bad year against other income with the eventual hope, if they so desire, of selling land or breeding stock at a capital gains rate has been the incentive to keep many of them in a business which has recently been a low-profit one and in which there are more hazards and risks than in other sections of the economy.

2. Among my personal friends and associates in the commission firms, order buyers, feed manufacturers, officers of purebred associations, and other people tied in with this business there are a majority who through early background and family tradition in agriculture have owned ranches, farms and breeding herds as a secondary interest and have had to hire resident managers or outside management firms because they have not personally had the time to do the work themselves. These people, relative to their numbers, have had an important effect on raising the quality of breeding animals, improving wornout farms, and maintaining the flow of quality-type cattle into stockyards and feedlots of Kansas and Missouri.

3. To my knowledge no one has recently criticized any other industry because it has required a tremendous amount of assembled capital from all sources in order to build a mill or fabricating plant. Likewise, the recent industrial revolution in agriculture has meant that an economically competitive livestock operation requires an enormous amount of capital in both land and cattle. For a young man starting out or for a small farmer trying to stay in and survive, one hope is to have available to him outside capital from people who will give him cattle on maintenance contracts or grazing or feeding contracts or permit him to lease land that they have developed. This type of thing is being done on an extremely large scale and is solving a good part of this transition phase in agriculture by private capital without Government assistance.

Combinations of all three of the points I have mentioned are occurring around the Kansas City area to an extent that an enormous amount of employment is involved as well as the prosperity of all types of business that are only indirectly involved with livestock but are nonetheless affected. It is my personal opinion that the proposed discrimination against people with over $15,000 in nonfarm income with its consequent cutting off of additional capital from this source and its possible liquidation of existing farm and livestock holdings because of a fear of this action is going to cause a disruption of the livestock industry as well as the general business economy of Kansas City and similar type cities far beyond the imagination of the people in the Treasury that have proposed this change in the law.

STATEMENT OF HAROLD W. HUMPHREYS,

Senior Vice President, First National Bank of Kansas City

The proposed discriminatory provision in the new tax bill specifically aimed at ranch and livestock owners with nonfarm incomes exceeding $15,000 annually will dry up the source of capital which has contributed so materially during the past decade in restoring the economic status of marginal farm areas to a position whereby they are now improving the productivity of the soil by fertilization and proper seeding. Pastures that formerly were of little value are presently furnishing the feed for cow herds and young cattle so that the available protein from red meats for human consumption is at an alltime high at prices within the reach of our people.

This program has also included land previously in a production of grain under agricultural price supports, and thereby removed the cost of these price supports from the already overburdened agricultural program. This could not have been true if outside capital in substantial amounts had not been attracted to the livestock industry, and the supply of livestock available for slaughter would not have reached its present totals, whereas the very necessary proteins would have been priced beyond the reach of millions of our consuming public.

To my personal knowledge, many small livestock men and farmers in central Kansas have received much-needed income for the pasturing and care of herds owned by those who would be penalized by this proposed discriminatory tax legislation which would dry up this source of risk capital, cut off the income of marginal farmers, likely force them into the role of a relief position, and allow the land which will be needed to produce food for livestock at a reasonable cost to be forced out of production.

The present program has in many cases taken land from the grain program which has been costing the Government stabilization program substantially more in direct supports than any income which may be derived by the proposed change in tax laws.

I am definitely opposed to any change in the present tax laws that would discriminate against those engaging in livestock production who enjoy substantial nonfarm income.

STATEMENT OF L. C. CARPENTER,

Director of Public Affairs, Missouri Farmers Association, Inc., Columbia, Mo.

Mr. Chairman and members of the committee, my name is L. C. Carpenter, director of public affairs of the Missouri Farmers Association, headquarters at Columbia, Mo.

The business of farming is becoming one of the most highly competitive and technical businesses in which any individual can engage. Furthermore, for a family, there are few businesses which require more capital outlay to successfully carry out than a farming enterprise. A tremendous amount of outside capital and financing is required under today's system of operation. Any punitive tax restriction that your committee places on the availability of this capital and financing will automatically become a detriment to the farm economy.

Specifically, may I make an issue of the purebred livestock breeder? This is the farm operation which by and large provides the high quality breeding livestock for average farm herds. This enterprise is generally carried on by persons with large amounts of capital, and in many instances financed and operated by persons who are gainfully employed elsewhere. To impose restrictive tax provisions that would make it virtually impossible, or at least impractical, for this farmowner to carry on such an enterprise, would prove to the disadvantage of the family farmer who needs a source of supply of high-quality breeding stock on his farm.

Secondly, the demand for capital investment has increased manifold over the past few years. In fact, the young farm family encounters much difficulty in securing adequate capital for this investment. In many instances there are active farmers now who are serving as managers of well-equipped and well-capitalized farms of others. Restrictive tax legislation should not prevail to eliminate this opportunity to those people.

Thirdly, the price of farmland has advanced rather rapidly over the past few years, and there are those who criticize persons engaged in other occupations for acquiring farmland at a relatively high price. We can well understand where by this situation prevailing would be a source of discontentment with some young farm families who wish to acquire farmland and go into the business of farming on their own. On the other hand, the retired farmer, those who are physically disabled, a widow, and various other comparably situated people, would find a much lesser demand for their real property and might be forced to sell it at a distressed price if outside capital could not be profitably invested in this farmland.

It is in the light of these three suggestions that we urge you and your committee to consider seriously any proposed tax reform which would prove a disadvantage to the entire farm economy.

STATEMENT OF W. D. DAVIS,

President, Farm Management Associates, Inc.

As president of one of the major professional farm management organizations, I desire to object strenuously to the provision in the President's 1963 tax message relating to capital gains and losses in the sale of farm properties. It is my judgment that the present method of treating such capital gains and losses must be retained.

The nonresident owner investing in farm property should receive the same tax treatment that he would receive when investing in urban property. Failure to receive like treatment will cause investors to discriminate against the purchase of farm property, thereby depriving the farm real estate market of their support.

Most farms that are offered for sale require a substantial amount of rehabilitation before they can be expected to operate profitably. In fact, they are many times offered for sale because they are losing money for their present owners. The proposed change in the tax treatment of these rehabilitation costs which must result in annual operating losses for several years will, in my judgment, make the purchase and improvement of such farms not possible.

Almost every farm offered to a professional farm-management firm for management is not currently profitable to its owner. Usually substantial expenditures for soil improvement and building remodeling are necessary before the farm can earn an annual profit. In my judgment, the proposed tax treatment of such expenditures will be so unsatisfactory that the professional farm manager will be unable to secure the approval of the client for the expenditures that are needed. Such farms will then continue to be "poor farms" that are a drag on the community in which they are located.

The number of persons engaged in farm management work in our country is in some measure indicated by the fact that there are about 1,300 members of the American Society of Farm Managers & Rural Appraisers and about 1,500 members of the National Institute of Farm Brokers. In almost every town of over 2,000 in population, there are one or two people who make most of their living in the management of farms belonging to others. Thus, it is probable that there are well over 5,000 persons or firms that manage farms belonging to others. If these firms average only 5 farms managed by each firm, more than 25,000 farms are managed serving that many individual farmowners. Since the great majority of these nonresident owners are either widows, orphans, or people who live too far away from their land to look after it themselves or are not trained in farm management, it is possible that these nonresident owners and their families may constitute a group of as many as 60,000 people who will be seriously injured by this proposed change. Estimating the average family of the farm manager at four persons and the average size of the tenant family at the same number indicates that another 130,000 people will be adversely affected making more than 180,000 in all. In fact, the inability to rehabilitate such farm properties will have an additional detrimental effect on the suppliers of materials and labor for such work and will affect many, many other persons.

Having spent more than 30 years in the management of farms belonging to others, I have had much experience with the problem of getting them to furnish the money needed to rehabilitate their farms so that they could earn a profit. This is an extremely difficult task under the present tax provisions. Under the proposed revision, it will be almost impossible. I, therefore, strongly recommend that no change be made in the capital gain and loss provisions of the Federal income-tax laws as they pertain to farm properties.

STATEMENT OF WINTHROP ROCKEFELLER

To the House Ways and Means Committee

Winrock Farms of Morrilton, Ark., was established in August of 1953 on approximately 1,000 acres of depleted land. From its inception, as is stated in publications relative to the farm, the objectives were to develop an outstanding herd of Santa Gertrudis cattle and, in the process, demonstrate what could be done in terms of the reclamation of submarginal land. A herd of approximately 30 head was purchased in 1954 and introduced to the farm the following year. Since that time the herd has been expanded to in excess of 2,000 animals, and the area to approximately 24,000 acres including rice, small grains, fodder, and an experimental fish farm. Although the majority of the farm's produce is marketed locally and in continental United States, quality Santa Gertrudis breeding stock, because of its adaptability and resistance to disease, is in considerable demand in the export market—particularly in Latin America.

The number of employees has grown to in excess of 125 people, including 8 college graduates on the management staff—one holding a degree in veterinary medicine and a second holding a Ph.D. in animal nutrition. Under the direction of this competent staff a long range, intensive, vigorous program of beef cattle improvement and land development is in progress, including drainage and soil conservation.

In excess of 70 miles of fences have been erected, 25 miles of roads built, and approximately 30 major buildings erected. Essentially all of this work has been done by local labor and the majority of the materials have been purchased locally. (During the period of peak construction in 1954, the third of drought years, the impact of the payroll, in excess of $2,000 a day, was sufficient to keep Conway County off the list of disaster aid counties.)

Consistent with the objectives of the farm, a veterinary center for research and routine procedures has been developed at a cost in excess of $100,000. The work done here under the direction of the veterinarian and the farm Ph.D. has been published and is the source of material for technical papers presented by members of the staff at colleges, universities, and professional association meetings. Additionally, in excess of 60 college students have each received 3 months training as part of a special student summer program.

Also consistent with policy, the farm is open to the public and receives in excess of 125,000 tourists a year from every State in the Union. (The majority of these visitors must travel in excess of 100 miles to visit the farm, thus creating a considerable consumption of gasoline with the resulting tax yield to both State and National treasuries. Similarly a large percentage of these people will enjoy at least one meal in local facilities, which also has a considerable economic impact on the area.)

Although the majority of the tourists are curiosity seekers they do include a considerable number of farmers and cattlemen who seek counseling from the staff relative not only to procedures at Winrock, but also advice in connection with their own operations. It is estimated that between one-quarter and one-half of staff time is devoted to rendering this service.

To the commercial cattlemen it would be readily obvious that the above sketched program could not have been undertaken without considerable supplemental capital resources, invested because of the incentive provided by the present favorable tax laws.

Finally, because Winrock Farms is our home and Mrs. Rockefeller and I do take an active part in civic affairs, plus the favorable publicity that Winrock Farms has enjoyed, the homestead has become a center of many meetings bearing on the economic and cultural development of the State.

The Chairman. Are there any questions of these gentlemen?

Mr. Keogh. Mr. Chairman.

The Chairman. Mr. Keogh.

Mr. Keogh. Colonel, on the letterhead of the National Livestock Tax Committee, the representatives of which preceded you at the witness table, is listed among others as sponsoring organizations the Missouri Livestock Association. I notice in the statements that you are submitting there is one of the president of the Missouri Livestock Association.

Is there any difference?

Colonel Oppenheimer. No, sir; they are the same outfit.

Mr. Keogh. Is that one of the statements you are going to submit for the record?

Colonel Oppenheimer. Yes, sir. We were late but I have a copy if you wish me to read it. It is very short.

Mr. Keogh. It will be in the record; won't it?

Colonel Oppenheimer. Yes, sir. He is supporting our position completely.

Mr. Keogh. From your knowledge of the industry and your experience in it, are you in a position to tell the committee how much of the cattle in the country are owned by people with nonfarm income?

Colonel Oppenheimer. Sir, I can't describe it exactly but in certain areas of the country with which myself and several of the people here are familiar, we will be able to give you a fairly good idea.

Mr. Greenough, can you tell them about what percentage of the people in Montana and Wyoming are running cattle with outside ownership?

Mr. Greenough. About 55 percent.

Colonel Oppenheimer. Mr. Furlong, in the Kansas Blue Stem what would you say the situation is on the ownership and the portion of the cattle economy that is tied up with outside risk capital?

Mr. Furlong. I would say it runs very high in the Flinthill area with which I am very familiar. It will probably run between 70 and 90 percent. Now, this is grass area.

Colonel Oppenheimer. May I ask you another question. Are those people who are running cattle in the Kansas Blue Stem that don't live in the ranches, that are buying them and putting them out on maintenance contracts, how many would you guess, just picking a figure out of the air, probably have an income of over $15,000 a year from nonfarm sources?

Mr. Furlong. I would say 65 percent.

Colonel Oppenheimer. Gentlemen, we just picked two areas of the country. It is not true so much in the Southwest where people have oil income with which to supplement their agricultural operations but it certainly is true in Wyoming, Montana, Idaho, Kansas, Missouri. I'm not sure about Arkansas.

Mr. Keogh. Would you say that any of those people engaged in those areas that you have mentioned who have substantial nonfarm income would fall under the definition of a legitimate rancher or farmer?

Colonel Oppenheimer. Sir, I am not sure what the term "legitimate rancher" means. If it means somebody born on the farm who has moved away; Mr. Puckett, who is a very prominent industrialist in this country, is a legitimate farmer. If Mr. Puckett was born in the city and moved to the farm and then moved away, I'm not sure, maybe he would not be a legitimate farmer. It so happened he was born on an Illinois farm and moved away.

(The following material was received by the committee:)

ADDENDUM TO TESTIMONY

Subsequent to the hearings, I have realized that my answer to Representative Keogh's question, "What is a legitimate rancher?" was quite inadequate. I suppose the technical answer would be: "A rancher who was operating in accordance with the laws and the statutes." Another definition could be that "a legitimate rancher is one whose mother and father were married." Seriously, I realize that he meant the term as it was repeatedly referred to all that morning by Mr. Stephen Hart of the American National Cattlemen's Association.

Rather than use the term "legitimate rancher," it would be better to use the term "established rancher" which Mr. Hart used in his interview with the Kansas City Star which was quoted 3 days before the hearings. I am enclosing a copy of the article. In essence, he did not want to see anything happen that would hurt the interests of the "established rancher."

Again, I am not certain what he meant by "established rancher," but I can give a few specific examples of what he did not mean:

1. The son of a small Texas dirt farmer who came out of World War II as a naval officer without a penny who got a Government lease away from a member of the executive committee of one of Hart's organizations and then got a west Kansas banker to put cattle on shares with him. He is not an "established rancher."

2. A millionaire director of one of the cattle associations had a tract of State land adjoining his ranch that had been leased by his family for two generations at about one-third normal market rent. It was put up for a public sealed bid sale and a Texas oilman looking for an inflation hedge outbid the director by 25 percent. The Texas man leased it to a young agricultural college graduate in the neighborhood at a 3-percent net rent. The young man stocked it with "tenant cattle" and now has about half as large an operation as the original rancher and is running at about 70 percent of the older rancher's per head operating costs. Mr. Hart and his group would not consider either the Texas owner or the young competitor as "established ranchers."

3. The small tenant farmers of Missouri, Illinois, and Tennessee would not be "established ranchers." When outside capital puts exhausted corn and cotton land back into permanent pasture and leases it or sells it with small downpayments to these people who now go into beef cattle as the Department of Agriculture has been recommending, this is not considered desirable. Neither are the tax laws that encourage it.

4. The recent policy of the Department of Defense to put all grazing rights on military land up for public sealed bid to any U.S. citizen that had a decent reputation and looked like he could pay the rent let all kinds of people into the game who were not established ranchers.

On a more positive note, what would be a typical "established rancher" of the last 30 years? He has upward of a 1,000-cow unit which at an average of 30 acres to a unit is 30,000 acres. His herd is worth $200,000; his land is worth $700,000; and he has $100,000 in machinery and improvements.

Because of the tremendous per head operating savings that can be made by expanding from 1,000 cows to 2,000 cows, he is attempting to squeeze out his smaller neighbors by purchase, lease, or maneuvers with various State and Federal agencies. If someone dies, he finds it quite objectionable to compete with outside capital on the purchase of adjoining land. As was mentioned in Mr. Hart's testimony, this causes "inflated land values." Whether the widow of the small rancher who died feels this way might be open to question.

In correcting the abuses described in Secretary Dillon's exhibit 15, there are five general areas of approach:

1. As Representative Curtis mentioned, a tax reduction that would narrow the gap between the top income rates and the capital gain rate would do most of it. The difference between 91 percent and 25 percent is 66 percent. The difference between 65 percent and 19 percent is 46 percent.

2. In the proposed draft of a minor change in sections 275 and 123 of the code, Mr. Arthur Levitt, Jr., of our firm, showed how most of the gimmick deals could be eliminated. This should have no adverse effect on the flow of risk capital to the small farmers or on the renewal of depressed rural areas in accordance with USDA policies.

3. If the country estate problem is bothering anyone, Congress can make a few small modifications in the limits on section 270, the Hobby law.

4. In the next area, if a modified EDA is demanded, the critical decision is on what end it will be modified. If it is in the direction of exempting certain expenses such as interest, taxes, drought, and a basic nominal per head feed allowance from the annual account, high bracket risk capital will still be attracted to the more efficient operations.

5. If it is in the direction of raising who is going to be discriminated against, from $15,000 in nonfarm income to $50,000 and considering oil income as farm income, for this purpose, as recommended by Mr. Hart, you create an exclusive bonanza for his southwestern established ranchers.

   a. The really significant sources of outside risk capital are cut off from their small rancher neighbors, eliminating competition.

   b. They may avoid the EDA altogether if their oil income does not count.

   c. Even if they get in the EDA pot, their oil income can offset livestock and land development cost and not cause any damage.

In summary, we feel that an extremely small clique of large oil rich ranchers, representing less than 2 percent of the industry have misled the Treasury into a new concept which will:

1. Keep young men from getting in the field.
2. Keep small ranchers from growing.

3. Depress land prices in order to further their own expansion.
4. Stop the conversion of land growing supported crops into permanent pasture in the Midwest and Southern States.

Mr. Keogh. Is that an application of the old adage that you can take the boy out of the farm but you can't take the farm out of the boy?

Colonel Oppenheimer. Mr. Puckett, do you have an answer to that?

Mr. Puckett. That is right.

Mr. Bass. He is legitimate because he has a farm in my district.

The Chairman. Mr Watts?

Mr. Watts. Mr. Oppenheimer and your group, I first want to compliment you on the fine way you have this proceeding organized. You have certainly portrayed in every facet just what will probably happen if this law is enacted. Let me ask you this question: What in your opinion, if this law is enacted, would happen to the quality of the cattle in this country?

Colonel Oppenheimer. We have one of the best experts in the country here. May I turn this over to Mr. Puckett?

Mr. Puckett. I don't think there can be any question whatsoever that if this law were passed, this suggested modification could only lead toward at least lessening the improvement in the quality of cattle. That is very far-reaching. If the future of this country is to have an adequate food supply at an appropriate price, raised by people who have a proper standard of living, it can only come about by improvement in the quality of the cattle themselves.

The variations between cattle, their ability to convert feed into beef, is a range of a hundred percent. That range of a hundred percent can be closed down and down and down by breed improvement. Without breed improvement you can only have in the future high-priced beef and undernourished ranch families.

Mr. Watts. Also, what do you think would happen to the fertility and quality of the various farms in the country if this were put into operation?

Mr. Puckett. Of course the big problem, which our Department of Agriculture recognizes very generously, I would say at times, is to maintain and increase the quality of our farmland and our natural resources. Department of Agriculture spends hundreds of millions of dollars encouraging people to take their land out of active grain cultivation and build up the soil along those lines.

That is what I meant when I said in my evidence grass farming—let me put it this way: This aid in the form of encouraging the cattle industry produces results in the protection of our natural resources in the future at one-tenth the cost of the other methods which have been approved by Congress.

Mr. Watts. In other words, this outside capital has been one of the principal methods?

Mr. Puckett. Certainly it has, and most effectively.

Mr. Watts. And the farmland has been revitalized and put back in production?

Mr. Puckett. The most economical method which has been devised yet has been this one which they have suggested to kill.

Mr. Watts. Let me ask you this question of one of you: Won't this law probably hurt the small rancher? The fellow who is just getting started does not have a lot of finances back of him.

Mr. Puckett. I think that is the one person who will be hurt. The big established rancher with thousands and thousands of acres and with thousands of head of cattle might like the monopoly position that he would have if everybody else went out of business. But the amount of capital it takes to equip and stock a farm, for a young person to go out and adopt farming, particularly cattle farming, as a life endeavor, he must have in very substantial quantities outside risk capital and capital that they won't call a bank loan the first time that cow prices go down a cent a pound.

Mr. Watts. Without the availability of that capital it is your thought that the cattle industry would have a tendency to channel itself into certain fixed operators?

Mr. Puckett. Yes. Of course, we don't know what the provision of the law is, when we talk about this amendment. I can well visualize the type of legislation coming out of the recommendation that would really cause a calamity in the cattle prices and be a loss to everyone, even those who think they might like to have their invested interests protected.

Mr. Watts. This law would also result in the lessening of the production of cattle income?

Mr. Puckett. Certainly. If you lessen the people in the ability to produce, the number of cattle would go down; the ability of people to handle them just would not exist. So there would be less meat at higher prices.

Mr. Watts. If there is any food that might in the—I won't say in the too near future but in some future date—become more scarce than other types of food, it is meat; is it not?

Mr. Puckett. That is right.

Mr. Watts. It takes so many acres to produce a certain amount, and, as the population grows, the consumption of meat increases. If we lessened our meat supply, we would have to become more grain eaters than we are today. That is all.

The Chairman. Are there any further questions?

If not, gentlemen, we thank you very much for your appearance and your statements before the committee. You have been very helpful to us.

Colonel Oppenheimer. Thank you.

Chapter IV

Outside Risk Capital in Cattle Industry[1]

In the last six months the Farmers Union, about No. 4 among the agricultural trade associations, in conjunction with Senator Metcalf of Montana and Under Secretary Surrey of the Treasury, has been sponsoring legislation to eliminate the tax subsidies, introduced by Congress over the last 30 years to encourage the entrance of outside risk capital into farming and ranching.

In general, the legislation attempts to parallel the unsuccessful attempt in 1962 to eliminate capital gains for anyone with over $15,000 in nonfarm income. In this case the mission is accomplished by forcing any ranch or livestock owner with over $30,000 in nonfarm income from the cash to the accrual method of accounting. Despite the many and complex provisions of the proposals the ultimate objective is simple—to keep the urban type of investor from putting money into agriculture.

Contrary to 1962, this legislation is now opposed by the American National Cattlemen's Association, the American Federation of Farm Bureaus, the American Hereford Association, the American Angus Association and many others with the National Farmers Union being in a minority. What are the objectives of the supporters of this legislation?

The Treasury is aware that the total amount of additional revenue recovery would be almost microscopic but is principally motivated by a "soak the rich" philosophy and the socialistic desire to bring all take-home incomes down to the same level. Whether this is good, bad, or indifferent is a matter of debate and is not the subject of this article.

The so-called tax advantages put into the law by Congress over a 30-year period to attract outside capital were not "loopholes." This implies something left out of the law by mistake through which someone can wriggle and get a special tax advantage. Items such as capital gain on breeding stock and exemption from the depreciation recapture clause were *put into* the laws after substantial debate and scrutiny by knowledgeable Congressmen. They had concluded, first, that these

[1]Reprint from article, "The Case for the Urban Investor," by H. L. Oppenheimer, *Farm Quarterly*, 1969.

were necessary to attract outside risk capital and second, that outside risk capital was desirable for agriculture.

On what basis have Senator Metcalf and the Farmers Union determined that this is no longer true? Their rallying cry has been, "Get the city guy out of agriculture and prosperity will return to the farm!" Insofar as the average "city guy" isn't going to compete with them on the seat of a tractor, what they really mean is get the city guy's investment dollar out of the business.

Presumably events like the following will occur:

1. Production of grain and livestock will go down and prices will go up.

2. Large "corporate type" farmers and ranchers with "outside money" won't be coming in with new improved breeding stock and large fancy equipment and the 200-head feeder, and the 100-acre corn farmer will move back onto the scene.

3. With the big guy out, the government will go back to spending $4 billion per year supporting and storing $2 per bushel wheat.

4. When a rancher dies, some outsider isn't going to come in and buy his property at $100 per acre but it will go to local neighbors at $20 per acre so they can expand to "modern economic units."

5. Without all of these "outsiders" banks won't make these ridiculous loans to allow "young squirts" to compete with the local "established ranchers."

Let's examine these premises one by one:

1. There is a given amount of agricultural land in the U.S. suitable for cultivation and grazing. With the exception of certain government actions, such as the Soil Bank or ASC crop restrictions, it is *all* going to be utilized. Eliminating outsiders is not going to change the numbers of cattle being put out on the Kansas Blue Stem. It might lower the summer grazing rents to the Blue Stem landowners on contract cattle but the grass is going to be utilized by somebody, and there will be the same number of feeders coming into the Kansas City market in October.

Without government restrictions on grain production, land suitable for corn and wheat is going to be put into corn and wheat. One thousand acres of corn can be farmed more economically than 10 tracts of 100 acres. Ten farmers on 100-acre farms cannot compete with one farmer on 1,000 acres. Whether he is a corporation, an employee of a New York landowner, or a farmers cooperative, it is unlikely that the clock will be turned backward to the 19th Century and the farm split back up to the 10 components from which it was formed.

Tax-subsidized risk capital has produced the Hereford steer which, on the same amount of grass and feed, produces three times the amount of top-quality meat of a Texas longhorn of 60 years ago. The development of improved blood stock is a high-risk small-profit game. In most countries it is not conducted by private enterprise but by the government and state-supported institutions.

There is little evidence that our government could have accomplished these spectacular advances for as little cost as they might have lost in these minor tax subsidies to the cattle breeders. Is Senator Metcalf advocating that we go back to the Texas longhorn? Does he believe that further improvement is unnecessary? Is he naive enough to think that a small farmer will put $500,000 into blood stock with the best expectation being about a 2% economic profit? Does he think the whole project ought to be taken out of the hands of private enterprise? The efforts of the purebred breeders have benefited all farmers and ranchers as well as the entire meat-eating population of the cities.

2. If all usable land is going to be utilized by somebody, even on a rent-free basis, a way of cutting back production would be to advocate less efficient techniques. We could reverse the modern trends, break up the larger land holdings (as Castro did in Cuba), stop the use of chemical fertilizers, order International Harvester to go back to horse plows. These procedures would eliminate the need of outside risk capital and the local country bank loans would provide all the cash needed.

There might be some grumbling from the cities on higher food prices, and the small farmers net position might not be greatly improved, but it would certainly be effective in eliminating any need of outsiders coming in with investment dollars.

3. Ten years ago the biggest news and most controversial issue of the day was the $15 billion the government was spending annually in agricultural subsidies. Today this has sunk to almost nothing. The elimination of outside risk capital is not going to make prices go back to the days when the government was buying half the grain. There is no connection.

Elimination of meat imports, removal of land from production (Soil Bank), forced export subsidies, cooperative marketing like the citrus growers—all of these can make prices go up. Cutting off your neighbor's source of risk capital isn't going to make 40¢/lb. steer calves.

4. On one point Senator Metcalf is correct. By eliminating all "outside interest" in farm and ranch land he will undoubtedly be successful in driving land prices down around 50%, making it more feasible for the "established farmers and ranchers" to "round out their holdings." Even better than this, the elimination of the absentee "float-

ing buyer" will make the *only* market for the small uneconomic size unit, the wealthy landed gentry on the perimeter. Recognizing this, the average bank and insurance company will be reluctant to make any loan on such a property, which will mean that the price will be driven down even further to where the powerful neighbor, particularly in times of distress, can now buy it at a price where he can make "a reasonable economic return."

As a matter of interest, 80% of the widows and estates do sell out to neighboring ranchers whether absentee or resident. The advantages of economic expansion with increased landholdings are so great that they meet the exorbitant offers of the "tax-motivated outsiders." However, its the fact that this outside group of purchase capital exists, that keeps the neighbor honest and forces him to pay a market price.

5. As a banker considering the marketability after foreclosure (or a rancher thinking about his estate), what would be your thinking if the Farmers Union were successful in driving out all potential buyers but the "neighbors"?

Banks loan 90% on listed securities; 80% on slaughter steers; 60% on registered cows; 50% on land; and 10% on oil paintings. Why the difference? The answer lies in flexibility and marketability of the collateral. Banks don't want their money tied up for 10 years in foreclosed farm land. The percentage they will loan depends on the speed they can get their money back if there's trouble.

The term "absentee speculator" has a bad ring in rural communities, but the bankers and widows like to know he's around with a ready checkbook, even if he never buys anything. Without this source of *potential* sale, the entire private farm loan-credit system could collapse. When there is only one or two potential buyers around for the collateral, a banker will view a loan differently than if there were a broad general market.

What is "outside risk capital"? By what channels does it enter agriculture? Is it needed in industry? Is it needed in modern agriculture?

The small village cobbler of the 19th Century, if he were reasonably frugal, could accumulate enough capital to buy his tools, buy his shop, and keep enough leather inventory to handle the needs of his limited customers. Very few individuals could do this with a $10 million-modern shoe factory.

How do you expand a cobbler shop into a shoe factory?

1. Borrow money from banks and insurance companies.
2. Borrow money from institutions or individuals on bonds or debentures.
3. Take in partners for part of the equity.

4. Incorporate and issue stock, taking in hundreds of "partners."

5. Get other investors to build you a factory or buy equipment. You then lease it from them and save a capital outlay.

What are some of the tax reasons that bring these "outsiders" into the shoe business?

1. They can get capital gains on the common stock you give them.

2. They can depreciate the buildings and equipment you rent from them.

3. They can deduct losses if your operation is slow getting started or if you default on your loans or debentures.

4. They get a 7% investment credit on the gross value of all the equipment they rent to you.

There is a parallel between the 19th Century-cobbler shop becoming a modern shoe factory and what has happened to U.S. agriculture in the last 25 years. Whether moral or immoral, good or bad, these are the facts:

The minimum unit on which a U.S. family unit with two adult hired hands can make a $10,000 annual income plus a 4% return on land value plus a 6% return on invested capital in equipment, livestock, feed, and supplies is as follows:

1. Midwest: 1,000 acres of good crop land.
2. Great Plains: 1,000-cow-breeding herd.
3. Grain-feeder operation: 2,000-head feedlot.

Each of these operations requires a minimum $600,000 gross investment. Four per cent on land, 6% on livestock feed and equipment, and a $10,000 salary is no bonanza for a high-risk game in 1968 when you can get 5½% on government bonds.

If you don't get up into this volume, you may get no return on your land, no return on your livestock, and a less than subsistence level for your family. If you are paying 7½% interest on a mortgage, you are in trouble. If you've got 100 acres of corn, 100 head of cows, or 200 head of feeder steers, you are in the same boat as the 19th Century-cobbler. You're in trouble. You've got to get an outside job if you want to make your mortgage payments and feed your family.

If you want to stay in full-time farming you've got to expand like the cobbler. Assuming the government isn't going to subsidize you, you've got the same alternatives the rest of U.S. industry has had—take in partners.

Here are the alternatives:

1. You can take in the government as a partner with ASC, Soil Bank, Grazing Districts, CCC contracts, loans, handouts, and subsidies.

Historically these have been great boondoggles but there is no permanency, and any moment they can change the ground rules.

2. You can borrow up to 50% from the banks if you have other net worth, but they want 7½% interest and a compensating balance.

3. You can incorporate and sell stock but this is hard to do on the narrow profit margin of present day farming.

4. You can take in straight partners who may be in high tax brackets who can get some benefits you can't. On the other hand they might irritate you with arguments on management decisions.

However, as long as the Farmers Union doesn't cut off your water with their tax changes, you have two other alternatives to expand with people who are willing to accept a 2% economic return because of certain tax subsidies:

1. You can take in "tenant cattle" on maintenance or "share the gain" contracts with all the decision-making elements reserved to you. The share you pay out will be less than the 7½% you have to pay your banker if you own them.

2. You can expand your landholdings by leasing at 4% net before depreciation from tax-subsidized investors who are willing to break even operationally because of eventual capital gain on resale.

The point here is that, if you need to put a $600,000 operation together to make a modern economic unit, the Congress has provided tax incentives to encourage high-bracket city people to provide you the cattle and the land to do it. They'll make up the difference between the 50% the banks will loan and what you have to come up with, and they'll do it for less than 7½% interest.

For a 100 years, the aggressive young rancher starting out has made it by running some cattle on shares and leasing part of his grazing land. Only in this manner has he been able to compete with the millionaire land baron subsidized by his oil revenue. In the Kansas Blue Stem, 70% of the stocking has been with "tenant cattle" since Civil War days. These have been owned by New Yorkers, Bostonians, and Englishmen. This has been a form of traditional outside capital that has always been welcome.

Looking at the whole controversy from another angle, has Senator Metcalf and the Farmers Union considered where these vast "deductible funds" are being poured? They are known to the economist as "high-velocity dollars." They are going into feed purchases, local labor, local supplies, local school taxes, farm improvements put in by local labor, calves produced by local farmers, rents to widows and farmers' estates, bank deposits in rural areas, local equipment and gasoline dealers, fertilizer stores, and young local managerial talent that couldn't put operative capital together without outside help. People like Winthrop Rockefeller and Robert Lehman have single-handedly salvaged entire destitute areas with outside capital.

It is questionable whether this would have occurred without the tax subsidies that Congress purposefully put into the law to encourage these types of activities.

In summary:

1. It is believed that existing crop and cattle production will fully utilize available land regardless of proposed tax changes. Consequently, volume of production and prices should in no way be affected by this legislation.

2. Elimination of outside risk capital might cause a decrease in land rents and land prices, but resident farmers' estates, widows, and land-borrowing power might sustain catastrophic results.

3. Obtaining "tenant cattle" at reasonable maintenance or share-the-gain contracts or land at reasonable rents from outside owners is the only way a young small rancher can expand to compete with the established millionaire oil ranchers of great inherited wealth.

Chapter V

The Battle of 1969

A second major attack sponsored by the Farmers Union and National Farmers Organization was launched in 1969 against absentee investors in ranches and cattle. In this instance the American National Cattlemen's Association and the American Hereford Association were firmly on the side of outside risk capital being welcomed. The following is extracted from the hearings before the House Ways and Means Committee.

General Oppenheimer. My name is H. L. Oppenheimer, and I am here with a group of other gentlemen, who are going to identify themselves.

We would like to handle ourselves as a group.

Personally, I am Chairman of the Board of Oppenheimer Industries.

I am going to introduce each one of the gentlemen. They will identify themselves as to what capacity they are appearing in, and on what subject they are experts.

Copies of their written testimony are in each one of your hands up there, if that is permissible, sir.

The Chairman. It is, but is your home office in Kansas?

General Oppenheimer. No, sir; my home office is in Kansas City, Mo.

The Chairman. All right. Go right ahead.

General Oppenheimer. We represent multiple facets of the livestock and rural economy: small ranchers, large ranchers, feedlot opators, bankers, farm cooperatives, heads of chambers of commerce, nonresident landowners, mayors of rural towns, and people from the farm management industry.

While all of us are, in general, opposed to the current Treasury proposal, our opinions and reasons are not necessarily the same.

I want to digress a second, here. I am the gentleman that was referred to by four other people earlier in the program as the horrible example within the field.

And I want to identify one more point, that this was not our firm that Congressman Byrnes referred to in his example this morning.

I personally am a brigadier general in the Marine Corps Reserve, and have returned to the firm after a two-and-a-half-year tour of active duty, the last part of which was in Vietnam. My firm and its subsidiaries are engaged in ranch management, rural and urban real estate brokerage, land development, livestock and ranch mortgage lending, and agricultural consulting, bookkeeping, and inspections. Directly or indirectly, we are involved in over 220,000 head of cattle placed on around 300 farms and ranches. We will have been responsible for a flow of about $20 million in risk capital during the past year into the western rural economy.

I am going to correct a few of the misconceptions regarding my own outfit, and the unfortunate publicity that we have been exposed to in the press, most of which is in error.

With the exception of a few bulls leased to clients, we own no cattle and operate no ranches. All of these funds flow to reputable, totally independent ranchers and feeders over a 16-State area. As agents, auditors, and inspectors for the owners, we charge an average of around $5 per head per year on the cattle portion of the business.

Outside of size, and possibly the percentage of ex-Marines we have in our organization, we consider ourselves no different from the other 1,500 members of the Farm Managers & Rural Appraisers Society or the 3,000 members of the National Institute of Farm Brokers, to both of which groups we belong.

It is our intent to prove that the outside risk capital, firms like ours are bringing into the rural economy through the tax incentives that Congress has provided, is doing the following:

1. Not costing the U.S. Treasury 1 penny in revenue.
2. Accomplishing long-range objectives of the U.S. Department of Agriculture less expensively than the Government could do it.
3. Giving the private independent rancher, many of whom are here today, some of whom are connected with us, and some of whom are not, a chance to compete against the "corporate conglomerate."

Because we wrongly estimated the length of time we would have before our appearance, a number of our scheduled group could not appear and are submitting written statements. These have been provided the committee. We have developed 18 points, each point covered by an expert in his field, backing up the statements above.

Because of our limited time allotment, I am going to give the title of each point and the name of the individual who is handling it. If the gentleman is present, I am going to introduce him, and he will give you a sentence or two summarizing his written presentation, which you have in front of you.

Mr. Charles McIlvaine.

The Chairman. Mr. McIlvaine.

Mr. McIlvaine. I am C. W. McIlvaine, from Saratoga, Wyo.

I came here with a prepared statement which has been presented, and am in a position to speak on the importance of outside capital in the development of ranching, and also the part that outside capital plays in the development of recreation, which is the third largest industry in our State of Wyoming, and also the fastest growing industry that we have.

Thank you.

(Discussion off the record.)

General Oppenheimer. Mr. Paul Etchepare.

The Chairman. Mr. Etchepare.

Mr. Etchepare. Mr. Chairman and members of the committee. My name is Paul Etchepare. I am from Cheyenne, Wyo., president of the Warren Livestock Co., and a past president of the National Lamb Feeders Association.

We operate a ranch that has been in existence since 1874.

We have talked about corporations. This ranch was incorporated in 1883. We run both sheep and cattle, and a statement that I have prepared has been filed with the committee, and I am prepared to discuss the current tax proposals and how, in my judgment, they would hurt the small operator and would not really affect the large corporation.

The Chairman. Thank you.

Mr. Etchepare. Thank you.

General Oppenheimer. Mr. Stephen Brock.

The Chairman. Mr. Brock.

Mr. Brock. Mr. Chairman, I am Stephen Brock, from Minneola, Kans., and I am here to testify after having 25 years of experience, of real struggle as a small stockman to totally disagree with some of the statements that have been made by the distinguished Senator from Montana here today, on this need of outside capital.

And I am prepared to speak on that subject, need of outside capital, as an example of a small operator in Kansas and New Mexico.

General Oppenheimer. Mr. Frank Kemp.

Mr. Kemp. Mr. Chairman, members of the committee, my name is

Frank Kemp. I live in Denver, Colo., and am in the ranch management and appraisal business, and am a small livestock feeder.

I have submitted a statement to the committee, primarily about a subject that gets very little attention these days, that the incentives talked about today in this tax legislation do not bring about Government subsidies. None of the money that goes out in the form of subsidies on the crops that are now produced in this country, primarily, of course, the grain crops and others, is involved in this area. There is no subsidy in the livestock business.

The Chairman. I notice you are a member of the State senate.

Mr. Kemp. Yes, sir; I am.

The Chairman. Go ahead, Mr. Oppenheimer.

General Oppenheimer. Mr. Buster Wheat.

Mr. Wheat. Mr. Chairman, my name is Buster Wheat. I am from Allen, Kans. My office is in Emporia, Kans. My business primarily is ranching and feedlot operation.

My statement is on file with you gentlemen, and I would be glad to answer any questions that you might ask me, if I can answer them.

General Oppenheimer. Gentlemen, I am going to amplify my introductory remarks for a second.

I want to lead off the group which is going to substantiate my previous statement that the present form of tax incentives are costing the Government nothing.

In this regard, I want to make four quick points in rebuttal to the totally erroneous newspaper and magazine reports many of you have been reading in regard to our particular clients' group.

First, the approximately $20 million expended by our clients last year did not go into a hole in the ground, nor is it going to all be converted into capital gains.

Most of it went to individuals and corporations in the rural areas, who will presumably pay their own income taxes on it or go to jail.

As a result of the above expenditures, our clients are going to be receiving about $15 million back this year, from the sale of slaughtered steers, calves, feed, interest, and rent.

The gain from this is subject to ordinary income tax, not capital gains.

They are going to pick up about $4 million in capital gain, or return capital, from the sale of breeding stock or ranch land.

Because many are in the development stage of their organization, about $3 million has gone into herd growth or land improvement, which will not produce taxable income for 2 or 3 years.

Second, assuming the present price level on cattle holds out for another 6 months, 90 percent of our clients will have had a substantial economic profit which has nothing to do with taxes—on all calf and steer sales. This is regardless of tax considerations.

A statement has been made several times this morning that these outsiders don't care how much money they lose.

I don't know about other farm management firms. We are on a 30-day agency contract. If we don't make them an economic profit, or have a damn good excuse, we get fired.

Fourth, a favorite thesis of—this guy was not here today, but he has been yelling about us all over the country—a favorite thesis of one prominent but misinformed public speaker has been that the outside investors are ruining American land by plowing up grass pastures and putting them into row crops and adding to surpluses.

To my knowledge, none of my 450 clients has ever plowed up a grass pasture for row cropping. On the other hand, they have spent very large sums of money in taking marginal, wornout corn and cotton land, fertilizing it, and putting it back into grass, thus cutting down on grain surpluses.

Now, because of the emphasis that has been given earlier on coming up with alternate solutions, Mr. Chairman, I don't think I am going to run over, but I would like the opportunity of having General Stiles read his presentation on alternate solutions, where these tax abuses could be corrected with either minor changes in legislation, or stricter enforcement of the existing laws. He will amplify that statement.

The Chairman. We will be pleased to hear you, General Stiles.

General Stiles. Thank you, sir.

Thank you, Mr. Chairman.

I will read most of this statement, sir, because it is pertinent.

The prevention of real abuses with respect to tax losses from farming can be carried out in large measure without any further restrictive legislation. Much the same as with other areas of control, it is simpler and more effective to enforce existing legislation on the subject at hand than it is to go to the trouble of legislating a new set of restrictions.

And there are in existence today ample provisions to present major tax abuses in the farming industry. Required, however, is diligent investigation and enforcement by technically qualified personnel. And I would underscore the word "technically."

There are three regulatory bodies of the Government with their own legislative enforcement authority that could handle all of the existing abuses, and they are adequately backed up by past court decisions.

I am referring to the Internal Revenue Service, to which the Supreme Court in the "Livingston Bond" case gave the right to use "reasonable expectation of economic profit," as the basis for disallowing a sham transaction; the Securities Exchange Commission, which in the "Howie Citrus Grove" case, the Supreme Court gave the authority to regulate "investment contracts"; and to the U.S. Department of Agriculture, which under the Packers and Stockyards Act has the authority to require registration, bonding, and inspection of anyone buying or selling cattle to the public, or engaged in interstate commerce with livestock.

Within the authority of one of the three agencies listed above, the following abuses could be corrected:

1. The sale of livestock at fictitiously high prices, with nominal downpayments, which creates an unrealistic depreciation expense.
2. Repurchase commitments and calf crop guarantees, which should establish a salvage value and eliminate depreciation or should be backed up by audited financial statements and other records normally required under the purview of either an SEC registration or the Packers and Stockyards Administration of the USDA.
3. Operating at a continuously higher level of production costs than sales value. In this case, an analysis of production costs relative to sales value can be made by the IRS.

For example, if an analysis of the operating history reveals that it has been costing $200 to produce a calf worth $100 over a period of time, this is not a "reasonable expectation of making an economic profit." On the other hand, a $5 or $10 per head operating loss with variations up and down from year to year would come within the limits of being a "reasonable expectation."

That is the majority of my statement, sir.

The Chairman. Thank you, General Stiles.

General Oppenheimer. That is all, sir. We are prepared for questions.

The Chairman. We thank you for coming to us with your testimony, General Oppenheimer, and the supplemental statements that all of you gentlemen have left. Without objection, the entire manuscript prepared by all of you, with all of your inserts, will be included in the record.

Extracts from the Document follows:

STATEMENT OF MR. BARRET HEDDENS, JR.,

President and Chief Executive Officer of
The First National Bank of Kansas City, Mo.

I believe the proposed legislation will seriously damage the rural credit structure of the midwest. The First National Bank of Kansas City, Missouri, and the Interstate National Bank, with which it merged 14 years ago, has been one of the principal sources of livestock credit in the Kansas, Missouri, Nebraska, Oklahoma and Nothern Texas areas since the 19th century.

Within the ranching field, slaughter steers, which are marketable within six months, are considered the most liquid. Breeding cows, which are a form of capital asset and need a specific buyer, are less marketable. Ranch land is like any other form of real estate . . . valuable but often slow to market. Consequently, most commercial banks generally welcome loans on slaughter steers, reluctantly make loans on breeding stock and tend to avoid making real estate mortgage loans on land.

However, when most banks make any agricultural loan, a major concern is the financial net worth of the borrower. To protect its depositors, a bank makes a careful evaluation of the liquidity of the assets, whether or not they are used for collateral.

Our bank attorneys have been making a careful analysis of the various tax changes now being proposed in the agricultural field, and we are viewing these proposed changes with considerable alarm. First, we feel that a substantial number of our customers are going to be adversely affected. Secondly, we feel that the removal of non-resident investors from this market is going to decrease the liquidity on land sales. Third, we feel that there will be at least a temporary depression of land value, which could snowball into a serious disruption of the market. Fourth, the elimination of land improvement programs employing local labor and locally purchased supplies might have repercussions. Fifth, the present timing is particularly unfortunate with the highest interest rates and tightest credit in almost one hundred years.

While most of these loans are handled by our country correspondent banks today and come to us only as participations in credit, we are well aware of the problem and know that the entire rural credit structure is in very delicate balance at this particular moment. It is my belief that anything which would unfavorably alter the financial statements of the small rancher and farmer, deny them the sources of outside risk capital, or disturb the liquidity of collateral that they use for loans could have adverse effects far beyond anything that the proponents of this legislation can imagine.

STATEMENT OF JAMES HARPER,

President, Harper & Handley

My subject is outside capital in agriculture versus other business enterprises. By way of introduction, I was raised on a ranch near Ashland, Kansas. My grandfather was one of the original founders and president of the Kansas Livestock Association, and both my father and brother have served as president of the Association. Since 1890, we have never run tenant cattle or cattle on shares, nor have we ever had any business connections with Oppenheimer Industries or similar agricultural management concerns.

My brother, who is currently operating the ranch, and I reviewed all of the Oppenheimer contracts in detail last year, and we feel that this method of using outside capital is a perfectly sound and legitimate method of operating a ranch and of expanding to an economically competitive size. We did not negotiate contracts with their investors because their 1968 maintenance rates did not, in my brother's estimation, equal in price what we hoped to obtain from running his own cattle. Subsequent market increases have vindicated his judgment.

On the other hand, our family is currently attempting to find adjoining property which "outside interests" could purchase, allowing my brother to lease it back. If this were possible, and if the 1968 Oppenheimer maintenance rates were to remain the same for 1969, I would be delighted to expand our operation with additional cattle from their clients.

In our particular case, contrary to several statements submitted earlier, we could obtain sufficient capital to handle these expanded operations. However, we would prefer contract cattle as a form of hedging against market risks, as well as keeping a greater degree of financial flexibility.

While my original background was in ranching, I have spent the last 25 years in business management and consulting, and I am thoroughly familiar with all of the normal methods of financing industrial enterprises. Expanding a single grocery store into a chain or a blacksmith shop into a steel mill cannot be done by borrowing from a bank, or your friends and relatives. You need additional equity capital as a base. You can incorporate and issue stock; you can find investors who will buy equipment and rent it to you; you can find insurance companies who will build a plant and lease it back to you, and you can find trucking firms who will haul by contract. All of the above are legal and conventional devices by which to use the capital of others.

In today's period of agricultural crisis where one must expand to survive and where credit is the tightest in the entire century, there is no reason why an agricultural enterprise should be different from any other. Taking cattle on contract or renting land for expansion should certainly be normal procedures with no stigma attached. Contracting to have your wheat harvested by a combine crew has finally become acceptable in row crop cultivation. Expanding one's cattle herd by contract should not be viewed any differently.

However, during this period of transition, the present tax incentives must be retained, at least until other sources of capital are available. I personally feel this should be accomplished by private enterprise rather than by the government.

SUPPLEMENT TO STATEMENT OF JAMES HARPER,

Los Angeles, Calif.

In reviewing my testimony and the question period before the House Ways and Means Committee on farm losses on 10 March, I would like to make a couple of additional points.

In cross examining Senator Metcalf, Congressman John Watts mentioned the young rancher who was engaged in no business but farming who had inherited sufficient securities to generate a dividend income of $30,000 per year. It was pointed out and acquiesced in by the senator that his bill would deny the rancher the deduction of any development expenses or net operational losses. The alternative was pointed out that he could sell his securities, buy additional land with the money and then properly qualify. The existing diversification would, of course, be denied to him.

I would like to point out a reverse of the above, applying to my own family, which would be equally damaging and will hit a great number of so-called traditional and established farm families. As mentioned previously, our Kansas ranch, established by my grandfather in 1890, was a satisfactory-sized economic unit in the past for one family. It has worked out well for my brother, but could not also support, full-time, my family and my sister's family.

We retained our ownership share, but I was forced to leave the ranch and go into urban life where I have been fortunate enough to have worked myself into the salary group Senator Metcalf feels is so undesirable. As the years have passed, we can see that the size ranch unit that was satisfactory in 1950 is no longer competitive in 1969. We have to expand or sell out. The expansion will require new development costs in additional breeding stock or additional land acquisitions.

We need the present tax incentives to make this feasible, whether it's our money we put up or whether we attract the risk capital of people like Oppenheimer Industries' clients. I would prefer going the latter route and letting somebody else take the market risks. However, this is my point: If the present proposal goes through, my brother gets a tax subsidy to help with the expansion; my sister and I do not. Also, if the present proposal goes through, there won't be the second alternative, as there will be no outside risk capital available.

While I am not complaining, I would like to bring to your attention a former automobile dealer in Wichita, whom we shall call Mr. A. He owns a substantial amount of wheat land in western Kansas and nets something in excess of $100,000 per year off of it. This "net" comes almost entirely from federal government payments from the "Feed Grain Program."

In addition, Mr. A owns a series of small grain elevators and processing plants which net him around another $100,000 per year. Under Senator Metcalf's "integrated operations" clause, this will also count as "farm income" with which he can develop breeding stock or improve new land acquisitions. While I recognize this as irrelevant, Mr. A's family came to Wichita about 20 years ago and got into farming about 10 years ago. Mine got into Kansas farming about 80 years ago.

I was not clear in answering a question of Congressman Byrnes. All during the testimony on both sides, the argument for the cash basis of accounting for the small farmer and rancher was that it simplified his bookkeeping over the accrual method. This is the least important part, and I was not clear on it. The cash method is critical for the survival of the under-capitalized small farmer.

In most of the U.S., hay, feed, and grain have to be put up or purchased at harvest time in the fall. On the cash basis of accounting, if the farmer purchases $60,000 of these items in November, he can deduct their cost. If he raises the feed stuffs, himself, and stores them, he has no tax liability. If he were forced to the accrual basis, in either of the above instances, he would have generated $60,000 of paper "income." At a 50% bracket, he would have to come up with $30,000 of cash equity for the government. I realize that this would equalize itself the following year, but my point is that he is borrowed to the hilt already and can't come up with the $30,000.

STATEMENT OF GEORGE HELLYER,

Rancher and Real Estate Broker, Buhl, Idaho
(Vice President, Blaine County Farm Bureau)

My name is George Hellyer. I am 31 years of age and I am a resident of the State of Idaho.

I own two separate ranches within the State of Idaho presently running one thousand head of young cattle. I am in the Real Estate business and therefore am acquainted with the land values throughout the State of Idaho.

In my dealings with ranch sales I would like to refer to a rancher presently desiring to sell his entire operation. He owns a large cattle operation, and in order to expand his carrying capacity he is in great need of large amounts of capital. His credit finally dwindles to the point that he is forced to put his entire ranch up for sale. An outside investor heard of this situation and went to the owner with the idea of buying the cattle herd and leasing it back to the owner. This temporarily relieved the credit situation. The outsider also offered to purchase the entire ranch and lease it back to the present owner. With the present tax benefits this entire transaction was beneficial to both parties concerned. My opinion is that the rancher would have gone bankrupt and been forced to sell his property for a much lesser value had this outsider not had the tax incentive to buy. The bankruptcy of this individual would have been entirely his own fault but in the State of Idaho and other areas the need for tremendous sums of capital is very apparent.

If we remove the tax incentive for outside capital, the further development of rural land, rural jobs, and an expanding economy would cease. Rural towns such as Buhl, Filer and Hailey declined drastically in population during the 1950's and when urban sources discovered the tax incentive of owning rural land, the economy and population of these towns began to increase. Idaho drastically needs these increases, more than surrounding States due to the lack of present population and tax monies.

If this bill passes, outside "risk capital" would be discouraged from buying lands in Idaho. My education dictates that the law of supply and demand would create a situation in Idaho where land prices would depreciate in value by the passage of this particular legislation. With lower land values the chances of bankruptcy occurring for many growing ranchers and farmers would multiply. Development of new land within the State of Idaho has come primarily from these outside "risk sources" of which I have previously spoken. Thousands of acres of what was formerly sage brush ground is now producing equally with other pasture areas.

The input of capital to make an acre of sage brush ground into producing pasture land requires an investment in land clearing, leveling, seeding, and irrigation facilities. When developing this new ground or promoting maximum production from existing grazing ground the possibilities of creating additional jobs is a very important issue. In the field of irrigation alone the manufacturing of sprinkler pipes, pumps, and well casings must be taken into account. The irrigation pumps in addition use tremendous quantities of electricity which is produced within the State of Idaho. For each improvement occurring on these new acres I could expound on the number of new jobs created.

While creating additional grazing capacity might add to production, the State of Idaho, which is largely underdeveloped, is in a special category. Relative to total national production this increase is microscopic. However, in order to get Idaho moving and bring it up to the level of other Western States I believe that this development of new land is a necessity.

Therefore, my stand, being involved in the business of Real Estate and ranching, would be that to discourage "risk capital" from such areas as New York and Los Angeles would decline the prices of land throughout the State of Idaho and cause an economic recession. The population trend within the State of Idaho presently reflects the migration from urban areas in the States of California, Oregon and Washington to the rural areas of Idaho and should this recession occur this population shift would automatically cease.

For these above reasons, I firmly believe that these Treasury Proposals for farm tax loss reform should not be approved.

STATEMENT OF CHARLES McILVAINE,

Rancher, Saratoga, Wyo.

I graduated from Colorado State University in 1932, and between that time and the start of World War II, I worked in extension work with the United States Department of Agriculture and was employed as a field secretary with the American Hereford Association. During World War II, I served in the United States Army, came out as a Lt. Colonel, and later retired as a Colonel. From 1946 until 1951 I was in ranch management work, and then went on my own with a pure breed herd until 1954. Since 1954 I have had a commercial cow

SUPPLY and DEMAND
DETERMINE THE PRICE OF BEEF

LAND NOW UTILIZED FOR FARMS AND RANCHES WILL CONTINUE TO BE...

BUT

KILLING TAX INCENTIVES WILL DRIVE DOWN LAND VALUES BUT NOT AFFECT PRODUCTION

HOW BIG MUST A FARM BE TO MAKE MONEY TODAY?

1000 ACRES OF CORN LAND, a 2000 HEAD FEED LOT
or 1000 ACRE COW RANCH

THEY'RE MINIMUMS For a $10,000/YEAR SALARY
plus 4.7% RETURN ON LAND
plus 6.1% RETURN ON EQUIPMENT
and REQUIRE AN INVESTMENT OF $600,000

TAX INCENTIVES DRAW ON CITY CAPITAL TO MAKE FARMS PROFITABLE

IT REALLY IS, TO SAY THAT FARMERS SUPPORT THE METCALF-CULVER TAX REFORMS!

- AMERICAN CATTLEMEN'S ASSOCIATION (largest)
- AMERICAN HEREFORD ASSOCIATION
- AMERICAN ANGUS ASSOCIATION and others...

ALL OPPOSE CHANGES in PRESENT TAX LAWS

CORPORATE INVASION?

METCALF-CULVER TREASURY PROPOSALS exempt all groups on accrual basis of accounting which includes almost all large corporations.

THEREFORE...

they would deprive small ranchers of outside capital but will not keep out large corporations.

ENCOURAGE YOUNG PEOPLE
TO MAKE CATTLE A CAREER

DO NOT CUT OFF THE
SUPPLY OF RISK CAPITAL

METCALF-CULVER TAX REFORMS WOULD
DISCOURAGE YOUNG MEN from BECOMING RANCHERS

HIGH VELOCITY DOLLARS

IF THE FEDERAL GOVERNMENT AVERAGES 20% IN TAX WHEN DOLLARS CHANGE HANDS, IT COLLECTS MORE MONEY THAN THE TAX INCENTIVES TAKE AWAY.

LET'S BE FAIR!

PRIVATE INVESTMENT.... NOT GOVERNMENT SPENDING, HAS GONE INTO CATTLE and CITRUS

The METCALF-CULVER TAX REFORMS would stop it

INVESTING MONEY IS A 2-WAY ROAD

Let's keep Capital **ON THE MOVE!**

operation, and have built my ranch up to the point it will now run about 3,000 animal units.

I want to discuss the supplementary sources of income which are now available to an agricultural land owner and the smaller rural communities, but which would not have been possible without the employment of outside capital.

In Wyoming, the number two source of revenue to the state comes from the use of recreational areas. These recreational areas have been developed primarily by people from the south or east who enjoy the country, and are willing to invest their money in the region. Multiple recreational facilities must be available to attract vacationers. In or near Saratoga, we have abundant wild game and fine trout streams; two golf courses; and are now in the formation stages of a ski resort that will require an investment of probably four million dollars.

City residents come to our country to relax, to hunt and fish, and to enjoy the natural beauty of the region. When they do, they spend money. During the summer months, one of the golf courses employs up to 60 people, the other about the same. In a community of 1,000 permanent residents, this is a significant source of income. During hunting season, many of our ranchers serve as guides and outfitters for hunters. The hunters buy equipment from our local stores, eat at our restaurants, and stay in our motels. I estimate hunters spend an average of $100 or more per day. Guide services are extremely important as supplemental income to our ranchers. For many this extra income is just the thing that lets them continue to operate. These jobs are created by development funds put in the country by people encouraged by the present tax laws. If we don't have risk capital, we're in trouble.

I feel that we have a much stronger community because of the influence of outside investment. Our retail merchants and other business people know they can anticipate income from the urban visitors and from the capital expenditures which are being made with outstanding funds to develop the recreational aspects of the community. They also are pretty well assured that the rancher can meet the financial obligations he has partially because of the additional income he receives from his services to hunters, fishermen, etc. At the same time, of course, the rancher is continually improving his range and the livestock which he runs. I think I can speak for all of the ranchers in the region when I say that our primary interest is operating our ranches at a profit, and I personally feel that outside capital is absolutely essential to us, whether it be to aid a young rancher who does not have sufficient cash or credit to start a cattle operation, or to develop a recreational activity. I further believe the bills which have been introduced by Senator

Metcalf and Congressman Culver, and the Treasury proposals to restrict the present tax laws relating to agricultural activities would seriously impair this flow of outside capital from urban to rural areas, and would be detrimental to the economic structure of our agricultural region.

STATEMENT OF PAUL ETCHEPARE,

President, Warren Live Stock Co., Cheyenne, Wyo.
(Past President, National Lamb Feeders Association)

The Warren Live Stock Company is presently one of the largest agricultural employers in the State of Wyoming, and has been in existence for 95 years. At one time it utilized 500,000 acres of land, and presently operates over approximately 200,000 acres of territory. The company was incorporated in 1883. I am aware that large corporations engaged in the ranching and farming business have come under criticism by the Farmers Union, the N.F.O., and various congressmen. I am also aware that the proponents of the Metcalf Bill, the Culver Bill, and the Treasury proposal of the past administration, which is currently being reviewed by this committee, have linked their attacks on outside capital coming into ranching with attacks on the so-called "Corporate Invasion."

I presume the term "Invasion" means somebody new entering agriculture and does not refer to the Warren Live Stock Company which was in operation before any of the gentlemen in this room were born.

Seriously, I think that the people advocating this legislation have missed the point that there is no connection between the two issues and actually the bills concerned will have not the slightest effect in any category whatsoever upon large corporaions.

All three of the bills exempt any entity which is on or is willing to switch to the "accrual basis of accounting." I have made inquiry to a number of the partners of various national accounting firms, whom I know, and they have told me that they have never heard of any corporations listed on either the New York Stock Exchange, the American Stock Exchange or of any size whatsoever any publicly owned, which are not already on the accrual basis of accounting. I presume that there are exceptions to everything, but they could not recall any.

In other words, these three proposals, which in my mind would be quite effective in cutting off the flow of available risk equity capital to smaller ranchers and farmers who need it, would not in any degree slow down the advancing corporate invading forces which seem to have got the entire industry in a state of turmoil. Apart from the current discussion, it is my personal opinion, and I believe I am backed up by the Department of Agriculture, that this entire subject has been ridiculously exaggerated, but this is another matter.

Further, I wish to point out that the Warren Live Stock Company has adequate capital to finance all of its present livestock and agricultural operations and does not even come under the category of some others on this program who may need this capital to expand.

I will make the additional statement that while we ran some cattle for Oppenheimer Industries one summer 4 or 5 years ago, that we have not run any of their cattle since. The reason was a market one—they wouldn't pay us enough money. With all of the above qualifications, I believe that I can speak as a totally disinterested observer as far as my opinion is concerned on the proposed changes in the tax laws.

I am now speaking as an American and as a rancher and not as President of the Warren Live Stock Company. I believe that if this industry and the country is to remain healthy socially and economically that we must provide an opportunity for under-capitalized small ranchers and farmers and their children to remain in the business if they so desire. Further, I see nothing immoral about any young American who currently wants to get in the business from entering. With the present large-scale capital investment required, this is totally impossible without either leasing land from one of these so-called "Absentee Owners" who are now in such disfavor or taking cattle in on shares or contract from people who have either retired or have sources of non-farm income.

Personally I have three sons who want to remain in the business, preferably without my help. They will have to have access to outside equity capitals from other people just like I did when I was their age or like my Father did in 1890 when he came to Montana as a 17-year-old immigrant from France.

In summary, the current legislative proposals will not hurt the large corporations but will remove the opportunity for the small and under-capitalized farmer and rancher to compete with them.

STATEMENT OF STEPHEN L. BROCK,

Rancher, Minneola, Kan.

I am Stephen L. Brock. With the Marine Corps so strongly represented, reluctantly I admit to having served in the Navy 3½ years during World War II. Maybe they still think the Navy is a part of the Marine Corps.

I have ranch holdings in both the State of New Mexico and Kansas. I am here in opposition to the Treasury proposals or any other legislation which would have the effect of drying up existing sources of risk capital now available to the agricultural community.

I am aware that certain farm organizations and individual ranchers support the bill in good faith in the belief that farmers and ranchers will benefit. As a former vice-president of the New Mexico Farm Bureau, and a local manager of this organization in New Mexico and Kansas for more than 20 years, I strongly disagree with the American Farm Bureau Federation's position on this particular issue. Many of us in Farm Bureau hold the view recently expressed by Senator R. C. Morgan, President pro tem of the New Mexico Senate and a farmer in Roosevelt County, New Mexico, who has been a member of the Board of Directors of the New Mexico Farm and Livestock Bureau, stating that passage of such legislation would be unquestionably damaging to the entire agricultural economy. I quote from his statement: "The legitimate farmer and stockman rely heavily on income from other pursuits in order to have a profitable business and make a living. If we prohibit the legitimate farmer from taking the non-farm business, together with his actual farming business, in computing his income tax, we will bankrupt many of our American farmers. The few that speculate and use agriculture as a write-off is of small consequence when we take into consideration the over-all effect the proposal of the Treasury Department would have on agriculture as a whole."

In support of my beliefs, I have been instrumental and hope played at least a small role in getting a "joint memorial" introduced into the 29th Legislature, State of New Mexico, expressing the opposition of the Legislature of the State of New Mexico to the proposed legislation now before the U.S. Congress. The joint memorial now before the New Mexico Legislature, a copy of which is appended to this statement, has very strong support, and I have every hope of it being passed in time to influence the Congress.

The reason for my strong stand on this matter may be of interest to the members of this committee. After service in the Navy during World War II, I returned to my native southwest without much more than my mustering-out pay. I went to work for a large established rancher, saved my money and bought a little land in New Mexico. I was able to find absentee owners who let me run their cattle on a share basis, with them furnishing the operating capital as well. With this risk capital as a basis, I acquired more land and expanded. As I expanded, I gradually replaced the "tenant cattle" with my own. While I have never reached the point of being debt free, I did acquire sufficient net worth to go it on my own. Today I operate what I think is one of the most desirable small ranches in the state of Kansas. My family has a nice home, near good schools and churches. You might say that my being helped to get equity in land and livestock was made possible through absentee owners and our present tax laws which encourage the flow of outside non-agricultural capital into the agricultural community.

New Mexico State Senate,
Santa Fe, March 4, 1969.

Mr. Stephen Brock,
Washington, D.C.

Dear Steve: The legitimate farmer and stockman rely heavily on income from other pursuits in order to have a profitable business and make a living.

If we prohibit the legitimate farmer from taking the non-farm business, together with his actual farming business in computing his income tax, we will bankrupt many of our American farmers. The few that speculate and use agriculture as a write-off is of small consequence when we take into consideration the over-all effect the proposal of the Treasury Department would have on agriculture as a whole.

Sincerely,

R. C. Morgan.

SENATE JOINT MEMORIAL

A Joint Memorial Expressing the Opposition of the Legislature of the State of New Mexico to Federal Legislation Which Would, in Trying to Stop Certain Tax Practices, Destroy Legitimate Members of the Business Community

Whereas, efforts have been made by the department of the treasury to present legislation to congress, in an attempt to prevent the use of agricultural businesses as a tax-avoidance technique, to prevent members of the legitimate agricultural community from using non-agricultural income to offset agricultural losses and thereby supplement agricultural income; and

Whereas, this would have the effect of driving some of the agricultural community out of business; and

Whereas, present proposals would have the effect of drying up existing sources of risk capital now available to the agricultural community; and

Whereas, present proposals would eliminate possible purchasers of agricultural land, and change current accounting procedures so as to impose ruinous taxes on legitimate members of the agricultural community; and

Whereas, there already exist, in the tax laws of the United States, numerous ways to eliminate the use of the "agricultural tax gimmick" by the tax-avoidance expert:

Now, therefore, be it resolved by the Legislature of the State of New Mexico, That it is opposed to inhibiting the free flow of capital into and from the agricultural industry; and

Be it further resolved, That the Legislature of the State of New Mexico requests that the members of the New Mexico Congressional Delegation work with the agricultural industry to bring about legislation which eliminates abuse without destroying the economic base of the agricultural industry.

STATEMENT OF HY OVERTON,

Sheep Rancher, Yeso, N. Mex.

I am past president of the National Wool Growers' Association and presently serve as Chairman of the Livestock Advisory Committee of the American Federation of Farm Bureaus.

My statement concerns the need for outside capital for a young man attempting to establish himself in the sheep industry.

A profitable sheep operation requires a basis herd of 4,000 to 5,000 ewes to produce an economical unit. We normally figure that land costs to maintain a sheep herd require an initial investment of $100 per breeding unit. Minimum land costs for an economical operation then can be estimated to cost approximately $500,000. Ewes cost about $25 apiece today, or another $100,000. Rams and replacement ewes are also needed to sustain and improve the herd, which may be worth another $25,000. Sheep do not require much sophisticated equipment, but we do need a lambing shed and a shearing shed, some wagons, three or four trucks, hay and grain machinery, camp tenders, and pack horses and mules. Altogether, this equipment might cost in the neighborhood of $50,000.

Adding all of these various costs components together, an economic sheep ranch would require approximately $675,000 capital to start up. Most of the sheep ranchers in existence today have come down through families. We have less sheep in the United States today than we did in 1870. Several reasons have contributed to this lack of growth in the industry. The American consumer eats less lamb than ever before and wool is imported from Australia, but the primary reasons we have fewer sheep is that the small units have switched to cattle operations which do not require the labor required in a sheep ranch, and outside capital has not been available to the young man wanting to start up a sheep operation. Sheep require constant human supervision and therefore, are not suited to absentee ownership.

Since absentee ownership is not well suited to the sheep industry, any new units, or expansion of the established ranches, must be initiated by men who want to live and work on the premises. Few young men have the $675,000 capital available for investment in land and cattle, and, of those who do, few are particularly interested in becoming sheep ranchers. At the same time, there are young men in my part of the country who very much want to be on their own and own their own ranch, but do not have enough capital to get a start. Any legislation which might inhibit the flow of capital from the more affluent areas of our country would hurt the economy of the rural areas which are geared to sheep operations.

I am opposed to the proposed changes in the tax laws which are being considered by this committee, because I believe these proposals would discourage the flow of funds into sheep country, and would ultimately have a detrimental effect on the value of our land, the economy of our rural communities, and the maintenance or expansion of our industry.

SUPPLEMENTARY STATEMENT BY BRIG. GEN. H. L. OPPENHEIMER

Amplifying my introductory remarks, I want to lead off the group which is going to substantiate my previous statement that the present farm tax incentives are costing the government nothing. In this regard, I want to make four quick points in rebuttal to the totally erroneous newspaper and magazine reports many of you have been reading in regard to our particular client group:

1. The approximately $20,000,000 expended by our clients last year did not go into a hole in the ground nor is it going to all be con-

verted into capital gains. Most of it went to individuals and corporations in the rural areas who will presumably pay their own income taxes on it or go to jail.

As a result of the above expenditures our clients are going to be receiving about $15,000,000 back this year from the sale of slaughter steers, calves, feed, interest and rent. All of this is subject to ordinary income tax, not capital gain. They are going to pick up about $4,000,000 in capital gain or return of capital from sale of breeding stock or ranch land. Because many are in the development state, about $3,000,000 went into herd growth or land improvement which won't produce taxable income for two or three years.

2. Assuming the present price level on cattle holds out for another six months, 90% of our clients will have had a substantial economic profit on all calf and steer sales, regardless of tax considerations.

3. A statement has been made that these "outsiders" don't care how much money they lose. I don't know about other farm management firms. We are on a 30-day-agency contract. If we don't make them an economic profit or have a damn good excuse, we get fired.

4. A favorite thesis of one prominent but misinformed public speaker has been that the "outside investors" are ruining American land by plowing up grass pastures and putting them into row crops and adding to surpluses. To my knowledge, none of our 500 clients has ever plowed up a grass pasture for row cropping. On the other hand, they have spent very large sums of money in taking marginal worn-out corn and cotton land, fertilizing it and putting it back into grass, thus cutting down on grain surpluses.

STATEMENT OF ROBERT M. GIFFORD,

Rancher and Attorney; President, Green City Feedlot Corp., Green City Bank Building, Green City, Mo. (Past President, Green City Chamber of Commerce; Former Mayor of Green City; Former Member, Missouri Legislature)

I am going to address the secondary tax recovery of development funds spent in the Green City, Missouri area.

Green City, Missouri, is a small rural farming community which might be located anywhere in the United States. A few years ago it had declined from a prosperous thriving community to an area of depressed economy and diminishing population. Railroad service, ceased; a new super highway missed Green City. The small farms could not support family units. There was no opportunity for the local youth and they migrated to cities immediately upon graduation from high school. Farm operations had dwindled to small grain farms with farmers utilizing their grain to feed out hogs and cattle. They were at an economical disadvantage with large commercial feedlots in purchasing and marketing cattle for feeding. Much of the local farmland was exhausted from years of continuous corn farming with no fertilizer or terracing.

About 8 years ago, a farm management agency interested outside capital in buying worn-out, abandoned farmland which had reverted to brush and converting it to livestock operations with improved grass pastures. At first, the local people were fearful of the effects of "outsiders" purchasing land. Frequently, snide reference to "tax dodgers" was heard.

Then they realized that the introduction of outside risk capital had revitalized the economy. Local people were hired to run the operation and local farmers were able to realize income by assisting in the time available from their farming. These salaries were spent locally. Local merchants benefited from the sale of building materials, seed, fertilizers, fencing, etc.

The grain farmer suddenly found he had a local source of high-quality feeder calves, and a market for excess silage. Farmers who did not have capital to stock their pastures were realizing income from leasing their grazing lands to their new neighbors. Stalk fields which were valueless before were now worth money.

The local people recognized the ready availability of good-quality cattle and obtained outside financing to establish a feed lot corporation. The feed lot provides employment for local farmhands during the fall and winter, their slack season. It also provides a local market for grain, hay and silage. In the past eight years, bank deposits have doubled. Time savings deposits have increased by 500 percent.

The local citizens realize that outside capital had completely reversed the economic trend in the area, and the atmosphere of gloom and depression had dissipated completely. A nonprofit cooperative has been formed with the aim of attracting new industry which is associated with agriculture. A few of the local citizens have recently had the opportunity to observe Mr. Winthrop Rockefeller's effect on similar areas of Arkansas, and I can assure you that such an additional outside investment enterprise would be most welcome in the Green City area.

This is what has resulted with the inflow to Green City of outside investment dollars. It is true the investor was afforded substantial deductions on his improvement dollars, but let's consider the entire tax picture. Gentlemen, these are high-velocity dollars; they flow through many hands. Outside money paid for building materials increases the local merchants' income and profit. A portion of this is paid as income tax, with the balance he may employ a carpenter to add a room to his house, thus increasing the income of the carpenter. Again a portion of the carpenter's income is paid as income tax and a portion is spent, perhaps, on new clothes. The store operator, in turn, pays a portion of his increased income in taxes and spends a portion of the increase for groceries. The chain flows on from merchant to merchant, each of whom contributes a part of it as income tax.

Thus, while at first blush, it may appear that the deductions allowed for these expenditures represent losses to the Federal Treasury, a more comprehensive examination reveals they are actually recovered as taxes from other sources. In closing, I should like to point out the merchants in Green City who eventually pay their individual 25-30% income tax on these "outside" dollars are all too happy to do so, because the memory is clear and vivid in their minds when there were no such dollars on which to pay their tax.

STATEMENT OF FRANK KEMP, JR.,

Ranch Management and Appraisals;
Member, Colorado State Senate

Mr. Chairman and gentlemen of the committee, in reviewing the material that has appeared in the public press, the benefits of maintaining a cattle industry without direct Federal subsidies are seldom mentioned. In my opinion, as a ranch manager and consultant, this point is important to a complete understanding of the tax revisions proposed by Senator Metcalf and Congressman Culver.

My own position in public life is as Senator in the Colorado Legislature. In this capacity, I have taken an active interest in the affairs of my constituents in all phases of western agriculture. The majority, I believe, have come to realize that Federal tax benefits help bring outside capital into Colorado and also assist local stockmen to find a degree of profit in a basic but hazardous industry. A minority, many of whom are primarily farmers, sincerely feel that outside investors constitute unfair competition and should be eliminated by changes in the tax law.

The segment of agriculture devoted to crops has enjoyed few of the benefits written into the present tax laws. Most of these benefits were designed for livestock and orchards. However, many other governmental advantages were extended to crop farmers. These included price supports, crop loans, and other subsidies. It is significant to note that most opposition to the present tax laws comes from this type of farmer and not from organizations like the American National Cattlemen's Association, which finds the present law equitable and opposes changes such as the Metcalf-Culver legislation.

In my opinion, much misunderstanding exists relative to the effect of tax benefited livestock on nontax benefited crop farming. For example, four acres of good farm land can produce, on the average, about 312 bushels of corn. In some form of subsidy, this production costs the Federal government perhaps 50¢ per bushel. If this same land were converted to improved pasture, it could support one cow. Therefore, the present tax incentive system which encourages investors to convert to grass (a) removes 312 bushels of grain from surplus, (b) eliminates a direct Federal subsidy, and (c) encourages higher grain prices for the farmer. Thus, it would appear that both the government and the farmer benefit.

Actually, the only likely member of the agricultural community with grounds to complain is the livestock producer who might face the prospect of over-production. But this is not the case, and stockmen continue to support with vigor tax principles such as capital gains and cash basis accounting. Maintaining the present system of tax incentives is important for ranchers and farmers alike. Except in instances where abuse exists . . . and these control the agricultural industry. There is much apprehension about adverse economic effects which could result from proposed legislation such as that introduced by Senator Metcalf and Congressman Culver, and I respectfully suggest that no such fundamental and far-reaching changes be considered by this Committee.

STATEMENT OF BUSTER WHEAT,

Rancher and Cattle Feeder, Allen, Kans.

My name is Buster Wheat. Members of my family have owned land and run cattle in the Kansas Blue Stem area since just after the Civil War. I am going to hit production and prices. Over the last 25 years, I have had cattle in Nebraska, Northern Texas, Northern New Mexico, Oklahoma and all over the State of Kansas.

I lease grass and winter wheat fields and run my own cattle. I have put cattle out with other people on contract. I have taken other people's cattle and run them on contract on my own land. I contract other people's calves often three or four months in advance. I have sold calves or yearlings of my own on future delivery contracts to other people, three or four months or sometimes as much as six months in advance.

I take other people in as partners on my deals; a lot of them take me in as partners on theirs. I have been on share-the-gain contracts, wheat-gain contracts, 50/50 deals on calf crops and deals where I furnish the management, somebody else furnishes the grass and a third guy furnishes the cattle.

I have been on each of these kind of partner-type deals with bankers, big wheat growers, feedlot operators and owners, grain elevator people, and from time to time, clients of Oppenheimer Industries, Inc. and other management firms.

If I think the market is likely to go down, I like to be running as many cattle on contract as possible. If I think the market is going to go up, I like to own them myself. Right now, one of my partners and I are running some cattle for Oppenheimer clients. The way the market is going this last month I think we made a mistake and should have kept them ourselves.

I believe I do as big an annual volume with grass cattle or winter wheat cattle as anybody in Kansas. In some years, some of my partners and I have been involved with over 100,000 head. My margin of profit or loss, either on buying or selling the cattle or on the gain contracts I am in and out of, is pretty small. One cent per pound in either direction means whether or not we have a real good year or a serious loss.

In other words, my whole livelihood depends on what I think the weather conditions are going to be, how good the grass is going to be, and what kind of gain is going to be put on. This is how I make my living. We have an old saying out where I come from that "nobody goes broke for having too much grass but plenty of them have gone broke when they run out." What I mean by this is that if you don't overstock your pastures and have a lot of grass left over at the end of the season, there is always going to be somebody who will rent it or some cattle you can buy and put on it and use it up. It's very unusual if it ever just goes to waste.

Today, and I guess it has been true for at least fifty years, a good part of the Blue Stem and the Oklahoma Osage country, and the Sandhill country in Nebraska, which is probably the best cattle land in the country, doesn't trade hands too much and a good part of it is held by estates, and widows. That's why the leasing of grass and contracting of animals in our particular section of the country has been the principal element of beef raising for as long as I can remember and I guess it goes back to before I was born.

What I am getting to in all of this, and I know I have been wandering around the barn some, is that it don't matter who owns the land, who is doing the leasing, who's got the cattle and whether they're on contract or not. The land in this country is pretty well going to be stocked to capacity and is going to be producing the same number of pounds of beef per acre. What does matter is how good the soil is and more important, how much rain do we get. Now, I've never had any courses in economics or whatever you call it but I sure know something about beef production, how many cattle there are and when they're coming to market and what is this going to do to prices. I guess wrong once in awhile but if I didn't guess right more often than I guess wrong, I'd be broke.

I finally got around to what I started to talk about and that is that these changes in the laws are not going to affect how much rain we are going to get in Kansas and Oklahoma, and that is what puts on the pounds of beef and makes the markets.

In other words, making it tough on some of my partners and the people I do business with is not going to affect the number of cattle that are going to be run on grass next year nor is it going to affect the prices. As far as I am concerned it might just mean I have to run more cattle on my own account and take a little more risk. However, there are lots of young guys in this business that don't have as good a bank connections as I've got, and, if they can't get partners, this is going to force them to quit. Right now the bankers seem to be short enough that, if you haven't been a good enough customer for years, you can't get any money at all no matter what interest rate you are ready to pay. All these laws are going to do is keep young guys from getting a hand in the game. This isn't the way the United States was built, or at least it isn't the way that Kansas was built.

SUMMARY AND SUPPLEMENT TO TESTIMONY OF OPPENHEIMER INDUSTRIES GROUP

As developed during the presentations before the House Ways and Means Committee on March 10 and the subsequent cross-examination by various Congressmen, we were asked to come up with some suggestions that would correct abuses within the livestock industry and still not curtail the cash flow and rural credit structure of the established operators.

I submit that the problem is a broader one than of just the tax laws and the Treasury and requires a coordinated piece of legislation overlapping into several other Departments.

In this supplement I plan first to summarize some of the previous testimony; second, to give a hypothetical desirable use of "tax incentive capital" in livestock; third, to give an undesirable example; fourth, to offer suggestions on how the latter could be curbed without harming the farmer.

Summary

1. Almost all tax incentive outside money goes into livestock and citrus.
2. These have not received a penny of the $2,000,000,000 to $3,000,000,000 annual subsidies for grain and cotton.
3. The only actual Treasury figures available indicate that the tax incentives cost $38,000,000 1964 and $23,000,000 1966, a decreasing amount.
4. All of the livestock associations (cattle, sheep, and horse) are opposing the legislation; only the small row crop farmers are supporting it. The wealthy individual attracted by tax incentives does not go into row crop cultivation. He is not driving down the price of corn and cotton. He is buying grain to feed his cattle. He is not competing with the row crop farmer.
5. Practically the only land transition accomplished by these "outsiders" is converting exhausted crop land back into pasture for livestock.
6. Beef prices, with no support, are currently at a five-year high. Grain prices are at a five-year low, and the CCC has just asked for an emergency increase of $1,000,000,000.

Desirable Example

1. The investor goes partners with a young local rancher, buying an adjoining property and leasing it to him and putting out cattle with him on shares or contract.
2. This permits the young rancher to triple the size of his operation and cut his per unit costs by 20%.
3. He converts 500 acres of crop land to permanent pasture or hay production, saving the Federal Government $10,000 per year in crop supports.
4. He goes into a land improvement program, hiring local labor

and buying local supplies. The local area has qualified for rural distress with an average per capita income under $2,500 and a 15% unemployment rate.

5. He gives the local farmer who's his partner an option to purchase the adjoining property he leases at a 60% mark-up in 10 years.

6. He hangs on to his breeding herd for 8 years and operates it in general conformance to the industry.

7. His contracts, purchases, sales, and general operations are right on the market for the area.

8. He makes an economic profit regardless of tax incentives.

Undesirable Example

1. He buys registered cows that would normally go at $600 cash for $4,000 each, with a $1 downpayment and a $3,999 mortgage.

2. He pays $500 per year maintenance plus a $50 per head management fee.

3. The outfit that sold him the herd also runs the farm in the Philadelphia suburbs where they are being kept.

4. His own accountant was paid a $1,000 undisclosed fee for selling him the program.

5. The managing outfit guarantees him a 100% calf crop and to buy all of his calves at $400 each.

6. They guarantee to replace any dead, barren, or aged cow with another one.

7. He depreciates his cows at $1,200/year.

8. At the end of two years he sells them back to the management firm for $300 each.

9. The management firm sells them and the calves that have been born and were purchased at $400 to another new customer at $4,000 each, $1 down.

10. Interest charges were at 8%, two years in advance; breeding fees on a "$500,000 bull" were $200/cow.

11. On around a $100,000 cash investment he is getting $130,000 in deductions, mostly depreciation.

12. His final cash recovery in two years is $60,000 or a $40,000 economic loss. At a combined federal-New York State bracket of 80%, his after tax cost is $20,000. On his $60,000 recovery he pays a tax of 25%, netting $45,000.

13. The management firm sells the entire package to a new "customer" and starts all over again.

14. On an operation of 500 cows and six employees, the manage-

ment firm spends $400,000/year in advertising, sales commissions, and split "fees" to accountants but still nets $1,000,000.

15. Cattle not "sold in the family" are generally "exchange sales" with similar firms to "establish the market." Example: "I'll sell you my '$200,000-bull' if you'll buy my four '$50,000-cows'."

Suggested Governmental Actions

On this basis, without singling out agriculture, I would like to suggest that Section 270 of the Internal Revenue Code be tightened up against all "hobbies," all activities, not run in a reasonably business like way. The present law permits losses of $50,000 per year for five years, with interest, taxes, and casualties excluded as "expenses." Capital gains count as regular income.

As an initial gambit why not change the guidelines to three years at $25,000 per year. This tightening of Sec. 270 would, of course, apply to timber, oil, yachts, equipment leasing, and many items besides farms.

Over and beyond the statutory tightening of Sect. 270, we still have the Supreme Court decision on "reasonable expectation of making an economic profit." Failure to qualify could make for the retroactive disallowance of expenses a number of years back. The threat of this alone should dissuade some of the more exotic abuses. By merely publicizing some new regulations and guidelines a great part of the abuses could be corrected. Here are some suggested regulations:

1. All steer calves and any bull calves above normal breeding ratios for replacement are to be considered items of inventory and not Sect. 1231 assets, thus not subject to tax free exchanges.

2. Failure to not have a bulk sale of these animals at least every other year will make suspect the "business purpose" of operation.

3. Sale of such livestock, grain or other produce will be analyzed in relation to total expenses and a per unit production cost arrived at. If this cost does not bear a reasonable relationship to historic or current price levels, economic motive will be challenged.

4. If annual per head maintenance costs substantially exceed those certified as normal to the area by the USDA for two consecutive years, entire operation will be challenged.

5. In event that collusion can be established among two or more breeders that they reciprocally sold cattle among themselves to establish fictitiously high prices to increase depreciation expense, then all parties will be criminally prosecuted for attempting to defraud the U.S. Government.

6. As a matter of policy on any female animal costing more than

$3,000 or male costing more than $10,000, the Treasury will appoint its own appraiser. The lower of purchase price or appraisal will constitute the basis for depreciation, unless adjusted by court action. A similar procedure will be used on gifts of animals to universities and institutions.

7. The deductibility of feed for a farmer on the cash basis of accounting will be limited to the amount that the livestock he has on hand at the end of the calendar year could normally consume during the 12 months following purchase. Any excess over this amount will be considered feed bought for inventory and not for feeding purposes.

8. In determining the amount of "maintenance" that can be prepaid it should be noted maintenance consists of feed, pasturage, rent, and labor. Only feed and pasturage (standing crop) can be deducted when paid. Rent and labor must be prorated monthly. Unless adjusted by notice from the USDA for local areas at certain times, all agents are directed that the maximum amount of "maintenance" that can be apportioned to feed will be $100/year for a beef cow and $175 for a dairy cow.

9. A default on any cattle mortgage, recourse or non-recourse, will be taken as evidence that the initial sales price was fictitious and all previously taken depreciation will be retroactively disallowed. Exceptions may be made if the buyer formally takes bankruptcy.

10. Any repurchase commitment or commitment to replace a purchased animal will automatically set up "salvage value" and all depreciation below this figure will be disallowed.

11. Any purchase and maintenance contact with the same party will be scrutinized. If the maintenance is substantially above industry averages, the excess will be added to the price of the animal and capitalized.

12. A purchase of cattle by a management firm with a resale to a customer at an "abnormal mark-up" will constitute grounds for challenging the depreciation base, particularly if the seller took back a purchase money mortgage.

It is believed that the Treasury has the authority to issue and make stick the above regulations under existing law and court decisions.

In the interest of eliminating the abuses, we should now leave the Treasury and the Tax Laws and move into other Departments of the Government. Here we are trying to protect the investor, whether he is tax-motivated or not, from the unscrupulous promoter. In absentee type livestock operations there are two quite different approaches.

In the first, the firm handling the deal sells the customer cattle it owns as a principal and subsequently runs them for the buyer at its own farms and ranchers. If the buyer is not technically qualified, there is no impartial agency to determine if the price is fair, the condition of the animals as specified, and the maintenance rates reasonable. If prepaid maintenance and long-term obligations are involved the buyer must rely on the net worth, reputation, and capability of the entrepreneur to live up to his obligations. There is no impartial inspection service to see what is going on.

In some of these operations, the cattle are not branded nor in the case of registered animals do the animals get transferred on the books of the breed association. The buyer has no evidence of title, such as the brand certificate or the registration certificate. (More sophisticated IRS agents could demand the normal evidence of title or disallow depreciation, as they would in real estate.)

In any case the novice investor on an inspection would have no easy way of seeing his own cattle unless the entire group was gathered and his sorted off by ear tattoo in the chutes. He has no way of checking the pedigrees with the breed associations independently or to know that the same cattle have not been sold twice as they are not registered in his name.

After the Supreme Court *Howey* citrus grove case, the SEC has the authority to require people selling "investment contracts" to register, and this is precisely the type of thing the law was designed for. On SEC registration a full disclosure of financial background would have to be made, optimistic advertising and false tax promises would be curtailed; repurchase commitments and guarantees would be studied, origins and history of cattle would have to be disclosed, prices and rates would have to be compared with industry figures, unconscionable markups and rates could be controlled, undisclosed splitting commissions with lawyers and accountants to get business could be stopped.

The second route, which is the safer for an investor, is to deal with a management firm that never sells cattle as a principal nor operates a ranch where they are run. This firm operates only as an agent conducting inspections and audits with no conflict of interest, paid solely by the owner on a published fee basis.

As agent the management firm sees that all cattle are branded in owner's name in accordance with local state, brand laws and that all contracts are between owner and rancher as independent contractor. As agent of owner, he must have man present at all roundups taking an independent tally and at the scales on weighouts. If such a firm is involved in the interstate sale of cattle, it can be made to register under the Packers and Stockyards Act of 1921 as a Dealer or Agent.

This act has even broader powers than the SEC. All employees have to be bonded, the firm's books must be open to USDA inspection at all times, full disclosure on price and origin must be made to all buyers. Fees and schedules must be approved by the USDA, and cannot be discriminatory or exorbitant. The Secretary of Agriculture has authority to stop any "deceptive advertising or unethical practices."

If the management firm operates as a principal he comes under the SEC; as an agent he comes under USDA. Either agency has adequate authority under existing law to issue regulations to clean up most of the abuses and gimmick-type operations.

The Chairman. Off the record.

(Discussion off the record.)

The Chairman. All right. It will be in the record at this point.

Are there any questions of Mr. Oppenheimer?

Mr. Gibbons. Mr. Chairman, first of all, I would like to thank this group of gentlemen for being as courteous as they have been. They dropped off their statements around our offices in advance, and I was given an opportunity to read them over the weekend, and I guess I learned a lot out of it.

We don't get that kind of treatment from all witnesses, so our heart goes out to you, and particularly my heart.

Let me ask you, gentlemen, how in the world did you ever get all these people together? How long have you been at this kind of organization?

General Oppenheimer. My family has been running cattle for quite a long time, and our firm has been in operation for 53 years. But we have been running cattle for outside people, and managing their ranches, for about 17 years.

Mr. Gibbons. Well, now, how do you find your investors?

General Oppenheimer. We do not advertise at all. And I would say almost all of our investors have come to us by word of mouth, and I hopefully say, based on our reputation, they tell their friends and associates, and that is how they come to us.

Mr. Gibbons. Now, I am not really familiar with what you do. Could you describe to me, to someone who is not really familiar with this technique, what you really do that makes it profitable for somebody, as outside risk capital, to come? What do you do?

General Oppenheimer. Well, the great majority of our operation does not relate to breeding herds at all, but the bulk of our sales last year was in steers and feedlot operations, where there was no capital gain, and there was ordinary income on the sale.

A further part of our operation relates to the ranch real estate brokerage business, where we buy and sell ranches, and very often we are given the management of the ranch after the client or somebody else has purchased it. Sometimes we get the management, sometimes we don't.

If a client wants to get into the breeding herd business, we do not run the operation ourselves. We find somebody like Jack Asay, here, and ask him if he would like to expand his existing operation with outside cattle, to try to bring it up to a more economic unit.

And if you would not mind, I would like to turn it over to Jack for a second and let him explain just how it works.

Is that satisfactory?

Mr. Gibbons. I would like to find out more about it.

General Oppenheimer. Fine.

Mr. Asay. I don't know exactly what you want.

Mr. Gibbons. What do you do to make money for this outside risk investor? How do you do it?

Mr. Asay. Well, you try to outguess the weather, for one thing.

Actually, those of us who run cattle as part of the Oppenheimer Industries do it and are compensated on a rate of gain, so much a pound for a calf produced, or so much gain on a yearling or 2-year-old. And additionally we have all of the operating problems and expenses but the market risk is underwritten by the people who own the cattle.

Mr. Gibbons. Generally, as I understand it, you make your money out of it, or your company makes its money out of it, charging so much a head.

General Oppenheimer. We charge a percentage of the total funds expended, which averages out to less than $5 per head.

The rancher, like Jack, here, has a contract with our client, and he runs the cattle. He deals directly with them. The client has his own registered brand on the cattle.

We supervise Jack, here. We send out an inspector once every 60 days, to be sure that everything is going all right. Otherwise, he runs this entire show himself, and if he puts a sufficient amount of gain on the cattle, and turns out a sufficiently good calf crop, our client makes an economic profit.

If he turns out a poor one, and does it a year or two in a row, next year our client does not renew the contract for Jack.

His incentive is to do a good job, and in every way that we know, we try to make the deal come out for him as precisely the same as it does as if he owned his own cattle.

Now, in his case, he happens to be working with us. We have other ranchers here who have nothing to do with us.

The one thing, where they have this outside capital that they all have in common, is that most have borrowed from the banks to the maximum that they are able to do, and they are unable to get additional equity capital to expand to meet the competition and to meet what is necessary in the industry today, which is a certain minimum size.

We have people here who can tell you what these sizes are in different sections of the country, but in order for them to stay in the business, or to enter the business, they have to get to a certain size, and the only way they can get to that size, unless they inherited a million bucks from their grandfather, is to get somebody to go put the cattle out with them on shares.

We will have plenty of people here that can give you more detail. This has been going on in areas like the Kansas Blue Stem, where Buster comes from, and Wyoming, where Mr. McIlvaine comes from, for about a whole century.

This is not anything new, and if something occurred to disrupt this flow of this capital today, when it is—well, would you care to talk about it, Jim?

Mr. Harper. General Oppenheimer probably referred to my situation because we are a little unique in comparison with some of these other people.

My grandfather trailed cattle. He bought our cattle ranch in 1890. It has been in the family since that time. We are fortunate, and we have not had to lay out additional capital for land, et cetera. At the present time, we have an economic operating unit.

However, in order to expand our unit, we would have to go out and borrow money, pay 7½, 8 percent interest, and in view of this situation, we are seriously considering utilizing the Oppenheimer approach for the expansion of our operation.

Since 1890, we have never taken cattle on shares, we have never leased any land to anybody, we have never brought outside capital. But at this point, we are seriously considering it.

General Oppenheimer. I would like to add another example, here. Mr. Brock at one time ran cattle for our clients and no longer does, but I think he feels kindly to the fact that we helped him get started.

Would you care to talk about that?

Mr. Brock. Mr. Chairman, my reason for being a stockman today in Clark County, Kansas, last year, just doubled. We had school bond issues, we had a reevaluation, and in order to cope with these rising costs, operating costs, to where our margin of profit per unit is just paper thin, we need additional outside capital to help enlarge our operation to continue to remain in the livestock business.

And, Congressman Gibbons, you or Congressman Chamberlain asked a question this morning or this afternoon, as to, if outside capital was being made available to a young operator today. It definitely is.

We extend you a hearty invitation to come to the Southwest, and see for yourself some small operations that this outside capital, such as Oppenheimer Industries is making available to these rural communities that it is providing opportunities for these young men, such as myself, to be in agriculture.

It is actually going on today, and I want to say this, Mr. Chairman, that we urge you to retain the part of the status quo, our present laws, that will enable this outside capital to continue to be made available to these rural areas.

Speaking for my family and myself, we would like to blow the trumpet; we would like to express deep gratitude for these present laws, and for these firms that are allowing us to work with them, to be in agriculture.

And, sir, we urge you to continue to make that possible.

Mr. Gibbons. Now let me ask this gentleman a question.

Really, what you need is capital. You don't care where you get it from, just so you get it?

Mr. Brock. That is correct.

Mr. Gibbons. That is the big problem?

Mr. Brock. Yes.

Mr. Gibbons. Now gentlemen, tell me something. In 1966 tax returns, you see adjusted gross income of over a million dollars, 88 of them, nonfarm income, and they lost $40,000 apiece, or on the average.

How does a fellow go about losing that much money in something like this?

General Oppenheimer. Well there are lots of ways it can be done. I mean, if these are at the development stage on a herd, a piece of land, he may be expensed out to his operating, he may have paid his operating costs, but he has been trying to build his herd up, or he is trying to develop it, or he is selling calves, let's say, they don't bring as much.

What was the year you said, 1966?

Mr. Gibbons. In 1966, there were 88 men who made an adjusted gross income of more than a million dollars, and they each lost, on the average, of over $40,000 a year in the cattle industry, which sort of—

General Oppenheimer. 1964 to 1966 was not—is that correct, this was a poor year, was it not, Buster?

Mr. Buster Wheat. 1964 was a real bad year.

General Oppenheimer. Let's look at that period. In 1964, there wasn't anybody in the industry that made any money, anywhere, that was keeping his books properly.

Now, with people who are developing land, who are trying to improve it, there is an initial period of 2 to 3 years where it will be unlikely that they would be showing an operating profit. For a guy that is in the business of starting a breeding herd, and trying to improve it, and develop it, by the time he has calves for sale, by the time he has got a good reputation to where he can sell them, for a purebred herd, that could very well take 2 or 3 years to get started.

By the way, as far as our operations are concerned, the purebred business, the registered business, represents approximately 1 percent of our total operations. We do not deal with registered cattle except for the production of bulls for our own use.

Mr. Gibbons. You are really just a capital supplier and a sort of overseer. Is that what you are?

General Oppenheimer. We are the negotiating agents, the inspector, and the bookkeeper. That is our function.

And I will tell you one more thing. Our office spends two-thirds of its effort not trying to find clients—we do not advertise—two-thirds of our effort goes around the United States trying to find guys like this, who will take our clients' cattle on contract. That is where our effort goes.

We try to find people who have a good reputation, who have a record of success in their own local area, who want to expand and don't have the capital to do so.

This is where our effort goes. And whenever we can find guys like this, we never have any problem finding 25 clients who would be delighted to put cattle out on contract with them.

Mr. Gibbons. On your contract, you don't specify they have to feed any particular kind of grain, or any particular kind of supplement, do you, or anything like that?

General Oppenheimer. On occasion, on feedlots, cattle going to feedlots, we will give them certain specifications. Normally, for commercial breeding herds, which most of these gentlemen here are involved in, we leave it to the rancher. He gets paid on the amount of weight he can produce on the animals, and if he does not do it, he loses. We require a sort of veto power, and if he does what is just generally normal, in his own local area, we go right along with that.

Mr. Gibbons. I guess what I was trying to get, the Oppenheimer Industries is not owned by any particular feed grain company, or anything like this?

General Oppenheimer. No sir; and we have made it a point, because we have had a lot of opportunities to go into these ranching operations ourselves. We have never done so, and we are extremely capable of doing so at a high level, but we feel that any absentee owner of livestock, if he does not have the technical capability or the time to inspect his own ranch and his own operation periodically, he is going to get in trouble, and he needs an arm's length third party in no way tied in.

We are not tied in with any of these people in any way. They are independent contractors. They have an independent contract with our client, and our only function is that we get paid by our client to go out and see that everything is being done properly. We have no relationship with any of these gentlemen present, except General Stiles, here, and Mr. Kemp. Everybody else here is absolutely independent of us.

To give you an idea, Mr. McIlvaine, here, does not even run any of our cattle.

Would you like to discuss this?

I have never met Mr. McIlvaine until yesterday.

Mr. McIlvaine. I am not associated with Oppenheimer Industries in any way.

I met the general yesterday for the first time, person to person. I had talked to him on the phone.

I came here at his request, on the importance of outside money and investments in agriculture and livestock development.

I came out of the Army, as a personal reference, and started into my stock business with no assets, on a ranch management basis, and later wanted to get in on my own. I had no assets to go to the bank with, to borrow money.

I was fortunate enough to have a friend who did have some money, which he was willing to invest in ranching operations, if I would run it, and this I did, and from that beginning, have developed the property that I have today.

It is absolutely impossible for a young man. I can hardly classify myself as young, but for a man who wants to get started in agriculture today, where you have an investment of $500,000 to $700,000 to have an economic unit, to be able to go to a bank with no assets and get established. So if you don't have a little encouragement and a little aid from the outside, I don't know how in the world I would have ever gotten started.

And I know of other people in my community that are in the same position.

Mr. Bush. Mr. Chairman.

I wonder if I could ask a question directly on that point.

Sam, would you yield?

Mr. Gibbons. Go ahead.

The Chairman. Mr. Bush.

Mr. Bush. I am troubled by the fact that the main congressional testimony we have had is from Iowa—and Senator Metcalf, of course.

Is there a difference between farming and cattle in this whole question?

I am beginning to feel there is, and I wonder mainly if there is a difference between the ranchers and the small 10 or 40 acre farmer who is raising a crop. Should we be trying to differentiate? When you said $500,000 to go into the business, that is a lot different figure than a guy with a hoe and a small lot raising some turnips or something like that might have, it would seem to me, so I am wondering if we made, in the testimony today, the proper differentiation between raising cattle, as opposed to farming.

Would you comment on that sir?

General Oppenheimer. Could I handle that?

I am going to refer this to Mr. Frank Kemp. I want to make one comment before he gets it, because he really knows what he is talking about. We have never put any of our clients into cultivated land, and the reason for it is that we do not have the manpower to do the inspection and the supervision. To my knowledge, most of the people that have been criticized all day long by the Farmers Union and by a lot of the smaller farmer groups in northern Missouri and Iowa have been these people coming into cultivated land and supposedly competing with them in crop production. To my knowledge, this is absolutely not so.

There may be exceptions to it, but as far as we are concerned, we have never placed any people of our clients into cultivated land, and we have never plowed up a grass pasture.

Mr. Kemp. This certainly is true, Congressman Bush, that in my knowledge, and I primarily see Oppenheimer Industries cattle in Montana, Wyoming, New Mexico, and Colorado, what the General has stated is certainly right.

None of the people that we have anything to do with are encouraged in any way, shape, or form, by the present tax laws, to convert the normal western grass range into cropland. There isn't any incentive.

They are in New York, California; they would not wish to invest in the tractors, the various other things, to do any type of cropping. They are primarily interested in livestock production, and the need that has been expressed very adequately here for outside capital in our area is in the area of additional livestock production, and certainly not in crops.

Mr. Bush. It seems to me that the cattle people, Mr. Chairman, testified mainly they wanted some improvement, but not doing away with it, and it is mainly the farmer, so far, who takes the opposing view.

Mr. Byrnes. There is all the difference in the world between a cattle operation and crop operation. In the cattle operation, one can work into a capital gains situation; there is no chance of that in the crop operation.

Isn't that at the heart of much of the criticism?

Mr. Kemp. It certainly is, Congressman Byrnes.

General Oppenheimer. To my knowledge, I cannot think of any.

But the thing that is interesting, if I am not interrupting, sir, is that every livestock association in the United States that I know of, every livestock association, is opposed to the Metcalf and Culver proposals.

The groups that are raising all the hell right now are the farmer groups, which is intriguing, because our people are not competing with them in any way, and we are not adding, we are not adding to any grain surpluses, and we are not competing with them on the grain market.

Now, one more little point—and I am not trying to say this is any cause-and-effect relationship, and I don't know anything about citrus groves, but the two areas where people seem to be putting this outside money in are livestock or citrus groves. These are the only two industries within agriculture that are not getting a nickel of this $2 billion that the Government is putting out in grain subsidies, price supports, and when I said that our operations don't cost the Government a nickel, that is one of the main factors I was talking about, and that is that we are using land for beef production and taking land out of crop production, and the money that the Government might be losing on some of these tax incentives, they are getting back three times in grain subsidies that they are not having to come up with.

Mr. Gibbons. Mr. Chairman, may I ask one more question?

General, as I understand, you are primarily in the business of supplying capital. Have you ever stopped to figure what the simple interest rate on your supply of capital might be to these people that are using the capital?

General Oppenheimer. I will tell you exactly how I approach feedlots when I try to convince them to run clients' cattle of ours.

I say I want you to figure out what you need to be a satisfactory price to sell, on cattle coming out of your feedlot. Then I say:

"Now figure out and give us a contract that would give you the equivalent of getting our clients a 5 or 6 percent return on the funds that they will put up for the feed, and figure out that our clients will be sharing the risk on market rises and falls."

Now, today, the average feedlot in the United States is having to pay 8 percent interest, if they can get it, and in most cases they cannot get it, and in the feedlot business, you may not realize, it takes about 5,000 head to run an economic, competitive feedlot today.

So if you get a feedlot that has got 2,000 or 3,000 head in it, and has an existing labor and equipment supply, this gives them enough additional cattle to bring themselves up to 5,000 and they get the use of money in advance feed purchases, use of these yearling steers, and so forth, at 5 or 6 percent, which is 2 percent better than they can borrow at.

Our clients, in this case, are getting no tax advantage, there is no capital gains; they are in the business of speculating on the beef on what they think the cattle are going to sell for when they come out.

Mr. Gibbons. I cannot imagine, though, that there are people going into that kind of business at 5 or 6 percent.

General Oppenheimer. Well, this last year, they came out making about 20 percent rate on their money, because the market went up, and they thought it was going up.

So on the amount of money they had out, relative to the time it was out, they made about a 20 percent rate of return.

Mr. Gibbons. Thank you.

The Chairman. Mr. Brynes.

Mr. Byrnes. General, on a number of occasions you have talked about "economic profit." Did you ever draw a distinction between the economic profit and taxable income?

General Oppenheimer. Yes, sir.

Mr. Byrnes. Why then, do you use the words "economic profit"?

General Oppenheimer. "Economic profit," in our terminology, refers to a profit, if you are at a zero tax bracket. In other words, it is plain money, forgetting taxes altogether.

You put in a hundred bucks, and you pull out $102. You made a $2 economic profit, if you are at zero tax bracket.

Mr. Byrnes. What concerns us is the mechanics by which people can get themselves into a zero tax bracket, and still make appreciable money.

General Oppenheimer. Well, in this case, by this I mean–

Mr. Byrnes. The average person goes to work, earns his wages, and never gets into this economic profit. He has to pay the taxes on his income.

General Oppenheimer. In this case, I mean plain dollars, without any consideration for taxes, that type of profit.

In other words, let's say he has no money from any other source. He has no other income at all–zero. And he puts in a $100, and he gets back $105.

Mr. Byrnes. In that example, no one is going to make any money through your operation.

General Oppenheimer. He might, if he were in feeders.

Mr. Byrnes. He has nothing to charge off against his original cost. He has to wait and hope that his loss is sufficient to carry forward to the time when he sells his interest. Is that not correct?

General Oppenheimer. Well, not necessarily, sir. This particular thing applies to the whole industry, not just to clients of ours who are not resident farmers, for example.

Mr. Byrnes. I understand that.

General Oppenheimer. Right. They have to make decisions assuming that a given operation of a given sort should produce "x" dollars of plain revenue.

If you want to go into something like breeding herds, you are going to get less dollars back for the same amount of land and capacity.

We have a real expert in this. In fact I got into a big argument with him a couple of years ago because he did not want to run cows for our clients any more.

Could I let him explain this. Mr. Wheat?

Mr. Byrnes. That would be fine.

Mr. Wheat. This is a good example of the reasons for dividing your operation, where the tax incentive is the reason where the people go into breeding herds versus steers. Is that—that was your question?

Mr. Byrnes. Yes. I did not think there was much doubt that a profitable operation, in terms of the general after-tax situation, could be effected by moving into those two areas which ultimately produce capital gains benefits.

As a result of the fact that one operates on a cash, rather than on an accrual basis, one's disbursements are charged off against ordinary income. It is, in many respects, a paper loss.

General Oppenheimer. No, it is an actual loss. There is no paper loss.

Mr. Byrnes. It would be a paper loss if figured on an accrual basis.

General Oppenheimer. I beg your pardon.

Mr. Byrnes. Figured on an accrual basis, it is merely a bookkeeping loss.

General Oppenheimer. No. I misunderstood your question.

There is a tax incentive for people, and we do all three of these type operations. We have people running cattle in feedlots; we have people running steers on grazing contracts, and we have people running breeding herds.

The latter guy gets use of these tax incentives we are talking about. The other two guys do not.

Mr. Byrnes. That is right.

General Oppenheimer. And a guy like Mr. Wheat, here, who has all three personally, he is in no other business, other than farming. He has to make decisions from time to time whether he wants to take advantage of being able to develop a breeding herd, expense it out, and get capital gain, whether that is more important than to take his own ranch, he has got a number of them, to put into breeding herds, or to put it into steers, or to put cattle out on full feed.

He makes this decision every day, and he is—

Mr. Byrnes. He makes it for himself, but you make decisions for clients?

General Oppenheimer. Right.

Mr. Byrnes. He is, in the general. Your operation, basically, is to find clients with money.

General Oppenheimer. Right.

Mr. Byrnes. Do you suggest to your clients that they put that money into either feeder operations—

General Oppenheimer. Yes.

Mr. Byrnes (continuing). Or into breeding operations?

General Oppenheimer. We have had clients, the same clients, in all three, last year.

Now, as I answered Mr. Gibbons, the clients who were in feeders last year made themselves about a 20-percent return on all the money they had up, and they did it in about a 6-month period, just plain profit, ordinary income profit.

They had the choice of going into breeding herds, and if we are lucky, making about a 3 or 4 percent return.

I am not talking about taxes.

Mr. Byrnes. But those people are not affected by the legislation before us, are they?

General Oppenheimer. Yes, sir. They sure are, because the fact that they switched into the breeding herd, and only are making 3 percent instead of the 20 percent is because they are able to convert expense money into capital gain. So part of this 3 percent they are going to make, a good chunk of it, is going to be capital gain money.

Mr. Byrnes. I am talking about the man who put his money into the feeder. As I understand it, there is nothing that is being proposed here, that would change either the tax situation of that investor, or of the farmer himself, who is engaged in the feeder operation.

General Oppenheimer. Yes, sir; it does affect him, because if the market went down this year, instead of up, he would have lost 20 percent.

Mr. Byrnes. My understanding was that even under the Metcalf bill, that kind of a loss was not considered a loss which was subject to the $15,000 limitation.

General Oppenheimer. You mean that–

Mr. Byrnes. Am I mistaken? Is that not one of the items which I suggested to the Senator when I pointed out that his bill did not cover all of the ordinary losses?

General Oppenheimer. I did not–

Mr. Byrnes. It should be included. I felt that the $15,000 limitation could not be applicable to all legitimate losses.

General Oppenheimer. You see, there's the feed, it is not all just a market loss on the sale. That is the end result of it, but let's say he buys feed, he has to pay too much for labor, his feed was too high, and his cost of producing these animals is more than what he sells them for, and I don't think, unless I misinterpreted this proposal, I am sure that guy cannot deduct it against nonfarm income. Maybe I am wrong.

Mr. Byrnes. There is some language in the bill on the subject of losses from sale and exchange.

It would seem to me that this is a loss on sale and exchange. If he is correct in saying that that kind of a loss is not deductible within the $15,000 limitation, then there isn't any proposal, really, that would affect feeder operations.

Mr. Harper. One problem–pardon me, sir.

One problem is that, if you were on the accrual basis, then what you are saying is correct, but if you are on a tax basis, you are writing these expenses off, you take these deductions; you see what I mean?

That is where the differentiation comes in, and it should be clarified.

Mr. Byrnes. Yes; I agree.

General Oppenheimer. Of course you know in the actual operation where you purchased or raised a steer, or purchased, you know, steer calf or something, and raised him up to a 2-year-old, a fat slaughter steer, and if you had a very inefficient operation, and let's say you were a tax-gimmick type operator, and don't care what you are doing, and so forth, and so on, and weren't trying to make a profit, and your operating costs were double what they were supposed to be, you would have an operating loss, I presume, that that is one that would certainly be affected by this, but if you were a legitimate operator and still doing the best you can, and were keeping within industry averages on what you are doing, and you still had an operating loss, my interpretation is that you could not expense that against nonfarm income.

I may be wrong. I just do not understand this point.

Mr. Byrnes. The Senator's language is ambiguous. He talks about recognized losses from sales, exchanges, and involuntary conversion of farm property. Does that include a loss which might occur to a feedlot operation?

When cattle are purchased, fed, and finally sold for less than the original price paid plus the cost of feed, a loss is felt which, it seems to me–

Mr. Harper. Right there is your problem.

Mr. Byrnes. There is an example of a loss on a sale.

Mr. Harper. You said plus the cost of the feed. Did you say that you could include the cost of the feed?

General Oppenheimer. I think that is the nut of the thing there, the cost of the feed.

Mr. Harper. You see, the cost of your feed on a cash basis would be an operating loss, and would not be encompassed.

Mr. Byrnes. It would be included on an accrual basis.

Mr. Harper. That is what he wants us to do, but the people in the cattle business could not stand up under that. You would virtually break the cattleman today if you insisted on the accrual basis for all of it.

Mr. Byrnes. It is apparent that there are two questions of tax advantage which arise in this area. One is the use of cash as opposed to accrual accounting, and the other is the nonrecapture of depreciation.

By taking deductions for, and by avoiding recapture of that depreciation when the lot is sold, one obtained the full advantage of all growth, even though some of that growth is equal to items that have been written off as book losses. These advantages are reflected in the appreciation which takes place.

General Oppenheimer. Mr. Byrnes, could I volunteer an answer to one of the questions you asked one of the other gentlemen this morning?

Mr. Byrnes. Certainly.

General Oppenheimer. On how these abuses could be corrected, and what some recommendations might be. The legitimate operator who is trying to operate for an economic profit and was doing a half-way decent job, how he could receive his flow of capital even though the gimmick operators and that whole crew were eliminated. One item that has not been, to my knowledge, brought forward in any testimony either now or in 1963 is that under the Packers and Stockyards Act, and the U.S. Department of Agriculture, the Secretary of Agriculture has the authority to regulate interstate commerce of dealers or market agencies. We reviewed our position in this thing, and while the Department of Agriculture had never asked us to register under this act, we voluntarily did it last week, just so we wouldn't be put in the same group with these other people. Under this act, the Secretary of Agriculture has executive authority to regulate fees charged by people like us; to have them posted; to see that any unethical practices are eliminated; to see that there be no discrimination between customers; and that fair prices and reasonable market conditions be maintained.

This means that if somebody was overpricing something, was charging exorbitant fees or was doing anything of that nature, after he had filed and was registered, and he were notified to desist by the Secretary or by his agent, he would be in criminal violation of the law if he continued. Thus, right within the present statutes, every one of these things that everybody has been talking about could be handled by the Department of Agriculture, which has the technical experts available to see that these things are being done properly and that reasonable and ethical practices are being maintained.

I repeat "ethical." The law specifically says that the Secretary has the right to maintain and issue regulations to establish a system of ethics in the business.

Now this is a very broad coverage, and I really think that this could get all of your abuses corrected, with no change in legislation at all. This is my opinion.

Mr. Byrnes. It is unlikely, however, that voluntary registration will correct the kinds of abuses outlined in the Sherbrook proposal.

General Oppenheimer. I think, sir–

Mr. Byrnes. The problems are inherent in the depreciation process, and the cost accounting procedures.

General Oppenheimer. May I interpose a point? I don't know the operation we are talking about. If the pricing were made exact and not fictitious, where an unreasonable price is established because of the depreciation benefits and the low downpayment and that type of thing, if a reasonable pricing were enforced, and I think the Secretary of Agriculture under this act has the right to enforce it, this would blow that thing right out of the water.

Mr. Byrnes. Thank you.

The Chairman. Mr. Watts.

Mr. Watts. Mr. McIlvaine, I have heard of your large operation. Did you ever need any of this tax incentive outside capital; did you get all yours on the outside?

Mr. McIlvaine. Mr. Watts–

Mr. Watts. I think you answered it once.

Mr. McIlvaine. I don't know whether it is tax incentive money, but I would rather classify it possibly as risk money.

Mr. Watts. Risk money.

Mr. McIlvaine. It is outside money which a bank isn't in a position to advance. If you are going to establish yourself in an operation, that is, an economic-sized operation, and when you have your investment in land, livestock, equipment, and operating expense, you are absolutely in need, and have to have this business capital, and this is the only place that I know that a man starting in the business can get it. And that is through association with somebody who has the money, and is willing to invest it in you as an individual, and not in your assets.

Mr. Watts. So, in other words, you do need this outside capital to establish a proper ranching operation.

Mr. McIlvaine. Very definitely.

Mr. Watts. Mr. Kemp, I heard you say that these outsiders put in money to put plowed land back into grass. Why would they not plow up some grass and collect some of these subsidies for feed grain?

Mr. Kemp. Congressman Watts, primarily the reason is the large investment that it takes to go into a farming operation. If they went and, say, plowed up grass and put it into corn or other crops, where there are subsidies involved, there are also quotas; there are many other things that are necessary to qualify them under our crop subsidy programs. This is as a general rule not an economic thing, that an outside investor, a man who is not living on the ground, is interested in. He is primarily, as has been well stated today, involved in the production of livestock, and therefore he would rather have that land in grass.

Mr. Watts. In other words, if the livestock industry was crippled in any way, he would go to raising crops.

Mr. Kemp. This is possible; yes, sir.

Mr. Watts. Mr. Harper, is it only the little rancher that the banker has turned down that takes on cattle from you people, your people?

Mr. Harper. First of all, they don't take them on from me. I represent people who invest in this kind of operation and am in business management. The size of the ranch, the ranch itself is not significant. It not only helps the little people, but it also helps the big people; as I stated before in my family's situation, we have an economic unit of 20,000 acres. We have handled a thousand breeding cows. That is considered an economic unit, and it will support my brother's family, and his sons, but this money gets spread around between my mother, my sister, and my brother and myself, because they are all involved. It is now not an economic unit, and that it is necessary for us to expand. Thit is why we are turning now to the Oppenheimer Industries approach.

Mr. Watts. And you have to have outside capital to do it.

Mr. Harper. That is right, and we can do it amazingly enough more economically through General Oppenheimer's operation than we can through going to the bank and borrowing it.

Mr. Watts. In other words, you have an economic operation as it is, and I assume you pay some taxes.

Mr. Harper. Oh, definitely.

Mr. Watts. If it was not for this outside money, your operation would not be as economic?

Mr. Harper. That is correct.

You see we are approaching that problem right now, because of the increase in size of the family; as the youngsters are growing up and becoming involved in the business, we have to expand our operation. We are using it for expansion capital. We presently have an economic unit, as it was once, but with the present increase in family we are now approaching the point of not being an economic unit. And so expansion is necessary, and we are using this method versus the bank method for this expansion.

Mr. Watts. Mr. Wheat, I can see why you might need a tax incentive to develop a fancy pedigreed herd. Why do you need it for a commercial breeding herd? The kind that produces the calves we eat?

Mr. Wheat. Well, in my case, I don't need it. But the main reason I use it, I handle a good many cattle on my own, and, as of this year, I tried with Oppenheimer, the first year in maybe, I believe, 7 years since I have had any of their cattle. I made a deal with them last fall on a thousand heifers. By doing so, I took the risk out of my own operation, but the market went right on up, and they have got me cheated now. (Laughter)

So, really, I didn't have to have it, but I thought the thing was going to go the other way. Well, it went the other way—it went the way I didn't think it was going to go. I would have been better off with the money on my—

Mr. Watts. But if it had gone the way you thought—

Mr. Wheat. If it had gone the way I thought it was going to go, I would have been much better off to have had them.

Mr. Watts. I see.

Thank you, Mr. Chairman.

The Chairman. Any further questions from this group?

Thank all of you again.

General Oppenheimer. Thank you, sir.

PART II

OPERATIONS AND MANAGEMENT

Chapter VI

New Dimensions in Leasing

As a rather unique phenomenon, rentals on grazing land until last year have not changed substantially in 15 years. With the average increase in agricultural land values of about 5% per year and the ever increasing real estate taxes, this has driven net rentals from a not spectacular 6% to about 3% of land value.

In the last two years there has been an increased awareness of the savings in labor and equipment of a land assemblage that could handle 1,000 head over one that could handle 500. Larger holdings have consequently been creeping up in rent.

Twenty-five thousand dollars in trucks, tractors, and haymaking equipment with three men can handle 1,000 head, but $15,000 of equipment and two men are needed for 500 head. As a sidelight for the future trend, $40,000 of equipment and four men can handle 2,000 head, with the addition of extra help for two weeks during roundups. The magic ingredient for these economic facts is *land*, land assembled in sufficient proximity so that your labor force and vehicles don't have to spend 30% of their time in going from pasture to pasture.

Unless you have inherited a fortune from your grandfather or have found an extremely trusting bank, you won't be able to own all of this land but must lease part of it. At one time within the industry there was a slight social stigma about being a "tenant." A rancher would brag at the local bar, "I own every hoof and acre on my place." Now 95% of all major operators are "tenants," at least for some of their land, whether leased from the government or private individuals or, as is becoming increasingly the case, from estates or widows. (To further horrify the memory of the old cattle barons, they might even have livestock on contract or "tenant cattle.")

These hard economic facts of operational size become annually more painful with the ever increasing cost of equipment and labor. Calculating rent on a per cow-unit of capacity basis, a tenant can afford to pay (and a landlord will demand) more rent per cow for a 1,000-head operation than for a 500-head spread. A further corollary is that a pasture for 50 head has no market at all and cannot be rented at any price except to an immediately contiguous neighbor. If there is no such neighbor, such as occurs on transition land near a city, it might be given to somebody who will just keep the weeds mowed.

For the purposes of this discussion let us define an economic unit as one large enough to run 1,000 cow-units. The common definition of a "cow-unit of land" is sufficient pasture and feed production land to run a cow and her spring calf for a 12-month period. Hypothetically it might be 9 acres of pasture to graze her for eight months and 1 acre of irrigated alfalfa to produce enough hay to get her through four months of snow cover. As a rule of thumb, a "cow-unit" is the equivalent of two yearling steers or three newly-weaned calves or two-thirds of a horse.

In most areas where grazing rentals are the standard practice, various services are also provided. Most commonly the landlord maintains the fences and "guarantees water." The latter is less common since the major droughts of the early 50's broke a bunch of landowners on this clause. Additional services could include labor for roundups, the furnishing of salt, protein blocks, etc.

Sometimes the "services" could be reversed. In some of the Indian Reservation leases in Montana and South Dakota, the tenant is supposed to "run" (and winter feed) a certain number of cattle and horses of the local tribe. This obviously raises the cost per head of his own animals. On most Department of Defense leases, such as the Sunflower and Lake City Ordinance plants near Kansas City, the tenant is required to do a certain amount of reseeding, fence construction, and nonagricultural mowing in lieu of rent as part of his competitive lease bid.

In this analysis, let's set the guidelines at a 1,000 cow-unit land assemblage in which the landlord does nothing but maintain the fences. Let us further assume that sufficient land is provided for the rental payment, that there is a reasonable safety margin of excess grass to handle a drought without having to move off.

Setting this as a standard, the factors governing the rent/cow-unit around the U.S. relate to the following:

1. Geographic differences of operation.
2. Rainfall conditions affecting local supply and demand.
3. Beef prices.

Because cows, contrary to yearly steers, cannot be moved from season to season without substantial costs of transportation or losses through new acclimatization, they are normally kept on the same ranch for both summer and winter. Consequently, the costs of winter feeding have a major effect on what a tenant could afford to pay on leasing a property on a year-round basis.

For example, in New Mexico a ranch might have a snow cover lasting only a few days at a time and only two months of the year in which any supplement is needed to be fed. The entire winter feed might be 100 pounds of cottonseed cake and one-half bale of hay, and the entire winter labor feeding period was confined to 60 days. The overall feeding cost on a 1,000-head ranch, attributable to winter feeding, was $7/head.

A ranch in northern Missouri might have three months of snow cover and six months when hay and supplement are needed to be fed. Forty bales of hay, 200 pounds of protein, and 160 days of labor and equipment, used in mud and snow, are necessary. (One hour of tractor time, pulling a hay wagon through one foot of mud, is the equivalent in wear and tear of five hours in dry country.) The overall cost for winter feeding comes to $40 per head.

A ranch on the west slope of Colorado has five months of heavy snow, seven months of winter feeding, and substantial irrigation costs during the summer. The overall costs for hay production and winter feeding come to $90 per head.

In the 15-year period, 1953 to 1968, the New Mexico operation rented for $40 per head per year, the Missouri operation for $30 per head, and the Colorado operation couldn't be rented at all. Because of the prohibitive costs of the winter, in case after case, the government grazing leases in this area are being abandoned or are going "non-use." A further factor here is that the competition of the ski resorts has made nonexistent the former cheap local winter labor supply. The local 18-year-old high school kid who formerly fed cattle after school at $1 per hour is now making $5 per hour serving drinks at the Red Onion bar in Aspen.

From 1969 to 1972 we have seen the amazing phenomenon of cattle prices going ever successively higher. This gives vent to the old Wall Street saying, "On a rising market everybody is a genius." There was a slow effect on the grazing rental market. As the industry says, "The market strengthened." This meant that large leases were a little harder to find; some landlords got back in the business; some of the services got cut back; and here and there you had to give another $5/head rent. Nothing really dramatic happened, and rents, in no case, went up in proportion to cattle prices.

It appears that something dramatic *is* about to happen. At a certain level, quantitative increases in prices can cause something qualitative to occur. This might have been associated with the movement this last December of 400-pound steer calves going to 48¢/pound and 700-pound yearlings going to 42¢/pound. If one can gross over $140 per cow and over $100 on yearlings and you are not being clobbered by increasing labor and equipment costs, a new dimension has been added.

Here's the arithmetic. On an 85% calf crop, 1,000 cows produce 850 mixed calves averaging 400 pounds worth 44¢/pound or $176 per head for a total of approximately $150,000. Direct costs (excluding rent) of labor, equipment, and feed supplements come to $30,000. Indirect costs of depreciation on cows, replacement heifer program, bull service, interest on capital, etc., come to $35,000. This leaves $85,000 in the pot. On this basis, for a ranch large enough to produce these results, one could afford to pay $60,000 rent and still make $20,000 profit after getting 7% interest on equity capital. (We are assuming that two-thirds of the value of the cow is borrowed out and you have one-third equity.)

On assumption a 1,000-cow capacity ranch can run, as an alternative, 3,000 steer calves averaging 400 pounds to a weight of 700 pounds in a year. Here is how this works out. Three thousand steers purchased at 48¢ or $192/head come to $576,000. Assuming 3% death loss you will have 2,910 steers weighing 700 pounds to sell at 42¢ or $855,540. This gives a differential gross of about $280,000. On assumption that direct costs (excluding rent) come to $75,000 and interest on your capital comes to $45,000, you have a total cost of $120,000, leaving $160,000 in the pot. This means you could pay $40/steer rent and still make $40,000 profit.

In summary, at slightly lower than the prices on December, 1971, on 1,000-cow-unit capacity ranches with an eight-month grazing season and not too much snow cover, an operator could afford to pay $60/cow rental or $40/steer, get a reasonable return on his capital investment in the animal, and still make a profit. These figures represent a 40% increase in rentals prevailing in the 1971 season. This is a 40% increase in *gross*. If real estate taxes and landlord type maintenance do not go up, this will represent a 60% increase in *net*.

This type of rental is not applicable to smaller ranches where labor and equipment costs per head skyrocket. It is not applicable where one can expect snow cover over four months. It is not applicable where the landlord is permitting overgrazing where there is no safety margin for drought.

The rumblings of what can only be called an "upheaval" are just becoming apparent. Some landlords are embarrassed to ask for a 40% increase where they have been dealing with a single tenant for 20 years. They get around this by saying that "they are cancelling him because they want to run cattle themselves next year." In other cases they have "a son-in-law who has offered a substantially higher rent." Or maybe this year they "want to run cattle on shares or on an incentive-type gain contract with price participation." Possibly it could be tied in with services such as "if you rent this pasture you will have to put up 500 acres of my alfalfa on this other farm for me for free."

Regardless of the national picture, there will be variations of local supply and demand due to weather conditions. In 1971 the Southwest had a very severe drought and Wyoming and Montana had one of their best seasons in history. There is still a major surplus of unused forage. Consequently there won't be as much of an increase here but, possibly, an even greater one in Texas and New Mexico.

Reviewing the preceding facts, one might gain the impression that large rural landowners are about to have a bonanza. This is not the case. They are only going to slightly narrow the gap with investors owning urban real estate. Over most of the U.S. an urban real estate owner has received about a 14% gross rental return based on the potential sales price of his property. Real estate taxes and maintenance take 4%, leaving him a 10% net return before depreciation and obsolescence.

Forgetting income tax factors, there is a real depreciation and obsolescence factor, and most buildings in the U.S. over 50 years old are about ready for demolition. At a given point, long before this, maintenance starts to go up sharply and net becomes microscopic. However, a real 7% average return can be legitimately anticipated.

Traditionally over the last 15 years on large agricultural properties (smaller ones can't be rented), a gross return of 5% on market value was tough to obtain. In remote areas real estate taxes came to 1%, leaving a net of 4%. In populous or fashionable areas like California, real estate taxes came to 2%, leaving a net of 3%. In areas within 100 miles of major metropolitan areas land prices and taxes have gone up to a degree that one was lucky to net 1% after taxes on sales price. *Nowhere* in the U.S. are agricultural rentals on principally deeded properties able to carry a 70% mortgage at 8% interest and 4% amortization. This is an absolute fact.

This mortgage just mentioned would generate a debt service which together with real estate taxes and essential landlord maintenance could cause an annual cash deficit of about 6% of the sales price of the ranch. If the current anticipated situation causes a 40% increase in gross rentals, the average ranch owner is still going to be substantially under what his city cousin is getting on urban property.

Because of the past dismal history on agricultural rentals, 90% of the ranch buyers have looked to a land value increase or a possible sale for nonagricultural purpose as a principal motivating factor for a purchase. In addition, they have received special tax subsidies not available to the owners of urban real estate. These factors should remain constant. Consequently, I do not see an increase of 2% in taxable gross income having a major effect on ranch sales prices. The recent application of the 7% investment credit to fencing, grain storage facilities, and other items connected with the "care and containment of livestock" will be considerably more significant on land values and marketing than a rental increase.

In a fluid free economy where capital "can go where the music plays the loudest," there has to be a reason why the sophisticated rural land investor is satisfied with a lesser rental return than he can get on urban property. It relates to a study of the past and a projection into the future.

1. He knows that large buildings, whether apartment or commercial, get worse with time, hopefully no faster than 2%/year.

2. He knows that neighborhoods can deteriorate or become unfashionable. If he is lucky and picked 57th and Madison in New York instead of 90th and Central Park West, his land values will have gone up enough to cover cost of demolition.

3. In event of wild inflation, war, or social upheaval, it has been the tradition of most modern governments, including our own, to slap on rent ceilings that have squeezed the urban investor into a zero net position. As far as voters are concerned, it is a fact of life that apartment dwellers will always outnumber apartment owners.

4. In a world of increasing population and the nonagricultural absorption of land, the rural landowner can look forward reasonably confidently to a continuation of a 5%/year increase in value. This is a nontaxable increment unless he sells.

5. While this is no insurance against the future, at least in this country, there have been no ceilings or rent controls imposed on farms and ranches. At the present moment most raw farm products are also exempt.

All of the preceding have existed in the past and have applied basically to all agriculturally usable rural land. A new factor relates to the scarcity and possibly unionization of farm labor, together with the doubling in price of farm equipment. As the gasoline tractor costing $1,000 put out of business the 40-acre corn farm being worked with one mule, so will the $50,000 alfalfa dehydrator-waferizer and associated equipment put out of business the 200-cow herd and associated hay field.

The name of the game is *land assemblage*. This is what will command the decent rents. This is what justifies the new equipment. If ranch labor goes to $4/hour with time-and-a-half on Saturday and double time on Sunday, this is what you must have to afford to hire it.

There are very few ranches in the U.S. that can run 1,000 cows or its equivalent of 3,000 steer calves. In northern Missouri it would take 5,000 acres. In western Kansas it would take 10,000 acres. In the Texas Panhandle it takes 20,000 acres. In northern Arizona it takes 50,000 acres.

This does not mean there is no place in ranching for the young man who is capable and energetic who was not lucky enough to inherit a fortune. It's quite the contrary. Let him look about him. On all of the neighboring farms or ranches the owner's average age is over 65. All of their sons want to go into the city. There is a total vacuum in the area of young aggressive leadership. Some of the properties are available for lease. Some are available for sale.

There is all kinds of outside risk capital available to buy these properties subject to one requirement—availability of young capable management to lease them or run them. The ideal tenant is a young longtime resident of the neighborhood who owns his own property but wants to lease the adjoining property to expand his operation into a modern economic size.

The young agricultural entrepreneur, engaged in or contemplating such an expansion with leased land, may look with misgiving on a forthcoming 40% rental increase. However, it's the old chicken and the egg story. Without the rent he is not going to get the investor to buy the land which will permit him to expand his operation, to cut his per head labor and equipment costs, and to be able to afford the rent. If, fortunately, cattle prices can maintain their present levels for a couple of years, both the landlord and the operator can make a profit during the transition period.

Chapter VII

Evaluating Resident Management

From the earliest days of Homo sapiens, when Neolithic Man first tamed *Bos taurus* and *Bos indicus,* the problem of livestock management has existed. It may have been responsible for one of the earliest examples of human division of labor.

Perhaps the very first example of human division of labor or economic specialization was in the hunting party. The younger boys and the swiftest runners were designated to beat the bushes, flush the game, and drive them toward the waiting spearmen. The spearmen were specialists picked for strength and accuracy. After the kill, women and other members of the tribe had the task of stripping off the hides and carrying the meat to the caves. It is quite possible that this organization and specialization existed with Neanderthal and Cro-Magnon Men by 20,000 B.C.

It is logical that the next major step in the development of man's civilization was his attempt to keep some of these animals herded in close to his camp so that his hunting parties would not have to travel so far seeking game. Outside of saving wear and tear on the feet of the hunting party, this had two other advantages: First, it kept a close-in food supply for emergency situations. Second, it kept the game out of the hands of a neighboring tribe, particularly during periods of drought or in winter when food was short. The task of keeping game herded around one's campsite had to be a full-time job. The first man a tribe assigned to do this was history's first "ranch manager." There is no question but that this procedure must have antedated the domestication of grain.

The planting of grain and the full domestication of most of our present forms of livestock seem to have occurred somewhere in the Nile, Euphrates, or Indus River Valleys about 5000 B.C. and this development has been classified by the anthropologists as the beginning of the "Neolithic Age." A process of herding or controlling the movements of the ancestors of these domestic animals could have easily occurred 3,000 years earlier during Paleolithic times.

From Neolithic times and on into the Biblical times of recorded history, techniques and problems identical with those of modern livestock operations appeared in full bloom. Neolithic Man had grain; he probably knew how to put up grass for winter hay; and he had grazing-type domestic animals which he used for meat, milk, hides, draft, and locomotion. There is very little evidence that by 3000 B.C. man was in any way physically or intellectually inferior to the average man today. Consequently, the following facts would have become very quickly self-evident:

1. It was best to set up your huts and your village in the rich bottom-land near a river, where there was a water supply. Here the greater part of your labor would be devoted to crops, and the soil could produce more crops than the highland meadows or the more remote plateau areas.

2. Grazing animals, that could be herded, could be moved wide distances from the village and could graze substantial areas of native grass with only one or two herdsmen to keep them together.

3. There were certain specialized areas, such as mountain meadows in the more northern climates that would produce grass in the summer but would be covered with snow in the winter and certain dry areas in more southern climates that would have grass for a few months during the rainy season but would be non-usable during the other seasons, that could be productively utilized by livestock for approximately half a year.

Even after private land ownership became the normal thing, these remote grass areas and the submarginal land fit only for grazing were often kept under the ownership of the tribe or the state. When things got more crowded and more complicated, grazing rights within these areas were often assigned to individuals. In Colonial times, you might have had the privilege in "common" with others, of grazing two cows on the "Boston Common," which was the origin of the name of the present park. Today you might have the "right" under the Bureau of Land Management to graze 200 head for six months on Federal land in the state of Wyoming.

During the same Neolithic times, before the dawn of recorded history, a local ruler, a tribal chief, or just a wealthy land owner became aware of some basic economic facts:

1. Work that you delegate never gets done properly unless you can supervise it yourself.

2. You have only two eyes, two hands, and two feet, so you cannot be everywhere at the same time.

3. Under these circumstances it is better to concentrate your efforts where they will do you the most good.

Having come to the same conclusion reached by the present-day head of General Motors, our Neolithic chieftain took a good look around him. There was a lot of action within about a 500-yard radius of where he was sitting on his bearskin rug. People were engaged in planting the barley and wheat fields, manufacturing a new supply of polished stone ax-heads, erecting a new addition to the log palisade around the fortified village, and replacing the pottery jugs that were broken on the last military expedition. Ninety-five percent of the tribal efforts were being concentrated on these pursuits.

Now he was well aware that the tribe had three herds of goats up in remote mountain meadows about five miles off and two herds of cattle in a plateau area about two miles off. The efficiency, reliability, and general intelligence of the five "resident managers" with them left something to be desired. Furthermore, he suspected that an occasional new-born animal belonging to the tribe got slaughtered, butchered, and eaten from time to time in an unauthorized manner. This was having an adverse effect on calf crop percentages.

However, to check out and visit the three goat herds in the mountain meadows and the two cow herds which were in a different direction on the high plateau would involve a two-day hike. In the meanwhile, if our chieftain left the village, he realized that without his personal prodding, stone ax production would drop by 50%. Furthermore, he did not relish the two-day hike because the arthritis in his hip was bothering him. What a dilemma!

As he thoughfully scratched a couple of flea bites, an absolutely brilliant and inspired idea occurred to him. Og Og, his nephew, was a bright young man. He could get around fast in the hills. He knew enough about goats and cattle to look at their bags and tell whether they had recently given birth and whether someone had stolen or had eaten a new-born kid or calf. The chieftain would send Og Og instead of going himself!

Og Og was particularly well qualified. First, he had a tendency of reporting exactly what he saw instead of making up a fairy tale. Second, he was big enough to knock a few heads together if things were not being done properly. Third, he had invented a fantastic new accounting system. Where people had previously used their fingers, setting a limitation to the taking of inventory at the figure 10, Og Og had worked out a system using not only one's fingers but also one's toes, which increased the capability to 20! Og Og thereupon became history's first "cattle inspector."

One thousand years before the invention of the alphabet, the livestock industry had already developed into the divisions of village dwellers who owned the cattle, resident managers and herdsmen who ran them, and inspecting agents who represented the owners' interests. Devices or letters burned into the hide as a brand to identify an owner's interest, apart from that of the herdsmen or neighboring owners, may even have been one of the origins of the alphabet.

This chapter covers the selection, supervision, and techniques of control, by an owner or his agent, of a resident manager or resident contractor who is physically in charge of the herds on a day-by-day basis. The next chapter deals with the selection and supervision of the intermediate but necessary level of managing agents who inspect the herds, audit the records, and supervise the execution of the owner's orders.

If everything else in the field of livestock ownership is forgotten, one rule should be remembered. That is, from the dawn of history to the present hour, that every cattle owner who has a herd that is being operated at a distance from himself is going to get into trouble unless he does one of two things:

1. Personally makes frequent physical inspections of his herd if he is qualified to do so.

2. Hires someone else to do it for him, if he is not qualified or is too busy to do so.

Because cattle are easily movable and are generally being run over wide areas of country and because the country is usually remote with poor communications, this is not always an easy thing to do and, for that reason, is even more important. Ninety percent of the scandals, bankruptcies, and defaults on cattle loans have occurred because the owners or the lending agencies have violated this principle.

The following items from the autobiography of the famous 19th-Century cattleman, Mr. John Clay, are typical:

> The cablegram I received stated that the Scotch investors accepted Mr. Stewart's book account as correct and would buy on this basis. My mission was to pass on the range, the quality of the cattle and report on the general outlook so far as cattle were concerned. Buying by "book count" was the method in those days. The Prairie Co. had done it. Their success was constantly being flashed upon the screen. Fortunes had been made under this system and incited by the success of the past, investors did not look far into the future. The result was an era of speculation in herds. It was a minor South Sea bubble. It is safe to say that in many cases not half of the cattle represented on the books were in actual existence. The owners were honest but the wastage was far greater than any of us ever expected. There was only one way to test your number, which meant gathering and rebranding. That was expensive and not advisable, as long as there were customers in the other free and easy way.[1]

---

[1] *My Life on the Range*, John Clay, 1924, reprinted by Antiquarian Press, Ltd., 1961, p. 35.

> One stormy day when a blizzard was sweeping across Wyoming and howling through the streets of Cheyenne, the boys who liked their noon dram leaned up against Luke's bar. Their faces very long and disconsolate, backed up by low mutterings of loss on the range and visions of unpaid notes in the fall, the witty but rather disreputable saloon keeper said: "Cheer up boys, whatever happens the books won't freeze."[2]

Going back to the subject of this chapter, the selection, supervision, and evaluation of the resident operator or manager, we will cover the following subjects:

A. Classification and degrees of resident management.
B. Judging potential capability of manager.
C. Management techniques.
D. Potential conflicts of interest.
E. Potential areas of trouble.
F. Summary.

A. CLASSIFICATION AND DEGREES OF RESIDENT MANAGEMENT

"Resident management" could involve a $300 per month working foreman or a $50,000 per year executive running the Matador. For the purpose of this chapter, the "manager" could actually own the land and own a half interest in the cattle. The term is being used in the sense that there is some interest held by a distant owner in part or all of the livestock and part or all of the land and that the actual physical operation is being conducted by another entity. The manager could be on a salary, he could be on shares, or he could be a prime contractor on a maintenance contract. He could actually be throwing the hay bales out in the morning, be living on the ranch and supervising someone else who is doing it, or be living in a nearby town and checking the herd out once a day. The owner could be living in the nearby town and checking out the manager once a day, or he could be living in a city 100 miles away and checking out the operation once a week, or he could be living a considerable distance away and personally visiting the operation once a year, with "non-resident management" being hired to make the intervening inspections.

The resident manager could have all degrees of responsibility and discretionary authority. He might have to telephone the owner to get permission to feed 25 bales a day instead of 24 bales, to spend $25 for a new tire rather than to get one re-capped, or to repair a leaking gasket

[2] *Idem*, p. 116.

on a water pump. On the other hand, he might have complete authority as to the number of cows to be culled in the fall roundup, where he should purchase bulls and how much he should pay for them, and negotiating and contracting relative to the sale of the annual calf crop.

Obviously, the size and type of the operation have a lot to do with all of the preceding points. If you had 200 cows out on an all-year-round grass contract where the principal action involved feeding a small amount of cottonseed cake during four months of winter weather, supervising the calving, and conducting two roundups per year, this would require one type of manager and one level of supervision. If you had 5,000 cows, a major hay production deal employing 20 men going on in the summer, and an irrigated crop project and if you fed out 2,000 calves per year and generally had to keep over $300,000 in mechanical equipment going, this would require quite a different type of management. At a certain high level, you would want a top-drawer executive and it would be immaterial as to whether or not he knew anything at all about the technical aspects of the livestock industry.

B. JUDGING POTENTIAL CAPABILITY OF MANAGER

The only true test of capability is performance. In ranch and livestock operations, performance can be divided into four general categories:

1. Producing the maximum pounds of beef for the size and type operation involved.
2. Producing these pounds at the least possible cost and with the least amount of damage to the land, facilities, and equipment.
3. Arranging the timing and the quality of these pounds of production best to fit market conditions.
4. Merchandising these pounds so that you can get the maximum amount of money.

Hundreds of books have been written on every one of these four subjects and thousands of people have gone bankrupt or made fortunes on their ability or failure to perform successfully within these four fields. A man who can perform outstandingly in all four fields is worth real money. Whether he is an employee on salary or your partner on a share deal or your contractor on a maintenance contract, you are justified in giving him considerably more liberal terms than a man who is not so competent. Obviously, such a man is in tremendous demand, and if you do not make it worth his while, somebody else is going to grab him or he will decide that he can make more money running his own cattle.

Now, having decided what you want in the way of a resident manager or contractor, how do you go about locating him? That is the $64 question. Anyone who is infallible in selecting this kind of manpower quickly becomes a multi-millionaire.

Obviously, the best criterion would be a long record of unbroken, brilliant performance. A manager who possesses this has been so successful that he is going to be too expensive. As alternatives, you might select a young man starting out who gives indication that he might develop into such a manager, or you might pick a more proven man who might not be of top capability in all four of the fields previously mentioned but is good enough in a couple of them that you feel that you personally can assist in certain phases and supplement him with other personnel so as to make an overall team.

Here are some of the things you should consider regarding a manager:

1. Does he have a reasonably good background of successful performance?

2. Is he young enough, not necessarily in years, but in mind, to be going upward or is he over the hill and going down?

3. Is he any good at leadership? Can he get support from his subordinates? Can he delegate authority or does he try to run a one-man show, work himself to death, and get bogged down in detail?

4. Does he have an adequate educational and technical background? This might mean agricultural college training for a smaller operation or a business administration and accounting background for a larger operation.

5. Has he jumped around from job to job or from lease to lease, indicating instability?

6. Has he the physical stamina and vigor to make it for a number of years, or are you looking at a person who might require a replacement in a year or two?

7. Has he the emotional and moral stability not to give you any trouble in this direction?

8. What do people think of him in his own neighborhood?

9. Can he get along with people like the forest rangers, Bureau of Land Management personnel, county agents, suppliers, and immediate neighbors, or are you going to have to be bothered with settling one feud after another?

10. Is he any good at negotiating? Can he buy feed cheap and sell cattle high?

11. How does he stand on perseverance? Will he be out saving a calf in the middle of the night during a blizzard? Will he keep a crew going 24 hours at a stretch to get hay in before a rainstorm?

12. How is he on machinery and horses? In some operations, two-thirds of the trucks are always broken down, and half of the horses are always lame. An operation next door, functioning under identical conditions and being of an identical size, never has more than 5% of its equipment or its horses out of action. This is a question of management.

13. If the manager is at a high enough level to have full authority over expenditures, is he "machinery happy"? This is a peculiar 20th Century malady. It means that every time a salesman comes by with a trick piece of push-button equipment and a good sales pitch, the manager will buy the machine. Whether it might take 100 years of its labor-saving qualities to amortize its cost is irrelevant. The fact that wheels whirl, indicators turn and colored lights flash on and off completely hypnotizes him.

14. Is he capable of using normal judgment on the allocation of his time and that of his subordinate personnel? In other words, is he going to spend all of his time doing things he likes to do and neglecting the things he doesn't like?

15. Is he a "prima donna"? Can he take orders and carry them out? Or does much time have to be wasted in argument?

16. Does he go off half-cocked? Can he use reasonable judgment in planning his actions, forsee the consequences, and analyze alternative courses?

17. Can he prepare a budget and carry it out?

18. Does he know anything about cost accounting? Can he analyze in advance what certain alternative operations are going to cost and make a decision as to which one is best?

19. Is he non-receptive to new ideas? Or does he go to the other extreme and jump at anything new just because it is new? For some reason, within the ranching and livestock business these two extremes seem more common than in almost any other industry. This is one field in which it pays to take a good look at the old proverb, "Be not the first to accept the new, nor the last to discard the old."

C. MANAGEMENT TECHNIQUES

The telephone, the airplane, the modern car, and a good roadway system have completely revolutionized this field in the last half century. When an owner in New York was two weeks by rail and four days by saddle horse from the man running his cattle, things were different. In the 19th Century it was quickly recognized that this was a different type of investment than an apartment building on Park Avenue.

Because of distance and lack of communications, bonus plans, incentive plans, and share-the-profit arrangements with distant managers or partners were absolutely necessary so as to give these men a financial interest in doing a good job. Even with modern communications, these are still important. The following is quoted from the chapter on "absentee ownership" in a previous book of mine, *Cowboy Arithmetic:*

"For the time being we will assume that the cattle owner also owns the land or has it under control by a primary lease with either the government or civilian land owners. These basic arrangements could be combined in various proportions:

"1. The owner pays the manager a flat salary.

"2. The owner gives the manager half the calf crop, but the manager furnishes hay, protein, equipment, and all outside labor.

"3. The owner keeps the heifer calves and the manager gets the steer calves.

"4. The owner furnishes everything except labor and permits the manager to run a certain number of his cattle on the owner's land in addition to the owner's herd. All proceeds from the manager's cattle belong to the manager.

"5. The owner pays the manager on the basis of a weight-gain contract. As an example, the owner hands the rancher a thousand heifer calves weighing 400 pounds each at the beginning of the year and pays the manager 16¢ a pound on all the gain these animals put on in the year. The manager furnishes everything and pays a land rent to the owner. If the manager furnishes less, the contract involves fewer cents per pound. These so-called weight-gain contracts are gradually becoming the most common form of managerial incentive plan in the industry.

"6. Occasionally the manager may be paid so many dollars per head on a flat fee to run the owner's cattle. This might be tied in with a weight-gain contract as a 'guaranteed minimum.'

"7. A common method used a number of years ago where the

manager owned the land, the feed, and furnished the labor was for the owner to put steers or calves and yearlings out on a 'share-the-gain' basis. A certain number of cattle were purchased at a given price. The owner would then hand the cattle to the manager, who would run them for a specified period of time, and the cattle would then be sold. The proceeds after the owner had been paid back his original cost would be split 50-50 between the owner and the manager. The owner would be receiving a return for the capital that he had tied up for the period, and the manager would be receiving a return for his land, feed, and labor out of the additional weight that had been put on the cattle while they were in his possession. However, in this particular case, risks and profits from market fluctuations would be partially borne by the manager as well as the owner. In recent years operating costs have risen so high that the manager would normally demand more than a 50% share of the gain if he furnished everything except the cattle."[3]

D. POTENTIAL CONFLICTS OF INTEREST

In a situation which is not at all uncommon where you may have one man owning the land, another man leasing it and taking cattle on contract, another man owning the cattle, and a fourth man owning machinery and doing custom work for combinations of the others, there is no way to avoid substantial conflicts of interest.

Outside of the normal ones common to all business transactions, such as the man doing the work wishing to get paid the most for his efforts, the man owning the land wishing to get the most rent for the least desirable part of the land and the man owning the machinery wishing to get the greatest rent for the least amount of wear and tear on his equipment you have a number of items which are special to agriculture:

1. If the man running the cattle for an absentee owner owns the land rather than leases it, he may try to protect the land at the expense of the cattle. For example, in the South or Mid-west in the early spring he may try to put the cattle on rocky, hilly pasture so that his better fields will not get trampled while they are still muddy. A similar situation would prevail in regard to grazing hay meadows in the fall.

2. Items like mowing weeds and repairing fences do not generally have any short-term benefits. Consequently, a landlord must carefully spell out the tenant's obligations on these and similar points in

[3] *Cowboy Arithmetic*, 3rd ed., Gen. Harold L. Oppenheimer, The Interstate Printers & Publishers, Inc., 1971, pp. 97-98.

order to protect his land. These items are so commonly causes of arguments and litigation that it is much simpler for the land owner to tend to them and charge the tenant an increased rent.

3. Where a share crop arrangement is being made between a landlord and his tenant, whether on calves, grain crops, hay, or some other item, the actual physical method of division, where the landlord's share of the crop is to be delivered, how it is to be treated, at what time it is to be gathered, and every other item concerning it must be spelled out in complete detail and in writing. Otherwise, one is asking for trouble. Even if landlord and tenant are close friends and have gotten along together for years, it must be remembered that one of the two of them might die and the other will have to be dealing with an estate.

4. Where cattle are owned by one party and are being placed with another on a maintenance contract contingent on weight gain, the manner of handling should still be spelled out. For example, if the cattle in question are a group of yearlings being held for breeding purposes and there is a sudden debacle in the corn market making very cheap corn available, it is very much to the disadvantage of the owner to have the contractor put the animals on a full-corn feed, raising them up to very heavy weights, costing the owner more money on weight-gain contracts, and making the cattle so fat that they are unfit for breeding purposes.

5. If heavy equipment is being leased, it is obviously extremely important to specify who is responsible for the repairs and maintenance. If one is hauling a $3,000 hay baler across the field, there is often the choice of going through a ditch or around it. If the man driving the tractor is responsible for maintenance and repairs, this could very well influence his decision.

6. Where cattle are being handled on a flat-fee contract or a per head per month contract without a weight-gain or incentive plan, the problems become innumerable. Is the contractor going to keep one man, two men, or no men in constant watch on the herd during the calving period? Later in the summer, is somebody going to ride the herd to keep the bulls evenly distributed or are they going to be allowed to congregate around the water holes in "bachelor clubs"? Who is responsible for the salt, extra supplement in case of drought, veterinary bills, gathering missing cattle at a neighbor's ranch, and the hundred other things that cause extra labor and increased expense or generally affect the welfare of the livestock?

E. POTENTIAL AREAS OF TROUBLE

1. An unweaned, unbranded calf gets stolen.

2. Somebody's brand other than your own is placed on a calf at the fall roundup at weaning time.

3. In the Mid-western area, where there are no enforced brand laws, one of your cows gets over the fence and hurriedly gets shipped by your neighbor along with a couple of his dries.

4. The hay and feed which you have purchased are also used to support some of your "partner's" cattle as well as to feed his horses.

5. A high proportion of your branded stock turns out to be "missing." On large western ranges, 1% is perfectly normal, as an animal can die in a ravine or disappear for several years, but when the figure gets much over 1%, there is carelessness or monkey business.

6. The entire neighborhood is fueling up at your gasoline pump.

7. Your maintenance and repair bills are two times what they should be because no one has even heard of "preventive maintenance." Also, your pickup is being used in the local Saturday night hot-rod races by your manager's 16-year-old son.

8. You have contracted for hay to be put up at so much per bale and you are consequently getting 50-pound bales instead of the normal 70-pound bales. This is happening because you have not contracted by the ton.

9. The silage that you expected and contracted for was shown to you out of a section of the field producing 60 bushels of corn to the acre. The other section of the field which was not looked at and which you also received is producing 30 bushels to the acre.

10. The haystack which you inspected and purchased had all the good hay on the outside. The "baled weeds" were two rows in.

11. When you divided the calf crop, you got a "gate cut." All of the cattle were trailed in and the first half through the gate went to your "partner." You got the second half. On a long trail drive, all of the stronger and better animals moved to the front. His half came out being worth approximately 25% more than yours. There is only one good way to divide cattle:

   a. "A" sorts them into two different groups.
   b. "B" gets to pick which of the groups he wants.

If both parties know what they are doing, there is no way for one to outwit the other on this gambit.

12. Twenty percent of the average group of bulls are deficient in potency or fertility. Buy bulls subject to a test.

13. Never do anything orally. If an arrangement has to be made by telephone, confirm it immediately by letter or telegram. Even the best written contracts are open to misunderstanding and misinterpretation. Oral agreements, where matters of consequence are involved, nearly always get misunderstood.

14. When leasing a ranch, look at it in the winter and look at it in August, and not just when it is in its most favorable condition in the spring. More people have gotten into trouble on this point than on any other. Check with the county agent and local banker to see what the off-season history of the ranch has been.

15. Be suspicious of any rancher taking "tenant cattle" on contract who employs an advertising agency, has expensive colored brochures, and has a fancy guest house. A good operator does not need to advertise and there is not enough margin of profit in the business to be able to afford all of this stuff.

16. If the farm is all cluttered with junk equipment, the weeds around the house have never been cut, and everything appears to be in a disorderly condition – watch out! This is the same way the contractor is going to treat your cattle. Things do not have to be fancy or expensive, but the minor amount of effort necessary just generally to clean up the place is an indication of the character of the man with whom you are dealing.

17. Never pay the full feed bill, pasture bill, or maintenance payment in advance, but always hold something back to use as leverage in order to get the contractor to perform properly on his contract.

18. Put some kind of regulating arrangement with a seal on your water gates and inspect them periodically to be sure that no one has been stealing your irrigation water.

19. In purchasing a farm or leasing it, always take the real estate agent's or owner's "estimate of capacity" and divide it by two. Check with the local Bureau of Land Management, forest ranger, or county agent.

20. Be suspicious of any tenant who has never rented a farm or ranch more than two years in a row. Something must have made the previous landlord unhappy. The best recommendation a maintenance contractor can offer is the name of a satisfied customer who has been with him for five years or more.

21. Avoid the dilettante who has lots of outside income and doesn't have to make a living from your maintenance fees or salary.

22. Avoid the newcomer who has just come into the area from another district and is not familiar with the climate, the range, the

neighbors, or the generally proven historical methods of operating in the area.

23. Avoid the amateur who is going to startle the world with his new approach or new techniques. On the other extreme, avoid the man who looks contemptuously on doing anything differently from the way his grandfather did it.

24. Avoid any tricky feeds or tricky new pieces of equipment put out by companies that you never heard of. Call the nearest agricultural college and ask what it thinks about them.

25. Avoid any rancher, manager, supplier, custom operator, or corporation that refuses to give you an audited financial statement. While many worthwhile people have personal reasons to be secretive, the chances are they have something to hide if they don't wish to furnish such statements. If you wish to proceed with them on the basis that they have a negligible net worth, that is still all right if you have other reasons to believe that they are capable.

26. When asking for bank references, never have the other person's bank write you, but always have your banker telephone his banker if you want the correct facts. Detrimental information will be put out over the telephone that would not be put into a letter. Furthermore, your banker can tell by the tone of voice of the other banker how enthusiastic he is about the individual concerned.

27. There are whole textbooks written on the conditions governing shrink, feeding and watering before weighing, and other items involved in purchasing or selling livestock by the pound. This is no game for amateurs. Whatever is going to be done should be spelled out in writing and in detail.

28. Never believe anybody who says that he can tell that a six-month pregnant cow is pregnant just by looking at her. Furthermore, the average veterinarian who is not a specialist on pregnancy tests is going to be wrong 10% of the time on the usual manual tests.

29. When you purchase something on the basis of its being guaranteed open, guaranteed bred, guaranteed fertile, or guaranteed something else, be sure to specify the dollar amount of penalty and precisely *what* happens if the guarantee is not met and *who* is to referee if there is an argument.

30. Never buy cattle by the herd on a "book tally." Buy them by the pound or by the head. In either case, you must be there yourself or have your own personal representative present when they are checked in and preferably rebranded.

31. If you are buying or selling livestock by the pound, a weight certificate from a "public scale" is not adequate. You *must* have a personal representative present. There is many a cattle purchaser who has also paid for the weight of a couple of heavy truck drivers on the scales. A "certified" public scale means only that it is occasionally checked by a government agent to see that the weights are correct. There is no one there to guarantee that the same cattle are not being weighed twice, that the truck drivers also are not standing on the scales, or that a substantial amount of manure is not accumulating on the scales, which are not being adjusted to take this into consideration. Scales must be zeroed after every few loads. Your only protection is to have an *independent inspector* present.

32. If your cattle are being mingled with others on a maintenance contract, it is necessary that they have your own personal brand on them. Chains, ear tags, and ear tattoos are not adequate even for registered animals. You are better off having the damage to the hide from a regular burned brand. The reason the ear tattoo is not adequate is that you want your inspector to be able to identify and count your animals from horseback without having to gather every single animal in the herd, run it through a chute, and inspect its ear number. In a larger herd, this is much too time-consuming to be practical. You can't afford the expense of this type of inspection.

33. In buying, be careful of rigged auctions. Be sure that you are not just bidding against yourself.

34. Have some assurance that the funds you advanced for maintenance and for feed are actually paid to the vendors. Remember that in most states a pasture lien or an agister lien can be thrown on the cattle for unpaid bills that might have priority over a recorded chattel mortgage as well as over the owner's interest. In the event of bankruptcy on the part of the contractor, you will not be able to recover the cattle unless the pasture bill has been paid.

35. Where there are any doubts in your mind concerning the financial stability of the contractor, record bills of sale, leases, chattel mortgages, brands, and all important contracts. Your protection will vary from state to state according to local law, but when the documents are recorded, they very often have priority over any subsequent liens, except for the agister liens referred to in the preceding paragraph.

36. Your best protection is to get the legal owner of record of the ranch, where a lease is involved, to subordinate his lease to your maintenance contract with the person who may be running your cattle. In this manner, if you have paid your maintenance bill, the land owner

cannot throw a lien on your cattle for unpaid pasture rent. This usually has the result of his making the contractor advance part of your maintenance funds against his rent, which is a further protection to you.

37. When you place mortgages on the cattle, try to place them with a local bank so that you will have the advantage of its inspection service. Try to get the bank to send you a copy of each report it makes when it checks out the collateral.

38. Furthermore, most local banks hear everything that is going on in the neighborhood, and if your contractor is getting in trouble, you will be able to get some advance knowledge of this.

39. Avoid the man who is too full of the "romance of the Old West." You are better off with someone who knows cost accounting and can keep his checkbook balanced.

40. Avoid the rodeo types who wave their ropes and yell, "Yippee!" Remember that every unnecessary step a steer takes makes him lose weight and costs you money.

F. SUMMARY

From the very dawn of history, livestock have been grazed on the less desirable, more arid, more rocky, more remote lands at distances from village and urban areas whose locations have tended to be concentrated in the better soil districts where grain cultivation can occur. Because of distance alone, one of the earliest divisions of labor in human society was among the man who owned the livestock, the man who took care of the livestock, and the man who inspected it on the owner's behalf.

This chapter has dealt principally with the selection, supervision, and problems of the man who takes care of livestock, whom we have designated the "resident manager," in relationship to the man who owns the animals. The next chapter will deal with the intermediate man, the "non-resident manager" or inspector, who represents the owner's interest.

Chapter VIII

The Functioning and Evaluating of Non-resident Management

A good analogy of the relationships in a large-scale enterprise can be found in an infantry division. The owner, whether he is an individual or the elected president of a corporate group of stockholders, is the Commanding General. The resident ranch managers described in the previous chapter are the regimental commanders. The entire echelon referred to as "non-resident management" corresponds to the Division Staff.

The functioning and organization of a military staff are not the invention of a single man but represent the composite thinking of some of the best brains of the world over the last 200 years. It was an outgrowth of war when battles became so large and complicated and spread over so much terrain that the General could no longer stand on a hill and direct his forces by aides and bugle calls. Initially, the staff was the eyes and ears of the General. In modern times, it has taken on a planning and supervisory function.

Essentially, a staff performs the following:

> . . . the staff secures information and furnishes estimates and advice as may be required by the Commander, prepares the details of his plans, translates his decisions and plans into orders and causes such orders to be transmitted to each command element. It assists, to the extent authorized by the Commander, in the supervision of the execution of plans and orders and takes other action necessary to carry out the Commander's intentions.[1]

At a division level the sequence of action by the staff may be as follows:

1. The staff assembles all possible information on the enemy, terrain, and friendly forces.

2. It prepares alternative courses of action and a recommendation for the General.

3. The General O.K.'s a course of action and this becomes his *decision*.

4. The staff prepares detailed plans, budgets, estimates, etc., to implement the General's decision. These are submitted.

---

[1] "Staff Organization and Procedures," *Staff Officers Field Manual*, FM 101-5, Department of the Army, July 1962, p. 4.

5. The General O.K.'s these and they become his *orders*.

6. The staff now transmits these orders to the regiments, explains them, and offers assistance and advice in carrying them out.

7. During the course of the action, the staff continues to supervise the execution of the orders, keeps the General informed as to what is happening, and, in the General's name, issues minor directives, to see that the General's main purpose is being accomplished.

Let us apply this to a large-scale livestock operation. Mr. "A" is a herd owner at a distant location who has three large operations, under Ranchers "B," "C," and "D" in three different states. They are his "resident managers," or regimental commanders. His "staff," a non-resident management firm that he employs, is required as part of its services to make market and weather studies on a continuing basis. The following corresponds to the previous paragraph numbers of the military analogy:

1. In the month of April in a given year, the "staff" reports that market prices look weak for future fall deliveries and that moisture conditions are good in the area where "B" has his operation but bad in the localities of "C" and "D," where drought is a possibility.

2. The following courses of action are available to meet this situation if it should get worse:

   a. Cull cows heavily at "C" Ranch and sell all steer calves. Sell yearlings and all steer calves at "D."

   b. Sell entire calf crops at both "C" and "D" Ranches, and cull cows and yearlings 30% at "C."

   c. Move heifer calf crops off both "C" and "D" to B; make decision on steer calves at later date; cull cows only 30% at "C."

Because of the advanced age of cows at "C" Ranch and the need to have access to heifer calves for replacement at a later date if the drought situation improves, the course of action "c" is recommended to the owner.

3. The owner gives his approval to this recommended course of action and it becomes a *decision*.

4. The staff now goes into consultation with "B," "C," and "D." "B" is helped to make plans to get additional pasture to carry the calves that will be moved in. Early roundup plans are set up with "C" and "D" for the culling. The latter two ranchers are instructed to start negotiating fall delivery contracts on the steer calves. Budgets are asked for on the winter feeding for the coming year from all three, based on the changed anticipated cattle inventories.

PRESSURES ON RURAL LAND

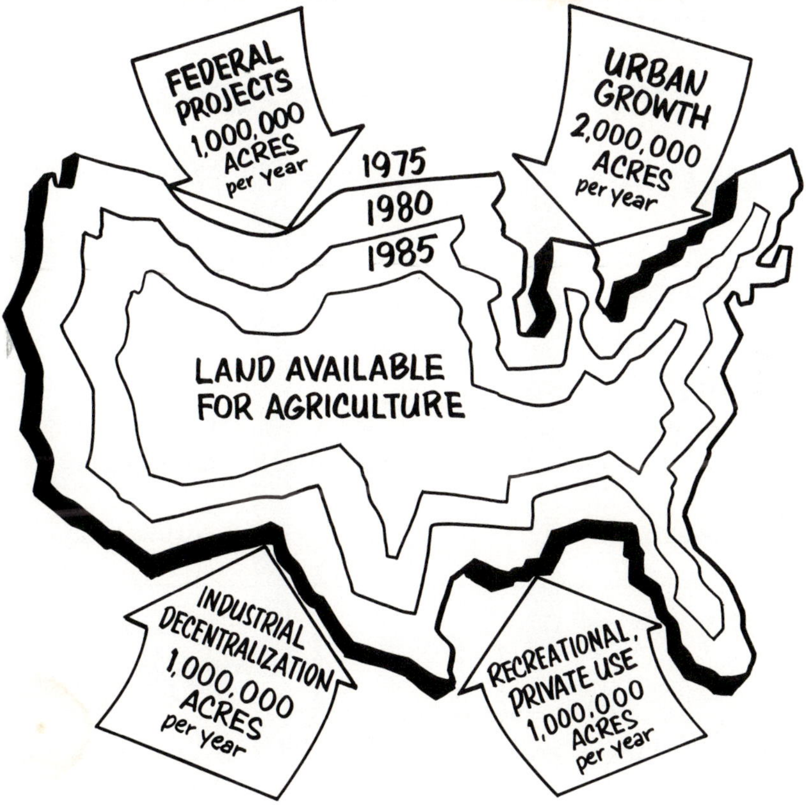

THE *BEST* TAX SHELTER HAS THE *LEAST* RISK

Consider the hazards:

REAL ESTATE

- Percentage of Occupancy
- Neighborhood Changes
- Mortgage Interest Rate
- Management

DRILLING FOR OIL

- Dry Holes
- Availability of Transport
- Flooding
- Geologist's Judgement

CATTLE (A BREEDING HERD)

- Variations in the Price of Beef
- Droughts or Blizzards
- Supervision

3 RURAL TAX SHELTERS

BREEDER HERDS

- Have flexibility to meet year to year needs of investor
- Help to convert Ordinary Income to Capital Gains

FEEDER CATTLE

- Can create a Roll Over of Income from One Year to Another

RANCH OWNERSHIP

- Acquisition of Land with Tax Deductible Dollars

Growth in Value of Farmland in 30 Years

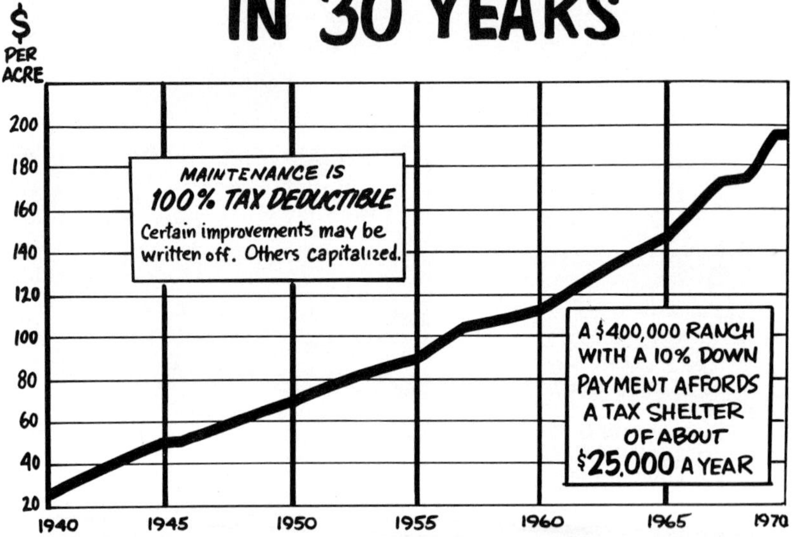

HISTORICALLY,

URBAN PROPERTIES DEPRECIATE *AT 3% A YEAR*

RURAL LAND INCREASES IN VALUE *AT 6% A YEAR*

4 BASICS OF A RANCH INVESTMENT	
LOCATION:	*Transportation . . . Near Urban Area?*
DOWN PAYMENT:	*Usually not over 10% — Might be Less*
MORTGAGE TERMS:	*Personal Guarantee - Not Always Needed*
GRAZING INCOME:	*Average 2% to 3% Income on Investment*

WHY CATTLE AND RANCHLAND ARE SOUND LONG TERM INVESTMENTS

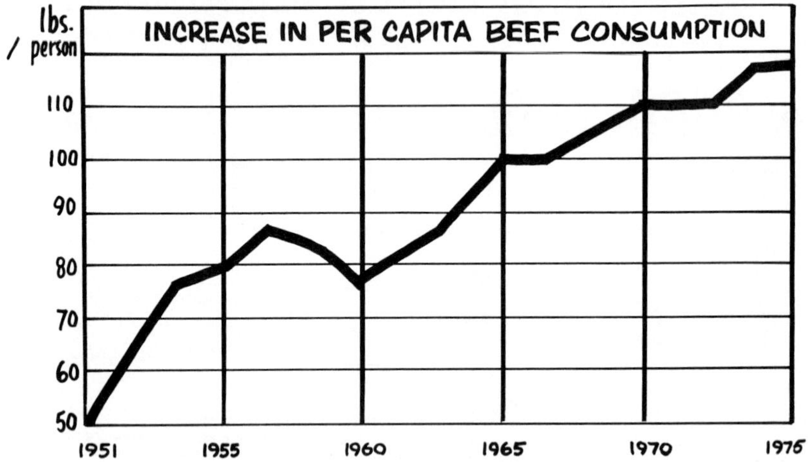

Experts project growth in consumption at 2 lbs. per year, reaching 130 lbs. per person by 1980

HOW A BREEDING HERD IS FLEXIBLE TO CHANGES IN INCOME

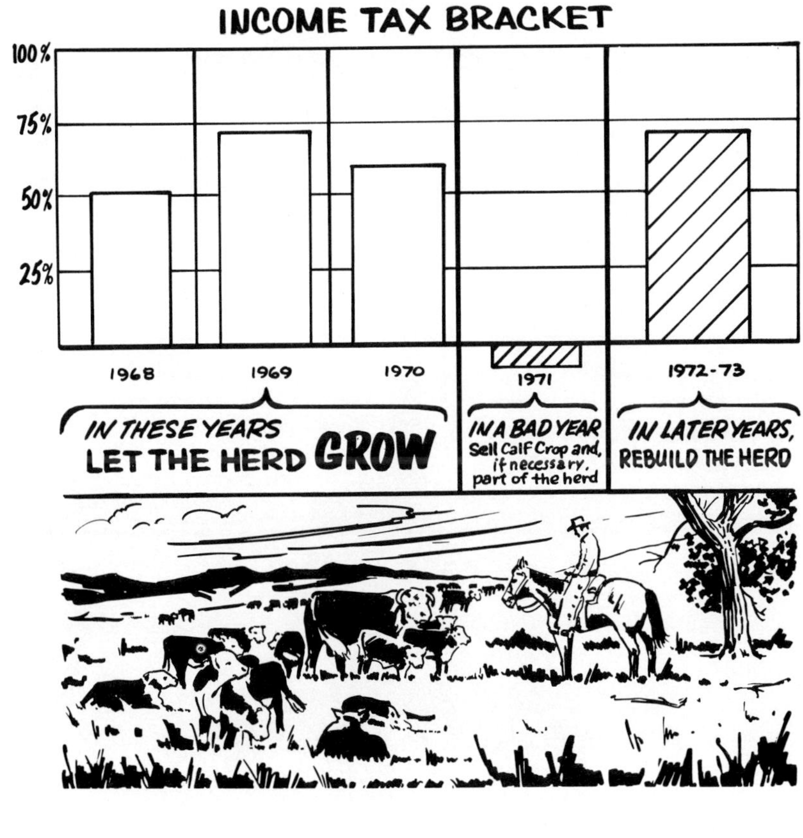

WEIGH THE TAX OPTIONS ON CAPITAL GAINS

5. When the plans, budgets, movement schedules, and fund requirements are prepared, they are submitted to "A" for approval. He O.K.'s them and these become *orders.*

6. The management firm so informs "B," "C," and "D," and various members of the "staff" now render assistance on the grouping of trucks, massing of feed purchases, detailed shifting of roundup personnel, coordination of interstate veterinary inspections, shifting of cattle between pastures on a given ranch to facilitate future sorting, etc.

7. By frequent inspections during the summer, members of the staff determine whether these preparatory actions are being conducted properly in accordance with the directive of "A." Concurrently, additional studies and estimates are being conducted to see if a change in conditions should cause new recommendations to be made for changes and alterations in the original plan. "A" has delegated authority so that the exact basis of culling and the decision as to where calves are to be marketed can be left to the discretion of "B," "C," and "D," but the staff should see that these are accomplished in an orderly and organized manner.

In both military and livestock operations, an overly enthusiastic and eager-beaver "chief of staff" and his associates may tend to get "drunk with power" and usurp too much authority without proper consultation and direction from the General. However, 90% of the failing is in the other direction, where the staff has to be whipped forward rather than reined back. The following is a description of "completed staff work":

> *Completed Staff Work* is the study of a problem, and presentation of a solution in such form that all that remains to be done on the part of the head of the division is to indicate his approval or disapproval of the *completed action.* The words *completed action* are emphasized because the more difficult the problem is, the more the tendency is to present the problem to the chief in piece-meal fashion. It is your job to work out the details, no matter how perplexing they may be.
>
> The impulse which often comes to the inexperienced to ask the chief what to do recurs more often when the problem is difficult. It is accompanied by a feeling of mental frustration. It is so easy to ask the chief what to do, and it appears so easy for him to answer. Resist that impulse. You will succumb to it only if you do not know your job. It is your job to *advise* your chief what to do, not to *ask* him what you ought to do. He needs answers, not questions. Your job is to study, write, restudy and rewrite until you have evolved a single proposed action—the best one of all you have considered. Your chief merely approves or disapproves.
>
> Do not worry your chief with long explanations and memoranda. Writing a memorandum *to* your chief *does not* constitute completed staff work, but writing a memorandum for your chief to send to someone else does. Your views should be placed before him in *finished form* so that he can make them his views simply by signing his name.

In some instances, completed staff work results in a single document prepared for the signature of the chief without accompanying comment. If the proper result is reached, the chief will recognize it at once. If he wants comment or explanation, he will ask for it.

The theory of completed staff work does not preclude a rough draft, but the rough draft must not be a half-baked idea. It must be complete in every respect except that it lacks the requisite number of copies and need not be neat. But a rough draft must not be used as an excuse for shifting to the chief the burden of formulating the action.

The *completed staff work* theory may result in more work for the staff, but it results in more freedom for the chief. The advantages of this theory is that the chief is protected from half-baked ideas, memoranda, and immature oral presentments, and the individual who has a real idea to sell is enabled more easily to find a market.

The final test of *completed staff work* is: If you were the chief, would you be willing to sign the paper you have prepared, and stake your reputation on its being right? If the answer is in the negative, take it back and work it over, because it is not yet completed staff work.[2]

A staff is supposed to be capable of creative thinking. There should be a steady production of original good ideas to be sorted, evaluated, and presented. In the military, in the livestock field, and in civilian industry in general, intermediate groups that can perform "completed staff work," can produce creative thinking, and have the necessary force to supervise the execution of orders do not grow on every bush. It takes a lot of time and effort to develop this kind of team or organization.

A general staff is divided into four functional fields: G-1, personnel; G-2, intelligence; G-3, operations; G-4, supply and logistics. It is assisted by the special staff composed principally of technical experts, such as the tank officer, the artillery officer, the civil affairs officer, etc. All are coordinated by the chief-of-staff.

In a large-scale management organization in the livestock business, similar functional divisions should exist. There may not be individual men to handle each division, but the job categories still exist.

Under the G-1 field come the screening, evaluation, and selection of resident managers. There should be an active and constant solicitation of universities to get replacement foremen, inspectors, and other personnel to be made available to the resident managers who may not be able to get them locally. Bonuses, salaries, incentive contracts—all the devices of remuneration fall into this field.

In the most competitive field in industry, the G-2 section, producing knowledge of what your competitor or "enemy" is doing is criti-

[2] *Directive to All Fleet Marine Force Units, Fleet Marine Force Pacific, 1945*, Maj. Gen. Merritt A. Edson.

cal. Furthermore, there is no section of American life so dependent on weather and terrain. Studies of these two are also a G-2 function.

In a military operation, the mission is to seek out the enemy and destroy him. In a livestock operation, the mission is to market the maximum pounds of beef in a manner to make the maximum amount of profit. The G-3, or operations, officer must direct the application of capital, labor, ranch land, and equipment to livestock under given market conditions so as to produce the maximum amount of money at the least possible cost.

The G-4, or logistics, officer is responsible for the supply and quality of the livestock, the acquisition of feed and equipment, the availability of trucks for movement, the grouping of purchasing to get a better price, the quantity and type of fencing, fertilizer, fuel, building material, etc. He handles the purchasing of land, the leasing of pasture, and negotiations with the Bureau of Land Management and other government agencies.

The special staff of the non-resident agricultural firm, corresponding to the special staff of an infantry division, could include such individuals as a veterinarian, an animal nutritionist, a soil expert, a grass expert, an agricultural engineer, a certified public accountant, and a machine records or data processing expert, as well as a permanent traveling inspection team. The inspections necessary to supervise the execution of the owner's or commander's orders are a responsibility of all staff sections and might be considered one of the principal reasons for the existence of a staff or a non-resident management service. However, in a large operation, routine traveling inspection teams hitting each area on an organized time schedule might be desirable to keep the flow of information coming in over and above the regular staff inspections.

Furthermore, with livestock, as mentioned in the preceding chapter, there are certain specialized operations, such as roundups, brandings, weighouts, and culling for which a diverse interest may exist between the owner and the resident manager and for which it is customary and traditional to have an independent inspector present representing the owner's interest. This is different from the military situation, where it is assumed that the interests of the division commander and his regimental commanders are always synonymous.

The operation of a professional management service within the farm and ranch field could involve every phase of the agricultural industry and could not be adequately covered in ten large volumes. However, as an example of such a firm's functioning, I will include a recent publication which a large management firm sent to its customers and will then go over the periodic inspection report form used by this firm to inform its cattle-owning clients.

AGRICULTURAL CONSULTANT AND INVESTIGATION FEES

1. It should be emphasized that we have no cattle deal or land deal, do not run cattle, and do not develop land but that we are solely a service organization which does the following:

a. Acts as a real estate broker.

b. Furnishes inspection services.

c. Furnishes bookkeeping services.

d. Acts as a financial advisor or consultant within the agricultural field.

e. Acts as an employment agency to secure farm and ranch managers.

f. Acts as a negotiating agency in securing farm and cattle mortgages.

g. Acts as a service agency for lending organizations holding mortgages in the agricultural field.

h. Makes appraisals on cattle herds and ranches.

i. Furnishes temporary, on-the-spot management teams to handle affairs for owners in emergency situations. The latter is not a permanent service but is only an emergency capability when a ranch manager dies or becomes ill or when some crisis occurs that needs immediate manpower brought in from the outside.

2. We have represented clients in almost every phase, type of contract, type of lease, and type of operation within the agricultural field. We do not favor any particular type of operation over another and try to render an impartial survey and analysis to the best of our ability when we are employed to do so.

3. In connection with an investigation on any agricultural operation, we have to charge a fee for anyone asking us to make an investigation other than clients who are already hiring us. Within recent years, a substantial portion of our administrative time has been spent investigating and analyzing ranches, special livestock breeds, fertilizer companies, farm equipment companies, grain storage companies, dairies, dairy pools, feed companies, veterinary supply companies, feed lots, agricultural lending agencies, and many others.

4. As a general guideline, the following fee schedule will be adhered to:

a. A credit check with local banks, suppliers, and people in the area by telephone or mail.................................$ 50

b. A one-day physical look-see by a qualified inspector and a one-page written report.................................... 200

c. A detailed financial analysis with recommendations. This would have to be negotiated, but a minimum fee would be..... 1,000

d. A detailed financial analysis and complete ranch appraisal. A part of this would ordinarily be sub-contracted to a full-time rural real estate appraisal firm. We are administratively not set up to handle anything that would come to a combined fee under 2,000

e. In some cases where we have been employed to make an investigation or have made it in connection with other management services for which we are employed and a new party wishes access to the same information, we must first get the permission of the initial party, but then we would have a minimum charge of.. 50

f. If additional or supplementary information is required or any further confirmation or investigation, the minimum fee will have to be.. 100

g. In the case of all of these fees, long distance telephone calls and travel expenses for investigative personnel have to be charged for extra.

5. A principal part of our activity has been an effort to locate adequate livestock operations on which to place clients' herds on leases or maintenance contracts. In general, our history has been that we have to screen 20 operations to find one that we wish to recommend. The point here is that we are not trying to find excuses to turn down given operations but are going to a great amount of expense and trouble to locate new ones for both additional clients and the expansion of herds of existing clients. In evaluating a ranch operation, the following general items are considered:

a. The liquid financial net worth of the corporation or individual on the contract.

b. The length of time that the existing management has operated the proposed type operation in the existing neighborhood.

c. The history of performance of this operation.

d. The conformance of this operation to normal practices in its neighborhood. We have no objection to new experiments on a small scale, but we recommend that the majority of a client's agricultural operations be confined for at least the first couple of years to methods that have proved successful in the past. We believe this is particularly important where the owner is not physically present to supervise his own holdings and the affairs are being supervised by a managing agent or a fiduciary.

e. The general reputation of the management within the local area concerned.

f. The prospects of financial stability in the type operation concerned as related to jeopardy of advanced maintenance fees and of the livestock or land itself, the possibility of agister liens being thrown on the cattle through failure of the maintenance contractor to pay his feed bills or his pasture rent, etc.

g. The degree of operational security as evidenced by the type of land tenure (does the rancher own his land or have it tied up in long-term leases?); the protection against overgrazing so as to have some security in the event of a drought; and the local presence of excess emergency feed for blizzard, freeze, drought, and crop failure.

h. The competitive position of the rancher on operating costs and charges.

6. Our evaluation of all of this is a combination of these factors. For example, a man of moderate net worth who has for a ten-year period turned out the best performance in his neighborhood might be considered more sound than an operator of greater net worth who is brand new to the area. An operation in which only half of the maintenance money was advanced at the beginning of the contract and half was paid when the contract was completed at the end of the year would be considered sounder financially for the owner than an operation in which he advanced two years' maintenance at the beginning of the contract and could look forward only to long-term litigation to recover his money if the contract were violated in the middle of its time period.

7. Over and beyond this, a critical point in the livestock or farm business is that even if an operation has a top score on every one of these points, it is absolutely essential that a completely impartial third party be physically present representing the owner, if he cannot be present himself, in order to approve the initial purchase, to keep an eye on things at the branding and at each roundup, to inspect the premises physically a minimum of once every 60 days, and to watch after the owner's interest at a detailed physical inventory and brand count a minimum of once a year or possibly twice a year.

8. For thousands of years cattle have been purchased by owners who operate with outside management, and anyone who has violated the principle stressed in the preceding paragraph has invariably gotten into trouble. Nearly every reputable rancher himself will insist that the owner have present at brandings and roundups a personal representative who is completely independent of the rancher and guards solely the owner's interest.

9. We are not trying to solicit such employment, but it is absolutely necessary that these physical inspections be made either by the owner himself or by some type of independent agency. There are 1,500 firms that are members of the American Society of Farm Managers and Rural Appraisers and another 1,500 firms that are members of the National Institute of Rural Brokers. At least half of these firms have personnel well qualified to handle this function.

Inspections have three general functions:

1. They produce information for the owner or his designated agent on which he can prepare plans, make decisions, and formulate orders.

2. They are a means of establishing that his previous orders have been carried out.

3. They are a means by which on-the-spot corrective action can be taken or advice can be given to correct or improve a given situation.

The most important part of a consistent inspection program is none of the aforementioned but is the point that the unit or operation which knows that it is going to be inspected is going to try a little harder to do a good job. The poor and lazy manager is going to work a little harder to avoid criticism. The efficient and capable manager is going to do even better because he knows that his good work is going to get some recognition and is not going to "flower unseen on the desert air." For a conscientious man who is doing an outstanding job in any field, it is very discouraging when no one comes to observe his work and he is given no more credit than the man who is doing a mediocre job. This is particularly true in livestock operations, which are often located at remote and inaccessible places and where a certain amount of difficulty in transportation is involved for the owner or an inspector to get there.

HERD INSPECTION REPORT FOR..........................
(Location)

Date of Inspection:..................................19....

BREED	TYPE		CLASSIFICATION
☐ Hereford	☐ Hfr. Calf	☐ 2-Yr. Hfr.	☐ Registered
☐ Angus	☐ Bull Calf	☐ 1st-Calf Hfr.	☐ Grade
☐ Brangus	☐ Hfr. Yrlg.	☐ Cow	
☐	☐ Bull Yrlg.	☐ Bull	
	☐ Unweaned Hfr. Calf		

TOTAL INVENTORY OF ALL CLIENTS ON LOCATION..............

Brand	No. Hd.	Brand	No. Hd.	Brand	No. Hd.	Brand	No. Hd.

1. Number of animals inspected at close range (under 50 yards):................
2. Average weight of top half of herd:........... Of bottom half:............
3.

Defects Observed	Number	Defects Observed	Number
....	....	....	....
....	....	....	....
....	....	....	....

4. Grade of condition based on following classification: 0—unobserved, 1—unsatisfactory, 2—fair, 3—average, 4—excellent, 5—outstanding, X—not applicable:

	X	0	1	2	3	4	5
a. Weight of animals							
b. Quality of animals							
c. General health and condition of animals							
d. Condition and quality of winter feed							
e. Adequacy of water							
f. Drainage and mud conditions around water holes							
g. Salt and minerals around water holes							
h. Condition of pastures							
i. Adequacy of pastures for existing herd for season							
j. Calf crop percentage for type operation involved							
k. Weight gain from last inspection for type operation							
l. Equipment and preparation for blizzard							
m. Isolation of diseased animals							
n. Indications from droppings as to type feed re contract							
o. Conformance to contract							
p. Conformance to instructions regarding branding, castration, vaccination, dehorning, etc.							
q. Maintenance of registration and other records							
r. Supervision of breeding							

5. Explanation of any of above marked unsatisfactory:

6. Were defects from last inspection corrected?

7. Other comments: (use reverse side if in detail)

INSPECTION TEAM:..

RANCH PROPERTY INSPECTION

Date of Inspection......................Name of Ranch......................

Location of Ranch......................

Operator..............................

	Poor	Fair	Average	Good	Excellent	Not Applicable
1. General over-all appearance and condition of ranch	☐	☐	☐	☐	☐	☐
2. Condition of the following:						
a. Buildings	☐	☐	☐	☐	☐	☐
b. Fences and gates..............................	☐	☐	☐	☐	☐	☐
c. Irrigation system..............................	☐	☐	☐	☐	☐	☐
d. Terraces, waterways, water outlets, etc.	☐	☐	☐	☐	☐	☐
e. Hay meadows..............................	☐	☐	☐	☐	☐	☐
f. Pastures	☐	☐	☐	☐	☐	☐
g. Corrals	☐	☐	☐	☐	☐	☐
h. Machinery	☐	☐	☐	☐	☐	☐
i. Other______________________..	☐	☐	☐	☐	☐	☐
______________________..	☐	☐	☐	☐	☐	☐
j. Status of ranch books and records.....	☐	☐	☐	☐	☐	☐

3. Did you notice any practices or acts that should be stopped, avoided or changed?

4. What are the most pressing problems?

5. What solutions do you propose?

6. Have deficiencies (if any) noted on last inspection been corrected?

7. Explanation of any inspection ratings less than "average":

8. Remarks:

Inspected by:

....

Two typical inspection forms used by one management firm for a cattle breeding herd and a ranch real estate property are shown on the preceding pages.

To be of value, an inspection grade should be taken in context with the general area of the country concerned. For example, the type of the condition of grass and pasture that would be marked "poor" in Missouri would be marked "outstanding" in northern Arizona. An item such as "adequacy of water" would have no meaning in certain sections of Florida where the big problem is draining water and not irrigating.

Tendencies of individual inspectors to mark "high" or "low" should also be taken into consideration. The categories of "excellent" or "outstanding" should not be used unless the particular item being marked is in the top 5% or 10% of all the ranches and farms within a 50-mile radius of the spot being checked out. Individual preferences or prejudices of an inspector must be taken into consideration. However, it is much better to give inspectors a free hand and discount these items in evaluating their reports than to try to correct them to achieve some kind of uniformity. The minute a group of inspectors attempts to color its reports in order to please the echelon receiving them or to avoid having to justify unusual markings, the reports lose half of their value. No report should ever be changed from the original, but where an extreme or unusual grade or comment is given, some explanation might be offered by the reviewing authority.

The following is a list of 40 items to which an intermediate or non-resident agricultural management firm should give attention:

1. Do not inspect only at regularly scheduled intervals. It is always better to have an occasional surprise inspection. Particularly when heavy winter feeding is going on, it is a good idea to have an inspector arrive in the early morning to make a spot check on what is specifically being fed that day.

2. Individual inspectors should be frequently alternated. It is better not to have the same man inspect twice. In this manner, several different opinions on a given operation or a given situation can be obtained and the chance of reports being colored by either excessively friendly or excessively hostile relationships between the inspector and the resident operator being inspected is reduced.

3. It is unwise to have cow herds of an absentee owner commingled with the cows of a resident manager because there might be an argument as to which calf belongs to which cow. In the case of weaned calves or yearlings with separate brands, there is no problem.

Where all of the cows belong to absentee owners, there is no problem in commingling and pro-rating the calf crops as long as the complete interest of the absentee group is separated from that of the resident owner and an inspector from the absentee owners is present during the branding.

4. When cattle bolt and panic on the mere sight of an inspector, this might be an indication that the resident manager has not worked them or checked them very frequently and they are not used to the sight of a man.

5. Cattle that are being regularly fed or caked will normally come up to someone in a truck or car.

6. Any new cattle brought onto a ranch should be isolated in a separate pasture and observed for at least a week to be sure that no disease or epidemic will be carried to other cattle.

7. Do not let a roundup or a movement take place unless a plan is prepared in *writing* at least one week before. The specific details of the plan are unimportant. What is important is that in this manner you are assured that the resident has *a* plan. When the cattle are milling around in corrals losing weight and empty trucks with cursing truck drivers are congregated in a traffic jam, that is no time for the ranch manager to start deciding how he is going to sort the cattle and what is going to be done to them.

8. Insist that the resident manager assign specific authority and responsibility for every detail of a roundup or a movement to a single individual and that this individual know that he is in charge of this specific point.

9. Insist that disaster plans be made months ahead of a possible contingency. The best time to plan for a winter blizzard is in the month of July. The best time to plan for an August drought is during the spring rains of April.

10. Insist that pastures be undergrazed and that a certain amount of extra grass be kept as an insurance policy. I have never heard of any rancher going broke because he had too much grass, but the woods are full of those who went broke because they ran out of grass.

11. On a beef cattle operation, take a good look at anyone who has a labor force in excess of one man to 400 cows. When you improve on that, you can make money. When your labor force is over that, look out for trouble.

12. Agriculture is seasonal. Administrative work load is too. Try to get routine things accomplished in the off-season.

13. Management staffs are trained, skilled, expensive personnel. No one can afford on an all-year-round basis the number of personnel for a peak load. Try to level off peaks and valleys.

14. Schedule roundups, weigh outs, and operations requiring inspection personnel to meet availability of manpower and travel requirements.

15. Buying, selling, and negotiating all take time and executive manpower. On both feed and livestock they tend to be seasonal. Make judicious use of future delivery contracts negotiated in off-seasons to cut down administrative workload in the rush season.

16. When responsibility for action is assigned, be sure that *one* person is in charge, that the assignment is in writing, and that everyone involved knows about it. This is as important in cattle as it is in the military.

17. It is impossible to do everything equally well. Everyone has limited time and resources. The decision as to whether to concentrate on repairing fences, moving pastures, or spraying cattle might have to be a high level staff decision on a big operation.

18. There is a major gap between people's knowing what should be done and their getting it done. Everyone knows that salt should be out and rub racks filled. These things will not get done unless a specific person has the specific job on a specific day of the week to take care of them over the entire ranch.

19. In a modern operation, the repairs and maintenance of mechanical equipment can spell the difference between a net profit and a net loss for the year. On two identical ranchers' trucks, tractors, and hay balers, there might be a 50% difference in longevity and a 100% difference in repair bills. This is big money. The answer could very well be that one rancher is practicing preventive maintenance and the other is not. Preventive maintenance is the type of thing that should be *enforced* by the owner's representative.

20. Budgets and operating plans should be prepared in advance in writing. It is absolutely true that many things work out on paper but not in practice. However, it is also true that if a project cannot show a profit even on paper, it is extremely unlikely that it will in the field.

21. Exert fiscal control on fund allocation. Some people are constitutionally unable to see a large sum in the bank without spending it on something foolish. The idea of keeping a cash reserve against contingencies is beyond their capability, and if any business has contingencies, agriculture does.

22. Work out legitimate depreciation rates. A bull is not immortal and a truck will not last forever. Their growing older is an *annual* expense and should be considered *before* they are purchased.

23. Get lines of credit and loan commitments from banks in writing and *before* you need them. If necessary, pay a standby fee. Do not go into an operation based on a future loan requirement that you have not pinned down.

24. Do not permit interest charges to be forgotten in budgets and operating plans. Even if the owner's capital is being used, it should be considered to be worth 6% and this should be charged against the operation, particularly in comparing it with some alternative that does not require the capital.

25. In appraising property for an owner, be sure to evaluate improvements in terms of the owner's intended use. For example, a $20,000 turkey shed is worth only scrap lumber to an owner who is going to run cows instead of turkeys. Furthermore, it may have a negative value as it may raise his real estate taxes.

26. In representing an owner, be sure to have a written agency agreement spelling out in complete detail what the owner wants to contract, what he wants you to be responsible for, and how much authority he wants you to exercise over the resident managers.

27. In every circumstance, always inform the owner of the worst that can happen. If it doesn't, you are a hero.

28. Where an operation or movement is concerned for which it is vital to have transportation properly coordinated, it is *not* adequate just to call the trucking company or railroad. Instructions must be confirmed in writing, and the day before the transportation is needed everything must be rechecked for last minute foul-ups.

29. Where cattle numbers between two geographic locations have to be adjusted, it is better to shift calves and yearlings than cows. A mature cow might take a whole year to adjust to new grass, new weather, and new terrain.

30. It is better to shift cattle from south to north than from north to south. It is better to shift from dry country to wet than vice versa. Where the wet is semi-tropical, such as in Louisiana or Florida, that introduces new problems.

31. Bulls moved from lush midwestern pastures to the rocky slopes of Colorado will have foot trouble for a year and it will take them two years to be able to do their job.

32. In moving into a new area, do not try to revolutionize traditional procedures the first year. The local people may have good rea-

sons for what they are doing. Observe for one year before you try anything radically new.

33. In a new area, be sure to have some local people on the payroll. This will give you access to feed sources, information, and tested methods of operating. Also it will improve your neighborhood relations.

34. Insist that the resident manager participate in community organizations and projects, such as chamber of commerce, ASC board, school board, etc. Many things require a joint effort, and it is better to have the neighbors with you than against you.

35. From an operational standpoint, the single most important item in differentiating success from failure is the habit of a successful operator of getting something done at the right time. One man works night and day with neither rest nor sleep to get a hay crop baled and in the barn while the weather is good. His next-door neighbor, working an eight-hour day with an hour off for lunch, gets caught with the bales on the ground by a rain that was not in the forecast. He calls this "hard luck." One man has his field planted and seeded ready to catch the rain. The next man delays and cannot get out into the field because it is too muddy and does not get his crop in. When he does get it in, there is no more rain to get it started. He also curses his "hard luck." It is rare when a resident manager operating a ranch or farm for an absentee owner has the internal fortitude to be sufficiently "self-generating" to put in a performance like that of the first man in each of these examples. It is the function of the "non-resident manager" to inspire him to do so.

36. Almost anybody can feed out ten yearlings. To feed out 2,000 yearlings requires organization, ability to delegate authority, budgets, operation plans, and cost accounting. In the customary use of the words, the operation has changed from an "agricultural" to an "industrial" enterprise.

37. Study your manpower and executive personnel. Some people get their terminal growth at a lower level, and if a person is advanced to an executive responsibility beyond his capacity, you might ruin a man who would be perfectly satisfactory at a simpler job. Contrary to the popular conception, ulcers, nervous breakdowns, and heart attacks are as closely associated with large-scale ranching operations as they are with any other form of modern industrial activity.

38. Carefully review all administrative procedures on a continuing basis. Very often change and additions make something that you are doing unnecessary, but you continue to do it just through inertia.

39. Never be afraid to sub-contract work to an expert in another field. This work may very well be something that people within your own firm are quite capable of doing but which would take them three times as long to accomplish as it would a specialist who does nothing else.

40. Insist that the resident operators make out lists of worthwhile productive rainy-day projects for slack periods. Review these lists with them. It is much better to have this kind of work well thought out and planned in advance rather than to try to drum up something on the spur of the moment. In modern-day operations, agricultural, military, or industrial, labor is the major item of cost. On its efficient use, the operation will rise or fall.

In final summary, a non-resident management firm occupies the same position between a ranch owner and his resident manager that a general staff occupies between a division commander and the regimental commanders. Like a general staff, the management firm must secure information, make inspections, prepare plans and budgets, and submit reports of these to the owners with a recommendation as to which one of the alternate courses of action he should take.

"Completed staff work" means that this recommendation should be in such a finished form that all the owner has to do is to sign it and it then becomes an order, or a directive. After this decision has been made, it then becomes the function of the staff or the management firm to supervise the execution of the order to be certain that it is carried out in accordance with the owner's wishes. Simultaneously with this supervision of the execution of the order, the staff should be preparing additional plans for a contingency that might arise, should be offering technical consulting services to the various resident managers, and should be insuring that a continual flow of information and new recommendations is being forwarded to the owner.

Differing from a military situation, there will be special occasions in which the financial interests of a resident manager may not be identical with those of the owner. In this case, it is the responsibility of the management firm to have a representative physically present during these occasions to represent the interests of the owner.

PART III

RURAL LAND TRANSACTIONS

Chapter IX

Buying a Ranch

At the time this chapter is being written, there are no bargains in ranch or farm land in the United States. Anybody that tells you he has a property that will consistently produce 10% in net agricultural income after all expenses is an outright liar. Anyone who says that he has a property that will produce 8% is an optimistic dreamer; at 6% he is extremely lucky; at 4% he might be telling the truth.

The foregoing figures are based on the net agricultural incomes averaged out over five years with a reasonable degree of security. They are further based either on a strictly net arm's-length rental or on an operation in which a proper allocation toward cost is given for the personal labor of the owner and his family. Specifically, these figures do not include the following situations:

1. You have a 100,000-acre ranch with 1,000 acres of deeded land and 99,000 acres of attached Federal and state leases, forest permits, and other grazing rights which can be canceled on you with no compensation, so you could see your whole investment evaporate overnight. In this case, a 20% temporary net return would hardly compensate for the risks.

2. The principal part of your investment is a dry farming wheat operation in which you get special rainfall conditions one year in five which permit you to make a killing, but you "burn out" the other four. "Net return" in these circumstances should be an average of the five-year period.

3. Not included is the situation where you inherited the land from your grandfather and it went through probate at one-fourth of its market value. When we say "4% net return," we mean 4% of its legitimate market value at this moment.

4. Not included is the situation where the owner personally is a highly educated, energetic, capable man, who could command a $20,000 per year salary in any other field, and he has two sons who could command $10,000 per year in any other line of activity, and he puts the entire labor of himself and his two sons into the operation at a value of 50¢ per hour. On this basis, he calculates that he is making a 10% return on a $300,000 ranch when he actually is making only "wages."

Why does this situation exist?

1. From the long-range security and speculative play inherent in large tracts of agricultural land, discussed in Chapter I, there is a steady ground swell of investment demand in this field.

2. There are such tremendous savings to be offered by increasing the size of one's holdings that there is an unusual demand from the immediately surrounding neighbors to increase their operations by acquiring adjacent properties. Two thousand acres of alfalfa meadow could be handled with a 20% increase in labor and equipment over the amount required for 1,000 acres of alfalfa. This is a phenomenon of the last 15 years and represents as dramatic a revolution as that which occurred in the cloth industry in the latter part of the 19th Century.

3. Enough people have had their fortunes made by hitting oil or uranium, having a ranch in the direction of the suburban growth of Phoenix, getting paid three times normal value because of a missile base, or having lightning strike in some other manner that such possibilities are always secretly in the back of the minds of most absentee investors.

4. The popularity of TV westerns over the last ten years has created such an aura of romanticism about the ownership of large tracts of western land either in the thoughts of the purchaser or, more likely, in those of his children that it has undoubtedly had some influence, although the land purchaser would be the last in the world to admit it.

5. Those Americans who have spent much time in Europe and Latin America in the last few years have become conscious of the enormous social prestige that goes with being one of the "landed gentry." If your grandfather had 5,000 acres in Herefordshire, you are a couple of notches further up the social scale than if your family had a shoe factory in Manchester for three generations.

For the purpose of this chapter, let us assume that you are an unromantic, money-hungry character who is in a high tax bracket from other investments and that you want to end up with the maximum possible dollars in your pocket after a ten-year program. Furthermore, you want to do this from an agricultural standpoint. You have no objection to striking oil or to having a fashionable summer resort put right next to you, but this is for another part of your portfolio, and for the moment you want to look only to the agricultural play and a long-range growth in the value of your investment. Also, you want your program to make some immediate sense from a current return basis, even if minor, with a hope that it could become reasonable if the current depression within the agricultural industry is overcome in the near future. At the risk of making a lot of people angry, I shall list some of the things to do and not to do:

1. Stay 50 miles away from any "rapid-growth city." In a city of under one million in population, it will probably be a number of generations before the suburbs move out another 50 miles, but the land speculators feel that the expansion is already upon them and you will have to pay corresponding prices. On top of this, the county assessors are also convinced that "the great day has arrived" and your real estate taxes will run neck and neck with your operating net income.

2. Avoid the glamour states. Totally non-productive land 100 miles from anywhere in Arizona and Florida is selling for four times the price of reasonably good land in such "old-fashioned" states as Missouri and Nebraska.

3. Be somewhat cautious about pretty scenery. Beautiful snow-capped peaks in the middle of the summer and high green mountain meadows in a 7,000-foot-high western slope ranch might also mean an eight-month winter feeding season on snow covered ground with alfalfa hay costing $50 per ton. Bright red sunsets and clear desert air might also mean that you will have to liquidate your herd every fourth year when the stock water runs out.

4. Avoid over-elaborate improvements for the type of operation you want to run if you have to pay a premium for them. One of the old sayings in the industry is: "Fancy white houses and big red barns don't put fat on cattle. You just need grass and water." On the other hand, if you don't have a telephone and power line, you don't have enough improvements. If you are trying to make money, there is considerable advantage when your tractor needs a spare part to being able to telephone a dealer in a town 40 miles away to find out if he has it or can get it before one of your employees makes a round-trip in a pickup and still doesn't get the part.

5. We have previously discussed a number of things for which you should not pay a premium. A major exception for you is to have immediate access to a concrete road, preferably a state or Federal highway. If your property is located in one of the central southern states, there are three or four months of the year when dirt and gravel roads turn into mush. If you are in one of the more northern states, at the end of a three-day blizzard, there is nothing more welcome than to see a great big yellow snow plow coming around the bend, particularly when the state is paying for it and you are not. There is nothing more annoy-

ing when you have cattle contracted to go out on a certain date than to see four or five truckloads of your calves mired in the mud while the animals are shrinking at the rate of about 2 pounds per hour.

6. As a somewhat unrelated corollary of this, if you are lucky enough to have a concrete road adjacent to a section of your ranch or farm, and you are in a wet area, be sure to have at least some holding pens and corrals as well as storage facilities adjacent to the concrete. These might not be beautiful, but when the mud is 2 feet deep everywhere else, this will seem like a great idea.

7. The best way to make money in this play on the land is to start out with a decent-sized operation and a headquarters facility and gradually assemble small lands around you, knowing that by acquiring an assemblage with its economic advantages, you are doubling the value of the individual acreage that you are picking up. Don't lose this assemblage play by moving into an area where all of the land is in strong

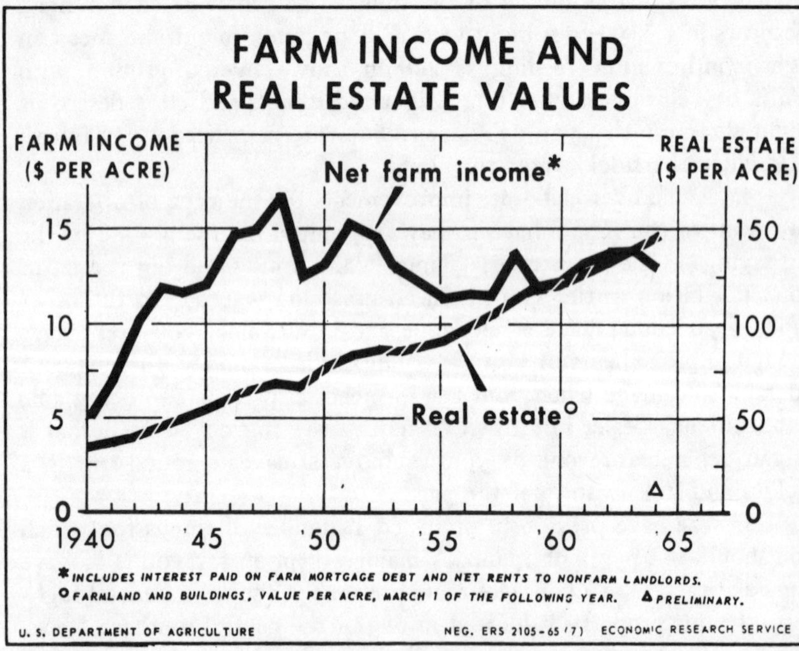

The above chart implying a 1960 $12 per acre annual income on $120 per acre land is a form of statistical reasoning that has plagued agricultural thinking for half a century. Possibly it means that the cost of the farmer's and his sons' personal labor is disregarded, that real estate taxes are ignored, and that depreciation on buildings and equipment is ignored. Nobody knows. The only absolute cinch is that no farm land in the United States nets 10% by an accepted accounting procedure. The slight reverse for 1964 probably comes from a more realistic analysis rather than from a change in input. (Courtesy U.S. Department of Agriculture)

hands and other people are doing the same thing you are. On the other hand, this might be counterbalanced by the fact that while your own growth is effectively stopped, you have a ready market if you want to make a short-term play.

Up to this point, we have principally covered a number of things not to do. Now let us take a more positive approach.

You have finally decided you really want to go ahead. You have sufficient capital to get a large enough operation that it can form an economic unit. You have generally selected the area of the country you want. You have received numerous ranch listings from real estate brokers in the area. You have narrowed your choices down to three or four, and now you are about to make a decision. You are a very strong character who is going to ignore completely his wife's preferences as to the layout of the kitchen and the main house and you are going to make your decision based totally on an appraisal of the agricultural value of the land.

There are many excellent books on this subject, so we are going to touch only on a few of the high points.

1. *Carrying Capacity:* In brief, the generally accepted yardstick is the number of cows and their spring calves (cow units) which the property can carry on an all-year-round basis. In other words, carrying capacity is determined by the amount of land required to graze the cattle in the summer, together with the winter grass or the hay meadows and cultivated land necessary to produce the winter feed, to carry them through the entire year all in one big package. For this purpose, two yearlings are supposed to be the equivalent of one cow unit, and three weaned calves the equivalent of two yearlings. When a real estate broker says that the land has a carrying capacity of 1,200 yearlings, he means a carrying capacity of 600 cow units. When he says 1,000 "head," pin him down and find out "head of what." On dual-use ranches that can be converted for use with either sheep or cattle, the general calculation is that five sheep equal one cow. The "sheep" refers to mother ewes.

Insofar as this is the most important estimate in the entire appraisal, it should be done by an expert completely familiar with the section of the country involved. As a general rule within the business, it is a good idea to take the estimate of the seller or the selling broker and subtract 40% from his figure on "carrying capacity," and you may be getting close to the mark. Generally, the seller tends to estimate carrying capacity on the best season he had in 20 years and he forgets the other 19 years. The buyer, of course, would like to calculate capacity based on a drought year. The legitimate figure is based on an average year.

2. *Attached Government and Private Leases:* In general, ranches made up principally of deeded land go for substantially more than those made up principally of government lease land. However, the type of government lease, as well as the way the area lies in relationship to your deeded land, can cause a tremendous variation in value. No matter what the history has been or what you are told by brokers and "old ranchers," never forget that all it takes is for the President of the United States to get up on the wrong side of the bed one morning and sign a document that will take away your leases without any compensation.

3. *Water Rights:* In most areas, you have unlimited rights on any flowing or sub-surface water for the purpose of stock water and water for your household. Rights for irrigation, manufacturing, and other purposes are the subjects of thousands of legal cases and entire careers for some lawyers. In brief, water rights on a stream are generally measured in so many cubic feet per second. On a precise formula, this figure can be converted into the number of acres you can irrigate in the particular area that you are in. If these rights are "adjudicated," this means that they are recorded in the various deeds of your property and the surrounding properties and are usually given a priority. During the spring overflow, everybody gets all the water he wants out of the main ditches or streams. However, as the dry season approaches and somebody downstream from you has an allocation of 10 cubic feet which is prior to your own, he gets his 10 cubic feet per second through the water gate before you are allowed to take one drop from your part of the stream for your own land. Water rights are often more valuable than the land itself and should be checked out by an expert before you buy. There has been so much litigation on the subject that most of the title insurance companies will refuse to insure water rights and you and your attorney are on your own on this point. Cities like Denver, for example, have purchased outright, without the land, the water rights on thousands of square miles in their watersheds. The remaining land might have one-fourth of the value that it would have had, had it retained the original water rights.

4. *Well Water:* This is highly speculative and a business of its own. The only accurate test of a well is to have it pumped dry and see how fast it fills up, or to see how much water can be pumped out of it and how fast without substantially changing its level. Here, the time of the year is tremendously important and there is also a variation

between years. Too, in most western areas, the general underlying water table is going down every year and it is impossible to predict what you might have ten years from the date of purchase. Artesian wells are the most risky of all. Nobody can predict when they are going to stop flowing.

5. *Grass and Soil:* These constitute another specialized field. However, the local county agent, ASC office, or office of the Bureau of Land Management probably has fairly good records and estimates on the property that you are considering to buy. This is public information at which anyone has the right to look. The local banker will also probably know something about the history of the district in this regard.

6. *Roads, Communications, Utilities:* These have been previously covered.

7. *Minerals:* It is often traditional for the seller to keep half of the mineral rights. If the property has been through three or four hands, possibly one-eighth of the minerals might be left for the new purchaser. It is customary for a deed to read that the owner of the surface has the right to negotiate and sign deals for all of the remaining owners with or without their permission. All of these points, however, are matters for negotiation. Oil leases usually include a cash bonus for getting the lease and a small annual payment for retaining it. When drilling is conducted and oil is hit, the usual lease gives one-eighth of the production to the owners of the mineral rights and this is divided the way their interest lies. In the better areas, it is normal to tie in a drilling requirement before one grants a lease to an oil company. Obviously, in many areas the mineral rights are more valuable than the surface.

8. *Timber:* This, again, is a game for an expert. Just because the trees look pretty does not mean they are worth anything. Also, the value of timber delivered at a market may have practically no relationship to its value as it stands. It is possible that the cost of cutting the timber and transporting it to where it is going to go may be more than it's worth when it gets there, so its value as a stand is zero. On both minerals and timber, there are special tax plays which no attempt will be made to cover in this book.

9. *Improvements:* Fences, windmills, stock tanks, irrigation ditches, barns, houses, and corrals should not only be looked at by somebody who knows what he is doing and can estimate current condition, but they should also be looked at with a view as to their intelligent location and their adaption to the purpose for which you are

going to use the ranch. If you are going to operate it as a beef cattle ranch, the most elaborate dairy barns and sheep sheds will have only limited value to you.

10. *Availability of Markets:* If you are a thousand miles away from the nearest packing plant or the nearest place where proteins are produced or the nearest area of heavy grain production, you can figure that the animals you are going to sell will be taking 3% more shrink and that a $5 to $10 freight bill will be subtracted before you get your net over what a rancher closer in will be getting. Likewise, your supplementary feed is going to be costing you $5 per ton more than his. These items can add up to a substantial change in the net operating picture. At one time, the proximity to a railroad was nearly the single most important element of value. This is no longer true, but it still has some advantages.

11. *The Possibility of Further Expansion by Purchase or Leases:* This was covered previously in this chapter and it probably is the single most important money-making item in the venture.

12. *Financing:* The general picture here is for insurance companies or the Federal Land Bank to make 50% mortgages based on a rather conservative estimate of land value. Today, a number of sellers take 29% downpayments and purchase money mortgages. By staying at 30% or under on the downpayments, the sales qualify as installment sales and the sellers don't have to pay the capital gains tax except as a proration when they get the money. In the event that one can find a seller with a big tax loss "carry forward" from previous years, it is possible sometimes to prepay several years' interest at once and get a reduced downpayment. Occasionally, a ranch can be acquired with almost nothing but deductible dollars and very little initial capital investment. Subsequent depreciation may match the amortization payments on this mortgage.

The following is a hypothetical example of how a deal like this would work out, together with a seven-year projection of its operation, cashwise and taxwise, from the standpoint of an absentee owner:

1. A 600-cow-unit capacity ranch in eastern Colorado, where it takes 15 acres to run a cow for a year.

2. A total of 7,000 acres deeded and 2,000 acres government lease land.

3. Price, $42.85 an acre on deeded land, or $500 per cow unit, for a total price of approximately $300,000.

4. Annual rent in this area, $36 per cow, or $21,600 a year. This goes up with increased capacity from improvement program.

SEVEN-YEAR PROJECTION STARTING NOVEMBER 1

9,000 acres, purchase price $300,000, 10% down, 3 years and 2 months' interest in advance at 6%, 20-year mortgage

	*1st Year**	*2nd Year*	*3rd Year*	*4th Year*	*5th Year*	*6th Year*	*7th Year*
Down payment	$ 30,000						
Interest	48,870				$13,770	$12,960	$12,150
Amortization		$13,500	$13,500	$13,500	13,500	13,500	13,500
Maintenance and improvements†	14,000	6,000	2,000	2,000	2,000	2,000	2,000
Taxes and government rent	300	1,200	1,200	1,200	1,200	1,200	1,200
Management	1,500	1,100	800	800	800	800	800
Total cash outlay	$ 94,670	$21,800	$17,500	$17,500	$31,270	$30,460	$29,650
Rent‡	1,000	21,600	22,100	22,600	23,100	23,600	24,100
NET CASH OUTLAY	$ 93,670	$ 200	$(4,600)	$(5,100)	$ 8,170	$ 6,860	$ 5,550
Deductible expenses	$ 64,670	$ 8,300	$ 4,000	$ 4,000	$17,770	$16,960	$16,150
Depreciation: straight line	2,000	12,000	12,000	12,000	12,000	10,333	2,000
Total deductions	$ 66,670	$20,300	$16,000	$16,000	$29,770	$27,293	$18,150
Rent	1,000	21,600	22,100	22,600	23,100	23,600	24,100
NET TAXABLE INCOME	$(65,670)	$ 1,300	$ 6,100	$ 6,100	$(6,670)	$(3,693)	$ 5,950

* Last two months only.

† Does not include non-taxable contribution of government ASC estimated at $800 per year average.

‡ Rent gradually went up as carrying capacity increased through improvements.

5. Taxes plus rent on government lease land, $1,200 a year.

6. Initial fence repair, reseeding, maintenance, and other expenses to put ranch in top shape and generate above rent, $20,000 in first 12 months.

7. Annual management and supervision at 5% of gross income, $800 after first two years.

8. Annual improvement expense after first fiscal year, $2,000.

9. Depreciation on $50,000 of fences at 20% and $40,000 of other improvements at 5% for a total of $12,000 per year for first five fiscal years and $2,000 per year thereafter.

Chapter X

Selling a Ranch

There is a story that one of the famous Wall Street financiers had a $3 million yacht. After the stock market crash, he decided to sell the yacht and called in a prominent advertising and sales promotion agency. "Now," said the financier, "I want to get rid of this yacht in a hurry and I am willing to spend a substantial amount of money in advertising and sales work. How much money do you need?"

"Ten cents will be perfectly adequate," said the broker.

"Ten cents?" said the financier. "Are you trying to be funny?"

"No. It's very simple. There are only five people in the entire United States who could afford to buy it or to maintain it. I shall write five letters and shall need five 2¢ stamps."

One interesting thing about real estate and particularly rural real estate is that no two farms or ranches are alike. They can be big or small. They can be scenic or non-scenic. They can have elaborate living quarters or modest ones. They can have varying proportions between cultivated land, irrigated land, grazing land, timber, desert lakes, water facilities, etc.

So that you do not waste a tremendous amount of energy and money in spinning your wheels, it is necessary to pick your market. The first step in picking your market is to take off your pink-colored glasses and make an honest, careful evaluation of what you have to sell. Most of us have inbred into us an element called "pride of ownership." When you own a property and have worked on it, developed it, and improved it, you subconsciously feel it is better than most comparable properties in the area. Its defects you have gotten used to and overlook.

It seems like yesterday that you and your son put in the "new" four-strand fence around the alfalfa field. Time has passed by rapidly and you have forgotten that ten years have gone by since the fences went up. In your own mind, you still think of it as "new," but anybody else looking at it would think of it as a ten-year-old fence. The house that you designed specifically to fit every one of your wife's changing needs over the years, with a room being added on here and there, is exactly the way you want it. To your family, it is infinitely better than the new house recently designed by an architect for one of your neighbors. However, you must remember that a new buyer may not like your specialized layout.

Now for a few obvious facts regarding agriculture in this latter part of the 20th Century which may or may not be pleasant but are nevertheless there. These relate to the principal element of market selection and are connected with size.

1. If your property is located in a "working-type" area and not a recreational area and you are not within the 50-mile commuting radius of a city or factory payroll, you must have a farm or ranch large enough to support a single family. You will not get much of a price from "part-time farmers" or the more sophisticated outside investors.

2. If your farm under these circumstances cannot support a single family, your principal market today has to be your immediate neighbors. The fact that it takes increased land holdings for proper use of modern equipment and techniques puts a lot of pressure on your neighbors to expand their holdings and better utilize their labor and equipment. A man already in the neighborhood can afford to pay substantially more than "market value" for the land, as his excess purchase price will be made up for in a very short period of time by his savings in the costs of other agricultural items.

3. If you have a "single family" farm or ranch and you plan to sell to someone who is going to move on it and work it himself, do not forget that items like proximity to towns, good schools, adequate roads, etc., are going to be significant. It might also be necessary to review the term "single family operation." This has changed substantially over the last 20 years. With regard to a beef cattle ranch, this means a ranch with a capacity to handle 300 cows. No matter how good his credit or what kind of financing terms he can drum up, a man will need a minimum of $50,000 in hard cash to handle this size deal. A person who wants to buy this type of property for an investment and doesn't personally plan to work on it and give it day by day supervision must have a property of this size or be able to combine properties of smaller size in order to hire a man to run his ranch and be able to pay sufficient salary to get a good enough man that he will not have constant problems.

4. If your property is not of this size and you can't sell it to one of your neighbors, your only alternative may be to lease it. You may be forced into leasing it to an adjacent neighbor or leasing it to someone who has bought other land in the neighborhood or who is acquiring other leases in the neighborhood to combine them with yours. If you make the mistake which so many other sellers have of selling to an under-capitalized operator on narrow mortgage terms, the land is probably going to bounce back in your lap in a few years in considerably worse condition than it was when you sold it. When times are bad,

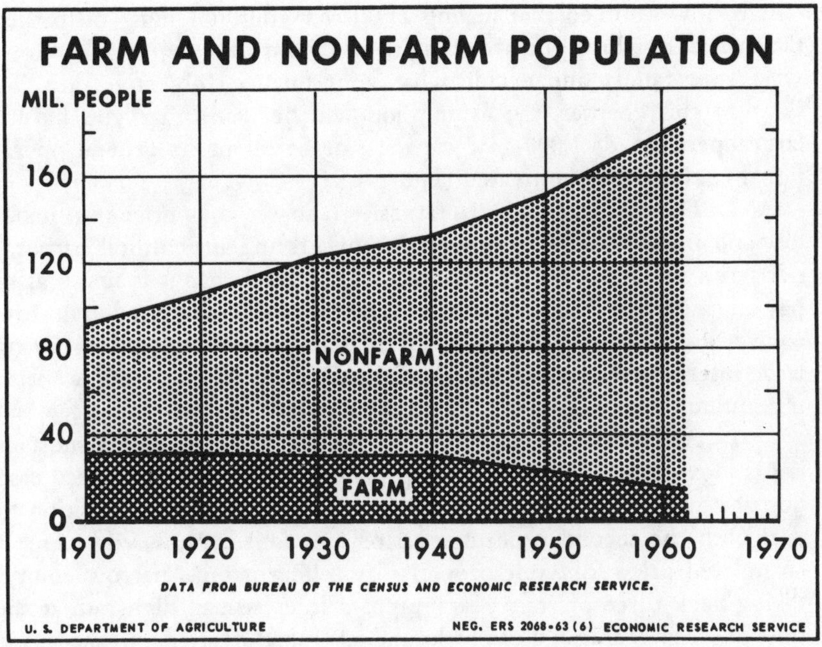

Where will these curves level off? Projected into 1975 we would have 230 million in the general population and less than 2 million on farms! (Courtesy, U.S. Department of Agriculture)

the operator is going to feed and clothe his children before he makes his mortgage payments and he is not about to spend any money on fertilizer or fence maintenance.

5. If you have a working ranch that will hold 1,000 cows or more or can combine enough long-term lease options or joint sales commitments from your neighbors to bring the capacity to this figure, you have opened up an entirely different market and have a highly negotiable asset. Now the land becomes attractive to big eastern investors as an inflation hedge; it becomes worthwhile as an insurance policy against drought by some of the big wealthy southwestern ranchers; it is a marketable entity to people in or out of agriculture all over the United States. The same factors as previously mentioned now apply in reverse on a 1,000-head operation. You can afford to hire aggressive resident management and national ranch accounting firms, take advantage of mass purchasing power in obtaining your supplies, and utilize modern equipment.

It is now assumed that having evaluated your holdings and picked the market at which you are going to aim, your next step is to sit down with your family and decide what your financial objectives are. To simplify this chapter, the assumption will be made that you have a large operation of 1,000-cow capacity or better or its general operational equivalent in cultivated land.

1. Do you need cash in a fast sale? If so, set your price reasonably low and aim for the big professional ranchers and agricultural corporations as a market. The big eastern investors feel that it is immoral to pay all cash, even if they have it, and they are more interested in narrow equity plays, leverage, and tax differentials. They don't mind paying large interest charges if these are deductible, but they do not want to put out any hard non-deductible dollars if they can avoid it.

2. Are you in a low income tax bracket and have you a substantial tax loss "carry forward" from previous years? You don't need cash but you want a future income? If so, you are in a perfect position to deal with the second type of investor mentioned. Now you can get an inflated price for your property by selling it on a narrow equity, taking back three or four years' prepaid interest at a high rate at the time of closing, and you can make the sale more attractive to the buyer (and still get a higher price) by giving him a long, strung-out amortization rate on the mortgage.

3. Do you wish to retire from large-scale ranching or farming but want to stay in the country on a smaller ranch within easy driving distance of a city for social conveniences? In this case, you should locate the property that you want to buy and then have the individual or corporation wishing to buy your ranch purchase the new property and trade it in on your old one in lieu of a downpayment. You avoid a capital gains tax on the value of the traded property and have to pay capital gains tax only as you receive principal installment payments on your mortgage. In this connection, the new property traded in on your old one must be worth less than 30% of your former ranch in order to qualify the entire deal as an installment sale. If you violate the 30% provision, you will still have to pay a capital gains tax immediately on the entire price of your old ranch, even though the money coming in on the mortgage will be strung out over a long period of years.

4. What if you want to retire, but you and your family have been in farming and ranching all of your lives and don't know anything about the securities market? You don't know how to reinvest your money and are nervous about jeopardizing the long-time security of your estate and family. All of you understand land and cattle, but

you remember what happened to pieces of paper during the depression that had "General Motors Common Stock" printed on them. Here again, you could take back a very narrow equity and a big mortgage, but you could give the mortgage a great degree of security by making the buyer plow improvement money back into your land so that you would be delighted to see him default. Right in the mortgage you could put a detailed schedule of the things he must build or improve on the property, and in the same document, you could restrict the number of head he could run on the ranch, specify the number of times he must paint the house, etc. Any failure to comply would be as much a default on the mortgage as his failure to pay interest, and you could move for immediate foreclosure.

Up to this time, you have done nothing but planning and thinking. You have estimated the situation, decided what your objectives are, and now you are ready for action. If you decide that you want to make the effective move two years hence, there are a number of things you can do to make a ranch more salable and to get a better price:

1. Go light on the grazing a year or two before you intend to sell. The appearance of the grass may make a big difference in price.

2. Spend a few dollars on paint, new wire, etc. Above all, pick up all junk around the property. Spending $2,000 on these kinds of things might mean getting 10% more on a $300,000 property, which is a return of 15 to 1 on your expenditures.

3. Have detailed, colored section maps prepared and get a professional to take pictures in the best season. Get your abstracts brought up to date. If yours is a large ranch, have a brochure prepared. It is possible that you will run into someone who wants to make a quick decision and he will be attracted if you have done most of the preliminary work for him.

4. If your operating history has been better than average, hire a certified public accountant to audit your records over the last three years and have copies of the audit made to hand to the prospect.

5. Get notarized statements from the water commissioner, the Bureau of Land Management, and your local county agent verifying the carrying capacity and water rights. Even if some of the information is unfavorable, you are better off presenting it yourself than having the buyer independently determine it. If yours is a $500,000 property or over, don't try to hide anything. Any buyer that can handle a deal that large is going to bring in a professional appraisal team. He might not know anything about ranches, but he didn't get that big by being stupid.

In summary of these last few points, remember that almost everybody in the world is lazy. Whether it is the purchaser himself, his broker, his attorney, or his financial advisor – everybody likes to see most of the work done by somebody else. When a presentation is neatly put together, with all of the financial records, legal documents, verifications, substantiating documents, maps, surveys, etc., all well prepared and organized in a tabulated manner, half of your selling mission has been accomplished. If the purchaser and his advisors are trying to make a decision between yours and two other comparable ranches, which one are they going to pick: the one that is slightly better than the other two for the price but where three months' hard work in analysis, investigation, mapping, and inspecting is necessary, or the one that may not be quite so good pricewise but where all of this work has been efficiently accomplished beforehand?

The firm of which I am the head has done a substantial amount of ranch management and appraisal work. One of our clients recently purchased a large western ranch where it took almost six months of work just to find what the actual deeded acreage, water rights, etc., were, and after the property had been acquired, it took another year before a final determination was made on many of these elements and before the Federal, state and private leases were completely worked out and assigned. We are only human. It will be a long day in June before we ever recommend to a client, no matter what kind of a price bargain is involved, a ranch whose ownership and lease records are messed up to the extent this one was. Outside of the advisory echelon that will always look on this kind of setup with a jaundiced eye, the average purchaser wanting to buy a major property would like to acquire it within a couple of months' time. The thought of standing by with his funds tied up in escrow for a year and a half, with the legal entanglements being worked out (and a possibility of the deal not even going through at the end), is going to make him have a few second thoughts before he gets into the mess.

Most legal and appraisal work is done on a time basis, particularly in this field. The fees are charged whether or not the deal is finally consummated. Consequently, $10,000 to $15,000 worth of expenses in straightening out items that could have been taken care of for one-tenth of this amount by the seller is an item that is not going to be overlooked by the prospective purchaser.

The next step for the ranch or farm seller is to decide about a broker. In urban real estate, the average fee seems to be around 5%. In rural real estate, which envisions that the seller is selling not only land but a business, the fee often goes to 7½%. In this case, the seller's broker might keep 2½% and offer 5% on a participating basis to other brokers over the country so as to make the sale more attractive.

The first decision, of course, is whether or not to have any broker at all. If you believe that you have a number of neighbors who are anxious to get your property to increase their own holdings and you feel that you are a pretty good negotiator, you may wish to handle the deal yourself. It is possible that even though you decide to hire a broker you may wish to reserve the right to handle personally, with no commission being involved, any deals made with 10 or 15 neighbors, a list of whose names you would present to the broker. This would enable you to see what kind of a price the broker could get from outside interests while still reserving for yourself the privilege of making a deal with your adjoining neighbors if the broker could not get enough of a price to pay his commission and still exceed what you could get locally.

Another obvious consideration here on whether or not to have a broker is your own time availability. Even if you are quite capable of presenting and negotiating, you may have outside interests that make your personal time valuable enough that you would still rather pay the commission than be bothered.

Now, assuming that you have decided that you want a real estate broker, what are some of the questions and factors?

1. Almost everyone today in American industry is a specialist. This is truer of the sales industry than any other. If you want to sell shoes, you hire a shoe salesman. If you want to sell horses, you hire a horse trader. If you want to sell a small farm or a ranch in a local area, you hire a local broker. But if you want to sell a million dollar ranch, you should hire a sophisticated broker who is accustomed to selling big ranches and whose clients and contacts are at the national and international investment level.

2. Do you want to select a single broker and give him an exclusive, or do you want to try the shotgun technique and list your property with numerous brokers? Generally, if you expect to get a really top level broker and expect him to put in a substantial amount of work on the property, you must give him an exclusive at a reasonable price. You should probably attempt to select one who is nationally known. Members of the National Association of Real Estate Boards, who can use the term "realtor," as well as members of the National Institute of Farm Brokers, are governed by a code of ethics and rules requiring them to perform certain functions if they accept an exclusive,

and in most cases they will. This does not mean that there are not plenty of good, competent brokers who are not members of these two national associations, but you have a slight additional degree of protection if you select one that is.

3. What can you expect on an exclusive listing? An exclusive listing can be made into as detailed a performance contract as any other contract. If you wish, and you can negotiate this with the broker concerned, you may require him to expend a given number of dollars in advertising in which you may or may not participate, you may require him to participate in the cost of preparing your brochure or possibly to prepare it entirely on his own, and you may demand that he produce a given number of salesmen who will work a given number of hours on your property. In return, he will demand of you that you give him a price to work on that is realistic and that you commit yourself to taking back financing terms, if necessary, that will give him a reasonable chance of making a rapid sale. If you decide on a 7½% commission within the listing contract, you can specifically tie into the agreement that the broker must cooperate with other brokers and give them a full 5% and must advertise this fact. This type of arrangement can be given a time limit. In other words, the broker might have 60 days to sell the property on his own and then after that must open up the listing to other brokers on a participating basis.

To protect yourself, you should have a very definite time limit on the exclusive listing arrangement. Six months is customary. At the end of the six months, you might permit the broker to give you a list of five or ten prospects that he wishes to reserve the selling rights on for a period of another three months. If this has not been accomplished before the time limit expires, then all bets are off. This should be explicitly spelled out, as there are many arguments on this point.

4. If you want to get real action out of one of the top national ranch brokers, you can help matters by contacting a number of your neighbors who might want to sell and who will go into the deal with you on a joint listing. The joint listing may not necessarily have to involve a sale on their part but could involve the commitment to make a long-term net net lease (the tenant pays everything, including taxes) of their properties that could be presented simultaneously with a sale of your own. If, in this matter, a joint operating capacity of 2,000 to 3,000 head can be put together, you will have a highly desirable and salable arrangement which will result in increased value for your own holdings.

Now, having done your preliminary planning, selected your market, prepared your property for sale, and picked a broker and having decided on a price, your next and final decision, which can be more important than the price, is, "What kind of financing terms will I take back?" Or, "If I don't want to take any back, will it make the property more salable if I place a mortgage on it myself from some other source prior to the sale?"

1. There is a lot of merit in this last point because you, as an existing operator, can probably get a better mortgage than a new buyer can. Particularly is this true in getting one out of the Federal Land Bank, which tends unconsciously to favor local people trying to get loans rather than outsiders coming in. If you can get one of the 33-year amortization 5½% Federal Land Bank mortgages that can be prepaid at any time without penalty for 60% of the value of the property, you have already added a substantial amount to what you can sell the property for plus greatly increasing its chance of a sale. Now if you decide to take back a purchase money mortgage, there will be only a small second mortgage and you will still have gotten most of your cash out. On Federal Land Bank mortgages, there is a safety factor in that in a time of complete agricultural distress the government traditionally waives some of the payments or makes some other arrangements rather than get involved in any large-scale foreclosures over a given geographic area.

2. Don't be afraid of taking back mortgages if you can get enough premium in price. If you have a tax loss carry forward from previous years, you can take big hunks of prepaid interest tax-free. On the other hand, prepaid interest items will be deductible to the buyer and might be very helpful in getting one.

3. The mortgage document itself can be made as explicit and complicated as you wish. You can tell the purchaser what to plant, how much fertilizer to use, and hypothetically even where his children have to go to school. To make it more palatable to him, you can lift certain restrictions and requirements when the unpaid balance of the mortgage is reduced to certain predetermined but specific levels.

4. As part of your own tax problems, if you are incurring a big liability on the sale, consider deeding portions of the land to your children, your grandchildren, multiple trusts, family corporations, etc. To avoid the collapsible corporation statute, you probably should do this three years before the sale. When a joint sale is made by all of the parties concerned, each of them throwing in his portion of the land, the income tax liability is spread around in smaller brackets.

5. Consider, rather than selling your equipment outright with the ranch, leasing it on a three-year lease with the lessee having an option to buy. This will spread the income into the next couple of years.

6. If you have cattle to liquidate, possibly you might wish to lease the ranch back for two more years after you have sold it. Then you can sell your cattle in different tax years and in a more orderly manner. The rent is deductible and will offset the interest you are receiving on the mortgage.

In summary, in this chapter, we have attempted to cover the following points:

1. Picking your sales market.
2. Selecting your personal financial objective in selling and the different routes to accomplish it.
3. Getting the property ready for sale, both physically and administratively.
4. Selecting a broker.
5. Considering various alternatives in your financing a sale and in arranging the sale so as to reduce your own tax liability.

Chapter XI

Water Rights*

Water rights have been of prime importance to the development of civilization. Nearly every early society had a system of regulating this limited commodity. According to the ancient *Ada*, the Bedouin "Code of the Desert," a traveler might drink of a well, but "should the well bear the *wasm* (camel brand) of a local tribe, and should he, without permission, water his flocks and camels, not bearing this brand, then should he be slain, and his body left to be devoured by the birds of the air and the beasts of the field." This law of the desert nomads could go back to the very dawn of neolithic culture.

Thousands of years later, around 1800 B.C., the famous Assyrian conqueror, Hammurabi, formed certain specific rules governing the use of water in agriculture. "In Babylonia, where the agricultural foundation of the state required efficient cooperation in regulating the irrigation canals, negligence could not be tolerated . . ." Laws No. 53-54 run thus: "If a man has neglected to maintain the dike of his field, and he has let the water ravage farmland, the man, in whose dike the breach was opened, shall make good the grain that he caused to be lost. If he cannot make good the grain, they shall sell him and his goods for silver, and the farmers whose grain the water carried off shall divide (the proceeds)."[1]

One of the first water rights laws to be published in North America was originated in the colonial ordinances of 1641-47. "The charter resulted from a grant of letters by James I of England to the Council at Plymouth, England, for the colonization of New England. . . ."

A portion of the Body of Liberties states:

> Every Inhabitant that is an howse holder shall have free fishing and fowling in any great ponds and Bayes, Coves, and Rivers, so farre as the sea ebbes and flowes within the presincts of the towne where they dwell, unlesse the free men of the same Towne or the Generall Court have otherwise appropriated them, provided that this shall not be extended to give leave to any man to come upon others proprietie without their leave.[2]

Water rights have always been essential in arid country where there

---

*This chapter has been reprinted with permission from two articles by H. G. Oppenheimer, of the Ranch Real Estate Department of Oppenheimer Industries, Inc., which appeared in 1971 issues of the *American Hereford Journal*.

[1] *Hammurabi's Code*, Cyrus H. Gordon, Holt, Rinehart & Winston, Inc., New York.

[2] *Law of Seashore, Waters and Water Courses, Maine and Massachusetts*, Moses Frankel, LL.B., Murray Printing Co., Forge Village, Mass., 1969, p. 1.

is a limited water supply. The necessity of understanding these laws is even more important in modern America because the future demand for water resources will possibly not be fulfilled by the inadequate supply. A 1965 study by the water resources council found that with present means of obtaining fresh water the United States could only produce 1,200 billion gallons a day. By 2020, in accordance with growing industry and population, the country will need 1,400 billion gallons a day. Thus, the water shortage is becoming increasingly significant. Consequently, it is crucial that landowners and their attorneys comprehend these laws applying to rights to this limited supply.

WRITTEN INTO RANCH DEEDS

In arid country, where the use of water is essential to the productivity of the land, and to all living things on the land, the use of waterways is written into the deed of the ranch. This water right then becomes a part and parcel of the land, meaning it cannot be separated from the land. This is because much of the value of the property depends on accessibility to water. The rights are vested, and thus are considered private property. No individual actually owns a stream but only has a usufructuary, or useful, right to the water in that stream. In the case of *Eddy* v. *Simpson*, 3 California–249, 252, (1853), the court decided, "The owner of land through which a stream flows, merely transmits the water over its surface, having a right to its reasonable use during its passage. The right is not in the corpus (body) of the water, and only continues with its possession." In other words, the individual has the right to benefit from the water. The state, not individual citizens, owns the waterways. He is entitled to an allotted amount of water from a stream but only that amount that he can use reasonably. The reasonable use is determined by state statute. If there is not enough water to justify a strict interpretation of reasonable use, then in many states, the allottment is determined by everyone's "fair share."

SEVERAL UNITS OF WATER MEASUREMENT

There are several different units of water measurement. One of the most commonly used measures is an "acre-foot" of water. This is the amount of water necessary to submerge an acre of land a foot beneath the water level, or approximately 326,000 gallons of water. The "water-inch" is a measure of the trickle from a pipe, one inch in diameter, with a one inch head, estimated at fourteen pints per minute. The "waterhead" is the height of the surface of a contained water source, *e.g.*, in a pipe, above the point of measurement. This determines the water pressure and speed of flow. Another means is a "miner's inch," which has no universality and changes frequently, but in many areas of the Old West, it refers to a flow of 1.5 cubic feet per minute. A "water flow" is measured in cubic feet per second.[3]

According to Wells A. Hutchins, author of *The California Law of Water Rights*, laws concerning water rights have two specific doctrines: rights applying to a *riparian owner, one who owns land adjacent to the body of water*, and rights applying to an *appropriatory owner, one who does not have land adjacent to the body of water, but uses some means of transportation such as irrigation ditches.*

RIPARIAN OWNER HAS SPECIAL RIGHTS

The main difference between these two doctrines is that the *riparian owner has special rights* superior to appropriatory owners. The riparian owner has the right to use the water as long as he doesn't harm it, which is determined by state statute. He also has the right to use water regardless of prior claims, including claims of other riparian owners. The reasoning is that riparian owner's rights are proportionate to other riparian owners, and not exclusively his own. In other words, all riparian owners have equal rights.

The riparian right cannot be separated from the land as it is a part and parcel of the land, nor can it be transferred to someone else or to a different unit of land other than specified in the deed. A riparian owner can only use his rights on land considered riparian. If he has land further away from the stream, riparian rights do not apply. In this case he is considered to be an appropriator. The distance is determined by state statute. "In a few states, notably California, the past history of the user's chain of title sets . . . a limit on the land which can be called riparian. Under this viewpoint, the riparian land is restricted to the smallest area, having the present frontage on the stream, which has ever been held by one owner in the chain of title of the present user."[4] The land cannot regain its riparian character by being rejoined to the existing riparian land.

The riparian owner may take as much water as he needs for household purposes and for watering his farmstead animals. If necessary he may consume all the water of the stream for that purpose.

---

[3] Seminar on Water Rights, University of Colorado, Boulder, July 2-4, 1969.

[4] *Powell on Real Property*, Abridged Edition, Richard R. Powell and Patrick J. Roban, Matthew Bender & Co., Inc., New York, 1968, p. 789.

RIGHTS MAY BE LOST

Appropriatory rights, concerning land not adjacent to the stream, refer to a specific quantity of water, diverted for beneficial use, and are good as long as the rights are exercised. If one does not use his rights, he loses them. These rights may be lost by abandonment; statutory forfeiture, adverse user; or estoppel. If the rights are abandoned, concurrently nonused and intentionally relinquished, it reverts to the state and is released to existing appropriators in order of seniority. This doctrine is somewhat limited by the fact that in all states, excluding Colorado, Montana, and Washington, if the water is unused, it automatically reverts back to the public in a certain allotted time by statutory forfeiture.[5] Powell herein cites Hutchins' four questions concerning adverse use: "(1) Whether the procedure to appropriate water through the state engineer is the exclusive method of acquiring a water right; (2) whether forfeiture results from illegal use of water on the part of others, that is, adverse use; (3) whether the statutory period of forfeiture is less than the prescriptive period in the statute of limitations; (4) whether the water right can be detached from the land to which it is appurtenant and whether the statutory procedure is the only way of changing the place of use."[6]

"Appropriative rights may be lost by estoppel. The basic principle of estoppel, that of injurious reliance, applies to water rights in the same manner as it does to other rights."[7]

APPROPRIATED WATER MAY BE TRANSFERRED

A riparian owner, however, cannot lose his rights by disuse in most states. Appropriatory rights have priority against other appropriatory rights by seniority. Whoever applies for appropriation first has prior rights over subsequent appropriators. This rule was first applied in the California gold fields where water was a necessary ingredient for extracting gold. In some states appropriated water may be transferred to another land. In other states this would entail a loss of priority. Just as with riparian owners, the water must not be wasted but must be used reasonably and beneficially.[8]

---

[5] *Idem,* p. 834.

[6] *Selected Problems in the Law of Water Rights in the West,* Wells A. Hutchins, N. 1, at 401, 1942.

[7] *Idem,* p. 836.

[8] *California Law of Water Rights,* Wells A. Hutchins, State of California Printing Division, Sacramento, 1956.

There are several limitations to the quantity of water to be appropriated. The four main limitations are:

1. The quantity of water first subjected to appropriation. An additional amount may be included for increased needs if within scope of "original intent."

2. The maximum quantity as stated in the permit application, the notice of appropriation, the permit itself and the final issued license, in terms of second feet or miner's inches for direct irrigation and in terms of acre feet for storage.

3. Capacity of ditch or the conducting mechanism.

4. Beneficial use.

Some states also contain:

1. Quantitative operative limitations, such as only so much water used for a certain function.

2. An apportionment of water among appropriators from an insufficient supply.[9]

According to the California Water Code, Section 1201, "All water flowing through natural channels, excepting as far as it has been or is being applied to useful and beneficial purposes upon, or insofar as it is or may be reasonably needed for useful or beneficial purposes upon lands riparian thereto, or otherwise appropriated, is hereby declared to be public water of the state and subject to appropriation in accordance with the provisions of this code."

Thus, unless water is put to other use, anyone can take a claim on it and have appropriatory rights subject to prior claims.

PRESCRIPTION IS ANOTHER METHOD

Prescription is another method of obtaining water rights. Prescription is the legal right obtained, determined by use for a specified period of time.

The essential elements of a prescriptive right are:

1. Beneficial to the user.
2. Open to the person whom a new right is later claimed.
3. Continuous and uninterrupted.
4. Adverse, hostile, and in violation of the rights or privileges of the person against whom a new right is later claimed.
5. For the required period of time.[10]

---

[9] Powell and Roban, *op. cit.*, pp. 826-827.
[10] *Idem*, p. 797.

The most common method used by appropriators for obtaining water is irrigation ditches. The ditch that draws directly from the body of water is the main diversion ditch. A headgate is placed on the ditch with a meter that measures the quantity of water passing through the gate in a certain time. Thus the correct amount of water can be measured, and no one will be allowed to take more than his proper share in a given time period. This measurement is controlled by local government authorities. Lateral ditches connected to the main diversion ditch carry the water to the areas where it is most needed and diverts it over the fields.[11]

Many times the rights of riparian owners and appropriators come into conflict. The first really important case, *Lux* v. *Haggin*, decided in 1884, became the cornerstone for the riparian doctrine. The case concerned Henry Miller, the cattle baron, and Haggin and Travis, the founders of the famous Kern County Land Co., now part of the Tenneco Corp. Haggin and Travis wanted to appropriate water from the Kern River to sell to the settlers in the San Joaquin Valley. This came into contest when Henry Miller, a riparian owner, claimed that his water rights were part and parcel of his land, and thus could not be taken away. It was a battle between the doctrines of appropriatory and riparian rights, and took eight years to decide.

The end result was a victory for Miller. The court's reasoning was that since the riparian rights were part of the land, this would entail a confiscation of private property which they considered most important. Thus riparian rights had priority over appropriatory rights.[12]

OTHER WATER RIGHTS PRINCIPLES

An important premise in water litigation is that there is no distinction between ground water and surface water in point of law in most states. Ground water is, of course, contained beneath the surface of the ground. The use of water obtained from a well must be limited to the same laws applying to the use of water from a stream. Thus, well water is limited to reasonable use, as defined by state statute, without sufficient damage being sustained to the supply or quality of the water.

The "water table" is the shallowest point to which a well can be dropped and still draw water. The deeper the well is sunk, the more

---

[11] *Encyclopaedia Britannica*, Encyclopaedia Britannica, Inc., Chicago, 1962, Vol. XII, pp. 684-684.

[12] *The Cattle King*, Edward T. Treadway, Valley Publishers, Fresno, Calif., 1931.

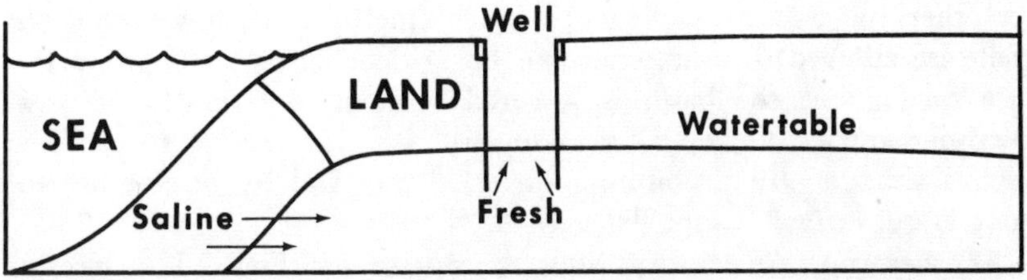

expensive becomes the drilling operation. In some areas, a great deal of harm can be caused by drawing too much ground water. In areas near a sea coast there is a particularly dangerous situation. An excessive drawing of water causes the saline (salt) water to take the place of the fresh water, causing pollution of the fresh water supply. If damage is caused to the water supply it is actionable against the defendant.

Another form of underground water is percolating water, or water that does not constitute part of a definite underground stream. "It is essential to the nature of percolating waters that they do not form part of the body or flow, surface or subterranean, of any stream."[13] This water is considered by the courts to be real property. But in the leading case, *Katz* v. *Walkinshaw* concerning an artesian belt, the laws of California concerning percolating waters were changed from private ownership of the water to public ownership. The proprietors were then limited to beneficial and reasonable use. "Owners of lands overlying the same supply of percolating water have equal rights therein for use on their overlying lands."[14] "Their rights are in the common supply, that is, are correlative."[15] The correlative, or public, rights prevail over the absolute private rights of proprietors. This ruling is limited to the state of California, and only in some degrees to other states. Most states use the doctrine of "reasonable" use to determine rights.

Sometimes reasonable use is affected by the fact that a user employed powerful pumps to obtain the water, damaging the quantity of water allotted to private owners.

The character of artesian belts has been taken into consideration in many statutes. Well water "rises by hydrostatic pressure, and, if wells are kept capped when not in use, a maximum of pressure will remain

---

[13] *Vineland Irr. Dist.* v. *Azusa Irrigating Co.*, 126 Calif. 486, 494, 58 Pac. 1057 (1899).

[14] *Katz* v. *Walkinshaw,* 141 Calif. 116, 135-136, 70 Pac. 663 (1902), 74 Pac. 766 (1903). See Hutchins, *op. cit.*

[15] *Burr* v. *Maclay Rancho Water Co.*, 160 Calif. 268, 273, 116 Pac. 715 (1911). See Hutchins, *op. cit.*

for other owners with wells tapping the same basin. If, however, such wells are allowed to flow when not being beneficially used, the pressure throughout the basin is lowered without any benefit to any overlying owner. Generally speaking, the statutes attempt to prevent such a situation by prohibiting surface waste and by attempting to control subsurface waste."[16]

Another type of priority right deals with overflows. If a stream overflows, flows over the banks of the stream, proprietors who have special overflow rights may use the waters available for their use before other proprietors. These rights are mostly seasonal, depending on rainfall and melting snow. As with all water rights, these rights are attached to the deed of the land.

Individual riparian and appropriatory rights are often superseded in priority in several cases. If a body of water is navigable, then its navigability must not be injured by private use.

> *Smart* v. *Aroostook Lumber Co.*, 103 Me. 37, involved a non-tidal river, the original channel of which was quite crooked but well defined for 30 miles and of sufficient width and depth to float logs and small boats at all times of the year except in seasons of unusual drought. The court held that this was a navigable stream. Navigability is a question of fact. A river capable of floating to market the products of the country and upon which boats, barges, rafts or logs may lie borne is a navigable stream and the public has a right of passage over all freshwater streams which are by nature capable of such general use. Also, waters capable of use for boating or sailing for pleasure should be considered navigable.[17]

This interpretation is based on the premise that the United States Government has the right and obligation to improve and protect navigation.

> The authorities, ancient and modern, are all consistent and point in one direction. Highways, whether on land or water, are designed for the accommodation of the public, for travel or transportation, and any unauthorized or unreasonable obstruction thereof is a public nuisance in judgment of the law. They cannot be made receptacles of waste materials, filth or trash, nor the depositories of valuable property even, so as to obstruct their use as public highways. All such obstructions in the eye of the law, are deemed unreasonable.[18]

This control of navigation and navigable water is basically an attribute of sovereignty and police power. In the *United States* v. *Gerlock Live Stock Co.* case, (1950), it was decided that the government also had the power to promote welfare through projects for reclamation, irrigation, and other internal improvements. Thus for these large

[16] Powell and Roban, *op. cit.*, p. 789.
[17] Franchel, *op. cit.*, p. 139.
[18] *Idem*, p. 145.

scale purposes the government by eminent domain also has prior rights to water over private owners.[19]

If a riparian owner loses right by confiscation he must be compensated because his rights are private property (*U. S.* v. *Gerlock Livestock Co.* 1950). The riparian owner can litigate and have appraisers estimate the damages. Not only is he paid in full, but he receives tax benefits because he suffered from "involuntary conversion," which means that his property was converted to money against his will.

A city has further potential rights over private ownership, even though the water is not presently needed. This is the "Pueblo Right." It insures future use of water for an expanding city. Others, however, may use this water until the municipality needs it.[20]

An important question is: what constitutes a water course to which these rights apply? In some early decisions it was said that a water course consists of bed, banks, and water. There must be a stream flowing in a particular direction that need not always be continually flowing, since a drought would cause it to dry up. It must also have a definite channel and be of such a well-defined existence as to be considered valuable to proprietors along its course. Sloughs or catchment areas concerned simply with flood control are not considered water courses. The "banks of watercourses are those boundaries which contain their waters at highest flow, that is, the fast land which confines the water in its channel or bed in its whole width as determined by its highest flow."[21] Professor Richard Powell defines a watercourse with four criteria:

1. A definite channel.
2. A current of flow having substantiality.
3. A definite source of supply.
4. An outlet into another body of water.[22]

In cases of flood, a proprietor may protect himself from the "common enemy" and guard against floods as long as he doesn't change the natural channel. Others downstream cannot sue for damages brought about by his acts for self-protection, even if this causes them an added burden. However, his acts must be considered reasonable under the circumstances, as determined by a court of equity. The leading case, *Weinburg Co.* v. *Bixby*, 195 Calif. 87, 95, 96, 101, 196 Pac 25 (1921), cites: Floods are considered common enemies

[19] Hutchins, *op. cit.*, p. 352.
[20] *Idem.*, pp. 256-257.
[21] *Lee Venture Land and Power Co.* v. *Meiners,* 136 Calif. 284, 290, 68 Pac. 818 (1902).
[22] Powell and Roban, *op. cit.*, p. 782.

". . . which may be guarded against or warded off by one whose property is invaded or threatened, by obstructions which are merely defensive in their nature and not calculated to interfere with the current of the water in its natural channel." This decision applies even if the ". . . result of such obstruction has been to throw an increased volume of the flood upon opposite or lower proprietors." However, the proprietor must exercise ordinary care, and cause as little damage as possible or his actions may be actionable by other landowners.

An increasingly important aspect of water litigation is water pollution. The riparian owners not only have a certain quantity of water by right, but also a certain quality. The upper riparian owner has the right to use water even if he necessarily impairs the quality of the water. He cannot, however, injure the water maliciously or unnecessarily. The important consideration is whether the upstream user substantially injures the downstream user. The downstream individual has the right to insist the water not be injured. This is particularly the case where the downstream use is for domestic purposes.

"The law is well settled that any use of a stream which materially fouls and adulterates the water, or the deposit or discharge therein of any filthy or noxious substances that so far affect the water as to impair its value for the ordinary purposes of life, or anything that renders the water less wholesome than when in its ordinary state will constitute a nuisance, which courts of equity will enjoin, and for which a lower riparian owner, injured thereby is entitled to redress . . . It is a matter of common knowledge that pure and wholesome water for domestic uses, and in farming operations, is a valuable asset, and its presence or absence naturally affects the value of farm property, and such rights cannot be destroyed by a riparian owner in a stream to such an extent as to render the water unfit for use."[23] However, a prospective right may be acquired to pollute a watercourse as long as the pollution does not become a public nuisance.

Appropriators have rights concerning pollution too. The prior appropriator, or the first one to record his right, is entitled to a stream of such purity as to fulfill the purposes for which he appropriated the water.[24] The law recognizes that some deterioration will occur, which, within reasonable limits, is *damnum absque injuria*, or damages without injury. The reasonableness of the use by each appropriator is decided in each individual case by state authorities.

Sometimes it is very difficult to determine how much pollution is

---

[23] *Joerger* v. *Pacific Gas & Electric Co.*, 207 Calif. 8, 25-26, 276 Pac. 1017 (1929). See Hutchins, *op. cit.*

[24] Hutchins, *op. cit.*, p. 122.

considered reasonable. This is particularly true when a major industry, beneficial to the whole community, is the offender.

Professor Richard Powell treats the following criteria as significant:

"1. The general character of the stream;
"2. The volume and velocity of the stream;
"3. The uses to which the stream has theretofore been put;
"4. The use and location of the plaintiff's land;
"5. The extent of the damage caused to plaintiff;
"6. The customs of the locality and of the industry involved;
"7. The comparative public concern in the positions of the plaintiff and defendants.

"It is this last factor which often has controlling force in pollution cases. Public interest can be involved either for minimizing of health hazards (thus helping plaintiffs), or for the minimizing of the difficulties of a locally dominant industry (thus helping defendants). Differences of judgments as to the wisdom of courts in weighing these considerations of public interest have led to many recent suggestions of a statutory coverage for the problems of stream pollution."[25]

The court will tend to find the use "unreasonable" if the pollution can be limited with a small expense.

If damage has been done, the superior rights of a prior appropriator entitles him to both injunctive and legal relief.

In summary, as the supply of water diminishes while the demand increases, it is becoming increasingly essential that lawyers and land owners familiarize themselves with water right laws in their areas. The laws concerning these laws are probably going to become more demanding and the penalties more severe. This applies particularly to reasonable use of water. None should be wasted if the supply is going to be able to meet our needs. Nor should any be damaged. Our well being in the future, as predicted by statesmen and conservationists, depends upon our ability to keep our water usable. This implies that future litigation concerning pollution is going to be more demanding upon those who pollute our streams and rivers. Nothing need be said concerning many of the rivers' conditions in our industrial areas. It has been said before, and will be repeated often. To be able to remain in contact with your present and future water rights, everyone should be aware of the fluctuating laws of water litigation.

[25] *Idem*, p. 792.

Chapter XII

Technical Documents

As indicated in previous chapters, the buying, selling, and leasing of ranch and farm properties is not substantially different from other forms of real estate. However, there are some technical terms, special situations, and occasional local ground rules that may be different. The easiest method of explanation is by example. In this chapter, we are going to go over in detail and give actual reproductions of the principal documents in the sale of a large western ranch and in the leasing with an option to buy of a major eastern Kansas farm. This will include reproduction of the sales contracts, mortgage documents, transfer of water rights, deed of trust arrangements, transfer of attached grazing rights, transfer of personal property on the ranch, and a copy of the title insurance policy. The leasing of the eastern Kansas ranch will include the lease document, the measures designed to prevent overgrazing with a graduated rent schedule, and an option agreement with a price contingent on subsequent improvement programs.

For the general reader, too much emphasis cannot be placed on the necessity of employing an attorney who not only knows the legal ramifications of ranch transactions, but is also familiar with the state laws and local customs where the ranch is located.

As a specific example, the term "controlled land," as used in many sections of Wyoming, is rarely found in an urban real estate book. This might mean several isolated sections (640 acres) located in the middle of your 100,000-acre ranch which were homesteaded 50 years ago but which were subsequently abandoned but where ownership was retained by distant parties. If the ranch is located in areas of the state that require 50 acres to run one cow, it means that a single isolated section can only handle 10 to 15 cows. Obviously, no one can afford to put a man on it or can come out and live on a property with this level of production, nor can he afford to erect a fence around the property to keep the neighboring landholder's cattle out of it. Because Wyoming is an open range state dating back to the old days, it was the obligation of the minority farming group to "fence the rancher's cattle out." The small farmer whose truck garden was damaged by a rancher's cows had no recourse to the rancher, as the law left the obligation of fence construction and maintenance to him.

The arrival of the Homesteader or "sod buster" in the 19th Century was greeted with less than enthusiasm by the cattle barons who controlled the "open range." Most of the early fencing laws passed by cattlemen-dominated legislatures favored livestock over the farmer. (Courtesy, Mr. Byron B. Wolfe, Kansas City Posse of The Westerners)

Consequently, such a section of land, where it is insufficiently productive to justify fence construction, has no economic agricultural value, particularly if there is no source of water on it. In these situations, the surrounding landholder will normally pay an extremely nominal rent, usually just sufficient to pay the real estate taxes. If the distant landholder says, "I won't rent it to you" or "I want more rent," the rancher says, "Okay then, fence my cattle *out*." This the landholder cannot afford to do, so the property then becomes what is known as "controlled land under private lease." Obviously, this type of thing does not appear in a mortgage document or a title insurance policy or a sales contract, but could be a significant asset of the ranch if sufficient of these tracts exist.

As a general orientation of the urban-type reader, before we get into the more technical material, I want to quote from *Cowboy Economics*:

"There are no bargains in ranch or farm land in the United States. Anybody that tells you he has a property that will consistently produce 10% in net agricultural income after all expenses is an outright liar. Anyone who says that he has a property that will produce 8% is an optimistic dreamer; at 6% he is extremely lucky; at 4% he might be telling the truth.

"The foregoing figures are based on the net agricultural incomes averaged out over five years with a reasonable degree of security. They are further based either on a strictly net arm's-length rental or on an operation in which a proper allocation toward cost is given for the personal labor of the owner and his family. Specifically, these figures do not include the following situations:

"1. You have a '100,000-acre ranch' with 1,000 acres of deeded land and 99,000 acres of attached Federal and state leases, forest permits, and other grazing rights which can be cancelled on you with no compensation, so you could see your whole investment evaporate overnight. In this case, a 20% temporary net return would hardly compensate for the risks.

"2. The principal part of your investment is a dry farming wheat operation in which you get special rainfall conditions one year in five which permit you to make a killing, but you 'burn out' the other four. 'Net return' in these circumstances should be an *average* of the five-year period.

"3. Not included is the situation where you inherited the land from your grandfather and it went through probate at one-fourth of its market value. When we say '4% net return,' we mean 4% of its *legitimate* market value at *this* moment.

"4. Not included is the situation where the owner personally is a highly educated, energetic, capable man, who could command a $20,000 per year salary in any other field, and he has two sons who could command $10,000 per year in any other line of activity, and he puts the entire labor of himself and his two sons into the operation at a value of 50¢ per hour. On this basis, he calculates that he is making a 10% return on a $300,000 ranch when he actually is making only 'wages'."[1]

It is hoped that the balance of this chapter will give some of the reasons for the unusual situation just described.

TRANSACTION DOCUMENTS

Sales Contract

Most arguments and law suits on a land transaction occur over misunderstandings and discrepancies on the sales contract. Here everything should be spelled out in detail. The contract could be a simple one such as we use here, or it could be one of many hundreds of pages covering complex assignments of water rights, mineral rights, and many other items. As a matter of custom, it often happens in the sale

[1] *Cowboy Economics*, 2nd ed., Brigadier General Harold L. Oppenheimer, The Interstate Printers & Publishers, Inc., 1971, p. 105.

of a western ranch that the seller retains half of the minerals with the buyer getting the surface land and the other half. In cases where the ranch has passed through 20 hands over the last half century, and where it was assembled from multiple small ownerships to start with, and where various of the owners have made certain assignments of the mineral rights, and where various drilling leases might be involved, the legal description of the mineral rights alone could very well take 50 typed pages.

Title Insurance Policy

The *abstract* is usually a lengthy document of everything that appeared on the record that happened to the property from the day it was purchased from the Indians. "Bringing an abstract up to date" is the process of having an attorney go to the county courthouse and pour through the records, finding everything that might have happened to the property since the last recorded item on the abstract. Principally, the attorney is looking for filed mortgages, mechanics' liens that may not have been released, evidence that some widow might still have "dower rights," evidence that some heir never gave his permission to some transaction, and items of this nature.

In modern times, most transactions in land are covered by title insurance. As explained previously, certain insurance companies, licensed to do this kind of business in a given state, will insure that everything is up to snuff, and if any damages occur to the buyer because of undisclosed "*title defects*," that the insurance company will make up the difference. When one finds something on the title (listed in the abstract) that can't easily be cleared up, such as a missing heir who never gave permission to a sale, this constitutes a "cloud on the title." In some cases you can have a friendly suit in court to "quiet the title." In this "quiet title" suit, the judge directs that every effort be made to find the missing heir, proper steps are taken to advertise the situation, and in the event that he can't be found or restitution or damages cannot be paid to his estate, the judge will "clear the title" for the present seller and all subsequent owners.

Closing Statement

The parties finally meet in an attorney's office or in the office

 Official Form approved by Legal Counsel—10-63-25

This is a legally binding contract. If not understood, seek competent advice.

Kansas Real Estate Sale Contract

1. THIS CONTRACT is made this..............day of.......................................19..........., by and between..

....seller,

and...buyer.

2. WITNESSETH: The seller hereby sells to the buyer the following described real estate, together with all improvements thereon, including, if any, gas heaters, ventilating, central air conditioning, attached T.V. antennas, lighting, heating and plumbing equipment and fixtures, attached mirrors and linoleum, window and porch shades, venetian blinds, storm windows and doors, screens, curtain and drapery rods, awnings and..

....

in...County, State of Kansas, to-wit:

3. Subject, however, to any recorded restrictions, easements, party wall agreements and community contracts. Subject, also, to any existing leases, tenancies and zoning laws.

4. The purchase price is...DOLLARS $.....................

which the buyer agrees to pay as follows:...DOLLARS $.....................

at the signing of this contract, the receipt whereof is hereby acknowledged by the seller and which is deposited with.....................

....

as part of the consideration of the sale; the balance to be paid in the following manner:

....DOLLARS $.....................

cash on delivery of deed as herein provided, and

5. All deferred payments not already secured by deed of trust or mortgage shall be evidenced by note........, signed by the buyer, secured by deed of trust or mortgage, at the option of the seller, on the above described property, containing usual provisions, drawing interest from date of delivery of deed, on the terms specified above.

6. The seller shall make any payments required on existing mortgages or deeds of trust until date of delivery of deed; and, if it is provided herein that such property is being sold subject to any existing mortgage or deed of trust, buyer shall, on such date, reimburse seller for any principal reductions not already considered in computing payment of purchase price and for any deposits held by the holder of the mortgage or deed of trust.

7. The rental from said property, and the interest on any existing mortgages or deeds of trust to which this sale is made subject, shall be pro-rated between the seller and the buyer as of the date of the delivery of the deed.

8. The seller shall pay all taxes, general and special, and all special assessments, against said property which are due and have accrued at the date of this contract and the buyer shall assume all of such taxes and assessments, and installments of unpaid special assessments becoming due and accruing thereafter, except that all general state, county, school and municipal taxes and special assessments and installments of unpaid special assessments (exclusive of rebates and penalties) becoming due and accruing during the calendar year in which the deed is delivered shall be pro-rated between the seller and the buyer on the basis of said calendar year, as of the date of delivery of the deed. If the amount of any such tax or assessment to be pro-rated cannot then be ascertained, pro-ration shall be computed on the amount thereof for the preceding year, except...

....

9. The seller shall, within twenty (20) days from the date hereof, deliver to the buyer or at the office of.......................................

....an abstract of title by competent abstractors showing all instruments of record affecting said property from the United States Government to this date, with the usual certificates as to bankruptcy, taxes, judgments and mechanics' liens. Subsequent acceptance of the abstract by the buyer shall be a waiver of time of delivery. The buyer shall have ten (10) days after such delivery of abstract to examine it. If there are objections to the title, the buyer shall specify the objections in writing, to be delivered to the office of...

.... The seller shall have any defects in the title corrected and shown on the abstract within thirty (30) days from date of delivery of such objections. The abstract shall become the property of the buyer.

10. In lieu of furnishing such abstract of title, or in lieu of correcting such objections, the seller may furnish the buyer an Owner's Title Insurance Policy in the amount of the purchase price from a company authorized to insure titles in this state, insuring a merchantable fee simple title in the buyer as of the date of recording the deed. The seller may, within twenty (20) days from the date hereof or the date of receipt of objections to said title, deliver to the buyer or at the office of...

....a commitment for said policy. The seller shall have an additional thirty (30) days to make any corrections in the title required by said company. In case such defects in title are not rectified within the time specified, or the title insurance commitment is not delivered, this contract shall be null and void, unless the buyer elects to waive such objections, and the money deposited aforesaid shall be returned to the buyer and the abstract returned to the seller.

11. If the seller has a merchantable fee simple title to said property, the seller shall deliver to the buyer at the office of said ....General Warranty Deed, properly executed and conveying said property free and clear of all liens and encumbrances whatsoever, except as herein provided; the buyer shall then and there pay the balance, if any, of said cash payment, and execute and deliver to the seller the note...... and deed of trust or mortgage, if any, hereinbefore provided for. The buyer shall furnish insurance policies necessary for the protection of the holders of mortgages or deeds of trust, containing loss clauses payable to the holders of the mortgages or deeds of trust as their interests may appear. The abstract and insurance policies shall be held by the holder of the first mortgage or deed of trust until paid.

12. If before delivery of deed any of the improvements on said property are destroyed or substantially damaged by fire, lightning or any cause that could be covered by what is known as extended coverage insurance, the buyer shall have the option of enforcing this contract or cancelling by written notice within ten (10) days thereafter. If cancelled, the deposit shall be returned to the buyer and the abstract returned to the seller.

13. If the seller has kept his part of this contract, and the buyer fails to comply with the contract on his part as herein provided, within five (5) days thereafter, then this contract may or may not be operative thereafter, at the option of the seller, and, in the event the seller shall declare the contract inoperative, the money deposited aforesaid shall be paid to the seller as liquidated damages. Time is of the essence of this contract.

IN WITNESS WHEREOF, said parties hereunto subscribe their names. Executed in triplicate.

.... (Seller)	.... (Buyer)
....	....

of the title insurance company, start signing papers, and passing checks. The closing statement is merely an itemization prepared by an attorney or the title insurance company of who owes what on the prorated insurance policies, prorated real estate taxes, adjustments of existing mortgages, proration of interest rates on the mortgages, and often who is responsible for what real estate agent's commission. At the bottom of the statement is the final amount owed by the buyer to the seller. Traditionally, the seller is responsible for the Federal revenue stamps that have to be paid on the deed.

Deeds

Traditionally, the most common deed is the *warranty deed*. Here the seller guarantees the buyer against any title defects and agrees to defend him against any law suits or problems that might arise. He "warrants" that everything that is stated in the deed or transfer of title is correct. A warranty deed from an outfit like the General Motors Corporation guaranteeing the new owner against problems of any nature whatsoever would probably be as good as a title insurance policy. On the other hand, a warranty deed signed by an individual of small means might leave something to be desired.

A *quit claim* deed is usually just a deed signed by the owner of record stating that he turns over all rights that *he* possesses in the property to the new buyer. This means that the new buyer is strictly on his own, and his attorney had better give everything a good looking at. It is common where there is a title defect and a questionable right of ownership in some heir or party, other than the principal seller, to pay such a person a small sum of money and get him to give a quit claim deed renouncing any rights he *might have* in the property and turning them over to the new buyer. Such a quit claim deed might be required by a title insurance company before they would issue the title policy from the principal seller.

The types, forms, manners of recording, and other items concerning deeds are governed by state laws and vary from state to state. The form of a corporate deed is usually different from that granted by an individual. It is important that the title company prove that the corporation is licensed to do business in the state and has paid its franchise taxes. A deed signed by the executors of an estate can be a complex matter involving the Probate Court and peculiar local laws. A deed signed by a guardian for a minor can be extremely complex. A deed obtained through a mortgage foreclosure sale is no simple matter.

Form No. 18—Class E | Demaree Stationery Co., 908 Walnut, Kansas City, Mo.

Corporation Quit-Claim Deed

This Indenture, ***Made on the day of , A. D., One Thousand Nine Hundred and , by and between***

a corporation, duly organized under the laws of the State of , of the County of , State of , party of the first part, and

of the County of , State of , party of the second part,

WITNESSETH, THAT THE SAID PARTY OF THE FIRST PART, in consideration of the sum of DOLLARS, to it in hand paid by the party of the second part, the receipt for which is hereby acknowledged, does, by these presents, REMISE, RELEASE and FOREVER QUIT-CLAIM unto the said party of the second part, the following described lots, tracts or parcels of land, lying, being and situate in the County of and State of to-wit:

THIS DEED OF QUIT-CLAIM being made to release

from the lien of certain bearing date day of 19
recorded in the office of the of Deeds within and for the County of
and State of , in Deed Book No. , at Page No.
which said was executed by
to secure the payment of a numbered
and described in said which said note and
are now held and owned by the said
grantor herein.

TO HAVE AND TO HOLD THE SAME, with all the rights, immunities, privileges and appurtenances, thereto belonging, unto the said part of the second part and unto and assigns forever; so that neither the said party of the first part, nor any other person or persons, for it or in its name or behalf, shall or will hereafter claim or demand any right or title to the aforesaid premises or any part thereof, but they and each of them shall, by these presents, be excluded and forever barred.

IN WITNESS WHEREOF, The said party of the first part has caused these presents to be signed by its President and attested by its Secretary, and the corporate seal to be hereto attached, the day and year first above written.

____________________ ____________________

____________________ ***By____________________***

President.

In some states the mortgagors may have certain rights to come back in and pay off their former obligation and claim the property at some future date. Particularly is this true where properties were picked up by a county or municipality on the foreclosure of a tax lien. There are certain areas of the United States where the laws are in sufficient confusion that title companies won't touch any properties obtained in this manner. Obviously, if a title company has insured your title with no exceptions and somebody comes back in 10 years later on a claim, they could be liable for damages. These could be enormous, for example, if you had originally bought vacant land, received a title insurance policy on it, and subsequently built a building and had then raised the limits of the title policy to the total value of both land and building.

Mortgages

Essentially, these are the same as mortgages on personal property except that land is being put up as security instead of livestock or other chattels. An example follows in the subsequent section.

Deeds of Trust

This is becoming more and more common and works like this: Mr. A owns the land and wants to borrow on it. Mr. B, a banker, decides to loan him the money. A Deed of Trust is then signed with Mr. C, a third party, usually a bank or an escrow agent, in which Mr. A actually deeds the property over to Mr. C, but with an arrangement that the transfer is not to take place unless he defaults on the loan to Mr. B. As part of the arrangement, Mr. C agrees to transfer the property to Mr. B in the event A does default. The whole procedure is designed to eliminate much of the legal red tape and expense connected with the conventional mortgage foreclosure in most states. This is particularly common in the sale of small houses, lots, and other items which are done on the installment plan with purchase money mortgages where the cost of mortgage foreclosure would be prohibitive because of the small sums involved. A variation of this, known as a "Contract for Deed" is contained in the ranch sale example which follows.

Leases

Leases can be simple one-page forms involving an owner, a tenant, a description of the property, and the rent, as shown under

"Leases." This is normally true where small amounts of money are involved or the lease is for one or two years. A much more complicated lease follows by way of illustration where 10 years are involved, combined with an option to buy, and with the rent contingent on the amount of cattle run during certain seasons of the year.

As previously mentioned, 999-year leases, common in England, transfer so many of the incidents of ownership that for all practical purposes they should contain everything that's in an involved sales contract plus warranty deed plus title insurance policy, and all of the

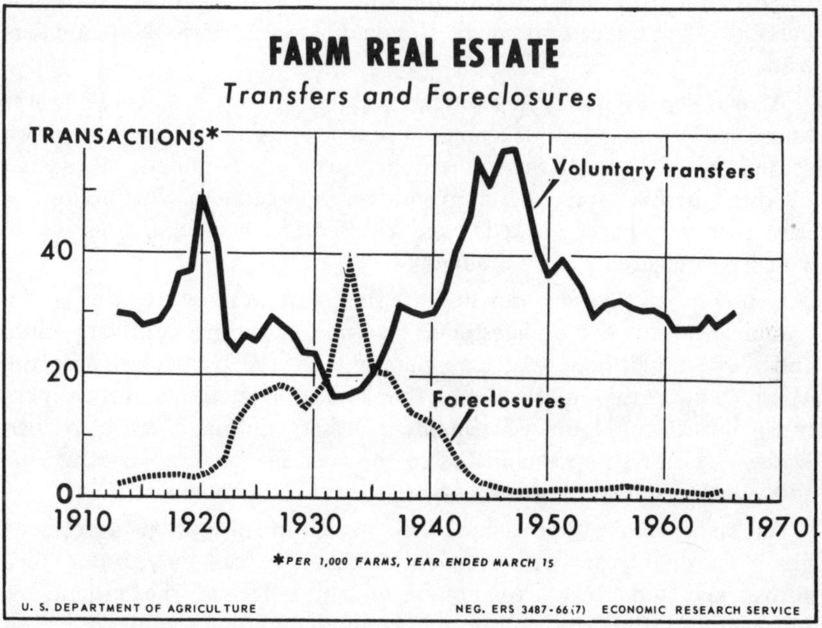

In times of rising values (1945-1968) there are very few foreclosures. If the land is equal to the value of the mortgage or more, the owner who gets in default will sell it rather than go through the embarrassment of foreclosure. (Courtesy, USDA, Washington, D.C.)

other features of a land sale. In major urban areas, it is quite common to construct buildings worth millions of dollars on land held not in fee but only by a 99-year lease. Obviously, the builder, the new owner, the mortgage company, and all other parties concerned are quite interested that there not be any gaps or loop holes in the lease arrangements.

SALES

Large transactions in agricultural land involve a number of factors not present in urban business properties. Part is due to the emotional and social connotations going back 1,000 years in western European history. For example, the term "landed aristocracy" carries plenty of weight today in England, France, Germany, and Spain. You are substantially further up the scale and your son has a better chance of getting into Eton if you have owned 2,000 acres in Herefordshire for four generations than if your family has a couple of shoe factories in Manchester. The German "Junkers" and the Spanish Grandees are all tied in closely with the land. Being the Earl of Northumberland doesn't mean so much if you no longer have Northumberland.

A man can be pretty sophisticated about buying or selling a warehouse in Wichita, but he chokes up when it's the Wyoming ranch settled by his grandfather where he spent his boyhood. Above all of this, there is some basic, primitive, non-economic attraction to land that you have worked, over a commercial structure on which you have repaired the plumbing.

Consequently, larger ranches are not just real estate, but are a combination of home, livestock, machinery, business, private club, and family heirloom. As an operating entity, particularly in the West, they may require above the land: water rights, forest permits, Bureau of Land Management leases, railroad leases, civilian leases, cattle or sheep acclimated to the area, custom feed contractors, and work exchange agreements with the neighbors.

As an example, the ranch may have an unwritten agreement going back 50 years with a neighbor that you can move your herd across his land to go to your summer range in the mountains. In return, during the month of August, you open your fence so his cattle can use your northeastern water tank which adjoins his property. None of this appears in the deed or title insurance policy. As part of old English common law, an "easement" that has existed in excess of 10 years may exist as a legal right which would hold up in court.

Furthermore, in recent years it has been the practice of both the Federal and state government to cut back the grazing permits whenever title to a ranch changes hands. There may be no way of knowing what will happen on the day the real estate closing takes place. Likewise, litigation may be taking place on water rights, miles upstream of your property, of which the eventual outcome may very well affect the available flow to your ranch. Title insurance companies have been burned so often on these points that they will not insure them. In some of the subsequent documents you will note devices to attempt to get some protection here.

One last point. In the old days most sales contracts gave the seller the choice of furnishing an abstract "brought up to date" by his attorney or furnishing a title insurance policy. If the attorney makes a mistake on the land description or fails to locate a title defect, you can sue him for negligence, many attorneys carry professional liability insurance which would back up any title of opinion. On the other hand, the Title Insurance Company presumably has large assets to back up their policy. When a local attorney says, "Why all ranches in this valley always change hands by abstract," use your own judgment as to whether you wish to go under a title opinion or a title insurance policy.

To renew an existing title policy costs about half of a new one. Today all insurance companies require them for mortgage loans and you will have to pay for one anyway if you borrow from this source. If you can tie in a mortgage title policy with the closing at the same time the seller is furnishing you the main one, you can often get it for a nominal additional charge such as $20.00.

EXAMPLE OF A MAJOR RANCH SALE

In the following blow by blow description of how a large western ranch changes hands, be alert to these points:

1. This $330,000 ranch is being purchased with a 10% down payment and 90% in mortgages. One is the assumption of an existing first mortgage, and the other is a substantial second mortgage.

2. The new buyer is taking no legal liability on either the assumption of the first mortgage, nor is he assuming personal responsibility on the second mortgage.

3. Note that Schedule "B" of the Sales Contract sets up an arbitration system in the event that the seller can't deliver all of the specified water rights. As will be discussed later, this is because title insurance companies generally refuse to insure water rights even if they are recorded.

4. Note that the various legal descriptions of the large tracts do not contain the phrase "being ________ number of acres, more or less." This is a handy thing to get into a legal description if the

seller is willing to do it. Most title companies will refuse to accept it as this is not part of the description that is a matter of record. The reason for this is that it offers some legal protection in the event that somebody makes a mistake in the legal description. It corresponds in urban real estate, after one is given a legal description of the property, to insert the phrase "popularly known as 1802-03-04-10 Main Street."

5. The mineral rights on this ranch are apparently intact. This is extremely unusual on most western ranches where each succeeding seller retains half of the mineral rights and only passes on half to the next buyer.

6. Note that the sellers of the ranch have taken a lease back on a 5% net basis. The sale-lease back transaction, made popular in ur-

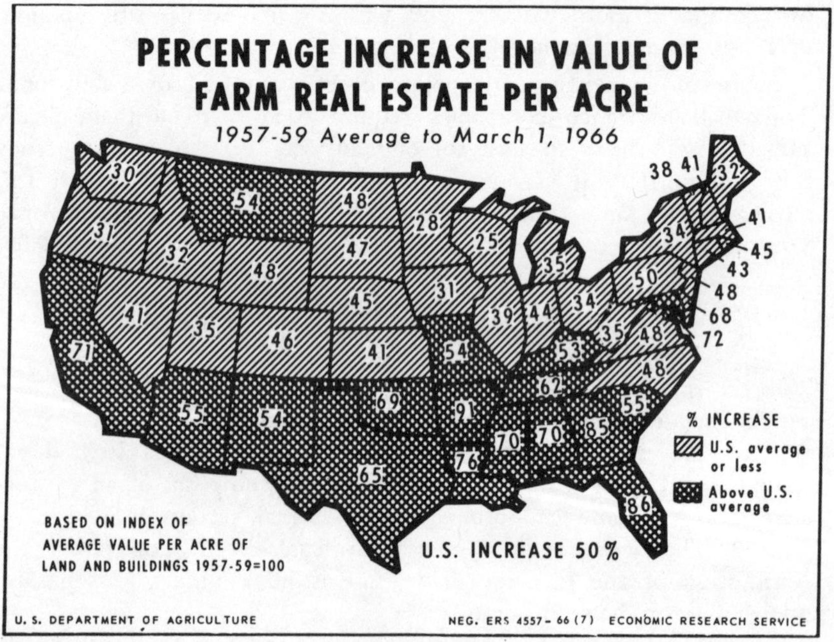

ban properties by the large grocery chains such as Safeway, was relatively unusual in farm and ranch properties until the last five years. It is now becoming an acceptable means for a ranch owner to attain additional capital to buy or lease surrounding lands and benefit from the savings that can be accomplished with larger volume type operations. Furthermore, if he can lease back at 5% net in periods when interest rates are around 7%, this interest differential plus the savings from larger type operations is very much to his advantage. The buyer on the other hand has a chance to speculate on the increase in land values which have recently been averaging four or five percent per year, plus the many tax benefits inherent in holding rural land.

Real Estate Contract

This agreement, dated this 20th day of January, 1967, between Jones Corporation, a Wyoming corporation, of Yellowstone County, State of Wyoming, hereinafter referred to as "seller," with mailing address of Route 1, Rawlins, Wyoming, and The Smith company, a California corporation, hereinafter referred to as "purchaser":

Witnesseth: seller hereby agrees to sell, convey, and assign to purchaser, and the purchaser agrees to purchase, free and clear of all liens and encumbrances, except as herein specifically noted, all of the real and personal property, leases, and water and mineral rights described in Schedules "A" and "B" attached hereto and hereby made a part hereof, said real and personal property, leases, and water and mineral rights being hereinafter collectively referred to as the "property," and such leases being hereinafter referred to as the "leases."

A. *Purchase Price*

The purchase price is three hundred thirty thousand dollars ($330,000), payable as follows:

1. ten thousand dollars ($10,000) by check payable to Kansas City Title Insurance Company, at the execution of this agreement. Said money shall be held by Kansas City Title Insurance Company, subject to the terms of this contract and shall be delivered to the seller at the closing provided for in "D" hereof. If there be no closing by reason of the termination of this contract as provided for herein, then Kansas City Title Insurance Company shall return such money to purchaser.

2. twenty-three thousand dollars ($23,000) by certified check of the purchaser to the order of the seller to be delivered to the seller at the closing.

3. one hundred twenty-one thousand five hundred dollars ($121,500) with interest from the closing date at the rate of six percent (6%) per annum payable in twenty equal annual installments of principal of six thousand seventy-five dollars ($6,075) together with interest on the unpaid balance outstanding with each succeeding installment. The first principal payment is due January 1, 1968. However, at the closing purchaser shall pay interest in advance equal to six months interest on the principal sum and shall pay the remaining interest due for the year 1967 on the first payment date. purchaser shall have the privilege of prepaying without penalty any or all of the principal amount above stated at any time during the term of this contract. The form of Contract for Deed to be executed at the closing is set forth in Schedule "C."

4. one hundred eighty thousand dollars ($180,000) by the purchaser accepting payment obligations when due on a promissory note secured by a First Mortgage of record with an unpaid principal balance on January 1, 1967, of said one hundred seventy-five thousand five hundred dollars ($175,500). A synopsis of the terms and conditions of this note and mortgage are set forth in Schedule "D" hereto. It is agreed that purchaser shall not assume liability for the unpaid principal of said promissory note or for the performance of the terms and conditions of said first mortgage. In the event that the principal amount as stated above is reduced prior to the closing, the principal amount stated in "3" hereof shall be increased by a like amount.

B. *Prorations*

Interest on the first mortgage described in Schedule "D" hereof shall be apportioned as of the date of the closing. No other items shall be apportioned and any and all taxes, rents, insurance premiums, irrigation charges, assessments and other charges with respect to the PROPERTY that are liens against the PROPERTY or that are due and payable prior to the closing shall be paid by the SELLER.

C. *Title Insurance*

1. SELLER shall deliver to PURCHASER within twenty (20) days of the date hereof a written commitment from the Kansas City Title Insurance Company to issue to the PURCHASER at the closing a policy of title insurance in the amount of the purchase price insuring to the PURCHASER that SELLER has a merchantable fee simple title to the PROPERTY included in this sale, free and clear of all liens and encumbrances (including filed and unfiled mechanics' liens) other than those subject to which PURCHASER has agreed to take title by the terms of this contract.

2. SELLER shall deliver to PURCHASER at the closing an owner's title insurance policy in accordance with the requirements of the commitment to insure delivered to the PURCHASER pursuant to "1" above.

3. If the commitment to insure delivered to PURCHASER, pursuant to number "1" above, specifies that title to the PROPERTY is subject to liens or encumbrances

a. that render title unmarketable;

b. that are not included in those subject to which PURCHASER has agreed to take title; and

c. that SELLER is unable to cure prior to the date fixed herein for closing, PURCHASER may, at PURCHASER's option, either terminate this contract or elect to accept such title as SELLER is able to convey.

D. *Closing*

The closing shall be held within thirty (30) days from the date of this contract at a time and place that is mutually agreeable to the parties hereto. If the SELLER has kept its part of this contract and the PURCHASER fails to comply with the contract on its part as herein provided within five (5) days thereafter, then this contract may or may not be operative thereafter at the option of the SELLER and, in the event that the SELLER shall declare this contract inoperative, the money deposited shall be paid to the SELLER as liquidated damages. Time is of the essence of this contract.

1. The following documents shall be delivered by the SELLER at or simultaneously with the closing against payment of the purchase price as provided herein and receipt of the documents to be delivered at the closing by the PURCHASER as provided in Paragraph D (2) hereof:

a. General Warranty Deeds, each of which shall be properly executed, acknowledged, and delivered to the escrow agent in accordance with an escrow agreement mutually agreed upon prior to closing, conveying to PURCHASER a fee simple title in the real estate included in this sale as described in Schedule "A" hereof together with all of the oil, gas, and other minerals and mineral rights in and under such real estate and such portion of the water rights included in this sale as may be conveyed by such General Warranty Deed. There shall be attached to the Deed to be recorded in Jefferson County all required United States documentary and other revenue stamps and SELLER shall deliver with such Deeds evidence of payment of all state and local transfer taxes and charges.

b. All documents, properly executed, required for the assignment to the PURCHASER of the LEASE (including any necessary consents of the lessors thereunder to such assignment and to the subletting by the PURCHASER to the SELLER of the property covered by the LEASES as contemplated in Paragraph D (2) (d) of this contract). SELLER shall also deliver evidence of payment by the SELLER of any consideration or fees required to be paid to the lessors under the LEASES upon the assignment or subletting (as aforesaid) of the LEASES.

c. Bill of Sale transferring to the PURCHASER all personal property described in Schedule "A" and such portion of any water rights described in Schedule "B" as may be transferred by Bill of Sale.

d. Instruments assigning to PURCHASER the shares of stock in the water and ditch companies described in Schedule "B" to which shall be affixed all necessary Federal or state transfer tax stamps.

e. Certificate of Mortgage Reduction or similar document, in recordable form, executed by the holder of the first mortgage described in Schedule "D" hereof, stating, as of the date of the closing, the unpaid principal balance, the rate of interest, the last date with respect to which interest and amortization was paid, and the maturity date of the mortgage.

f. Certificates from all water or ditch companies furnishing water to the real property described in Schedule "A" hereof, showing the amount of any unpaid assessments or other charges with respect to the interest of the SELLER in such companies.

g. Policies of insurance duly endorsed to reflect the interest of the PURCHASER in the PROPERTY as PURCHASER under Contract for Deed.

h. Instruments transferring to PURCHASER the grazing permits described in Schedule "A."

i. Any documents required by the title insurance company, such as Corporate Resolutions, Stockholders' Consents, Registration Certificates, etc.

2. The following documents shall be delivered by or on behalf of PURCHASER at the closing, against receipt of the foregoing documents to be delivered by the SELLER:

a. A cashier's check representing part payment of the purchase price described in Paragraph A (1) hereof.

b. A certified check representing part payment of the purchase price as described in Paragraph A (2) hereof.

c. Contract for Deed in the form set forth in Schedule "C" of this contract.

d. Assumption agreement pursuant to which PURCHASER assumes performance of all of the obligations of the lessee arising from and after the closing under the LEASES.

e. Signed lease in the form attached hereto as Schedule "E" under which the SELLER becomes the lessee and the PURCHASER becomes the lessor of PROPERTY. SELLER hereby agrees to execute said lease at the closing.

f. Any documents required by the title insurance company, such as Corporate Resolutions, Stockholders' Consents, Registration Certificates, etc.

E. *Interim Maintenance*

Pending the closing SELLER shall operate the PROPERTY in accordance with good ranch management and shall not permit any of the PROPERTY to deteriorate, reasonable wear and tear excepted, nor shall SELLER commit waste on any of the PROPERTY between the date of this contract and the closing. In addition to the foregoing, SELLER agrees to continue to maintain the fire and extended coverage insurance policies now owned by the SELLER in full force and effect and to renew any of such policies which might otherwise terminate between the date of this contract and the closing.

F. *Fire or Other Casualty*

If, prior to the closing, a fire or other casualty shall damage any of the buildings or improvements included in the PROPERTY, this contract shall remain in full force, and PURCHASER shall not be entitled to any abatement of the purchase price as a result of any such damage. However, the SELLER shall promptly repair any such damage and restore any such building or improvement to its prior condition and shall collect and apply the proceeds of the fire insurance to the cost thereof.

G. *Interim Condemnation*

In the event of the commencement of any condemnation proceedings between the date of this contract and the date of closing with respect to any portion of the PROPERTY, PURCHASER may terminate this contract by written notice to SELLER. If PURCHASER fails to terminate this contract as aforesaid, SELLER shall assign to PURCHASER at the closing the right to receive any condemnation award or other compensation payable to the SELLER.

H. *Condition of the* PROPERTY

SELLER should represent to PURCHASER that there are no existing building and/or land requirements pursuant to any laws, codes, or ordinances in any municipality, county, township, or state government requiring any improvements to be made to such property. SELLER has not made and does not make any representation as to the physical condition, expenses, operation, or any other matter affecting or relating to the property to be sold, except as in this contract (including the Schedules attached hereto) specifically set forth, and PURCHASER hereby acknowledges that no such representations have been made. Except as otherwise provided in this contract, PURCHASER agrees to take the PROPERTY "as is" in such condition as the same may be on the date of closing.

I. *Previous Understandings*

It is understood and agreed that all understandings and agreements heretofore had between the parties hereto are merged in this contract, which alone fully and completely expresses their agreement, and that this contract is entered into after full investigation, neither party relying on any statement or representation not embodied in this contract (including the Schedules hereto).

J. *Notice*

Any notice which either party may desire or be required to serve hereunder shall be given by registered or certified air mail, return receipt requested, addressed to the party upon whom such notice is intended to be served, at such party's address as hereinbefore set forth, with postage and registration or certification charges paid for. A copy of any notice sent hereunder shall be sent by first class air mail to Kansas City Title Insurance Company, Kansas City, Missouri 64108.

K. *Agents and Commissions*

PURCHASER represents that he has dealt only with Oppenheimer Industries, Inc., and that, insofar as PURCHASER knows, no other broker is entitled to any commission payable in connection with this transaction. SELLER agrees that said Oppenheimer Industries, Inc., was the only real estate broker negotiating this sale and further agrees to pay said Oppenheimer Industries, Inc., FOUR THOUSAND DOLLARS ($4,000) at the closing of this sale, and FIVE THOUSAND DOLLARS ($5,000) on the first and second anniversary dates of the closing of this sale or a total of FOURTEEN THOUSAND DOLLARS ($14,000).

L. *Representatives and Assigns*

This contract shall bind and inure to the benefit of the SELLER, his personal representatives and assigns; and shall bind and inure to the benefit of the PURCHASER and its successors, representatives, or assigns.

M. *State Laws*

This contract and all exhibits hereto shall be governed and construed in accordance with the laws of the State of Wyoming.

IN WITNESS WHEREOF, the parties hereunto subscribe their names.

PURCHASER:	SELLER:
THE SMITH COMPANY	JONES CORPORATION, a Wyoming Corporation
By: /s/ Joe Smith, President	By: /s/ Tom Jones
Joe Smith, President	Tom Jones, President
Attest: /s/ Robert Smith	Attest: /s/ Mary Jones
Secretary	Secretary

There are four types of legal descriptions generally used:

1. Rectangular Survey
2. Lot Numbers of Plot or Map
3. Metes and Bounds
4. Monuments

The *Rectangular Survey* was adopted by Congress as early as May 20, 1785 and is used outside the original 13 states. This (rectangular survey) refers to a grid of north and south (meridians) and east and west (parallels) lines surveyed by the government. Identification of property is east or west so many ranges or vertical rows of checks from the north and south line called a "Principal Meridian" and so many horizontal rows of tiers or townships north of an east and west line called the "Base Line."

Distance between the parallels and meridians is 24 miles and the area contained therein is called a check. In this area are 16 townships and the townships are further divided into 36 sections of a mile square each. The section is further divided into halves, quarters, and smaller subdivisions.

Fractional sections on the north and west side of the townships are due to corrections made of the survey lines for the curvature of the earth. This results in these sections having more or less 640 acres, depending upon corrections. In describing these sections the words "Fractional Sections" should be used.

Lot Number. The lot number is used in urban centers where there has been a concentrated development of land, a property is transformed from a farm or vacant land into a subdivision laid out in numbered lots. The plan, if approved, is accepted by the municipality and recorded.

Metes and Bounds. The oldest method describing land is by "Metes and Bounds." Metes are measures of length—feet, inches, perches (1 perch = 16 1/2 feet). Bounds are artificial and natural boundaries such as streets, roads, adjoining farms, roads, and streams. Metes determine the certain quantity of land (acreage) while bounds confine that quantity within certain fixed limits. Such a description should have a definitely ascertained starting point, . . . and then proceed clockwise, tracing the lines by directions distances back to the point of beginning.

Monuments. In rural areas, descriptions of monuments are still frequently used. Land is cheap and a survey to determine the exact courses and distances would be of appreciable cost. At the end of the description it is customary to insert "containing 64 acres, more or less." The description by monuments does not lend itself readily to an examination of the title, particularly for one not familiar with the locale of the property. A description conveying "10 acres more or less" of other lands, and not locating the particular 10 acres, would be void, owing to uncertainty.[2]

Note that in the legal description of the Smith Ranch which follows, that combinations of all four types of description are used for various portions of the property.

Exhibit "A"

The following described lands situate, lying and being in Jefferson County, Montana:

TOWNSHIP ONE (1) SOUTH, RANGE FOUR (4) WEST

All of that portion of the Southwest Quarter of the Northwest Quarter (SW¼NW¼) and the Northwest Quarter of the Southwest Quarter (NW¼SW¼) of Section Seven (7), Township One (1) South, Range Four (4) West of the M.P.M., lying South of the South boundary line of that tract above described as conveyed to W. S. Gillespie by deed of record in the office of the County Clerk and Recorder of said Jefferson County in Book 43 of Deeds at page 450, and lying West and North of the Jefferson River.

TOWNSHIP ONE (1) SOUTH, RANGE FIVE (5) WEST

Lot Four (4) of Section Two (2).
All of Section Three (3).
Lot numbered Two (2) and that portion of Lot numbered Three (3) and the Southwest Quarter of the Northeast Quarter (SW¼NE¼) and the Northwest Quarter of the Southeast Quarter (NW¼SE¼) lying East of the Silver Bow-Jefferson County line in Section Six (6), Township One (1) South, Range Five (5) West, M.P.M.

[2] Robert W. Semenow, *Questions and Answers on Real Estate*, 4th Edition, Prentice-Hall, Inc., 1961, pp. 25-29.

All of Section Nine (9), save and except for a tract of land containing twenty-eight (28) acres, more or less, being described as in the shape of a triangle with the base to the North and the East line of which extends from a point about one thousand (1,000) feet East of the Northwest corner of said Section Nine (9) and runs Southwesterly to a point on the West section line of said Section Nine (9) about five hundred (500) feet North from the Northwest corner of the Southwest Quarter (SW¼) of said Section.

The Southeast Quarter (SE¼) and the East Half, Northeast Quarter (E½NE¼) of Section Ten (10).

All of Section Eleven (11), save and except that portion of the Northeast Quarter of the Northeast Quarter (NE¼NE¼) conveyed to C. W. Winslow by deed recorded in Book 44 of Deeds at page 112, records of said Jefferson County, and being that portion lying East of the County Road, and also, save and except for that portion of the Southwest Quarter of the Southeast Quarter (SW¼SE¼) of said Section Eleven (11) used as a cemetery.

All of Section Twelve (12), Township One (1) South, Range Five (5) West of the Montana Principal Meridian, save and except for the following described tracts of land:

(1) The Northwest Quarter of the Northwest Quarter (NW¼NW¼).

(2) The Southeast Quarter of the Southeast Quarter (SE¼SE¼).

(3) That portion of said Section Twelve (12) lying East of the East boundary line of the Ruby Valley Branch of the Northern Pacific Railway Company, and North of the South boundary line of a tract of land heretofore conveyed to W. S. Gillespie by deed of record in the office of the County Clerk and Recorder of said Jefferson County in Book 43 of Deeds at page 450, the West end of said South boundary line bears South 24° 06' West 6984 feet from the point of intersection of the East side line of said right-of-way with the North boundary of Section One (1), in said Township and Range, and running thence South 85° 12' East along said South boundary line 5335 feet as it intersects the East boundary line of said Section Twelve (12) and continues on to the West bank of the Jefferson River in Section Seven (7), Township One (1) South, Range Four (4) West of the M.P.M.

(4) All of that portion of said Section Twelve (12) described by metes and bounds as follows: Beginning at the Southwest corner of the tract herein excepted, which is the Southwest corner of the Northeast Quarter of the Northwest Quarter (NE¼NW¼) of said Section Twelve (12), and running thence easterly along the South boundary line of said Section Twelve (12) a distance of 796.6 feet to the West boundary line of the Ruby Valley Branch of the Northern Pacific Railway Company right-of-way; thence, North 24° 06' East along the West boundary line of said right-of-way 1446.5 feet to the North boundary line of said Northeast Quarter of the Northwest Quarter (NE¼NW¼) of said Section Twelve (12); thence, South 86° 43' West along the North boundary line of said Northeast Quarter of the Northwest Quarter (NE¼NW¼) of said Section Twelve (12) a distance of 1389.5 feet; thence, southerly 1240.8 feet to the Southwest corner of the tract described, being the place of beginning, and containing 31.83 acres, more or less.

The North Half (N½) and all of that portion of the North Half of the Southwest Quarter (N½SW¼) and the Northwest Quarter of the Southeast Quarter (NW¼SE¼) lying North of the Jefferson River, all in Section Fourteen (14), Township One (1) South, Range Five (5) West, M.P.M.

TOWNSHIP ONE (1) NORTH, RANGE FIVE (5) WEST

The North Half (N½); the Southeast Quarter (SE¼) and that portion of the Southwest Quarter (SW¼) of Section Thirty-One (31) lying North and East of the Silver Bow-Jefferson County line in said Section Thirty-One (31), Township One (1) North, Range Five (5) West, M.P.M.

TOWNSHIP ONE (1) NORTH, RANGE SIX (6) WEST

The Northeast Quarter of the Northeast Quarter (NE¼NE¼) of Section Thirty-Five (35), Township One (1) North, Range Six (6) West, M.P.M., lying North and East of the Silver Bow-Jefferson County line.

The following described lands situate, lying and being in MADISON COUNTY, MONTANA:[3]

TOWNSHIP ONE (1) SOUTH, RANGE FIVE (5) WEST

Lots numbered Three (3), Four (4), Five (5), and Six (6); the Southeast Quarter of the Northwest Quarter (SE¼NW¼); the Northeast Quarter of the Southwest Quarter (NE¼SW¼); and that portion of the Southwest Quarter of the Northeast Quarter (SW¼NE¼); and the Northwest Quarter of the Southeast Quarter (NW¼SE¼) of Section Six (6), Township One (1) South, Range Five (5) West, M.P.M., lying West of the Silver Bow-Jefferson County line.

All of Section Nine (9), Township One (1), Range Five (5) West of the M.P.M., save and except for that certain tract of land containing twenty-eight (28) acres, more or less, described as in the shape of a triangle with a base to the North and the East line of which extends from a point about one thousand (1,000) feet East of the Northwest corner of said Section Nine (9) about five hundred (500) feet North from the Northwest corner of the Southwest Quarter (SW¼) of said Section Nine (9).

All of the South Half of the Southwest Quarter (S½SW¼) of Section Ten (10), Township One (1) South, Range Five (5) West which lies in said Silver Bow County.

All of the following described lands lying in Section Fifteen (15), Township One (1) South, Range Five (5) West of the M.P.M.: The North Half (N½), the Southwest Quarter (SW¼), the West Half of the Southeast Quarter (W½SE¼) and the North Half of the Northeast Quarter of the Southeast Quarter (N½NE¼SE¼) of said Section Fifteen (15) lying North of the County Road; save and except for that portion of said lands lying South of the County Road and beginning at the West end of the tract herein excepted at a point on the South boundary line of said Section Fifteen (15) and the center of the County Road from which the Southwest corner of said Section Fifteen (15) marked

[3] The attached diagrams will show the reader how the legal description of that portion of the ranch in Silver Bow County would look plotted out on a section map.

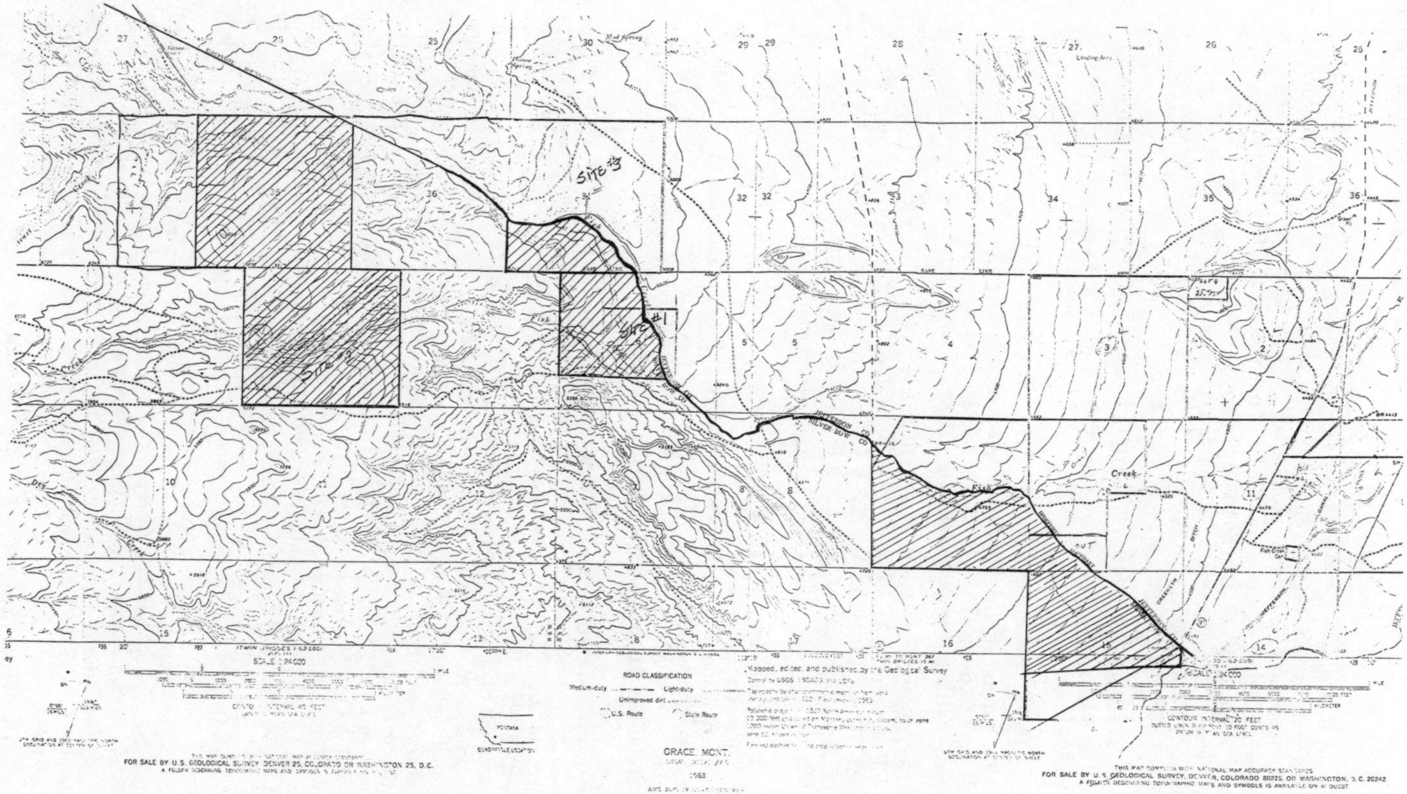

Site #3
Site #1
Site #2
Fish Creek
Mud Spring
Landing Field
JEFFERSON CO
SILVER BOW CO
BASE LINE
SCALE 1:24 000
ROAD CLASSIFICATION
Medium-duty
Light-duty
Unimproved dirt
U.S. Route
State Route
Mapped, edited, and published by the Geological Survey
CONTOUR INTERVAL 40 FEET
CONTOUR INTERVAL 20 FEET
MONTANA
QUADRANGLE LOCATION
GRACE, MONT.
1963
FOR SALE BY U.S. GEOLOGICAL SURVEY, DENVER 25, COLORADO OR WASHINGTON 25, D.C.
THIS MAP COMPLIES WITH NATIONAL MAP ACCURACY STANDARDS
FOR SALE BY U. S. GEOLOGICAL SURVEY, DENVER, COLORADO 80225, OR WASHINGTON, D. C. 20242
A FOLDER DESCRIBING TOPOGRAPHIC MAPS AND SYMBOLS IS AVAILABLE ON REQUEST

by an iron pipe bears West 950.4 feet, and thence East along the South boundary of said Section Fifteen (15) a distance of 3009.6 feet to the Southeast corner of the West Half of the Southeast Quarter (W½SE¼) of said Section Fifteen (15); thence, North along the East boundary of the West Half of the Southeast Quarter (W½SE¼) of said Section Fifteen (15) a distance of 1792.8 feet to a point in the center of the County Road; thence, South 59° 13' West along the center of the County Road 3503 feet to the place of beginning.

TOWNSHIP ONE (1) SOUTH, RANGE SIX (6) WEST

All of Section Two (2), Township One (1) South, Range Six (6) West, M.P.M.

TOWNSHIP ONE (1) NORTH, RANGE FIVE (5) WEST

That portion of the Southwest Quarter (SW¼) of Section Thirty-one (31), Township One (1) North, Range Five (5) West, M.P.M., lying west of the Silver Bow-Jefferson County line.

TOWNSHIP ONE (1) NORTH, RANGE SIX (6) WEST

All of Section Thirty-five (35), Township One (1) North, Range Six (6) West, M.P.M., except for a 9.4-acre tract in the Northeast Quarter of the Northeast Quarter (NE¼NE¼) lying in Jefferson County, Montana.

The following described lands situate, lying and being in MADISON COUNTY, MONTANA:

That portion of the Southwest Quarter (SW¼) and the West Half of the Southeast Quarter (W½SE¼) of Section Fifteen (15), Township One (1) South, Range Five (5) West, M.P.M., lying North of the State Secondary Highway to Whitehall, Montana, as now constructed.

SUBJECT, however, to such reservations and exceptions as are contained in conveyances to the present owners or their predecessors in interest, and further subject to such rights-of-way and easements over and across said premises as appear of record.

Excepting therefrom the tracts, conveyed by and subject to the reservations, covenants, conditions, and rights-of-way contained in the following instruments:

1. Deed, dated March 1, 1938, Excelsior Realty Company to Montana Power Company, the rights to erect and maintain electric transmission system and telephone system over and across NE¼NW¼ and W½NW¼, Section Fifteen (15), Township One (1) South, Range Five (5) West and SE¼SE¼ Section Ten (10), Township One (1) South, Range Five (5) West and NW¼ Section Eleven (11), Township One (1) South, Range Five (5) West.

2. Deed dated November 18, 1897, by A. B. Knight, *et al.*, to Gaylord and Ruby Valley Railway Company for strip of land 100 feet wide being 50 feet on each side of the center line of said Railway over and across: W½, NW¼NE¼NE¼NW¼, Section Twelve (12), Township One (1) South, Range Five (5) West.

3. Deed dated December 27, 1897, by Walter Bumby, single, to Gaylord and Ruby Valley Railway Company, a similar strip of land over and across E½NE¼, Section Fourteen (14), Township One (1) South, Range Five (5) West.

4. Deed dated January 11, 1934, Excelsior Realty Company to State of Montana, for easement for State Highway over and across W½SW¼ and SW¼, Section Nine (9), Township One (1) South, Range Five (5) West.

5. Deed dated August 20, 1907, executed by Creeklyn Stock Farm to

Madison River Power Company for right-of-way for electric pole line as constructed from switch house of second party near town of Parrot to Green Campbell Mine across ranch belonging to party of first part, situated on and near Fish Creek.

6. Deed dated September 14, 1938, executed by George Bonawitz, *et al.*, to Excelsior Realty Company for a strip of land 10 feet wide abutting Creeklyn Ditch on east side thereof, as ditch crosses W½W½NW¼ of said Section and also an additional one-half acre parcel in said W½W½NW¼ on the lower side of said ditch next to Jefferson River.

7. Deed dated April 15, 1952, by Caroline McGill and Jack Doyle to State of Montana for tract in E½, Section Fifteen (15), Township One (1) South, Range Five (5) West as recorded in Book 226 of Deeds, page 223, Silver Bow County, Montana.

8. Deed dated September 18, 1960, executed by Jack Doyle, a single man, to Robert W. Thometz, for strip of land for right-of-way easement 15 feet wide, over and across the S½S½ of Section Twelve (12), Township One (1) South, Range Five (5) West, as recorded in Book 83 of Deeds, page 416.

9. Final Order of Condemnation, dated March 8, 1961, in action, The State of Montana, *et al.*, vs. Jack Doyle, *et al.*, condemning a perpetual easement for right-of-way over a tract of land in the W½, Section Fourteen (14), Township One (1) South, Range Five (5) West for highway purposes, as recorded in Book 84 of Deeds, page 287, records of Jefferson County, and in Book 36 of Real Estate Misc., page 325, records of Silver Bow County.

Together with all water, water rights, water ditches, dams, flumes, reservoirs, and rights to the waters or water rights, whether acquired by Decree, Appropriation or Location, appurtenant, appendant, or in anywise belonging or appertaining or used in connection with or appurtenant to any part of said lands, including, but not limited to, the following:

75 miner's inches of the waters of Big Fish Creek.

All of the waters of Little Fish Creek.

250 miner's inches of the waters of Fish Creek, decreed, with priority of 1888, and a flood right of 1,000 miner's inches.

450 shares (dry shares) of the capital stock of the Jefferson Canal Company, a Montana corporation.

400 shares of the capital stock of the Fish Creek Irrigating Ditch Company, a Montana corporation. (400 shares of said stock entitles the owner thereof to 400 miner's inches of water.)

1,500 miner's inches of the waters of the Jefferson River, by appropriation, undecreed.

23/40th of the Class A" rights of the Creeklyn Ditch, an unincorporated association (also described as 23/52nds of the ditch rights of the Creeklyn Ditch, an unincorporated association).

Schedule "B"

I. The Water Rights included in this sale are:

A. That attributable to the upper ranch are:

1. 75 miner inches of water from Big Fish Creek.
2. All of the water from Little Fish Creek.

B. That attributable to the lower ranch are:

1. 1,250 miner inches of water from Big Fish Creek.
2. 450 miner inches of water from the Jefferson Canal.
3. 400 miner inches of water from Fish Creek Canal.
4. 1,500 miner inches of unadjudicated water from the Jefferson River.
5. 23/40ths of "A" stock of the Creeklyn Ditch Company.

II. SELLER represents and warrants that (1) SELLER has title to the water rights described in "I" above and that such rights will in fact be transferred to the PURCHASER at the closing; (2) that all water used in connection with the operation of the PROPERTY described in Schedule "A" during the *three* years last past was received by virtue of the water rights described above and no water was received from other sources; (3) that there will be no reduction in the rights to receive water described above during the period of one year from the date of closing.

In the wide arid lands of the Great Plains, water rights are often more valuable than the land and can be sold separatey. (Courtesy, Mr. Byron B. Wolfe, Kansas City Posse of The Westerners)

III. PURCHASER shall have the right, at its cost to hire an attorney to check and determine that the water rights described above actually do exist. In the event that it is found that there is a substantial variation in the water rights from that described above, the PURCHASER, at its option, shall have the right to cancel this contract, in which event it shall be null and void and the money deposited returned to the PURCHASER.

IV. It is agreed that the PURCHASER will suffer substantial damages if any person, firm, or corporation claims within a period of one year from the date of closing (and is ultimately successful in maintaining such claim) that the PURCHASER is not the owner of any portion of the water rights described above. The amount of such damages shall be determined by appraisers appointed as described below and the amount of such damage shall be deducted from the unpaid principal amount of the purchase money second mortgage. Appraisers shall be appointed as follows:

A. Each party shall appoint one appraiser who shall be a member of the faculty of a university which has as its primary purpose the study and teaching of agriculture.

B. The two appraisers thus appointed shall appoint a third appraiser having similar qualifications.

C. If the appraisers appointed by the parties are unable to agree upon a third appraiser, such third appraiser shall be selected in accordance with the rules of the American Arbitration Association.

The determination of a majority of the appraisers shall be binding upon both parties and may be entered as an arbitration award in accordance with the laws of the State of Montana.

The representations and warranties and provisions relating to appraisal contained in this Schedule "B" shall survive the closing and the delivery of the Deed.

SCHEDULE "C"

Contract for Deed

THIS DUPLICATE CONTRACT, made and entered into this ____________ day of January, 1967, by and between JONES CORPORATION, a Wyoming corporation, of Yellowstone County, State of Wyoming, hereinafter referred to as "SELLER," and ____

____

hereinafter referred to as "PURCHASER."

WITNESSETH: SELLER agrees to sell, and PURCHASER agrees to purchase the real estate described in Schedule "A" attached hereto, together with all improvements and appurtenances thereto, subject to the easements and restrictions set forth.

1. PURCHASER hereby agrees to pay for said premises the sum of THREE HUNDRED THIRTY THOUSAND DOLLARS ($330,000) as follows:

a. THIRTY-THREE THOUSAND DOLLARS ($33,000) upon the execution of this agreement, the receipt of which is hereby acknowledged.

b. ONE HUNDRED TWENTY-ONE THOUSAND FIVE HUNDRED DOLLARS ($121,500) with interest from ________________________, 1967, at the rate of six percent (6%) per annum payable in twenty equal annual installments of principal of SIX THOUSAND SEVENTY-FIVE DOLLARS ($6,075) together with interest on the unpaid balance outstanding with succeeding installments. The first principal payment is due January 1, 1968. However, at the closing PURCHASER shall pay interest in advance equal to six months interest on the principal sum and shall pay the remaining interest due for the year 1967 on the first payment date. PURCHASER shall have the privilege of prepaying without penalty any or all of the principal amount above stated at any time during the term of this contract.

c. ONE HUNDRED SEVENTY-FIVE THOUSAND FIVE HUNDRED DOLLARS ($175,500) to be paid by PURCHASER accepting payment obligations when due as provided by a promissory note secured by a first mortgage on the herein described property for the above amount between the SELLER and John Hancock Mutual Life Insurance Company dated ____________________________ and which is attached hereto as Schedule ________ and made a part of this contract. PURCHASER shall be responsible for the payments only when due and shall not be responsible for the unpaid principal to the John Hancock Mutual Life Insurance Company beyond the principal and interest payments when due.

2. PURCHASER shall pay all taxes and special assessments that may hereinafter become a lien against said property as they become due and at least ten (10) days before they become delinquent.

3. PURCHASER shall keep the buildings on said real estate in good repair and condition, and insured against loss or damage by standard form of fire insurance policy with "extended coverage" endorsements, in the sum of not less than eighty percent (80%) of the full insurable value thereof, in some good insurance company; loss, if any, to be payable to said parties as their interests may appear; and PURCHASER shall deliver policies of insurance to SELLER. In case the buildings on said premises shall be so destroyed or damaged, the proceeds from said insurance shall be used in the reconstruction or repair of said buildings, if PURCHASER so elects, or the same shall be applied on the balance due on this contract, but, in any event such funds shall stand as security for the payments herein required to be made.

4. Should the PURCHASER fail to pay the taxes and special assessments upon said premises as agreed or should fail to keep the buildings thereon insured as herein provided, SELLER may do so and all amounts so paid together with interest

thereon at the rate of seven percent (7%) per annum shall constitute additional consideration to be paid by PURCHASER; and such payment by SELLER shall not be construed as a waiver of rights accruing to SELLER by reason of breach of the contract of PURCHASER.

5. If any default is made in any of the payments or agreements above mentioned to be performed by PURCHASER, SELLER may notify PURCHASER as specified herein and PURCHASER shall have sixty (60) days from the date of such notice to correct such default. If default is not so remedied in the time specified, then the SELLER may, at his option, either declare the entire remainder of the purchase money due and collectable at once or he may declare this agreement forfeited by reason of such default and at once retake possession of said real estate; and in the event of such forfeiture all payments theretofore made by PURCHASER shall be retained by SELLER, and all such payments be deemed as having been made in consideration of the advantage secured to PURCHASER under this agreement; and this condition and the time of payments are declared to be an essential element of this contract. The failure of the SELLER to declare such forfeiture upon any such default shall not stop it from so doing at any time thereafter in case such default should continue, or upon the occurrence of any subsequent default. In case the rights of the PURCHASER under this agreement shall be declared forfeited as aforesaid, PURCHASER and any other person who may be in possession of said real estate will peaceably remove therefrom and in default thereof may be treated as tenants holding over unlawfully after the expiration of a lease, and may be ousted and removed as such.

In the event any notice of forfeiture is caused to be served upon the PURCHASER or if suit is commenced to enforce payment of any sums due under this agreement or to enforce any of the terms of this agreement, SELLER's reasonable attorney's fees are to be considered as part of the costs of service of notice or of suit and shall be added to the total amount necessary for redemption.

6. In case the rights of the PURCHASER under this agreement shall be declared forfeited as aforesaid, any and all improvements of whatever nature made by PURCHASER upon the above described real estate shall become and be the property of the SELLER.

7. The following documents shall be delivered to ____________________

____,
or such other place as may be mutually agreed upon from time to time by the parties hereto, by the SELLER to be held in escrow until the entire amount to be paid under Paragraph number 1 (b) hereof has been paid in full:

a. General Warranty Deeds, each of which shall be properly executed and acknowledged, conveying to the PURCHASER a fee simple title in the real estate included in this sale as described in Schedule "A" hereof, together with all of the oil, gas, and other minerals and mineral rights in and under such real estate and all portions of the water rights included in this sale as may be conveyed by General Warranty Deed. There shall be attached to the Deed to be recorded in Jefferson County all the required United States Documentary and other revenue stamps and evidence of the payment of all state and local transfer taxes and charges, if any.

b. Bill of Sale transferring to PURCHASER all personal property described in Schedule "A" and such portion of any water rights described in Schedule "B" as may be transferred by Bill of Sale.

c. Instruments assigning to PURCHASER the shares of stock in the water and ditch companies described in Schedule "B" to which shall be affixed all necessary Federal and state transfer tax stamps.

d. Instruments transferring to PURCHASER the grazing permit described in Schedule "A."

When the entire amount to be paid under Paragraph 1 (b) hereof has been paid in full, the documents so deposited shall be given the PURCHASER, the Deeds to be recorded, and this contract shall have been fulfilled and shall come to an end. In the event of a default by the PURCHASER, which shall not have been remedied within the time specified, the documents so deposited shall be returned to the SELLER and it shall retake possession of the premises as provided in Paragraph number 5 hereof and this contract shall thereafter be null and void. All payments to be paid under this contract shall be made to the ____________ ______________________________ or to such other escrow agent as may be mutually agreed upon from time to time by the parties hereto. Such escrow agent shall disperse the funds so paid to the proper parties as stated herein and all costs of such escrow agent shall be paid by the SELLER.

8. Any notice to be sent hereunder shall be given by registered or certified United States air mail, return receipt requested, addressed to the PURCHASER at ____ or such other place as it may specify from time to time to the SELLER, and to the SELLER at ____ or such other place as it may specify from time to time in writing to the PURCHASER.

It is agreed by and between the parties hereto that for the purpose hereof, the words "PURCHASER" and "SELLER" shall denote the plural thereof as well as the singular and that the word "it" denotes the feminine and masculine gender as well as the neuter, as may be applicable. It is also agreed by and between the parties hereto that this contract shall be binding upon the heirs, personal representatives, successors and assigns of the respective parties.

IN WITNESS WHEREOF, the parties hereto have executed this contract the day and year first above written.

SELLER
JONES CORPORATION, a Wyoming corporation
By: /s/ Tom Jones
President

ATTEST:
/s/ Robert Smith
Secretary

BUYER
THE SMITH COMPANY a California corporation
By: /s/ Joe Smith
President

ATTEST:
/s/ Robert Smith
Secretary

SCHEDULE "D"

Know All Men by These Pres.

That, JONES CORPORATION, a Wyoming corporation, of Yellowstone County, State of Wyoming, party of the first part, hereinafter called the mortgagor (which term wherever used in this mortgage, so far as the context may permit or require, it is hereby agreed shall be construed to include and shall include the heirs, executors, administrators, successors and assigns of the party of the first part), in consideration of the sum of ONE HUNDRED EIGHTY THOUSAND DOLLARS ($180,000) paid by John Hancock Mutual Life Insurance Company, a corporation duly established and existing under the laws of The Commonwealth of Massachusetts, with its principal office at 200 Berkeley Street, in Boston, Suffolk

Percentage of all farm land purchases financed, by type of lender, 1955-65

Year	Seller contract	Seller mortgages	Commercial banks	Insurance companies	Federal land banks	Other
	Percent	Percent	Percent	Percent	Percent	Percent
1955	13	9	13	12	6	11
1956	12	13	13	12	7	10
1957	14	13	12	11	7	10
1958	16	13	11	10	6	11
1959	17	12	12	9	7	10
1960	19	9	9	11	8	11
1961	20	8	9	10	8	12
1962	18	11	11	10	7	14
1963	21	7	14	9	7	15
1964	21	7	13	10	7	15
1965	21	7	13	12	7	13

Note that the highest percentage and growing greater is the "Contract for Deed" taken back in the seller's contract. The one just described in the text as Schedule "C" was a "second." The insurance company mortgage that follows is a "first." The holder of the first mortgage gets paid in full before the holder of the second gets anything.

County, Massachusetts, party of the second part, hereinafter called the mortgagee (which term wherever used in this mortgage, so far as the context may permit or require, it is hereby agreed shall be construed to include and shall include the successors and assigns of the party of the second part), have granted, bargained, sold and conveyed and do hereby grant, bargain, sell, convey and confirm unto said John Hancock Mutual Life Insurance Company, its successors and assigns, forever the following described real estate in the County of Madison, Jefferson, and Silver Bow and State of Montana, to wit:

(Legal description same as Sales Contract, Exhibit "A")

together with all water, water rights, ditches, aquaducts, appropriations and franchises upon, leading to, connected with or had and enjoyed in connection with said real estate and each and every part thereof, whether represented by shares of capital stock in any ditch company or by actual individual ownership or otherwise or which may hereafter be acquired by the mortgagors during the existence of this mortgage and used in connection with said real estate or any part thereof.

To HAVE AND TO HOLD the same, with all and singular the tenements, hereditaments and appurtenances thereunto belonging or in any wise appertaining, and all rights of homestead exemption and every contingent right or estate therein (all of which are hereinafter called the mortgaged premises) unto the mortgagee forever. And the mortgagor does hereby covenant and agree that at the delivery hereof it is the lawful owner of the mortgaged premises and seized of a good and indefensible estate of inheritance therein, free and clear of all encumbrances, except as aforesaid, and that it will warrant and defend the same in the quiet and peaceable possession of the mortgagee, against the claims of all persons whomsoever.

THE MORTGAGOR HEREBY COVENANTS AND AGREES:

FIRST. That this mortgage is given as security for the performance and observance of the covenants and agreements herein contained.

SECOND. To pay the principal amount of ONE HUNDRED EIGHTY THOUSAND DOLLARS ($180,000) (which amount the mortgagee has actually loaned to the mortgagor and for which amount the mortgagor is justly indebted to the mortgagee), with interest thereon, according to the terms of a certain note of even date herewith, executed by JONES CORPORATION to the order of said John Hancock Mutual Life Insurance Company, principal to be paid in installments as follows: $4,500.00 on January 1, 1967 and $4,500.00 each on the first days of January thereafter to January 1, 1985, inclusive; and $94,500.00 on January 1, 1986.

THIRD. To keep the buildings now or hereafter standing on the mortgaged premises insured against fire and such other casualties as the mortgagee may from time to time require and against which insurance is written at the time of such requirement, whether or not such insurance is now written, all such insurance to be in forms, in companies and in sums (not less than sufficient to avoid any claim on the part of the insurers for co-insurance) satisfactory to the mortagee; that all insurance policies shall be held by and be for the benefit of and shall be first payable in case of loss to the mortgagee and that at least fifteen (15) days before the expiration of each such policy a new and sufficient policy to take the place of the one so expiring shall be delivered to the mortgagee. The mortgagor hereby assigns to the mortgagee all moneys recoverable under each such policy. The mortgagor hereby appoints the mortgagee attorney irrevocable of the mortgagor to assign each such policy in the event of the foreclosure of this mortgage.

FOURTH. To pay before delinquent all taxes, assessments and charges of every nature and to whomsoever assessed, that may now or hereafter be levied or assessed upon the mortgaged premises or any part thereof, or upon this mortgage or the debt hereby secured.

FIFTH. To pay all sums the failure to pay which may result in the acquisition of a lien prior to the lien of this mortgage before such a prior lien may attach.

SIXTH. That, in case of default in the performance or observance of any of the covenants and agreements contained in paragraphs number "THIRD," "FOURTH," and "FIFTH" herein, the mortgagee, without prejudice to any rights given under subsequent paragraphs herein, may make advances to perform the same in behalf of the mortgagor and the mortgagor hereby agrees to repay all sums so advanced in its behalf, on demand, with interest from the date advanced at the highest rate per annum for which it is lawful to contract and all sums so advanced, with interest as aforesaid, shall be immediately due and payable and be secured hereby having the benefit of the lien hereby created, but no such advance shall be deemed to relieve the mortgagor from any default hereunder or impair any right or remedy consequent thereon, and the exercise of the rights to make advances granted in this paragraph shall be optional with the mortgagee and not obligatory, and the mortgagee shall not in any case be liable to the mortgagor for a failure to exercise any such right.

SEVENTH. To keep all fences, buildings, and other improvements now or hereafter standing on the mortgaged premises in good condition and repair and not to suffer strip or waste nor to do or permit any act by which the value of the mortgaged premises may be impaired.

EIGHTH. To pay to the mortgagee any moneys received as compensation for the taking of, or any possession of, or any interest in, the mortgaged premises or any part thereof by virtue of the right of eminent domain or in any other manner whatsoever, and all moneys received as damages for injury sustained by the mortgaged premises or any part thereof, said moneys to be applied on the indebtedness hereby secured;

NINTH. That the mortgagee shall be subrogated for further security to the lien, although released of record, of any and all encumbrances paid out of the proceeds of the loan secured by this mortgage.

TENTH. That, in case the mortgagee shall hereafter appear in any of the land departments of the United States Government, or in any court or tribunal whatsoever, to defend the title or possession of the mortgaged premises or the lien of this mortgage, or in case the mortgagee shall be made a party defendant to any action at law or suit in chancery by reason of the mortgagee being the holder of this mortgage and shall make an appearance in defense of said action or suit, all the costs and expenses of such appearance shall be allowed the mortgagee, and such costs and expenses shall bear interest from date of payment at the highest rate per annum for which it is lawful to contract, and said sum or sums so paid shall be immediately due and payable with the interest thereon as herein provided and shall be an additional lien upon the mortgaged premises and be secured by this mortgage, and may be collected in the same manner as the principal debt hereby secured, provided such action is not due to any act of the mortgagee exclusively. The term "costs and expenses" used in this paragraph shall include a reasonable attorney's fee.

PROVIDED, that, if payments are made as herein contemplated, then this conveyance shall be void.

But upon any default in the performance or observance of any of the covenants and agreements of any instrument now or hereafter evidencing or securing the principal debt hereby secured,

1. While any such default exists, the principal then remaining unpaid shall bear interest at the highest aggregate lawful rate per annum, as provided in said note.

2. Whether the mortgaged premises are homestead or not and without proof of any other ground for his appointment than the said default, if the mortgagee so elects, the mortgagee shall be entitled to the immediate appointment of a receiver to take possession and charge of the mortgaged premises, to rent the same and receive and collect the rents, issues and profits thereof under direction of the court and any amount so collected by such receiver shall be applied under the direction of the court.

3. If the mortgagee so elects, the principal then remaining unpaid, with accrued interest, shall at once become due and payable and the mortgagee may immediately cause this mortgage to be foreclosed in the manner prescribed by law.

In case of one or more defaults in the performance or observance of any of the covenants and agreements of any instrument now or hereafter evidencing or securing the principal debt hereby secured, the failure to exercise any right or remedy given herein in case of one or more subsequent defaults and notice of the exercise of such right or remedy is hereby waived, except for such notice as may be required by law.

In case of suit to foreclose this mortgage or to enforce the performance or observance of any of the covenants and agreements herein contained, the mortgagor shall pay such additional amount as the court may adjudge reasonable as attorney's fees in such suit, which attorney's fees are also secured hereby.

Notwithstanding any provision herein or in said note, the total liability for payments in the nature of interest shall not exceed the limits now imposed by the usury laws of the State of Montana.

Mortgagor hereby assigns to the mortgagee all rents, issues and profits of the mortgaged premises from and after default.

IN WITNESS WHEREOF, the said mortgagor has hereunto subscribed its name and affixed its seal this 5th day of August, 1966.

JONES CORPORATION

ATTEST: /s/ Mary Jones
Secretary

By /s/ Tom Jones, President

(Acknowledgments and Legal Descriptions added. All legal descriptions are the same as in Sales Contract, Exhibit "A.")

FEDERAL RANGE AND STATE LAND MORTGAGE RIDER

In addition to the agreements, covenants and conditions contained in the mortgage to which this rider is attached and of which it forms a part, the mortgagor hereby further covenants and agrees with the mortgagee, as follows:

In addition to the premises described in said mortgage, said mortgage shall extend to and include as part of the mortgaged premises and as security for the payment of the indebtedness, the payment of which is secured by said mortgage, all leases, permits, licenses, or privileges, written or otherwise, appurtenant or non-appurtenant, to said mortgaged premises now held by the mortgagor or hereafter issued, extended, or renewed to him by the United States or the State of ______________ or any Department, Bureau, or Agency of either, to rent, lease and/or use any of the public lands of the United States or said State for the purpose of grazing, pasturing and/or feeding livestock thereon.

To pay all rents, fees or charges now due or to become due under the terms of each lease, permit, license or privilege, written or otherwise, appurtenant or non-appurtenant, to said mortgaged premises, now held by the mortgagor or hereafter issued, extended or renewed to him by the United States or the said State, or any Department, Bureau or Agency of either; and to perform and observe every act, covenant, condition and stipulation necessary to keep each of the same in good standing as required by the terms thereof and by the laws, rules and regulations of the United States or said State; and, on the expiration of the term of each of the same, to apply for, and take every necessary step to secure the re-issue, renewal or extension of each of the same; and to assign, waive, pledge or endorse to the mortgagee each lease, permit, license or privilege hereafter issued, extended or renewed by any agency of the United States or said State.

That in the event the mortgagor fails to pay when due any rent, fees or charges payable under said leases, permits, licenses or privileges or any renewals or extensions thereof, or under the laws, rules and regulations of the United States or said State or any Governmental Agency thereof, the mortgagee may make such payments and the amount paid therefore shall become a part of the indebtedness secured by said mortgage and bear interest from the date of payment at the same rate specified in the note secured thereby on the principal thereof after default or maturity.

That in the event the mortgagor fails to perform all and singular the covenants, conditions, and agreements contained in said mortgage, including this rider, or upon receipt by the mortgagee of notice of the failure of the mortgagor to comply with the terms of said leases, permits, licenses or privileges, and/or the laws, rules and regulations of the United States or said State applicable thereto; then the mortgagee may exercise any and all rights provided by the terms of the mortgage to which this rider is attached in case of any default on the part of the mortgagor.

The word "mortgagee" as used in this rider shall be construed to mean the owner and holder of the security instrument to which this rider is attached, or any assignee, or transferee thereof. The word "mortgagor" as used in this rider shall be construed to mean any maker or makers of said security instrument, and also the vendee, devisee, successors, heirs and assigns of such mortgagor; and the word "mortgage" as used in this rider shall be construed to mean the security instrument to which this rider is attached.

This rider is attached to and forms a part of mortgage for $180,000.00, dated August 5, 1966, to the same extent as if it were set out in full therein and is identified therewith by the following signatures:

JONES CORPORATION
By: /s/ Tom Jones
President

ATTEST:
/s/ Mary Jones
Secretary

ATTACHED NOTE

$180,000 August 5, A.D. 1966

FOR VALUE RECEIVED, we the undersigned, JONES CORPORATION, a Wyoming corporation, hereby promises to pay to the order of JOHN HANCOCK MUTUAL LIFE INSURANCE COMPANY at its Home Office in Boston, Massachusetts, or at such other place as the holder of this note may from time to time designate, the principal sum of ONE HUNDRED EIGHTY THOUSAND DOLLARS ($180,000) with interest to be computed from August 5, 1966, at the rate of 6½ per centum per annum, payable on the first day of each January 1, beginning January 1, 1967, upon all principal remaining from time to time unpaid; principal to be paid in installments as follows: $4,500 on January 1, 1967 and $4,500 in the first day of each January thereafter to January 1, 1985, inclusive; and $94,500 on January 1, 1986.

Upon any default in the payment of principal or interest or in the performance or observance of any of the covenants or agreements of any instrument now or hereafter evidencing or securing this indebtedness; the principal then remaining unpaid shall bear interest at the rate of ____________ per centum per annum while such default exists, and the holder of this note may apply payments received on any amounts due hereunder or under the terms of any instrument now or hereafter evidencing or securing this indebtedness as said holder may determine. Upon any such default, if the legal holder of this note so elects, notice of election being expressly waived, the principal remaining unpaid and accrued interest shall at once become due and payable.

The undersigned agrees to pay all costs of collection when incurred, including reasonable attorney's fees. No extension of the time for the payment of this note or any installment hereof made by agreement with any person now or hereafter liable for the payment of this note shall operate to release, discharge, modify, change or affect the liability under this note of any of the undersigned not a party to such agreement. Notwithstanding any provision herein or in any instrument now or hereafter securing this indebtedness, the total liability for payments in the nature of interest shall not exceed the limits now imposed by the usury laws of ______________.

This note is given for a loan of ONE HUNDRED EIGHTY THOUSAND DOLLARS, and is secured by a first mortgage of even date herewith which is a lien on real estate in Madison, Jefferson, and Silver Bow, Montana, and shall be construed by the law of said state.

OPTION: The privilege is reserved of paying on the principal $100,000 or any multiple thereof on any interest paying date but not to exceed $36,000 in any one year, such privilege to be non-cumulative.

JONES CORPORATION
By: /s/ Tom Jones
President

ATTEST:
/s/ Mary Jones
Secretary

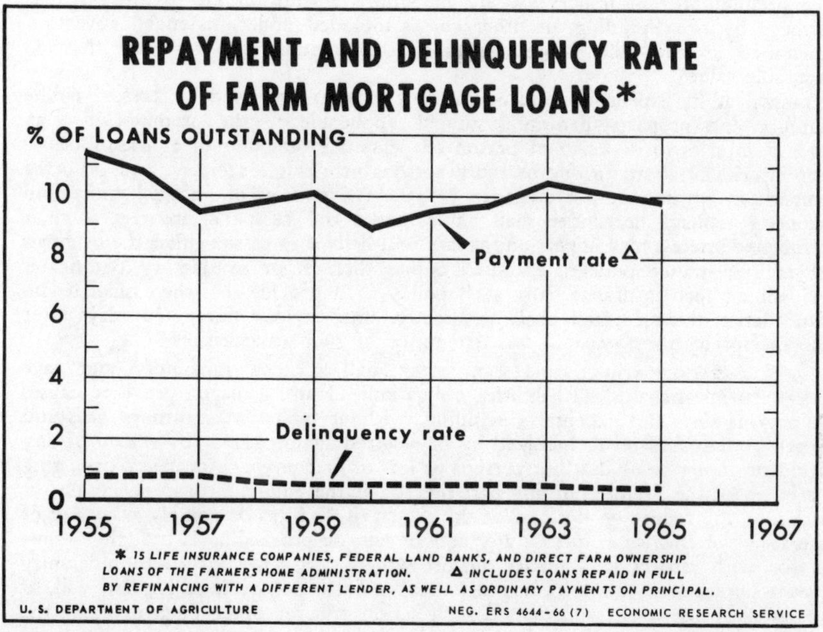

Delinquency rates on farm loans since 1940 have been lower on farm property than urban, principally because insurance companies and Federal Land Banks will not loan over 50% of value. Rapidly rising land values have salvaged many of the private loans. (Courtesy, USDA, Washington, D.C.)

SCHEDULE "E"

Lease

This lease is dated this ____________ day of ______________________, 1967, by and between THE SMITH COMPANY, Route 1, Rawlins, Wyoming, hereinafter designated as "LESSOR," and THE JONES CORPORATION, a Wyoming corporation, of Yellowstone County, State of Wyoming, hereinafter designated as "LESSEE."

WITNESSETH: That the LESSOR in consideration of the rent and covenants herein specified does hereby let and lease unto the LESSEE the property described in Schedule A attached hereto and a part hereof, for a term of three years, commencing on the ____________ day of ______________________,

1967, and ending on the ____________ day of ________________________, 1970.

1. RENTAL. LESSEE shall pay to LESSOR rent in the amount of FIFTY-SEVEN THOUSAND SEVEN HUNDRED DOLLARS, ($57,700) as follows:

a. SEVEN THOUSAND NINE HUNDRED FIFTY DOLLARS ($7,950) on the first day of September, 1967, and like amount on the 15th day of December, 1967;

b. TEN THOUSAND FOUR HUNDRED FIFTY DOLLARS ($10,450) on the first day of September, 1968, and a like amount on the 15th day of December, 1968, and on the first day of September, 1969, and the 15th day of December, 1969.

2. INSURANCE. As additional rental hereunder, LESSEE will pay when due the premium for insurance insuring the improvements on the premises against damage by fire, lightning, or other causes included under "extended coverage" insurance insuring said improvements in the amounts not less than the full insurable value.

LESSEE, at its expense will maintain with insurers approved by LESSOR, public liability and property damage insurance applicable to the premises, insuring against injuries to or death of person or persons in amounts of at least $300,000 per injuries or death to one or more persons in a single accident, and property damage in an amount not less than $25,000. All policies of public liability and property damage hereunder shall name LESSEE and LESSOR as insurers as their respective interest may appear and LESSEE will deliver to LESSOR either the originals of such insurance policies, executed copies thereof, or satisfactory certificates evidencing such insurance. Any such policy shall provide that there shall be no cancellation thereof which shall be effective until at least thirty (30) days after the receipt by the LESSOR of written notice of such cancellation.

3. INDEMNIFICATION BY LESSEE. LESSEE will protect, indemnify and save LESSOR harmless against all liabilities, obligations, claims, damages, penalties, causes of action, costs and expenses (including, without limitation, attorneys' fees and expenses) imposed on or incurred by or asserted against LESSOR by reason of any accident, injury to or death of persons or loss of or damage to property occurring on or about the Premises or any part thereof or the adjoining property, roads, or ways, or any failure on the part of the LESSEE to perform or comply with any of the terms of this lease. In case any action, suit, or proceeding is brought against LESSOR with respect to a matter against which LESSEE has agreed to indemnify LESSOR pursuant to the preceding sentence, LESSEE, upon LESSOR's request, will, at LESSEE's expense, resist and defend such action, suit, or proceeding, or cause the same to be resisted and defended by counsel designated by LESSEE and approved by LESSOR. The obligations of LESSEE under this Section shall survive any termination of this LEASE.

4. CARE, MAINTENANCE, USE, INSPECTION AND REPAIR OF THE PREMISES. LESSEE agrees at all times during the term hereof, at LESSEE's expense to:

a. keep the Premises and all improvements thereon and appurtenances thereto in good order, repair, and condition;

b. conform to and observe all laws, codes, ordinances, rules, and regulations of the County, State and Federal Government and all other public authorities, relating to the Premises or the use thereof;

c. not permit waste or nuisance on or about the Premises nor use nor permit the Premises or any part thereof to be used in such a way as to invalidate or prevent the obtaining of insurance on the improvements on said Premises or any part thereof, or increase the present premiums for such insurance;

d. refrain from over-grazing the Premises or committing or permitting any act whereby the leases from the State of Montana or any other leases will be breached or jeopardized in any manner;

e. maintain the present irrigation system on the Premises in as good a condition as received at the commencement of this term, normal wear and tear excepted;

f. maintain all fences in good condition;

g. prevent the growth of noxious weeds;

h. maintain the roads within or about the Premises in good condition;

i. exercise the same diligence and competence in caring for the Premises that would reasonably be exercised by a prudent rancher observing normal agricultural standards characteristic within the area of the Premises;

j. not remove nor allow anyone else to enter upon and remove from the Premises, during the term of this LEASE, any part or portion of the fences, improvements, trees, shrubbery of any kind or nature whatsoever upon the Premises at the commencement of the term of this lease;

k. at the expiration or termination of the term of this lease, to promptly deliver peaceable possession of the Premises to LESSOR as LESSOR's property, without compensation to LESSEE, in good condition and repair, normal wear and tear excepted;

l. permit LESSOR or any of its representatives, at any reasonable time during the term of this lease to enter upon the Premises or any part thereof, to inspect the same or to do anything therein that LESSEE is required to and shall have failed to do, any such corrective action to be at the expense of LESSEE.

5. CONDITION AND USE OF THE PREMISES. LESSEE is fully familiar with the physical condition of the Premises and has received the same in good and clean order and condition. LESSOR makes no representation or warranty with respect to the condition of the Premises or its fitness or availability for any particular use, and LESSOR shall not be liable for any latent or patent defect therein.

6. CLAIMS AGAINST LESSOR. Nothing contained in the LEASE shall constitute any consent or request by LESSOR for the performance of any labor or services or the furnishing of any materials or other property in respect to the Premises or any part thereof, nor as giving LESSEE any right, power or authority to contract for or permit the performance of any labor or services or furnishing of any materials or other property in such fashion as would permit the making of any claim against LESSOR in respect thereof.

a. LESSEE agrees that LESSOR may make any improvements at the sole cost and expense of LESSOR to subject Premises at sole discretion of LESSOR.

b. LESSOR reserves the right in event that rental payments are delinquent to deduct from LESSOR's obligation under contract for deed any payments due LESSEE. LESSEE shall also have the right in the event LESSOR fails to make payments pursuant to contract for deed to deduct rental payments therefrom.

7. RIGHT OF LESSOR TO PERFORM LESSEE'S COVENANTS. If LESSEE shall fail to perform any act required to be made or performed hereunder, LESSOR without notice to or demand upon LESSEE and without waiving or releasing any obligation or default may (but shall be under no obligation to) at any time thereafter perform such act for the account and at the expense of LESSEE. All sums so paid by LESSOR and all costs, fees, and expenses so incurred shall constitute additional rent hereunder with interest thereon at 8% per annum, payable with the next installment becoming due and payable of the net basic rent.

8. ASSIGNMENT OR SUBLETTING. The interest of LESSEE in this lease may not be assigned or otherwise transferred by LESSEE except with the prior written consent of LESSOR, nor shall any part of the Premises be sublet by LESSEE without such written consent of the LESSOR.

9. INCREASE IN TAXES. LESSEE shall pay as additional rental hereunder any

increase in the Real Estate Taxes or assessments, both general and special coming due in any calendar year during the term hereof that are in excess of the Real Estate Taxes, both general and special coming due in the calendar year 1966. Any additional rent, if any, should become due hereunder, shall be paid in a lump sum within ten (10) days after notice thereof has been sent to LESSEE by LESSOR.

10. DEFAULT. Each of the following shall be deemed a default by LESSEE and a breach of this LEASE:

a. The filing of a petition by or against LESSEE for adjudication under the Bankruptcy Act of 1898, as now and hereinafter amended or supplemented for adjudication as a bankrupt;

b. The appointment of a receiver or a trustee for the property of LESSEE;

c. The making by LESSEE of any assignment for the benefit of creditors;

d. A default in the payment of any rent herein reserved, or any part thereof or default in any other payment required to be made by LESSEE hereunder which default in payment is not corrected within thirty (30) days after written notice of such default from LESSOR to LESSEE;

e. A default in the performance of any other covenant or condition of this LEASE on the part of LESSEE which default shall continue and not be corrected for a period of thirty (30) days from written notice of such default from LESSOR to LESSEE.

In the event of any such incurred default of LESSEE, and at any time thereafter, LESSOR may serve written notice upon LESSEE that LESSOR elects to terminate this LEASE upon a specified date and this LEASE shall then expire on the date so specified as if the date had originally been fixed as the expiration date under the term herein granted, but any such notice of termination shall not prejudice the further rights of LESSOR as provided herein.

In the event that this LEASE shall be terminated as above provided, or by summary proceedings or otherwise, or in the event that the Premises, or any part thereof, shall be abandoned by LESSEE, it shall become vacant during the term of this LEASE, LESSEE, or its agents, servants or representatives, may, immediately or at any time thereafter, re-enter and resume possession of the Premises or such part thereof, and remove all persons and property therefrom, either by summary proceedings or by suitable action or proceeding at law without being liable for any damage therefor. No re-entry by LESSOR shall be deemed an acceptance of a surrender of this LEASE, and LESSOR shall be entitled to collect damages therefor as provided by law.

11. WAIVER. No failure by LESSOR to insist upon the strict performance of any term hereof or to exercise any right, power or remedy consequent upon a breach hereof, and no acceptance of full or partial rent during the continuance of any such breach, shall constitute a waiver of any such breach or of any such term. No waiver of any breach shall affect or alter this LEASE, which shall continue in full force and effect, or the rights of LESSOR with respect to any other then existing or subsequent breach.

12. NOTICE. Any notice applicable or required to be given by either party hereto to the other, pursuant to this LEASE shall be in writing, and shall be deemed to be due and given when mailed by registered mail, return receipt requested, and a postdated envelope, to LESSOR at ______________________________
____________________ and to LESSEE at ______________________________
____________________. Either party may at any time change the address for such notice to the other party by notice stating the change and setting forth the changed address.

13. CAPTIONS. The captions as to particular sections herein are inserted only for convenience, and are in no way to be construed as a part of this LEASE or

as a limitation of the scope of the particular paragraphs or sections to which they refer.

14. SUCCESSORS. The provisions, covenants and conditions of this LEASE shall bind and inure to the benefit of the legal representatives, successors and assigns of each of the parties hereto, except that no assignment, encumbrance or subletting by LESSEE, without written consent of LESSOR, shall vest any right in the assignee, encumbrances or sublessee of LESSEE.

IN WITNESS WHEREOF, the parties hereto have executed this LEASE as of the day and year first above written.

LESSOR:	LESSEE:
	JONES CORPORATION, a Wyoming Corporation
____________________	By: ____________________
	President
____________________	Attest: ____________________
____________________	Secretary

DEED

THIS INDENTURE, made the 15th day of February in the year of our Lord one thousand nine hundred and sixty-seven between Jones Corporation, a Wyoming corporation, party of the first part, and The Smith Company, a California corporation, party of the second part. WITNESSETH: That the said party of the first part, for and in consideration of the sum of One and no/100 Dollar ($1.00), lawful money of the United States of America, to it in hand paid by the said party of the second part, the receipt whereof is hereby acknowledged, has granted, bargained, sold, and conveyed, and by these presents does grant, bargain, sell and convey unto the said party of the second part, and to its successors and assigns forever, all of the following described property situate, lying and being in Silver Bow, Jefferson and Madison Counties, State of Montana, and particularly bounded and described as follows, to-wit:

(The complete legal description of said property
is the same as in Exhibit A of the Sales Contract.)

TOGETHER with all and singular the tenements, hereditaments and appurtenances thereto belonging or in anywise appertaining and the reversion and reversions, remainder and remainders, rents, issues and profits thereof, and also all the estate, right, title, interest, in and to said property, possession, claim and demand whatsoever, as well in law as in equity, of the said party of the first part, of in or to the said premises, and every part and parcel thereof, with the appurtenances.

TO HAVE AND TO HOLD, all and singular the said premises, together with appurtenances unto the said party of the second part, and its successors and assigns forever. And the said party of the first part, and its successors, the said premises, in the quiet and peaceable possession of the said party of the second part, its successors and assigns, against the said party of the first part, and its heirs, and against all and every person and persons whomsoever lawfully claiming or to claim the same, shall and will warrant and by these presents forever defend.

IN WITNESS WHEREOF, the said party of the first part has hereunto set its hand and seal the day and year first above written.

JONES CORPORATION, a Wyoming Corporation
By: /s/ Tom Jones
President

ATTEST:
By: /s/ Mary Jones
Secretary

STATE OF WYOMING } ss.
County of }

On this 15th day of February, in the year one thousand nine hundred and sixty-seven, before me John Doe, a Notary Public for the State of Wyoming, personally appeared Tom Jones, known to me to be the President of the corporation that executed the within instrument, and acknowledged to me that such corporation executed the same.

IN WITNESS WHEREOF, I have hereunto set my hand and affixed my official seal, the day and year in this certificate first above written.

/s/ John Doe
Notary Public for the State of Wyoming
Residing at ____________, Wyoming.
My commission expires April 25, 1969.

OWNER'S POLICY
KANSAS CITY TITLE INSURANCE COMPANY
(A Stock Company)
Kansas City, Missouri

AMOUNT—$330,000

THIS POLICY OF TITLE INSURANCE WITNESSETH, That KANSAS CITY TITLE INSURANCE COMPANY, herein called the Company, in consideration of the payment of the premium for this Policy, does hereby covenant and agree that it will pay to THE SMITH COMPANY hereinafter called the Insured, the heirs, devisees, or personal representatives of the Insured, all loss or damage not exceeding Three Hundred Thirty Thousand & No/100 Dollars ($330,000), which they, or any of them shall sustain by reason of any defect or defects in the title of the Insured to the estate or interest of the Insured in the real estate described under Schedule A, hereto annexed, or by reason of liens or encumbrances against the same as of the date of the final examination of the title thereto, to-wit:

March 30, 1967, at 2:00 P.M.,

which date shall be deemed the effective date of this Policy, excepting the defects, estates, interests, objections, liens or encumbrances mentioned in Schedule B, hereto annexed, or excepted by the conditions or stipulations of this Policy hereto annexed and incorporated herein as a part of this contract. Any loss hereunder shall be established and the amount thereof ascertained in the manner provided in said conditions and stipulations and be payable upon compliance with the provisions of same and not otherwise.

IN WITNESS WHEREOF, KANSAS CITY TITLE INSURANCE COMPANY has caused its corporate seal to be hereto affixed and these presents to be signed by its duly authorized officers in facsimile to become effective as its original seal and signatures and binding on the company as of the day and date countersigned by its designated home office authority or by its duly authorized agent, whose identity as authenticating signatory is subjoined hereto for reference and whose authority is guaranteed as of such date, all in accordance with its by-laws.

KANSAS CITY TITLE INSURANCE COMPANY

Local Service Unit:
MAURICE A. MAFFEI (SEAL)

/s/ W. M. McAdams
President

Validating Signatory:
Maurice A. Maffei
206-209 Professional Bldg.
Butte, Wyoming

ATTEST:

/s/ John D. Petterson
Secretary

Countersigned and validated this 30th day of March, 1967, at 2:00 o'clock P.M. (Here insert date of Special Counsel's final certificate of title.)

/s/ Maurice A. Maffei
Authorized Signatory

SCHEDULE A

1. The estate of the Insured in the real estate described below covered by this Policy is Fee Simple Title.

2. The deed or other means by which the estate or interest covered by this Policy is vested in the Insured is described as follows: Contract for Deed, dated February 15, 1967, wherein the Jones Corporation, a Wyoming corporation, is Seller and The Smith Company, a California corporation, is Buyer. Short form of Contract for Deed recorded in Book 318 of Deeds, page 493, Silver Bow County, Montana, and Book 219 Miscellaneous, page 89, Madison County, Montana. Above-mentioned documents, including Contract and accompanying Deeds, etc., deposited in escrow with Metals Bank and Trust Company, Butte, Montana.

3. Description of the real estate in which the Insured has the estate or interest covered by this Policy:

Real Estate situated in Silver Bow, Jefferson, and Madison Counties, Montana, more particularly described in Exhibit "A" attached hereto. (The legal description of property is the same as that shown in the sales contract.)

SCHEDULE B

This Policy does not insure or indemnify against the estates, interest, defects, objections to title, liens, charges, and encumbrances affecting said real estate, or the estate of interest therein insured, as are scheduled below:

1. The title to appliances installed on deferred payments whether attached to or otherwise used in connection with the premises hereby insured.

2. Rights of parties in actual possession of all or any part of the premises other than the Insured.

3. Mechanics' and materialmen's liens not of record at the effective date of this Policy.

4. Any discrepancies, conflicts, encroachments, or shortages in area and boundaries which a correct survey would show.

5. Unrecorded easements, if any, on or below the surface.

6. Exceptions, reservations, prior conveyances and easements, shown on Exhibit "A" attached hereto.

7. General taxes for the year 1966 and subsequent years, not now due and payable.

8. Water, water rights, minerals and mineral rights, no matter how acquired or evidenced of record.

9. The terms and provisions of mortgage executed by The Jones Corporation, a Wyoming corporation, dated August 5, 1966, recorded August 29, 1966 in Book 6 of Mortgages, at page 24, Records of Jefferson County, Montana, and in Book 182 of Mortgages, at page 475, Records of Silver Bow County, Montana.

10. The terms and provisions of that certain Contract for Deed and Assignment thereof, which Contract for Deed and Assignment are described in Schedule A (2) hereof.

Conditions and Stipulation of This Policy

1. The Company shall have the right to, and will, at its own cost and expense, defend the title insured by this Policy in any action of ejectment, or other action or proceeding founded upon a claim of title, encumbrance or defect, which existed, or is claimed to have existed, prior in date to the effective date of this Policy, and not excepted herein. In case any such action or proceeding shall be begun, it shall be the duty of the insured at once to notify the Company in writing of the full particulars thereof and secure to the Company the right to defend such action or proceeding in the name of the Insured and to give all reasonable assistance therein. Failure to notify the Company as aforesaid at its Home Office, in Kansas City, Missouri, within ten (10) days after process or notice in such action or proceeding shall be served upon the Insured, shall operate as a full release and discharge of the Company from any and all liability with respect to the subject matter of such action or proceeding; provided, however, that failure to notify the Company as aforesaid shall not prejudice the claim of the Insured if the insured shall not be party to such action or proceeding; nor be served with summons, process or notice therein; nor have any knowledge thereof. The Company reserves the option of settling the claim or paying this Policy in full; and the payment, or tender of payment, to the full amount of this Policy shall operate as a full release and discharge of the Company from any and all liability under this Policy. It shall be the duty of the Insured, within ten (10) days after learning of any claim of title, encumbrance, or defect not expected in this Policy, and before payment or settlement of the same, to notify the Company, in writing thereof, and failure to so notify the Company at its Home Office in Kansas City, Missouri, shall operate as a full release and discharge of the Company from any and all liability with respect to such claim, encumbrance or defect.

2. Whenever the Company shall have settled a claim under this Policy, it shall be subrogated to the rights and remedies of the Insured against any other person or property in respect to the subject matter of such claim and the Insured shall transfer or cause to be transferred to the Company such rights, securities and remedies and permit the Company to use the name of the Insured for the recovery thereof. Any such sum collected on such rights, securities and remedies over and above the amount of loss paid by the Company shall belong, and on demand shall be paid, to the Insured. The Insured warrants that such rights, securities and remedies shall vest in the Company unaffected by any act of the Insured.

3. Nothing contained in this Policy shall be construed as insuring against loss or damage by reason of claims arising under any act, thing, or trust rela-

tionship done, created, suffered or permitted by the Insured; or that the acquisition of the estate or interest hereby insured contravened the laws of the United States establishing a uniform system of bankruptcy; or against the rights of dower and homestead, if any, of the spouse of the Insured, nor will the Company be liable in any event for any loss or damage arising from the refusal of any party to carry out any contract to purchase, lease or loan money on the estate or interest insured.

4. A statement in writing of any loss or damage for which it is claimed the Company is liable shall be furnished to the Company within sixty (60) days after such loss or damage, and no right of action shall accrue under this Policy until thirty (30) days after such statement shall have been furnished and no recovery shall be had under this Policy unless action shall be commenced thereon within one year (or within the time allowed by the law of the state of the forum) after the expiration of said last mentioned period of thirty (30) days; and a failure to furnish such statement of loss or damage, and to commence such action within the times hereinbefore specified, shall be a conclusive bar against the maintenance of any action under this Policy.

5. All payments under this Policy, or any owner's policy issued to the Insured's vendee or vendees covering any part of the property described herein, shall reduce the amount of insurance pro tanto, and no payment can be demanded without producing the Policy for endorsement of such payment. If the Policy be lost or destroyed, indemnity satisfactory to the Company must be furnished. It is expressly understood and agreed that any loss payable under this Policy may be applied by the Company to the payment of any mortgage mentioned in Schedule B, the title under which is insured by the Company, or which may be held by the Company, and the amount so paid shall also be deemed a payment to the Insured under this Policy. The aggregate liability of the Company under this Policy and any policy issued to the holder of any such mortgage shall not exceed the amount of this Policy.

6. Nothing contained in this Policy shall be construed as insuring (a) against the consequences of any law, ordinance, or governmental regulation (including building and "zoning" ordinances) limiting or regulating the use or enjoyment of the property herein described or the character, dimensions or locations of any improvements erected or to be erected thereon, or (b) against the consequences of the exercise or attempted exercise of "police power" or the power of "eminent domain" over said property, or (c) the title or rights of the Insured in any property beyond the line of the property described in Schedule A, or in any streets, roads, avenues, lanes or ways in said property or upon which said property abuts, or to tide lands or lands comprising the shores and bottoms of navigable rivers, lakes, bays, ocean or gulf, or lands beyond the line of the harbor or bulkhead lines as established or changed by the United States Government, or to filled-in lands or artificial islands or riparian rights.

7. The Company shall not be liable hereunder for the cost and expense incurred in the satisfaction or removal of liens upon or objections to the title, which were found upon examination of title to exist at the effective date of this Policy, but which shall have been satisfied or removed prior to the date of the actual delivery of this Policy.

8. If the property described in Schedule A is divisible into separate independent parcels and a loss is established affecting one or more of said parcels, the loss shall be computed and settled on a pro rata basis as if the face value of this Policy were divided pro rata as to the value of each separate independent parcel, exclusive of the improvements made subsequent to the date of this Policy, to the whole.

9. Defects and encumbrances arising after the effective date of this Policy, or created, suffered, assumed or agreed to by the Insured, and taxes and assess-

ments which have not become liens up to the effective date of this Policy, or which, although they have become liens, are not payable until some future date, or in future installments, are not to be deemed covered by this Policy.

10. Any untrue statement made with respect to any material fact; any fraud perpetrated; any suppression of or failure to disclose any material facts; any untrue answer by the Insured, or the agent of the Insured, to material inquiries before the issuing of this Policy, shall void this Policy.

11. The term "the Company," as herein used, means Kansas City Title Insurance Company, and the term "the Insured" means the person or persons in whose favor this Policy is issued.

12. No officer, agent or other representative of the Company, shall have the power to waive any of the conditions or stipulations of this Policy, except the President or one of the Vice Presidents of the Company, and such waiver, if any, shall be written upon or attached hereto.

This Policy necessarily relates solely to the title prior to and including its "effective date" as herein defined.

This Policy is not transferable to subsequent owners. A Reissue Policy in favor of new purchasers should be obtained.

Note that Paragraph 8 in Schedule B of the Title Policy states that "water, water rights, minerals, and mineral rights, no matter how acquired or evidenced of record" are excepted from the insurance policy and are not insured. This has been caused by a volume of painful experiences the title companies have had in recent years on this type of litigation. If any of the water rights were recorded in the 19th Century where legal matters were pretty loose, it is quite possible to have "duplicate priorities" and you may or may not be entitled to water ahead of somebody upstream. This is one place where you may be on your own and you had better have an attorney who knows what he is doing.

The final *closing* where deeds and checks are exchanged may occur in the office of an attorney or title company. The financial transactions are summarized in the *closing statements*. One is prepared from the standpoint of the seller and one from the standpoint of the buyer. Examples follow.

LEASES

Background

The principal difference between an agricultural lease and an industrial lease is that the land may contain some non-replenishable assets which can be dissipated by misuse. For example, a Wyoming range may contain forage that was three years in the growing. Over-

SELLER'S STATEMENT

APPROVED BY MISSOURI REAL ESTATE ASSOCIATION

Date..............................

NAME OF BROKER..............................

NAME OF SELLER..............................

NAME OF BUYER..............................

SALE OF YOUR PROPERTY AT..............................

	Dr.	Cr.
Price		
Deed of Trust		
Deed of Trust		
Interest Accrued		
Tax Adjustment		
Insurance Adjustment		
Rent Adjustment		
Recording (W. D.)		
" (D. of T.)		
" (Misc.)		
Loan Fee		
Attorney Fee		
Revenue Stamps		
Abstracting		
Commission		
Federal Judgment Search		
Check herewith		
Total		

I, we have examined the above statement and find it correct.

Date.............................. ....Seller

..............................Seller

FORM R. E. 502 5M 10-61 55117
Printed and for sale by The Joplin Printing Co., Joplin, Mo.

BUYER'S STATEMENT

APPROVED BY MISSOURI REAL ESTATE ASSOCIATION

Date.......................................

NAME OF BROKER.......................................

NAME OF BUYER.......................................

NAME OF SELLER.......................................

ADDRESS OF PROPERTY PURCHASED.......................................

		Dr.	Cr.
Price			
Earnest Money			
Deed of Trust	(1)		
Interest Accrued			
Tax Adjustment	(2)		
Insurance Adjustment	(3)		
Rent Adjustment	(4)		
Recording (W. D.)			
" (D. of T.)			
" (Misc.)			
Attorney Fee			
Abstracting			
Balance due from you			
Total			

(1) Your loan of $.................... payable to.......................................

at the rate of $.................... per month plus including interest at....................%.

....

Your first payment will be due as of.......................................

(2) Tax adjustment. Total Annual Estimated Taxes $....................

We have given you credit for.......months.......days taxes. You are therefore to pay your own taxes for this year when payable.

(3) Insurance. Your policy is for $.................... covering the above property against fire and the Extended coverage provisions. The policy expires as of.......................................

Name of Insuring Agent.......................................

(4) Rent. Name of Tenant.......................................

Monthly rental $.................... Date rent is paid to.......................................

Name of Rental Agent.......................................

(5) ....

....

....

I, we have examined the above statement and find it correct.

Date.......................................

.... Buyer

.... Buyer

FORM R. E. 503 5M 10-61 55117
Printed and for sale by The Joplin Printing Co., Joplin, Mo.

grazing could upset the balance of the new grass coming on and require expensive reseeding to bring back. A Kansas bluestem grass ranch plowed up to get one or two wheat crops could make it unfit for cattle for 10 years. An Illinois farm extensively "corn farmed" for three years without putting any fertilizer back into the soil could be extensively damaged. Failure to mow pastures could permit brush growth of 2- and 3-inch trees that would have to be taken out with a bulldozer. This could cost more than the land was worth.

The example of a short form lease which follows is a typical one signed on a small Midwestern-type farm for the usual one or two year period. It covers the parties involved, the rent, method of payment, description of the land, and general protections against land abuse. This would not be adequate for large tracts of land leased for long periods of time involving big sums of money.

One will note in the previous form such broad brush treatments as "to cultivate in good and proper manner all of the tillable land," or "to allow no waste," or, as is often common in such short form leases, to "not overgraze the pastures." If big tracts of ground and long leases are involved, such clauses are a direct invitation to a lawsuit and are highly unfavorable to the tenant.

What is "overgrazing"? 1,000 cows? 1,500 cows? 2,000 cows? If you run twice as many in the winter when the ground is frozen and half as many when the grass is growing, is this satisfactory? Who is to determine it? What kind of damages are to be paid if the landlord thinks there was overgrazing? Can the tenant put more cattle on the premises if he puts fertilizer on the pastures? How much fertilizer? Obviously, it is impossible to pin down everything, but the tenant and his attorney should not leave too much dangling if possible.

If it's the type of property where the total amount of such damages might range from $500 to $1,000, this is not a matter of significance as it is unlikely that the landlord will go to court and pay legal expenses to recover this type of compensation. On the other hand, if overgrazing could result in a claim of $50,000 to $100,000 of damages, this is a totally different matter.

Because over the last 20 years agricultural rents have rarely exceeded 4 to 5% net on the value of the property, and because land owners feel that the future will bring an improvement, and because the tenant's misuse of the property could cause so much potential damage, it has been customary to rarely rent agricultural land more than one or two years.

This is not true in Europe, and particularly in England, where agricultural leases go on for centuries.

On the other hand, if the tenant is willing to put a substantial amount of money back into the property in improvements or fertilizer, or if the owner grants him an option to buy, this is quite a different story. We follow with an example of an actual agricultural lease made in eastern Kansas for a 10-year period with a graduated rent based on the amount of cattle run, tied in with an improvement program and a purchase option.

OPTIONS

Webster defines an option as "the power or right to choose." It is usually acquired through the payment of a monetary consideration, the rendering of some service, or as an adjunct to some other transaction. In the preceding example, a tenant in consideration for his entering a firm 10-year lease with a farm owner, acquired an option to buy the property. Any default in his rental payments would have resulted in an immediate forfeiture of his option rights.

You can possess an option to buy a herd of cattle at a given price, an option to extend a lease for a given number of years at either the same rent or a different rent, an option to purchase a piece of real estate for a given price for a given number of years.

The man who has this right of choosing to make a decision to lease, buy or do something is generally called the *holder* of the option. The man who has given him this right or owns something or is willing to be required to do something is normally called the *grantor* of the option.

With violently fluctuating types of personal property such as grains, cattle, or securities, options are normally of fairly short duration—probably less than one year. With real estate they might go on for 5, 10, or more years, particularly if they are tied in with a lease or some semi-permanent arrangement. Often on the basis of holding such a purchase option, a tenant might be willing to put in substantial improvements during the course of the lease which he would be unwilling to do otherwise. Commonly the consideration paid for an option is often applied to the eventual purchase price or to the first year's rent in the event of a lease.

Carelessly written options frequently cause litigation, particularly when the property has gone up in value in the meanwhile. Options should be drawn up by an attorney with the same care of a sales contract or a lease. A frequent procedure, in preparing an option, is to actually prepare a lease or a sales contract between the two parties in the exact detail that would be desired if the option were exercised, leave it unsigned but identify it as "Exhibit A." Then, when the option agreement is drawn up refer to the exhibit as part of the option document and indicate that should the option be exercised both parties agree to sign the attached exhibit.

An extremely frequent cause of misunderstanding, hard feeling, and potential litigation in the cattle industry is the confusion on future delivery contracts between an option payment and a deposit on a firm purchase contract.

There is a substantial difference if Mr. A, a feedlot operator agrees in April to buy 1,000 yearlings owned by Mr. B for an October delivery at 25¢ per pound and gives him a $10 per head *deposit* on the contract. This has no relationship to a document in which Mr. A pays $10 per head for an option to buy Mr. B's yearlings next October at 25¢ per pound. Obviously if Mr. A does not take the cattle he has lost his $10 per head which Mr. B keeps. However, in the first case, Mr. A has a legal and moral obligation to continue and accept delivery on his purchase, paying the balance of the cost. In the case of the first contract he can walk away from it and be out only his $10 and Mr. B should have no complaints as this is a perfectly normal business arrangement.

In the area of mineral rights and oil exploration, options have a long and involved history and usage. When someone is about to go in to a very expensive, exploratory drilling he can normally not afford it unless he secures a substantial number of options on surrounding land so that if he does "hit" he will be able to recover his cost. A common practice is to give the owner of the land a ⅛ interest in the gross value of any oil or other minerals acquired. The drilling group very often makes a fairly substantial initial payment for the option with the right to renew it year after year for a relatively nominal payment. The land owner on the other hand often puts into the option agreement, a requirement that after so many years the driller must drill a well of such-and-such specifications or forfeit his right to renew the option. Because of the large sums of money involved, these "drilling options" are almost always recorded in the local county seats in the same manner as a land deed and they appear as a matter of record or as exceptions on a title policy when property is transferred. An example of a mineral rights option follows:

April 28, 1967

Re: Oil and Gas Lease
Lots 6 & 9-15
Lot 2-22-12-92
Moffat County, Colorado

Baggs Land and Cattle Corporation
1808 Main Street
Kansas City, Missouri

Gentlemen:

Baggs Land and Cattle Corporation, hereafter called "Baggs," has executed as Lessor an oil and gas lease dated April 28, 1967, in favor of Calvert Drilling & Producing Co., hereafter called "Calvert," as Lessee, covering the undivided mineral interest owned by Baggs under Lots 6 and 9 of Section 15 and Lot 2 of Section 22, Township 12 North, Range 92 West, Moffat County, Colorado, hereafter called the "leased premises."

The purpose of this letter is to express our understanding of the agreement reached with you with respect to said oil and gas lease and when approved and accepted by you shall, along with said oil and gas lease, constitute a binding agreement between us, inurring to the benefit of our respective successors and assigns.

In addition to the considerations, royalties and other payments and mutual obligations as provided in said oil and gas lease, we have agreed that in the event Calvert successfully completes a producing well on the leased premises, Baggs shall be paid in addition to the royalties specified in said lease an overriding royalty of 1/16th of 8/8ths of all oil and gas produced, saved and sold from the leased premises, such overriding royalty shall be free of all costs and expenses, except taxes, and shall be subject to a reduction to the proportion that Baggs mineral interest in the lands covered by said lease bears to the entire undivided mineral estate in said lands.

At such time as Calvert has recovered out of the proceeds from sale of production from the leased premises all of Calvert's costs in drilling, completing, equipping and operating the well or wells on the leased premises to that time, Calvert shall notify Baggs in writing at the above address of such fact. Baggs shall have the period of 30 days after receipt of such written notice within which to make an election as to whether Baggs will retain its overriding royalty interest of 1/16th of 8/8th, as set out in the above paragraph, or to convert such overriding royalty interest into a net profits interest of 25% of Calvert's net profits from its operations on the leased premises. Such net profits shall apply only to that portion of Calvert's operation which the mineral interest owned by Baggs bears to the entire undivided mineral estate in the lands covered by said lease. Attached to this letter marked Exhibit "A" and incorporated in this agreement by reference is an accounting procedure which shall be used for the computation of operating costs in the determination of the payout period and net profits in the event Baggs elects to convert its overriding royalty interest.

Prior to commencement of any well on the lands covered by said lease, or as soon thereafter as is practicable, Calvert shall use due and reasonable efforts to obtain a voluntary agreement pooling all of the following described lands into one drilling unit:

Township 12 North, Range 92 West

Section 15: Lots 1, 2, 6, 9
Section 22: Lot 2

In the event of formation of any such unit, the overriding royalty interest provided herein and the net profits interest provided herein shall be payable to Baggs in the proportion that the leased premises bears to all of the lands included in the unit. Baggs, by this agreement, agrees to execute such pooling agreements as may be required to accomplish the intent and purpose of this paragraph.

If the above is in accordance with your understanding of our agreement with respect to the oil and gas lease referred herein, we would appreciate your indicating your approval and acceptance by signing and returning two copies of this letter to us.

Very truly yours,
CALVERT DRILLING & PRODUCING CO.
/s/ J. V. Boxell
J. V. Boxell, President

Approved and accepted this
__________ day of __________________, 1967,
BAGGS LAND AND CATTLE CORPORATION
By: __________________________
H. L. Oppenheimer, President

EXHIBIT "A"

Attached to and made a part of Letter Agreement dated April 28, 1967, between Calvert Drilling & Producing Co. and Baggs Land and Cattle Corporation

ACCOUNTING PROCEDURE
(Joint Operations)

I. General Provisions

1. *Definitions*

"Joint Property" shall mean the real and personal property subject to the agreement to which this "Accounting Procedure" is attached.

"Joint Operations" shall mean all operations necessary or proper for the development, operation, protection and maintenance of the Joint Property.

"Operator" shall mean the party designated to conduct the Joint Operations.

"Non-Operators" shall mean the nonoperating parties, whether one or more.

"Joint Account" shall mean the account showing the charges and credits accruing because of the Joint Operations and which are to be shared by the Parties.

"Parties" shall mean Operator and Non-Operators.

"Material" shall mean personal property, equipment or supplies acquired or held for use on the Joint Property.

"Controllable Material" shall mean material which at the time is so classified in the Material Classification Manual as most recently recommended by the Council of Petroleum Accountants Societies of North America.

2. *Conflict with Agreement*

In the event of a conflict between the provisions of this Accounting Procedure and the provisions of the agreement to which this Accounting Procedure is attached, the provisions of the agreement shall control.

3. *Collective Action by Non-Operators*

Where an agreement or other action of Non-Operators is expressly required under this Accounting Procedure and if the agreement to which this Accounting Procedure is attached contains no contrary provisions in regard thereto, the agreement or action of a majority in interest of the Non-Operators shall be controlling on all Non-Operators.

4. *Statements and Billings*

Operator shall bill Non-Operators on or before the last day of each month for their proportionate share of costs and expenses, for the preceding month. Such bills will be accompanied by statements reflecting the total charges and credits as set forth under Subparagraph A below:

A. Statement in detail of all charges and credits to the Joint Account.

B. Statement of all charges and credits to the Joint Account, summarized by appropriate classifications indicative of the nature thereof.

C. Statement of all charges and credits to the Joint Account summarized by appropriate classifications indicative of the nature thereof, except that items of Controllable Material and unusual charges and credits shall be detailed.

5. *Payment and Advances by Non-Operators*

Each Non-Operator shall pay its proportion of all such bills within fifteen (15) days after receipt thereof. If payment is not made within such time, the unpaid balance shall bear interest at the rate of six per cent (6%) per annum until paid.

6. *Adjustments*

Payment of any such bills shall not prejudice the right of any Non-Operators to protest or question the correctness thereof; provided however, all bills and statements rendered to Non-Operators by Operator during any calendar year shall conclusively be presumed to be true and correct after twenty-four (24) months following the end of any such calendar year, unless within the said twenty-four (24) month period a Non-Operator takes written exception thereto and makes claim on Operator for adjustment. No adjustment favorable to Operator shall be made unless it is made within the same prescribed period. The provisions of this paragraph shall not prevent adjustments resulting from a physical inventory of the Joint Property as provided for in Section VII.

7. *Audits*

A Non-Operator, upon notice in writing to Operator and all other Non-Operators, shall have the right to audit Operator's accounts and records relating to the accounting hereunder for any calendar year within the twenty-four (24) month period following the end of such calendar year; provided however, the making of an audit shall not extend the time for the taking of written exception to and the adjustment of accounts as provided for in Paragraph 6 of this Section I. Where there are two or more Non-Operators, the Non-Operators shall make every reasonable effort to conduct joint or simultaneous audits in a manner which will result in a minimum of inconvenience to the Operator.

II. Direct Charges

Subject to limitations hereinafter prescribed, Operator shall charge the Joint Account with the following items:

1. *Rentals and Royalties*

Delay or other rentals and royalties when such rentals and royalties are paid by Operator for the Joint Account of the Parties.

2. *Labor*

A. Salaries and wages of Operator's employees directly engaged on the Joint Property in the conduct of the Joint Operations, and salaries or wages of technical employees who are temporarily assigned to and directly employed on the Joint Property.

B. Operator's cost of holiday, vacation, sickness and disability benefits and other customary allowances paid to the employees whose salaries and wages are chargeable to the Joint Account under Paragraph 2A of this Section II and Paragraph 1 of Section III; except that in the case of those employees only a pro rata portion of whose salaries and wages are chargeable to the Joint Account under Paragraph 1 of Section III, not more than the same pro rata portion of the benefits and allowances herein provided for shall be charged to the Joint Account. Cost under this Paragraph 2B may be charged on a "when and as paid basis" or by percentage assessment" on the amount of salaries and wages chargeable to the Joint Account under Paragraph 2A of this Section II and Paragraph 1 of Section III. If percentage assessment is used, the rate shall be based on the Operator's cost experience.

C. Expenditures or contributions made pursuant to assessments imposed by governmental authority which are applicable to Operator's labor cost of salaries and wages chargeable to the Joint Account under Paragraphs 2A and 2B of this Section II and Paragraph 1 of Section III.

D. Reasonable personal expenses of those employees whose salaries and wages are chargeable to the Joint Account under Paragraph 2A of this Section II and for which expenses the employees are reimbursed under Operator's usual practice.

3. *Employee Benefits*

Operator's current cost of established plans for employees' group life insurance, hospitalization, pension, retirement, stock purchase, thrift, bonus, and other benefit plans of a like nature, applicable to Operator's labor cost; provided however, the total of such charges shall not exceed ten percent (10%) of Operator's labor costs chargeable to the Joint Account under Paragraphs 2A and 2B of this Section II and Paragraph 1 of Section III.

4. *Material*

Material purchased or furnished by Operator for use on the Joint Property. So far as it is reasonably practical and consistent with efficient and economical operation, only such Material shall be purchased for or transferred to the Joint Property as may be required for immediate use; and the accumulation of surplus stocks shall be avoided.

5. *Transportation*

Transportation of employees and Material necessary for the Joint Operations but subject to the following limitations:

A. If Material is moved to the Joint Property from the Operator's warehouse or other properties, no charge shall be made to the Joint Account for a distance greater than the distance from the nearest reliable supply store or railway receiving point where like material is available, except by agreement with Non-Operators.

B. If surplus Material is moved to Operator's warehouse or other storage point, no charge shall be made to the Joint Account for a distance greater than the distance to the nearest reliable supply store or railway receiving point, except by agreement with Non-Operators. No charge shall be made to Joint Account for moving Material to other properties belonging to Operator, except by agreement with Non-Operators.

C. In the application of subparagraphs A and B above, there shall be no equalization of actual gross trucking costs of $100 or less.

6. *Services*

A. The cost of contract services and utilities procured from outside sources other than services covered by Paragraph 8 of this Section II and Paragraph 2 of Section III.

B. Use and service of equipment and facilities furnished by Operator as provided in Paragraph 5 of Section IV.

7. *Damages and Losses to Joint Property*

All costs or expenses necessary for the repair or replacement of Joint Property made necessary because of damages or losses incurred by fire, flood, storm, theft, accident, or any other cause, except to the extent that the damage or loss could have been avoided through the exercise of reasonable diligence on the part of Operator. Operator shall furnish Non-Operators written notice of damages or losses incurred as soon as practicable after a report thereof has been received by Operator.

8. *Legal Expense*

All costs and expenses of handling, investigating and settling litigation or claims arising by reason of the Joint Operations or necessary to protect or recover the Joint Property, including, but not limited to, attorneys' fees, court costs, cost of investigation or procuring evidence and amounts paid in settlement or satisfaction of any such litigation or claims; provided, (a) no charge shall be made for the services of Operator's legal staff or other regularly employed personnel (such services being considered to be Administrative Overhead under Section III), except by agreement with Non-Operators, and (b) no charge shall be made for the fees and expenses of outside attorneys unless the employment of such attorneys is agreed to by Operator and Non-Operators.

9. *Taxes*

All taxes of every kind and nature assessed or levied upon or in connection with the Joint Property, the operation thereof, or the production therefrom, and which taxes have been paid by the Operator for the benefit of the Parties.

10. *Insurance Premiums*

Premiums paid for insurance required to be carried on the Joint Property for the protection of the Parties.

11. *Other Expenditures*

Any other expenditure not covered or dealt with in the foregoing provisions of this Section II, or in Section III, and which is incurred by the Operator for the necessary and proper conduct of the Joint Operations.

III. Indirect Charges

Operator may charge the Joint Account for indirect costs either by use of an allocation of district expense items plus a fixed rate for administrative overhead, and plus the warehousing charges, all as provided for in Paragraphs 1, 2, and 3 of this Section III OR by combining all three of said items under the fixed rate provided for in Paragraph 4 of this Section III, as indicated next below:

Operator shall charge the joint account under the terms of:

☒ Paragraphs 1, 2 and 3. (Allocation of district expense plus fixed rate for administrative overhead plus warehousing)

☐ Paragraph 4. (Combined fixed rate)

1. *District Expense*

Operator shall charge the Joint Account with a pro rata portion of the salaries, wages and expenses of Operator's production superintendent and other employees serving the Joint Property and other properties of the Operator in the same operating area, whose time is not allocated directly to the properties, and a pro rata portion of the cost of maintaining and operating a production office known as Operator's District Production office located at or near Williston, N. Dak. (or a comparable office if location is changed), and necessary sub-offices (if any), maintained for the convenience of the above-described office, and all necessary camps, including housing facilities for employees if required, used in connection with the operations of the Joint Property and other properties in the same operating area. The expense of, less any revenue from, such facilities may, at the option of Operator, include depreciation of investment or a fair monthly rental in lieu of depreciation. Such charges shall be apportioned to all properties served on some equitable basis consistent with Operator's accounting practice, with a drilling well being treated as the equivalent of six producing wells.

2. *Administrative Overhead*

Operator shall charge administrative overhead to the Joint Account at the following rates, which charge shall be in lieu of the cost and expense of all offices of the Operator not covered by Paragraph 1 of this Section III, including salaries, wages and expenses of personnel assigned to such offices. Such charges shall be in addition to the salaries, wages and expenses of employees of Operator authorized to be charged as direct charges as provided in Paragraphs 2 and 8 of Section II.

WELL BASIS (RATE PER WELL PER MONTH)

	DRILLING WELL RATE (Use Total Depth)	PRODUCING WELL RATE (Use Current Producing Depth)		
Well Depth	Each Well	First Five	Next Five	All Wells Over Ten
0-4000′	240	40		
4-8000′	300	50		
8-12,000′	390	65		
Below 12,000′	480	80		

The cost and expense of services from outside sources in connection with matters of taxation, traffic, accounting, or matters before or involving governmental agencies shall be considered as included in the overhead rates provided for in this Paragraph 2 of Section III, unless such cost and expense are agreed upon between Operator and Non-Operators as a direct charge to the Joint Account.

3. *Operator's Fully Owned Warehouse Operating and Maintenance Expense*
(Describe fully the agreed procedure to be followed by the Operator.)

None

4. *Combined Fixed Rates*
Operator shall charge the Joint Account for the services covered by Paragraph 1, 2 and 3 of this Section III, the following fixed per well rates:

WELL BASIS (RATE PER WELL PER MONTH)

Well Depth	DRILLING WELL RATE (Use Total Depth) Each Well	PRODUCING WELL RATE (Use Current Producing Depth) First Five	Next Five	All Wells Over Ten

Said fixed rate (shall) (shall not) include salaries and expenses of production foremen.

5. *Application of Administrative Overhead or Combined Fixed Rates*
The following limitations, instructions and charges shall apply in the application of the per wall rates as provided under either Paragraph 2 or Paragraph 4 of this Section III:

A. Charges for drilling wells shall begin on the date each well is spudded and terminate on the date the drilling or completion rig is released, whichever is later, except that no charge shall be made during the suspension of drilling operations for fifteen (15) or more consecutive days.

B. The status of wells shall be as follows:

(1) Producing gas wells, injection wells for recovery operations, water supply wells utilized for water flooding operations and salt water disposal wells shall be considered the same as producing wells.

(2) Wells permanently shut down but on which plugging operations are deferred shall be dropped from the well schedule at the time the shut-down is effected. When such a well is plugged a charge shall be made at the producing well rates.

(3) Wells being plugged back, drilled deeper, converted to a source or input well, or which are undergoing any type of workover that requires the use of a drilling or workover rig shall be considered the same as drilling wells.

(4) Temporarily shut-down wells, which are not produced or worked upon for a period of a full calendar month, shall not be included in the well schedule, provided however, wells shut in by governmental regulatory body shall be included in the well schedule only in the event the allowable production is transferred to some other well or wells on the Joint Property. In the event of a unit allowable, all wells capable of producing will be counted in determining the charge.

(5) Gas wells shall be included in the well schedule if directly connected to a permanent sales outlet even though temporarily shut in due to overproduction or failure of purchaser to take the allowed production.

(6) Wells completed in multiple horizons, in which the production is not commingled down hole, shall be considered as a producing well for each separately producing horizon.

C. The well rates shall apply to the total number of wells being drilled or operated under the agreement to which this Accounting Procedure is attached, irrespective of individual leases.

D. The well rates shall be adjusted on the first day of April of each year following the effective date of the agreement to which this Accounting Procedure is attached. The adjustment shall be computed by multiplying the rate currently in use by the percentage increase or decrease in the average weekly earnings of Crude Petroleum and Gas Production Workers for the last calendar year compared to the preceding calendar year as shown by "The Index of Average Weekly Earnings of Crude Petroleum and Gas Production Workers" as published by the United States Department of Labor, Bureau of Labor Statistics. The adjusted rates shall be the rates currently in use, plus or minus the computed adjustment.

6. For the construction of compressor plants, water stations, secondary recovery systems, salt water disposal facilities, and other such projects, as distinguished from the more usual drilling and producing operations, Operator in addition to the Administrative Overhead or Combined Fixed Rates provided for in Paragraph 2 and 4 of this Section III, shall charge the Joint Account with an additional overhead charge as follows:

A. Total cost less than $25,000, no charge.

B. Total cost more than $25,000 but less than $100,000, ________% of total cost.

C. Total cost of $100,000 or more, __________% of the first $100,000 plus ________% of all over $100,000 of total cost.

Total cost shall mean the total gross cost of any one project. For the purpose of this Paragraph the component parts of a single project shall not be treated separately and the cost of drilling wells shall be excluded.

7. The specific rates provided for in this Section III may be amended from time to time by mutual agreement between the Parties hereto if, in practice, the rates are found to be insufficient or excessive.

IV. Basis of Charges to Joint Account

Subject to the further provisions of this Section IV, Operator will procure all Material and services for the Joint Property. At the Operator's option, Non-Operator may supply Material or services for the Joint Property.

1. *Purchases*

Material purchased and service procured shall be charged at the price paid by Operator after deduction of all discounts actually received.

2. *Material furnished from Operator's Warehouse or Other Properties*

A. New Material (Condition "A")

(1) Tubular goods, two inch (2") and over, shall be priced on Eastern Mill base (i. e. Youngstown, Ohio; Lorain, Ohio; and Indiana Harbor, Indiana) on a minimum carload basis effective at date of movement and f. o. b. railway receiving point nearest the Joint Property, regardless of quantity. In equalized hauling charges, Operator is permitted to include ten cents (10c) per hundred-weight on all tubular goods furnished from his stocks in lieu of loading and unloading costs sustained.

(2) Other Material shall be priced at the current replacement cost of the same kind of Material, effective at date of movement and f. o. b. the supply store or railway receiving point nearest the Joint Property

where Material of the same kind is available.

(3) The Joint Account shall not be credited with cash discounts applicable to prices provided for in this Paragraph 2 of Section IV.

B. Used Material (Condition "B" and "C")

(1) Material in sound and serviceable condition and suitable for reuse without reconditioning, shall be classified as Condition "B" and priced at seventy-five per cent (75%) of the current price of new Material.

(2) Material which cannot be classified as Condition "B" but which,

(a) After reconditioning will be further serviceable for original function as good secondhand Material (Condition "B"), or

(b) Is serviceable for original function but substantially not suitable for reconditioning, shall be classified as Condition "C" and priced at fifty per cent (50%) of current new price.

(3) Obsolete Material or Material which cannot be classified as Condition "B" or Condition "C" shall be priced at a value commensurate with its use. Material no longer suitable for its original purpose but usable for some other purpose, shall be priced on a basis comparable with that of items normally used for such other purpose.

(4) Material involving erection costs shall be charged at applicable percentage of the current knocked-down price of new Material.

3. *Premium Prices*

Whenever Material is not readily obtainable at prices specified in Paragraphs 1 and 2 of this Section IV because of national emergencies, strikes or other unusual causes over which the Operator has no control, the Operator may charge the Joint Account for the required Material at the Operator's actual cost incurred in procuring such Material, in making it suitable for use, and in moving it to the Joint Property, provided, that notice in writing is furnished to Non-Operators of the proposed charge prior to billing Non-Operators for such Material. Each Non-Operator shall have the right, by so electing and notifying Operator within 10 days after receiving notice from Operator, to furnish in kind all or part of his share of such Material suitable for use and acceptable to Operator.

4. *Warranty of Material Furnished by Operator*

Operator does not warrant the Material furnished. In case of defective Material, credit shall not be passed to the Joint Account until adjustment has been received by Operator from the manufacturers or their agents.

5. *Equipment and Facilities Furnished by Operator*

A. Operator shall charge the Joint Account for use of equipment and facilities at rates commensurate with cost of ownership and operation. Such rates shall include cost of maintenance, repairs, other operating expense, insurance, taxes, depreciation and interest on investment not to exceed six per cent (6%) per annum, provided such rates shall not exceed those currently prevailing in the immediate area within which the Joint Property is located. Rates for automotive equipment shall generally be in line with the schedule of rates adopted by the Petroleum Motor Transport Association, or some other recognized organization, as recommended uniform charges against Joint Property operations. Rates for laboratory services shall not exceed those currently prevailing if performed by outside service laboratories. Rates for trucks, tractors and well service units may include wages and expenses of operator.

B. Whenever requested, Operator shall inform Non-Operators in advance of the rates it proposes to charge.

C. Rates shall be revised and adjusted from time to time when found to be either excessive or insufficient.

V. Disposal of Material

The Operator may purchase, but shall be under no obligation to purchase, interest of Non-Operators in surplus Condition "A" or "B" Material. The disposition of surplus Controllable Material, not purchased by Operator, shall be subject to agreement between Operator and Non-Operators, provided Operator shall dispose of normal accumulations of junk and scrap Material either by transfer or sale from the Joint Property.

1. *Material Purchased by the Operator or Non-Operators*
Material purchased by either the Operator or Non-Operators shall be credited by the Operator to the Joint Account for the month which the Material is removed by the purchaser.

2. *Division in Kind*
Division of Material in kind, if made between Operator and Non-Operators, shall be in proportion to the respective interests in such Material. The Parties will thereupon be charged individually with the value of the Material received or receivable. Proper credits shall be made by the Operator in the monthly statement of operations.

3. *Sales to Outsiders*
Sales to outsiders of Material from the Joint Property shall be credited by Operator to the Joint Account at the net amount collected by Operator from vendee. Any claim by vendee related to such sale shall be charged back to the Joint Account if and when paid by Operator.

VI. Basis of Pricing Material Transferred from Joint Account

Material purchased by either Operator or Non-Operators or divided in kind, unless otherwise agreed to between Operator and Non-Operators shall be priced on the following basis:

1. *New Price Defined*
New price as used in this Section VI shall be the price specified for New Material in Section IV.

2. *New Material*
New Material (Condition "A"), being new Material procured for the Joint Property but never used, at one hundred per cent (100%) of current new price (plus sales tax if any).

3. *Good Used Material*
Good used Material (Condition "B"), being used Material in sound and serviceable condition, suitable for reuse without reconditioning:
A. At seventy-five per cent (75%) of current new price if Material was charged to Joint Account as new, or
B. At sixty-five per cent (65%) of current new price if Material was originally charged to the Joint Account as secondhand at seventy-five percent (75%) of new price.

4. *Other Used Material*

Used Material (Condition "C"), at fifty per cent (50%) of current new price, being used Material which:

A. Is not in sound and serviceable condition but suitable for reuse after reconditioning, or

B. Is serviceable for original function but not suitable for reconditioning.

5. *Bad-Order Material*

Material (Condition "D"), no longer suitable for its original purpose without excessive repair cost but usable for some other purpose at a price comparable with that of items normally used for such other purpose.

6. *Junk Material*

Junk Material (Condition "E"), being obsolete and scrap Material, at prevailing prices.

7. *Temporarily Used Material*

When the use of Material is temporary and its service to the Joint Property does not justify the reduction in price as provided for in Paragraph 3 B of this Section VI, such Material shall be priced on a basis that will leave a net charge to the Joint Account consistent with the value of the service rendered.

VII. Inventories

The Operator shall maintain detailed records of Material generally considered controllable by the Industry.

1. *Periodic Inventories, Notice and Representation*

At reasonable intervals, inventories shall be taken by Operator of the Joint Account Material, which shall include all such Material as is ordinarily considered controllable. Written notice of intention to take inventory shall be given by Operator at least thirty (30) days before any inventory is to begin so that Non-Operators may be represented when any inventory is taken. Failure of Non-Operators to be represented at an inventory shall bind Non-Operators to accept the inventory taken by Operator, who shall in that event furnish Non-Operators with a copy thereof.

2. *Reconciliation and Adjustment of Inventories*

Reconciliation of inventory with charges to the Joint Account shall be made, and a list of overages and shortages shall be jointly determined by Operator and Non-Operators. Inventory adjustments shall be made by Operator with the Joint Account for overages and shortages, but Operator shall be held accountable to Non-Operator only for shortages due to lack of reasonable diligence.

3. *Special Inventories*

Special inventories may be taken whenever there is any sale or change of interest in the Joint Property. It shall be the duty of the party selling to notify all other Parties as quickly as possible after the transfer of interest takes place. In such cases, both the seller and the purchaser shall be governed by such inventory.

Oil and Gas Lease

THIS AGREEMENT, made and entered into this 1st day of August, 1967 by and between Baggs Land and Cattle Corporation of 1808 Main Street, Kansas City, Missouri, hereinafter called lessor (whether one or more) and Calvert Drilling & Producing Co., P.O. Box 1655, Bismarck, N. Dak. hereinafter called lessee:

1. WITNESSETH: That the lessor, for and in consideration of $ One and No/100 cash in hand paid, receipt of which is hereby acknowledged, and of the covenants and agreements hereinafter contained on the part of the lessee to be paid, kept and performed, has granted, demised, leased and let and by these presents does grant, demise, lease and let exclusively unto said lessee, with the exclusive right of mining, exploring by geophysical and other methods and operating for and producing therefrom oil and all gas of whatsoever nature or kind, and laying pipe lines, telephone and telegraph lines, housing and boarding employees, building tanks, power stations, gasoline plants, ponds, roadways, and structures thereon to produce, save, market and take care of said products and the exclusive surface and subsurface rights and privileges related in any manner to any and all such operations and any and all other rights and privileges necessary, incident to, or convenient for the economical operation alone or conjointly with neighboring land for such purposes, all that certain tract or tracts of land situated in the County of Moffat, State of Colorado, described as follows, to-wit:

Township 12 North, Range 92 West	
Section 15:	Lots 6 and 9
Section 22:	Lot 2

This lease is subject to the terms and provisions of an agreement between the Lessor and Lessee herein dated April 28, 1967, the terms of which agreement are incorporated herein by reference.

2. It is agreed that this lease shall remain in force for a term of six months from date and as long thereafter as oil, or gas of whatsoever nature or kind, or either of them is produced from said land or premises pooled therewith or drilling operations are continued as hereinafter provided. If prior to discovery of oil or gas on said land, or on acreage pooled therewith, lessee should drill a dry hole or holes thereon, or if after discovery of oil or gas production thereafter should cease for any cause, this lease shall not terminate if lessee commences additional drilling or reworking operations within sixty (60) days thereafter, or (if it be within the primary term) commences or resumes the payment or tender of rental on or before the rental-paying date next ensuing after the expiration of three (3) months from the date of completion of a dry hole or cessation of production. If, at the expiration of the primary term of this lease, oil or gas is not being produced on or from said land or said pooled premises but lessee is then engaged in drilling or reworking operations thereon, then this lease shall continue in force so long thereafter as drilling or reworking operations are being continuously prosecuted on said land or on a drilling or development or operating unit which includes all or a part of said land; and drilling or reworking operations shall be considered to be continuously prosecuted if not more than sixty days shall elapse between the completion or abandonment of one well and the beginning of operations for the drilling or reworking of another well. If oil or gas shall be discovered and/or produced from any such well or wells drilled, being drilled or reworked at or after the expiration of the primary term of this lease shall continue in force so long thereafter as oil or gas is produced from the leased premises or from any such unit which includes all or a part of said lands.

3. In consideration of the premises the said lessee covenants and agrees:

(a)) To deliver to the credit of lessor, free of cost in the pipe line to which lessee may connect his wells, the equal one-eighth part of all oil produced and saved from the leased premises, or at the lessee's option, may pay to the lessor for such one-eighth royalty, the market price for oil of like grade and gravity prevailing on the day such oil is run into the pipe line or into storage tanks.

(b) To pay lessor for gas of whatsoever nature or kind produced and sold, or used off the premises, or used in the manufacture of any products therefrom, one-eighth, at the market price at the well for the gas sold, used off the premises, or in the manufacture of products therefrom. Where gas from a well producing gas only is not sold or used, lessee may pay or tender as royalty One Dollar per year per net royalty acre retained hereunder, such payment or tender to be made on or before the anniversary date of this lease next ensuing after the expiration of 90 days from the date such well is shut in and thereafter on or before the anniversary date of this lease during the period such well is shut in, to the royalty owners or to the royalty owners' credit in the rental depository bank herein designated. If such payment or tender is made, it will be considered that gas is being produced within the meaning of this lease.

4. If operations for the drilling of a well for oil or gas are not commenced or if there is no oil or gas being produced on said land or on acreage pooled therewith as hereinafter provided on or before one year from the date hereof, this lease shall terminate as to both parties.

5. Lessee, at its option, is hereby given the right and power at any time and from time to time as a recurring right, either before or after production, as to all or any part of the land described herein and as to any one or more of the formations hereunder, to pool or unitize the leasehold estate and the mineral estate covered by this lease with other land, lease or leases in the immediate vicinity for the production of oil and gas, or separately for the production of either, when in lessee's judgment it is necessary or advisable to do so, and irrespective of whether authority similar to this exists with respect to such other land, lease or leases. Likewise, units previously formed to include formations not producing oil or gas, may be reformed to exclude such non-producing formations. The forming or reforming of any unit shall be accomplished by lessee executing and filing of record a declaration of such unitization or reformation, which declaration shall describe the unit. Any unit may include land upon which a well has theretofore been completed or upon which operations for drilling have theretofore been commenced. Production, drilling or reworking operations or a well shut in for want of a market anywhere on a unit which includes all or a part of this lease shall be treated as if it were production, drilling or reworking operations or a well shut in for want of a market under this lease. In lieu of the royalties elsewhere herein specified, including shut-in gas royalties, lessor shall receive on production from the unit so pooled royalties only on the portion of such production allocated to this lease; such allocation shall be that proportion of the unit production that the total number of surface acres covered by this lease and included in the unit bears to the total number of surface acres in such unit. In addition to the foregoing, lessee shall have the right to unitize, pool, or combine all or any part of the above described lands as to one or more of the formations thereunder with other lands in the same general area by entering into a cooperative or unit plan of development or operation approved by any governmental authority and, from time to time, with like approval, to modify, change or terminate any such plan or agreement and, in such event, the terms, conditions, and provisions of this lease shall be deemed modified to conform to the terms, conditions, and provisions of such approved cooperative or unit plan of development or operation and, particularly, all drilling and development requirements of this lease, express or implied, shall be satisfied by compliance with the drilling and development requirements of such plan or agreement, and this

lease shall not terminate or expire during the life of such plan or agreement. In the event that said above described lands or any part thereof, shall hereafter be operated under any such cooperative or unit plan of development or operation whereby the production therefrom is allocated to different portions of the land covered by said plan, then the production allocated to any particular tract of land, for the purpose of computing the royalties to be paid hereunder to Lessor, be regarded as having been produced from the particular tract of land to which it is allocated and not to any other tract of land; and the royalty payments to be made hereunder to lessor shall be based upon production only as so allocated. Lessor shall formally express lessor's consent to any cooperative or unit plan of development or operation adopted by lessee and approved by any governmental agency by executing the same upon request of lessee.

6. Lessee may, at any time, release this lease as to any stratum or strata and as to part or all of the lands above described, after which all payments and liabilities thereafter to accrue, as to the lands released, shall cease and determine. In the event of a partial release, the annual delay rental above mentioned shall be reduced proportionately.

7. Lessee shall have the right to use, free of cost, gas, oil and water produced on said land for its operation thereon, except water from ditches, ponds, reservoirs, or wells of lessor.

When requested by the lessor, lessee shall bury its pipe lines on cultivated portions below plow depth.

No well shall be drilled nearer than 200 feet to the house or barn now on said premises, without the written consent of the lessor.

Lessee shall pay for damages caused by his operation to growing crops on said lands.

Lessee shall have the right at any time to remove all machinery and fixtures placed on said premises, including the right to draw and remove casing.

8. If the estate of either party hereto is assigned, and the privilege of assigning in whole or in part is expressly allowed, although it is agreed that no change or division in ownership of the land, rentals or royalties, however accomplished, shall operate to enlarge the obligations or diminish the rights of the lessee, the covenants hereof shall extend to their heirs, executors, administrators, successors or assigns, but no change in the ownership of the land or assignment of rentals or royalties shall be binding on the lessee until after the lessee has been furnished with certified copies of muniments of title deraigning title from lessor; and it is hereby agreed in the event this lease shall be assigned as to a part or parts of the above-described lands and the assignee or assignees of such part or parts shall fail or make default in the payment of the proportionate part of the rents due from him or them, such default shall not operate to defeat or affect this lease insofar as it covers a part or parts of said lands as to which the said lessee or any assignee thereof shall make due payment of said rental. In the event of death of any person entitled to rentals hereunder, lessee may pay or tender such rentals to the credit of the deceased or the estate of the deceased until such time as lessee is furnished with proper evidence of the appointment and qualification of an executor or administrator of the estate, or if there be none, then until lessee is furnished with evidence satisfactory to it as to the heirs or devisees of the deceased.

9. Lessor hereby warrants and agrees to defend the title to the lands herein described, and agrees that the lessee shall have the right at any time to pay for lessor, any mortgage, taxes or other liens on the above-described lands in the event of default of payment by lessor, and be subrogated to the rights of the holder thereof, and lessor hereby agrees that any such payments made by

the lessee for the lessor may be deducted from any amounts of money which may become due the lessor under the terms of this lease.

10. If said lessor owns a less interest in the above-described land than the entire and undivided fee simple estate therein, then the royalties and rentals herein provided shall be paid the lessor only in proportion which his interest bears to the whole and undivided fee. Any interest in the production from the lands herein described to which the interest of lessor may be subject shall be deducted from the royalty herein reserved.

11. Lessee shall comply with all laws and regulations of any Governmental body purporting to exercise taxing authority over the lands covered by this lease or the person of the lessor herein and in so complying lessee shall not be responsible for determining the legality, validity or constitutionality of any such law or regulation enacted or issued by any such Governmental body. In determining the residence of lessor for purpose of complying with such laws or regulations lessee may rely upon the address of lessor herein set forth or upon the last known address of lessor. Neither any error in the determination of the residence or status of lessor nor an error in the payment of any sums of money due or payable to lessor under the terms of this lease which is made during the course of or as a result of lessee's good faith efforts to comply with any such laws or regulations shall terminate this lease or constitute grounds for any cause of action against lessee. All of lessee's obligations and covenants hereunder, whether express or implied, shall be suspended at the time or from time to time as compliance with any thereof is prevented or hindered by or is in conflict with Federal, State, County, or municipal laws, rules, regulations or Executive Orders asserted as official by or under public authority claiming jurisdiction, or Act of God, adverse field, weather, or market conditions, inability to obtain materials in the open market or transportation thereof, war, strikes, lockouts, riots, or other conditions or circumstances not wholly controlled by lessee, and this lease shall not be terminated in whole or in part, nor lessee held liable in damages for failure to comply with any such obligations or covenants if compliance therewith is prevented or hindered by or is in conflict with any of the foregoing eventualities. The time during which lessee shall be prevented from conducting drilling or reworking operations during the primary term of this lease, under the contingencies above stated, shall be added to the primary term of the lease; provided, however, that delay rentals as herein provided shall not be suspended by reason of the suspension of operations and if this lease is extended beyond the primary term above stated by reason of such suspension, lessee shall pay an annual delay rental on the anniversary dates hereof in the manner and in the amount above provided.

12. Should any person, firm or corporation have an interest in the above-described land, not leased to lessee, or should any one or more of the parties named above as lessors not execute this lease, it shall nevertheless be binding upon the party or parties executing the same.

13. The undersigned lessors for themselves and their heirs, successors, and assigns, hereby expressly release and waive all rights under and by virtue of the homestead exemption laws of said state, insofar as the same may in any way affect the purposes for which this lease is made as recited herein.

IN WITNESS WHEREOF, the undersigned execute this instrument as of the day and year first above written.

BAGGS LAND AND CATTLE CORPORATION

ATTEST: By:

Ronald Jarvis, Jr., Secretary H. L. Oppenheimer, President

ACKNOWLEDGMENTS

State of ______________ } ss.
County of ______________ }

INDIVIDUAL, North Dakota, South Dakota, Nebraska

On this ______________ day of ______________, 19______, before me, personally appeared ______________, to me known to be the person described in and who executed the foregoing instrument, and acknowledged to me that ______________ executed the same as ______________ free act and deed.

My commission expires:

______________ ______________
Notary Public.

State of ______________ } ss.
County of ______________ }

INDIVIDUAL, North Dakota, South Dakota, Nebraska

On this ______________ day of ______________, 19______, before me, personally appeared ______________, to me known to be the person described in and who executed the foregoing instrument, and acknowledged to me that ______________ executed the same at ______________ free act and deed.

My commission expires:

______________ ______________
Notary Public.

Dated ______________, 19______
No. Acres ______________
______________ County
Term ______________

This instrument was filed for record on the ______________ day of ______________ 19______, at ______________ o'clock ______ M., and duly recorded in Book ______________, Page ______________ of the ______________ records of this office.

____
Register of Deeds.

By ______________, Deputy

When recorded return to

____

State of Missouri } ss.
County of Jackson }

CORPORATE, North Dakota, South Dakota, Nebraska

On this 4th day of Aug. in the year 1967, before me, a Notary Public, personally appeared H. L. Oppenheimer and Ronald Jarvis, Jr., known to me to be the President and Secretary of the Corporation that is described in and that executed the within instrument and acknowledged to me that such Corporation executed the same.

My commission expires:
October 25, 1967

Doris S. D. Palermo
Notary Public.

AREAS OF LITIGATION

Land Sales

Other than problems of inheritance, foreclosures of mortgages, mechanics' liens thrown on properties for failure to pay construction costs, the principal area of litigation of land sales comes through either the buyer or the seller failing to live up to the provisions of the sales contract. Problems could arise in the mortgage documents, deeds, or title policies, but these are of a lesser frequency.

The biggest source of trouble occurs when the property either goes up or down rapidly in value between the time the sales contract is signed and the time the deed is transferred. This is a place where the "sharpie" type speculator starts to look for some kind of clause or clause violation by which he can wiggle out of the contract. This is the point where if, as a "gifted amateur" you wrote up the contract yourself, you will sincerely regret that you did not have a competent real estate attorney or real estate broker do it for you.

A few of the ways that sales contracts can be voided or rendered unenforceable follow:

1. There is a major error in the legal description.

2. There is a minor exception on the title which legally may render the title "unmerchantable." This may be of no consequence but the seller cannot quickly get it removed and the buyer can seize it as a means of getting out of the contract because it cannot be cleared up prior to the time limits set for a delivery. If the defect is of a monetary nature such as a lien that has not been removed, the seller may be able to hold the buyer to the agreement in a court of law by quickly putting up a bond to cover the precise amount of the potential obligation with his bond being released when he does get it cleared up at a later date.

3. The "seller" on the sales contract is not the owner of record on the title.

4. The seller is a married individual and signed a sales contract himself but the buyer failed to get the wife's signature on the sales contract and the seller's wife (possibly at the instigation of the seller who wants to get out of the contract) refuses to go along on signing the deed. In some states this does not necessarily void the sale but the wife may have subsequent "dower rights" which would form a permanent cloud on the title or require a future "quiet title

suit." In any case, the absence of the wife's signature would be noted as an exception on the title insurance policy.

5. The buyer may put a "straw name" on the sales contract and subsequently refuse to go through with it. The term comes from a man stuffed with straw such as one of the principal characters of the *Wizard of Oz,* i.e. a person of no net worth or substance, from whom one would be able to recover nothing if he or she were sued. Often this device is used with the knowledge of both parties if secrecy is required and it is desired that the identity of the buyer not be revealed on the public record. The "straw" takes title and gives an unrecorded deed to the actual buyer with only the name of the "straw" appearing on the public records. When this device is used as a means of defaulting on a sales contract, and it can be established that this was the original intent, the seller, in most states, can probably force the buyer to go through with the sale anyway.

6. The buyer puts a "straw corporation" on the contract. This is a different arrangment altogether as it is up to the seller to check the net worth, ask for a financial statement and make his own investigation of the corporation if he feels that it might not have sufficient assets to go through with the deal. In most cases, the officers and stockholders of a corporation take on no personal liability provided that there was no intent to defraud. Normally, such a default on a contract is due to lack of resources. All of these are very fine points which might go either way in a court action.

7. One of the commonest areas of litigation is where the seller agrees to something in the contract that he can't deliver and he is sued for damages by the buyer or for a commission by either his agent or the buyer's agent. This might occur if he specifies that he can deliver the property free and clear of all mortgages and finds that he has a mortgage on it which has no prepayment clause and the holder of the mortgage refuses to release it under any conditions. The buyer may or may not be willing to accept an escrow deposit equivalent to the mortgage. Technically, the mortgagee could ask that all future interest be paid as well as the principal before he would release it. This could be quite expensive and may or may not satisfy the problem depending on the local state laws.

In the same general catagory but on the other side of the fence the buyer may not be able to get the mortgage financing that he expected and cannot come up with either the cash or an adequate substitute, and both parties end up in court. The answer to this extremely common problem is "never sign a sales contract until you have an ironclad mortgage commitment from a responsible lending agency in advance or have a financing contingency clause in the contract."

8. If either party thinks he is dealing with a "fast operator" there is nothing wrong in having a sales contract notarized and recorded just as you would a deed. If you think there is a chance that the seller might sell the property to someone else at a higher price before closing and then let you go to court and try to collect damages and yet you still would prefer not revealing the terms of the sale contract to the entire world, a simple device is to have your real estate broker sign an affidavit establishing that he is a broker, that he is licensed, giving his license number, and state that on such-and-such a date such-and-such parties signed a sales contract on property legally described as blank-blank and then have this affidavit recorded in the county where the property lies. The existence of such a document filed as a matter of record should effectively stop any "monkey business." On the other hand, you had better be sure you know what you are doing and that a valid contract does, in fact, exist because otherwise you would be "slandering the title" and lay yourself open to a major lawsuit if a subsequent sale were blocked.

Leases

Outside of the failure to pay rent (which could result in a "pasture lien on the cattle"), most litigation in this area derives from the landlord failing to provide a contracted service or the tenant abusing the property. Before the 1953 drought, it was customary in Kansas bluestem leases for the landlord to "guarantee salt and water." The drought saw land owners having to buy trucks and trailers and haul water from as far away as 50 miles at enormous expense.

Landlords who didn't fulfill this clause were hauled into court and there were hundreds of lawsuits. It is left out today. Many tenants hauled the water themselves and then sued the landlords for the cost. In some cases, they moved the cattle hundreds of miles away and sued the landlords for the new rent and transportation.

Damage suits on land abuse can often be eliminated by use of a camera. On one particular five-year lease in Missouri, the landlord claimed he had suffered $20,000 damages by the tenants failure to mow. The case blew up when the tenant produced pictures that he was able to establish were taken at the time the lease commenced. He also introduced pictures taken at the time the lease terminated. He then brought forth a tree expert who testified that scrub oak-type brush with trunks 7 inches in diameter could not have grown up during the lease period and had to have existed before.

Commissions

The easiest way to avoid lawsuits on commissions is to actually insert into the sales contract who is the agent of record that negotiated the sale, who is to pay him, and how much he is to be paid. When more than one agent is involved or when each party has their own agent or broker, both names should be entered and the relationship of the brokers stated with the amounts of who is to pay to whom and how much. This action would eliminate most of the lawsuits in this area.

Traditionally, if this is left out, the agent representing both parties normally attempts to collect his commission from the seller. If no commission is specified or if the amount of the commission is not specified he can usually get a court to award him the customary commission rate for the type of transaction as established by the real estate board in the area. It is the responsibility of the agent to be able to prove that he was employed by one of the parties to find a buyer or find a property and that he was the "procuring cause of the sale." When an agent writes an owner and says "I have a buyer for your property at such-and-such a price" and the owner subsequently sells the property to the man named but through another agent, the first agent has no claim but will probably go to court and try to collect something anyway.

The agent must prove he has a written or an oral agreement from the owner that he can represent him before he is entitled to any commission. The big problem here is that oral arrangements in this area are often recognized for *commission* purposes even though they are not recognized in most states for the *transfer* of real property. The end result of most "oral arrangements" in this type of situation is a major court action.

One way that an owner can stop himself from this type of harrassment is to *state in writing* to the agent that he will recognize him only if he can produce a written statement from the buyer that he is willing to make such-and-such an offer or that he is giving the agent an exclusive right to represent him. This statement should be further amplified as to whether the buyer is willing to pay the commission or expects the seller to pay the commission.

On a really large transaction it is certainly prudent to have a check made of any agent that you plan to employ as to his credit, reputation, and whether or not he has had any trouble with the ethics committee of the local real estate board or the state real estate commission. If he has ever had his license suspended this is a matter of public record and can easily be determined by a simple letter of inquiry.

PART IV

URBAN LAND TRANSACTIONS

Chapter XIII

Evaluating Urban Vacant

DEFINITIONS

For the purpose of this analysis, we are going to define "vacant land" as that whose income from either parking, agricultural use, or inadequate improvements for the location represents, after real estate taxes, so little net that it can be considered almost negligible relative to the sales price of the property. Specific examples could be the following:

1. You own 100 acres on the edge of the suburban growth of a large urban area where the land in your neighborhood is going for $500 per acre. You are receiving $600 per year in rent for your property as a horse pasture, and the real estate taxes are $500 per year.

2. You own a 30,000-square foot property in an expanding area of a fringe district in a moderate size city. The property could be sold rapidly for $2 per square foot, or $60,000. You are currently getting $3,000 per year for public parking. Your real estate taxes are $1,000 per year; the cost of a parking attendant is $1,500 per year; and the property is costing you $500 per year in clerical effort.

3. You own a 10,000-square foot tract in an urban area where land values are going for $5 per square foot, giving you a potential quick sale price of $50,000. The property has on it a 30-year-old apartment house with 20 units. You have normally been running a 20% vacancy factor. Your gross revenue is $12,000 per year; your real estate taxes are $1,000; your direct operating expenses are $8,000; and every second or third year you can count on a major expense with the furnace, the roof, the window frames, or the sidewalk, that will cost you $2,000.

For the purposes of this chapter, all three of the preceding are to be considered "vacant land." The income from the present improvements and use does not bear a realistic relationship to its sales value for other purposes. To simplify the study, let us assume that there is sufficient revenue from one source or another to match the real estate taxes and insurance so that no cash loss is involved. If you have an annual cash deficit, the problem is aggravated.

TAX CONSIDERATIONS ON SALE

For further purposes of simplification, let us assume that all properties were purchased for 10% of their present value or that they stand on the owner's books at 10% of the present value and that they have been fully depreciated or the depreciation is of such a minor amount as to be negligible and that there is no particular advantage of holding the property for depreciation and tax loss. Let us further assume that the owner is in a tax bracket higher than 50%. On this basis, a sale will cause the owner to sustain capital gains tax of 90% of 25%, or 22½%.

In the event he sells his property on an installment basis and takes less than a 30% downpayment, he does not have to pay his tax except as he receives the principal balance of his mortgage. Consequently, he is able to make his interest rate not only on his money but also on the money that he will eventually have to pay the government.

For example, Mr. "A" owns a property which has been held for a number of years which he sells for $110,000, $10,000 down and a $100,000 mortgage. The property had a remaining capital base of $10,000 so he has a capital gain of $100,000 and a tax of $25,000 to eventually pay. His mortgage draws 6% interest. The 6%, of course, is fully taxable each year as he receives it as ordinary income. On his downpayment of $10,000, he is going to owe a tax of 1/11th of the $25,000, or approximately $2,300. However, on the balance of his mortgage, he is going to draw the full interest of 6% on the $100,000, or $6,000 per year, even though about $22,000 of this $100,000 really does not belong to him but belongs to the government and will eventually have to be paid to the government as the mortgage balance is reduced.

The principal point in all of this is, that even for a man who is in the very highest tax brackets and who holds his property almost at a zero on his books, the tax liability involved in this kind of sale is not really so painful that it should materially affect his business judgment on whether or not to sell.

For a person whose bracket runs from 20% to 30%, the alternative method of calculating capital gains tax would put him in a 10% or 15% tax. If on top of this he has not depreciated the property to zero and has any kind of capital base, the tax liability in the event of a sale may be small enough that it should hardly be considered at all.

ALTERNATIVE USE OF SALE PROCEEDS

We finally get down to the $64 question—"Is the potential annual growth in land value of the tract concerned greater than the owner could expect to make from the sale funds after paying his income taxes and re-investing the proceeds in other real estate, mortgages, common stocks, or in his own business?"

To simplify the situation even further, let us assume that the owner could re-invest the proceeds in an impeccably secure 6% mortgage. It might even be on a purchase money mortgage on the property that he has just sold which would at least have the security of his original investment and would have avoided most of the capital gains tax described previously. By equal security, I mean that, should the borrower default, the seller of the property would recapture the same property that he had before. We will further assume that any down-payment that the seller received was also safely invested at 6%.

The following is a table of $100,000 invested at 6% compounded semi-annually. You will note that on the twelfth year the money has reached $200,000, and the holder of the mortgage has doubled his money. Again, for the sake of simplification, we will use a broad brush treatment and assume that government income taxes have taken a sufficient bite out of the interest income to delay this doubling of

$100,000 INVESTED AT 6% COMPOUNDED SEMI-ANNUALLY

$100,000		$142,577	
3,000		4,277	
$103,000		$146,854	
3,090		4,406	
$106,090	First year	$151,260	Seventh year
3,183		4,538	
$109,273		$155,798	
3,278		4,674	
$112,551	Second year	$160,472	Eighth year
3,377		4,814	
$115,928		$165,286	
3,478		4,959	
$119,406	Third year	$170,245	Ninth year
3,582		5,107	
$122,988		$175,352	
3,690		5,261	
$126,678	Fourth year	$180,613	Tenth year
3,800		5,418	
$130,478		$186,031	
3,914		5,581	
$134,392	Fifth year	$191,612	Eleventh year
4,032		5,748	
$138,424		$197,360	
4,153		5,921	
$142,577	Sixth year	$203,281	Twelfth year

one's money by an additional 2 years and it could take 14 years to double one's money after taxes on interest.

Now, the question comes up—"Can the owner anticipate his property being worth $200,000 at the end of the fourteenth year?" Remember also that if he sells the property for $200,000, he will be subject to a $25,000 additional capital gains tax at that time and would only net $175,000, but we will disregard this point.

REALISTIC APPRAISAL OF GROWTH

All of us have read countless stories of the Texas rancher's grandfather who bought land at 50¢ an acre which his heirs eventually sold for $1,000 per acre. We have heard of properties that were bought in 1870 around 57th and Madison Avenue in New York for $2 per square foot that are now selling for $50 per square foot. We know of midwestern farm land that went for $100 per acre and was resold 15 years later for suburban housing at $2,000 per acre. These are the tales that make good reading.

There are also the tales of frenzy, boom, and bust, where properties that were purchased at $1,000 per acre on the basis of the railroad or highway going through which never happened, and the properties were eventually resold for $100 per acre. There are urban stories—properties on a street that looked like it was going to go fashionable that went for $2,000 per front foot, with the properties eventually being sold for $200 per front foot. These sales were not necessarily in the middle of a depression, but were after the glamour had worn off. All of these extremes are the exceptions.

The normal pattern of urban growth which doesn't make dramatic reading is the property that was bought at $3 per square foot and 15 years later was sold for $5 per square foot. "Close-in" acreage for suburban development was bought for $600 per acre, and 10 years later was sold for $1,000 per acre. With good judgment, good negotiating ability on both the buying and selling end, and a reasonable amount of luck, this type of thing can be accomplished in a country with an expanding population and an expanding economy with a mild touch of annual inflation. The question is—"How does this relate to the same amount of money invested at 6% compounded semi-annually?" I believe that the answer is that it takes a bit more than the average amount of skill and judgment and a bit more than the average amount of luck to make it match.

Land values move in spurts and vary tremendously from state to state, city to city, and districts within cities. As a base of reference, chronologically, it would probably not be realistic to take the bottom of the depression in the 1930's nor the height of the boom in 1929, but to use as sort of a base year, say, 1925. This is approximately 45 years ago. Again, it is not realistic to take the spectacular examples, such as the residential area of Beverly Hills or Third Avenue in New York, where values have gone up 10 times, nor to take 16th and Main in Kansas City where the properties are now selling at one-third of what they were doing 40 years ago.

If the reader would pick 10 rural tracts with which he is generally familiar, determine their land value in 1925, and find their values today, I believe the average would show a growth of 5% per year. This is the national average on farm land in this century.

Let us look at urban "vacant," leaving out the dozen or so spectacular cases that you might be able to find in a growing city and leaving out the half-dozen spectacular cities, such as Phoenix, Houston, Beverly Hills, and Miami. I believe that the reader would find that the average of the 10 properties that he selected as far as land tracts are concerned are going now, 40 years later, at about three times what they were bringing in 1925. The same funds invested at 6% compounded semi-annually would multiply over seven times at the end of a 40-year-period (they double every 14 years).

The price status at a given moment has a lot to do with the results that you can expect. For example, urban property that you can either buy or sell at $3 per square foot has historically more chance of going to $6 per square foot than property that you could buy for $6 per square foot going to $12 per square foot. Likewise, suburban type acreage that you can buy for $500 per acre has substantially more chance of going to $1,000 per acre than land costing $2,000 per acre going to $4,000 per acre.

In both cases, as you get into the larger numbers as far as real estate is concerned, you get into a much more limited development market. For example, $5 per square foot land in the middle of a city might justify one- and two-story buildings with attached parking, for which there is a substantial demand. Twelve dollars per square foot land in an average city of under 2 million in population could only be used for high-rise buildings or for 100% retail shopping areas in downtown districts. It is relatively unlikely that lightning will strike here, as districts of this type of development are usually fairly limited. Likewise, residential land that could be sold at $1,000 per acre can be developed into lots for homes selling around $15,000 to $20,000 of which there is a substantial demand. Land selling for $4,000 per acre needs homes in the $35,000 to $40,000 bracket, and these are pretty hard to sell.

In most business successes, planning has been everything. If you bought land at $2 per square foot, have held it for 10 years, and can now sell it for $4 per square foot, should you do this or should you hold it another 10 years with the hope of being able to sell it for $8 per square foot? There are several factors involved here:

1. The second 10 years will be tougher.
2. At the present sales price of $4 per square foot, you would now have more money to invest at 6% interest for your comparative analysis purposes, and the 6% of the larger figure may be a matter of some consideration where 6% of the original $2 per square foot figure was negligible.
3. In cases where a small amount of net income has been achieved, one should recognize that it might bear a favorable relationship to the original $2 per square foot purchase price but is no longer favorable when compared to the 6% interest one could be making on the potential $4 per square foot sales price of the present moment.
4. A steady growth in land value such as 4% per year does not compound semi-annually; interest does.

THE "BID"-"ASKED" APPROACH

If an owner is holding land as a business investment and not because of family tradition, prestige, or emotional reasons, then he should not let himself get too far away from the "bid" versus "asked" frame of reference. This is the way of life of the security dealers and the commodity brokers.

At a given day at a given hour, someone would pay "X" amount of dollars for 100 shares of General Motors. Someone else would sell 100 shares of General Motors for "Y" amount of dollars.

Real estate is not so simple because no two pieces of property could ever be exactly alike. Even if there were buildings that were absolutely identical, they would have to be on two pieces of land, and one location might be slightly more desirable than the other.

Vacant land or land with negligible income-producing improvements would, however, fit into this "bid"-"asked" picture better than most forms of real estate. In other words, within the same block or two in the city area or within the same general suburban district, land, that was not noticeably different from another piece as far as grading and usability were concerned, should be dispassionately studied by an owner in connection with other market sales as they appear from time to time. I am assuming that the owner is interested in money and is not emotionally involved with his property.

We now get into the "spread" situation. It would be extremely unusual if on a given day the bid price of General Motors stock was $45 and the asked price was $50, with there being a "spread" of $5. This would be a spread of 10% of the value and would be almost unheard of in any security or commodity that had a broad market. In real estate vacant land, however, a 10% "spread" would occur more frequently than it would not.

For example, in a given business district in more or less identical locations, it would be very common to see properties being bid for at $4.50 per square foot with the owners asking $5 per square foot. Owners holding out for $5 per square foot would be not at all disturbed to see actual sales going through at $4.50 per square foot, and this would in no way cause them to lower their prices. Generally, this should not be called an unrealistic attitude.

However, where this "spread" should go from 10% to 25%, then possibly an owner who really wished to sell should re-evaluate his position. For example, if he were holding his property at $5 per square foot and saw frequent sales at $3.75 per square foot or less, then he might consider that he would have a few years to wait before he could even get $4.50 per square foot, or that if he got an offer of $4.50 per square foot, that it might be better for him to take it and start making a 6% return on the money rather than to wait five years and hope to get his $5 per square foot. Likewise, if he had cash available and really thought that his property was worth $5 per square foot, then he should go out to try to snap up any properties that might be hitting the market at the $3.75 figure.

At times, one may fall heir to special windfalls such as a developer who needs to round out an assemblage or a building owner who wishes to expand his property or acquire adjacent parking. In these instances where a price of possibly 20% over what some "like" properties in the district are going for can be obtained, the offer should be carefully evaluated and the original price that one paid for one's own property should not enter into the equation. For example, if you own a lot that you bought for $2 per square foot and someone offered you a price, because of a special situation, of $5 per square foot for your own, you should not hesitate to accept it and, if you liked the neighborhood, go out and replace it with a similar property at $4 per square foot. The fact that you had originally paid $2 for your own should not influence you as the 20% spread between $4 and $5 is better than most investors can do in most fields.

If a tax situation is involved, have the proposed purchaser buy the other property and trade it for yours with a $1 per square foot "boot." Before you hold out on your sale for a $6 or $7 per square foot figure, feeling that the purchaser has to have it, you should carefully analyze the situation and his estimated requirements. The most successful big money that has been made by real estate operators has been by those who have sold on prices that were "high but not ridiculous." In turn, they reinvest in land that may not be in distress but is priced "realistically."

Naturally, you would prefer a "spread" of 50%. In other words, you would like to be able to sell property at $6 per square foot and replace it with something of equal value and use at $3 per square foot, or with something comparable in price with what you paid for the original tract. This is usually impossible at a given time and place and you may have to wait a long time. Waiting a long time is expensive if you are sitting on nonincome producing property that could be sold, with the proceeds reinvested at 6% compounded semi-annually.

REVERSE CASH FLOW

All of the preceding analysis was on the basis that there was enough net income from agriculture, parking, or the improvements to at least equal real estate taxes and carrying charges. If this property is held on a mortgage, and interest charges are going out, this may be hard to do.

For example, you hold a vacant suburban tract with no income worth $100,000 at the present time, and real estaate taxes are $1,000 per year and interest charges are $5,000 per year for a total of $6,000. Here you have to reverse the previous table showing what happens to $100,000 invested at 6% interest compounded semi-annually. In other words, the property has to double in value in 12 years for you to just break even.

A common failing in this type of analysis by an owner is his failure to put a dollar tag on his own time and effort in management. If one is evaluating a slum-type apartment that takes 40 hours per month to collect rents, answer phones, pay bills, show tenants, and do bookkeeping for, and you feel that your time is worth $5 per hour, then you have a legitimate management charge of around $2,400 per year that should be tossed into "carrying charges," even if it is not actually paid out.

Another common "hidden cost" is to be practically self-insured on liability insurance and not be aware of it. For example, a $200,000 liability policy on a 50,000-square foot old apartment building would cost upwards of $4,000 per year. With the kind of judgments juries are now awarding in personal injuries, the customary $10,000 or $20,000 policy is totally inadequate. Furthermore, owning the property corporately in a small family corporation may not be adequate, as in these types of cases, judges and juries often "pierce the corporate veil." Consequently, your insurance is low because you are inadequately covered, and you should still throw a factor into your cost analysis representing the dollar value of the risk you are personally carrying.

On operating and maintenance costs, don't be an optimist. If the property you are carrying for land speculation has a 50-year-old building on it, be realistic. Each year you are going to have a major expense, and each year it is going to be a different one. If it isn't the wiring, plumbing, roof, screens, furnace, or window sills, it will be the city inspectors on a new fire escape.

Depreciation (not tax-wise, but actual) proceeds in a geometric pattern. Your annual costs in a 60-year-old building will be double those at 40. When you get to 80, they will double again. At a certain level, costs of major repairs in an old building can be substantially greater than new construction. If you are not trying to preserve an historic landmark, it just isn't worth it.

TAX CONSIDERATIONS IN DEMOLITION

If you can establish your intent that you bought a property with certain improvements on it for the purpose of using them; actually used them for a number of years; lost money while doing so; demolished the improvements; and used the land for something else—it is possible that the government would permit you to deduct the remaining undepreciated value of the improvements on your books.

This is not simple and you will have to be prepared to document everything as the practice has been highly abused. For example, you buy a farm with elaborate chicken house facilities to which you assign a value of $10,000 from your purchase price. You never raise chickens on the farm, but only dairy cattle. In a couple of years, you tear out the chicken facilities and put up another dairy barn. The chances are you will not get to write off the $10,000, as the government will claim you intended to do this in the first place and make you ascribe the $10,000 to land and other items on the farm. If you ran chickens for a couple of years, you would be on firm ground.

The same principles would apply to old apartment buildings or rooming houses on urban land. Here the sums involved are bigger, and the documentation must be even more thorough. Demolition immediately after purchase would rarely be accepted for tax write-off. If improvements were never occupied or used, you are on weak ground. Your allocation of value between improvements and land will have to be substantiated. The Internal Revenue Service is very sophisticated in this area.

EMOTIONAL FACTORS

Anthropologists tell us that the desire to hold land, the desire to take exclusive possession of a particularly favorable hunting ground, the desire to keep intruders out of a favorite berry patch and retain the berries for the exclusive use of oneself and one's immediate relatives, is a primitive instinct that goes back to the distant recesses of man's evolutionary forebears. Not only is it characteristic of a large number of the primate families, it is also an attribute of many lower forms of animals. Hunting rights, fishing rights, and grazing rights on given tracts of forest and meadow were the direct or indirect cause of most of Primitive Man's wars and conflicts. This became more pronounced when Modern Man first started cultivating crops.

Because no two tracts of land can ever occupy the same area of the earth's surface, all land has to be unique in character. Because of this uniqueness, it is rare that an owner would consider it in the same nature as 1,000 bushels of wheat which could be almost identical to another 1,000 bushels of wheat. For this reason it acquires some of the quality, in an owner's eye, of a rare old painting. One has gotten used to it; there is no other like it; one is proud to display it; and the longer it has been in one's family, the more prestige it has.

In medieval times, the titles of nobility went to the men who had seized land by force of arms and whose castles were able to repel successive waves of intruders. The longer you had held your land, the more important and prestigious was your title. This basic concept still exists today.

How often has one heard the statement, "Our ranch is on the land that my great-great-grandfather homesteaded in 1810 after he seized it from the Indians." "This shoe factory that I own is on the site where my great-grandfather set up his blacksmith shop after he founded this town." These are emotional attributes of property ownership; they are not to be sneered at; and you cannot put a dollar sign on them.

To a lesser degree when one has held a building for 30 years, personally repaired the plumbing when it was necessary, driven by it every day on one's way to work, hopefully watched the neighborhood for signs of progress, and told its good points to dozens of potential tenants over the years, one convinces onself of its many virtues. Because of the natural instinct of pride of ownership, one does not see the cracks in the sidewalk, the deteriorating woodwork on the side, and the gradual encroachment of slum and second-rate tenancies in the neighborhood. One passes over the annual deterioration of the financial statement, where the annual rents seem to be going down and the vacancies and maintenance going up, on the basis that this is a "temporary" situation and not the encroachment of time and obsolescence. Some miracle or windfall is going to come along, and the property will again produce a handsome net as in its former glory. One can always look at Third Avenue in New York! For a whole century it went downhill, and today it is booming with leaps and bounds. The same thing is going to happen to Main Street in Podunk, Indiana. Look at Phoenix and Colorado Springs!

The preceding statements represent emotional attitudes associated with the "pride of ownership" and bear no relationship to the ordinary economic and real estate formulae. Even where sophisticated and intelligent owners are involved, who could make a coldblooded analysis of someone else's property, the books go out the window when their own property is concerned. A reference to the laws of probability, comparative returns from other real estate, or other investments, or the possible further deterioration of their investment—all of these only serve to irritate the property holder.

SUMMARY

We defined "vacant land" in this chapter as property whose net return from its present agricultural or commercial use bears so little relationship to its market value that it can be considered negligible. Its retention can only be justified on the speculative possibility of further value increase or its development for another economic use. Where the owner is not planning to develop it himself for another use, his reasons for retention are usually stated as follows:

1. If I sold it, I would be killed by income taxes.
2. Where would I reinvest the money after I sold it?
3. Because of the shortage of this kind of property and the growth of the town, I will make a fortune if I just sit on it.

Before taking a completely hard-nosed stand and attempting to disregard any emotional factors involved, the owner should look at the following:

1. Precisely what are the tax liabilities if the property is sold?

If there is a small capital base, and with the capital gain bracket only being half of the ordinary tax bracket, and with most of the tax being deferred in the event of an installment sale, it is possible that the tax may not be substantial.

2. On the basis that the funds derived from a sale can be reinvested at 6% compounded semi-annually, one would see one's investment doubled in a geometric progression every 14 years (after a moderate tax bracket). How does this compare with property's growth potential?

Chapter XIV

Effect of Assemblage in Condemnation Proceedings

On April 24, 1963, the Missouri State Highway Commission seized five tracts of land owned by the Airport Auditorium-Motel Corporation totaling 74,000 square feet. The state's position was that the tracts were worth about $5 per square foot because of previous sales. The owner's position was that they were worth $10 per square foot because of assemblage (plottage).

Because of the dearth of any recent sales in the area that could be introduced as evidence, five tracts not being condemned were evaluated by formula. In a condemnation suit, neither party is permitted to use the price of acquisition of a parcel being condemned as evidence, nor can they use any property in the area that was seized by condemnation, nor sold under threat of condemnation.

The following plat map (Exhibit I) indicates the properties seized by the Highway Commission and the Nicholas, Armacost, Hutchings, Brown and Holland properties used as examples of the pricing formula.

The other exhibits for the appraisal are:

Exhibit II: Appraisal Summary
Exhibit III: Appraisal Technique
Exhibit IV: Plottage Factors
Exhibit V: Application of Formula to Area

Prior to the seizure, the owners had tentative approval from the City Plan Commission of Kansas City for an urban renewal project taking in a much larger assemblage which the seizure disrupted. Part of the evidence presented to the Condemnation Board was a feasibility study and an outline of how this would be handled as a public corporation. An outline of the pertinent features of a future prospectus is shown as Exhibit VI. The values and construction costs relate to Kansas City in the year 1964.

EXHIBIT I

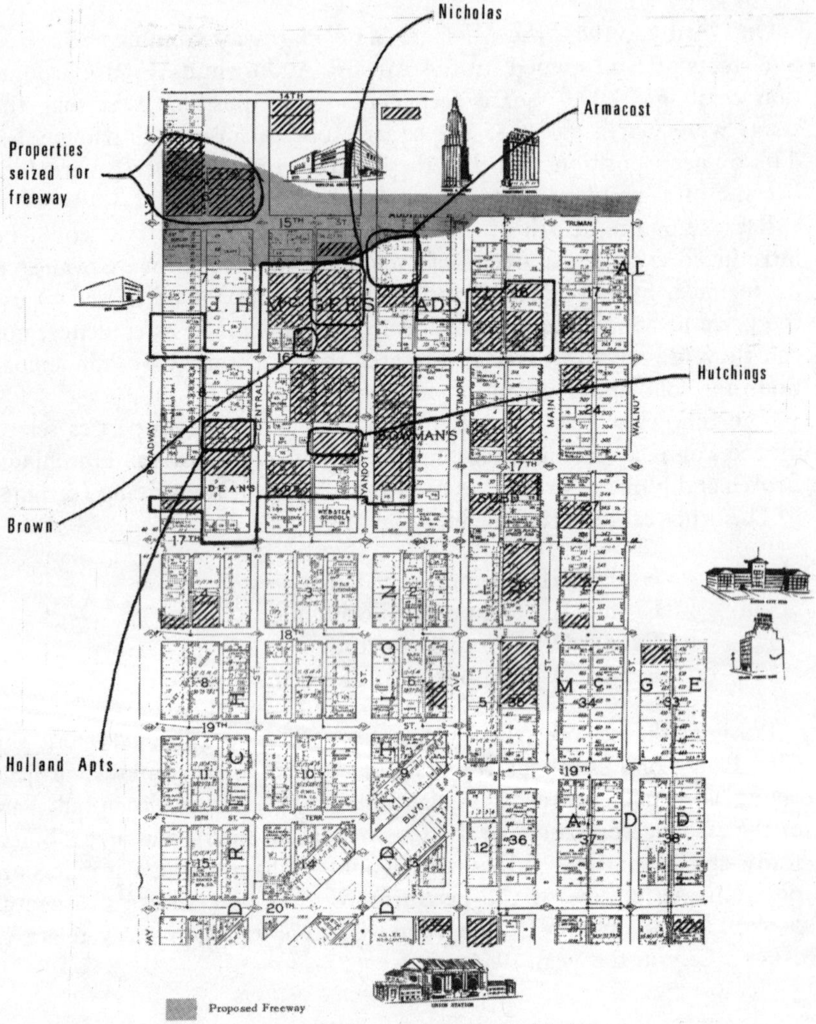
Nicholas
Armacost
Properties seized for freeway
Hutchings
Brown
Holland Apts.
J. H. McGEES ADD
BOWMAN'S
DEAN'S
14TH
15TH ST.
17TH ST.
18TH
19TH
20TH
BROADWAY
CENTRAL
WYANDOTTE
BALTIMORE
MAIN
WALNUT
TRUMAN
WEBSTER SCHOOL
Proposed Freeway
Properties owned, managed, or under option ,by Oppenheimer Industries, Inc. and associated companies.

EXHIBIT II: APPRAISAL SUMMARY

Appraisal Airport-Auditorium Motel Corporation in Vicinity of 15th, Broadway, and Central, Kansas City, Missouri

A. General

As of 24 April 1963, the Airport-Auditorium Motel Corporation, a Missouri corporation, had legal title to an assembled tract of approximately 74,000 square feet (including its half of alleys that could be closed) made up of the following legally described parcels:

1425 Broadway: Lot 13, Block 12, REID'S ADDITION, and Lot 73, Block 6, J. H. McGEE'S ADDITION, subdivisions in Kansas City, Jackson County, Missouri, according to the respective recorded plats thereof.

1417-23 Broadway: Lots 14, 15 and 16, Block 12, REID'S ADDITION, a subdivision in Kansas City, Jackson County, Missouri, according to the plat thereof.

1426-32 Central: All of Lots 70, 71 and 72, Block 6, J. H. McGEE'S ADDITION, and all of Lot 12, Block 12, REID'S ADDITION, both subdivisions in Kansas City, Jackson County, Missouri, according to the recorded plat thereof.

1415 Broadway: Lot 17 and the south ½ of Lot 18, Block 12, REID'S ADDITION, a subdivision in Kansas City, Jackson County, Missouri, according to the recorded plat thereof.

1433 Broadway: Lots 74, 75, 76, and 77, Block 6, J. H. McGEE'S ADDITION, a subdivision in Kansas City, Jackson County, Missouri, according to the recorded plat thereof.

B. Basis of Appraisal

This appraisal is based solely upon the market value of a vacant assembled tract of this size in this location in the central business district of Kansas City, Missouri.

1. It is felt that the following items are of such negligible value as related to the preceding that they should be disregarded:

   a. Cost of demolition, grading, or fill necessary to make the property usable for a major development. The present assemblage is principally vacant, graded to street level (except one corner), and total costs of this nature would be unlikely to exceed $5,000.

   b. Capitalization of rental income from various improvements on the property bears no relationship to its value as a single vacant tract of assembled development land.

   c. The appraisal technique of working backward from the

replacement costs and depreciation of improvements should also be disregarded as 95% of the land is principally vacant.

d. The sales and purchases of isolated small tracts of under 25,000 square feet either within this tract or within a one-block radius of this tract within the last three years have *no* relationship to the valuation of this tract as an assemblage and are being disregarded.

2. The following are provided for general background:

a. The present zoning is M-1, which permits almost any type of commercial development.

b. All utilities are presently available and the property is close enough to "city steam heat" so as to make the use of this facility practicable.

c. For general location reference, this property is one-half (½) block from the Municipal Auditorium and one-and-one-half (1½) blocks from the Kansas City Power & Light Building, the largest office building in Kansas City.

C. *Appraisal of Site As Single Tract Within Frame of Preceding Reference*

1. Comparative value appraisal technique.

a. It is recognized that a single assembled tract of 74,000 square feet within the central business district of a metropolitan area of approximately 1 million people is unique enough that a proper appraisal would include an analysis of similar tracts in similar-sized cities. While this is not being done at this time, it is felt that such an analysis will give a substantially greater value than would be obtained at the present time in Kansas City, Missouri.

b. While it is understood that an "offer" is not permissible evidence in a condemnation suit, we wish to point out that affidavits can be produced that a major hotel chain, approximately six years ago, authorized the purchase of any assembled tract of 55,000 square feet within a one-block radius of the Kansas City Municipal Auditorium for the sum of $700,000. Sites south of the Auditorium were only disregarded because of the threat of potential condemnation.

c. Using a 60,000-square foot assemblage as an entity, it is felt that north, east, and west of the Municipal Auditorium that it would be totally out of the question to assemble 60,000 square feet within a one-block radius for anything under $15 per square foot.

This leaves only the area Baltimore to Broadway, 14th to 15th, within the range of feasibility at any price under $14. Within this area there are only three possibilities of such an assembly and they are the properties held by the Greenlease interests, the Borserine interests, and the present site of the Airport-Auditorium Motel Corporation.

d. The Greenlease tract of approximately 76,000 square feet was purchased by the Missouri Highway Commission recently for a price in excess of $12 per square foot ($915,000).

e. It is felt that the recorded lease between the Yellow Cab Co. owned by the Murchison interests and the property between Wyandotte and Central owned by the Borserines, after a capitalization of the rent and after subtracting the value of the improvements or giving credit to the construction of equivalent facilities, would generate a land value of this assemblage between Wyandotte and Central of somewhere between $13 and $15 per square foot. In this case it is recognized that the principal value of the land was for an assemblage of parking space for the operation of a cab company adjacent to the central business district. For this particular use, there seems to be no appreciable difference in value between such an assemblage in the Wyandotte-Central area as opposed to a similar assemblage between Central and Broadway.

f. In a comparative analysis between the Greenlease site, the Borserine site, and the site in question, the following factors should be considered:

(1) Baltimore is a more "fashionable" street in this area than Wyandotte, Central, or Broadway. This gives Baltimore a plus factor of 15% over any of the others.

(2) Access to 14th Street of a large tract should create a value factor of an additional 15%. This is possessed by the Borserine tract but not by the Greenlease tract or the Airport-Auditorium Motel Corporation tract.

(3) However, Broadway is one of the principal north-south arteries of downtown Kansas City and the direct access route between the Municipal Airport and the most fashionable residential area past the County Club Plaza. Baltimore, Wyandotte, and Central all terminate to the south at the railroad tracks and have substantially less traffic than Broadway. We believe that this consideration should give Broadway a plus factor of 5%

(4) Subtracting this 5% from the plus 15% thrown in on the other two properties, we believe that the site under con-

sideration would have a desirability of 10% less than the two sites used for comparison.

(5) Further, we feel that the distinctly slum atmosphere to the west of Broadway, which, however, is definitely being eliminated by new construction in the last three years, should still cause an additional negative factor of 10%.

(6) This would net a total negative factor of 20% and would give a valuation to the site in question of approximately $10 per square foot on a comparative analysis basis to the *only* two comparable sites in Kansas City, Missouri.

D. Equation of Land Assemblage to Garage Construction

1. Equivalent construction factors:

a. From a construction cost standpoint relating to elevators, fire escapes, and increasing costs of height to square footage of space, there are considerable merits to motel or hotel construction under five stories and office building construction under eight stories.

b. With normal scenic setbacks, a 250-room motel-hotel, or a 120,000-square foot office building, should require 22,000 square feet of ground plat.

c. Disregarding actual city requirements and looking only at the competitive market, it is almost a necessity that either entity be able to provide off-street adjacent parking for a minimum of 225 cars.

d. Two hundred twenty-five (225) car spaces would require a minimum of 50,000 square feet for surface parking.

e. In the event that large attached garage parking on multiple levels is constructed, the neccessity of having columns, ramps, and other non-usable space would add a minimum of 20% to provide parking for the same 225 cars. In other words, it would require 60,000 square feet of construction to provide the same thing that 50,000 square feet of open surface parking would do.

f. Within the downtown district's No. 1 fire zone, multiple level garage construction could not be put up at under $7 per square foot.

2. Capitalization of extra operating costs:

a. A 225-car multi-level garage would require attendant livery service and a minimum of 5 extra employees over what would be necessary to supervise a park-and-lock-your-car surface operation. In addition, there would be some special insurance and maintenance costs on the structure.

b. Grouping all of the extra costs at $20,000 per year and capitalizing them at a 10% rate, we arrive at a figure of $200,000.

3. Conclusion: Now multiplying $7 per square foot times 60,000 square feet of garage construction, we arrive at a figure of $420,000. Adding to this the capitalization of additional expenses at $200,000, we hit a total figure of $620,000. Now by relating this figure on a constructed garage and completely ignoring the value of the actual land that the garage would sit on and dividing the $620,000 by the purchase price of 50,000 square feet of surface land, we can see that a building owner or a motel owner would be wise to pay $12.40 per square foot for the additional land rather than to construct a garage necessary to handle the 225 cars which would be necessary to put his operation in a competitive condition in the present Kansas City market.

E. Summary

1. A substantial portion of the transient and hotel traffic of downtown Kansas City is centered around or connected with Municipal Auditorium activities.

2. Within recent years, there have *only* been three tracts of assembled land in excess of 70,000 square feet within a one-block radius of the Municipal Auditorium. They are the Borserine tract, the Greenlease tract, and the Airport-Auditorium Motel Corporation tract.

3. The first two can be established as having a market value at the present moment in excess of $13 per square foot. In any direction other than south, 70,000 square feet cannot be assembled for under $15 per square foot. It can be demonstrated that a balancing of desirable factors and undesirable factors indicates that the Airport-Auditorium Motel Corporation site is not more than 20% less desirable per square foot than the other two.

4. In any type of commercial structure involving concentrated human occupancy, substantial amounts of adjacent automobile parking are necessary to make the structure competitive in the present market in Kansas City.

5. For factors enumerated in the body of this analysis, it is cheaper to purchase land for surface parking at $11 per square foot than to construct basement or multi-level garage parking.

F. Final Conclusion

As vacant assembled, graded, development land under single ownership within a one-block radius of the Municipal Auditorium, the approximate 74,000-square foot tract owned by the Airport-Auditorium Motel Corporation has a present worth of $10 per square foot, or $740,000.

EXHIBIT III: APPRAISAL TECHNIQUE

General Principles in Land Value Allocation for Projected Ownership of Atlas Properties As of September, 1964

A. Where property is not planned to be surfaced and graded on 1 September, about 5% of value is subtracted.

B. Where property is over 80 feet of frontage or can be combined with presently owned property so as to make over 80 feet of frontage, an additional value of 5% is added.

C. Where combined property can be put together immediately contiguous so as to make in excess of 150 feet of frontage or 15,000 square feet, the values have been increased by about 15%.

D. A corner is considered to be worth 5% more than an inside lot.

E. Where substantial grading costs, such as would exist where the average level of the lot is 8 feet over street level, 5% is subtracted.

F. It should be noted that the total amount of these appraised valuations as isolated tracts or in small contiguous tracts is 3% or approximately $40,000 over what we used in the projected Atlas figure on "market value." This decrease was to allow for "optimism."

G. Furthermore, it is believed that footages in excess of 150 feet and plottages in excess of 25,000 square feet pick up an added 20% of value. No consideration was given to this element.

H. Where existing improvements are bringing in a net return in excess of 4% of appraised valuation, a small amount of consideration was given because of the revenue that would be produced before actual demolition occurs.

I. In only three of the tracts was the appraiser's ordinary recognition given to the improvements. This is the case where the improvements produce a substantial amount of income, which was the case on the Allied Motors Building (northeast 16th & Baltimore), the 1715 Main Building, and the three buildings at 1601-15 Wyandotte.

J. Substantial improvements, in size at any rate, exist on a number of the other properties such as 1620-24 Central, but no recognition was given to them and demolition and grading costs were subtracted from land value.

EXHIBIT IV: PLOTTAGE FACTORS

A. *On land costing over $3/square foot, it is impracticable to build under two stories.*

B. In this area, city code requires one parking space for 300 feet of office or residency.

C. Any tract under 5,000 square feet or 40 front feet is almost valueless except to adjoining land owner.

D. For construction or a commercial parking lot, you need minimum of 12,000 square feet or 100 front feet. The latter would be 50% more valuable than the sum of its component parts.

E. For assemblages over 7,000 square feet on Baltimore and Main, add 50¢/square foot.

Over 10,000 square feet, add $1.00.
Over 15,000 square feet, add $2.00.
Over 25,000 square feet, add $3.00.

F. For assemblages over 10,000 square feet on Wyandotte, Central, and Broadway, add 50¢.

Over 15,000, add $1.00.
Over 25,000, add $1.50.
Over 40,000, add $2.00.
Over 50,000, add $2.50.
Over 100,000, add $4.00.

G. Example: Using a base price of $4/square foot on Wyandotte between 15th and 18th for small tracts and a plottage factor of $4 for tracts over 100,000 square feet gives a total of $8/square foot. Question: *Where on Wyandotte could a contiguous tract of 110,000 square feet be put together at a price under $8/square foot? Where could this be done on Central or Broadway?* We are not talking about 1934, but Kansas City in the year 1964.

EXHIBIT V: APPLICATION OF FORMULA TO AREA

Formula for Midtown Evaluation

A. Basic Principles

1. On assumption that all land will produce 4% net from public parking, use this as *base* condition.

2. If present improvements generate less than this, subtract cost of grading and surfacing to bring it to this condition.

3. If present improvements produce more than this, add value to base price of all such rent over 4% net capitalized at 12%. There will be very few properties where this factor will be involved (see examples later).

4. Plottage value factors.

For Contiguous Assembly:	*Add:*
Over 10,000 square feet	$ .50/square foot
Over 20,000 square feet	1.00/square foot
Over 30,000 square feet	1.50/square foot
Over 40,000 square feet	1.90/square foot
Over 50,000 square feet	2.20/square foot
Over 60,000 square feet	2.40/square foot
Over 70,000 square feet	2.60/square foot
Over 80,000 square feet	2.80/square foot
Over 90,000 square feet	2.90/square foot
Over 100,000 square feet	3.00/square foot
Over 200,000 square feet	3.50/square foot
Over 300,000 square feet	3.80/square foot
Over 400,000 square feet	4.00/square foot

5. Basic reasoning behind previous calculations:

a. 12th and Main is the 100% corner of Kansas City.

b. Within a 6-block radius of this corner it might be possible to assemble 30,000 square feet without hitting a valuable improvement but highly unlikely that one could get 40,000 and extremely unlikely that one could get 50,000.

c. Zoning as well as market conditions now require that one car space be provided for every 300 feet of residential or office construction in land areas now selling in the $4-$5/square foot brackets.

d. If land costs more than $3/square foot, one cannot afford a one-story building.

e. It is uneconomical to put modern elevators, stairways, and fire escapes in if you have less than a 5,000 square foot/floor.

f. A four-floor building of 5,000-square foot floors would involve 20,000 square feet. City regulations and present market conditions require adjacent parking for 66 cars.

g. Unless one wants to go to expensive attendants, it requires 250 square feet/car space, minimum.

h. This means 16,500 square feet of parking, plus the building site of 5,000 for a total assemblage of 21,500 square feet.

i. In the No. 1 fire zone, basement sprinkler, parking, or adjacent garage construction will cost $6/square foot. Constructed parking with walls, columns, and ramps will be 30% less usable than ground surface parking.

j. Conclusion: You can pay $9/square foot for the adjacent land rather than try to construct your own parking.

k. *If your original 5,000-foot site cost $5/square foot, you are better off paying an average premium of $4/square foot extra to get 16,500 more feet than attempt to construct your own parking.*

l. From a practical standpoint you would probably pick up another 5,000 square feet at $6.00. Then you would find you had to buy and demolish a fairly good building to get your last 11,500 square feet of land.

m. Final conclusion: *In an intermediate urban area of land values over $4/square foot, it requires an excess of 20,000 square feet average rather than try to construct parking, i.e.,* four contiguous assembled tracts of 5,000 feet each are twice as valuable as each tract would be separately.

B. Base Land Values, Unimproved, Graded to Street Level, and Surfaced (Under 10,000 Square Feet)

1.	Main Street 14th to 15th	$12.00
2.	Main Street 15th to 16th	10.00
3.	Main Street 16th to 17th	9.00
4.	Main Street 17th to 18th	9.00
5.	Baltimore 14th to 15th	15.00
6.	Baltimore 15th to 16th	11.00
7.	Baltimore 16th to 17th	9.00
8.	Baltimore 17th to 18th	9.00
9.	Wyandotte 14th to 15th	7.00
10.	Wyandotte 15th to 16th	4.00
11.	Wyandotte 16th to 17th	3.75
12.	Wyandotte 17th to 18th	3.75
13.	Central 14th to 15th	7.00
14.	Central 15th to 16th	4.00
15.	Central 16th to 17th	3.75
16.	Central 17th to 18th	3.75
17.	Broadway 14th to 15th	6.00
18.	Broadway 15th to 16th	5.00

19. Broadway 16th to 17th 4.50
20. Broadway 17th to 18th 4.50

C. *Specific Examples Applying Formula*

1. Nicholas Property.

a. One hundred eighty feet on west side of Wyandotte between 15th and 16th; 164.25 feet deep; 29,565 square feet.

b. Base price $4.00/square foot.

c. Add $1.00/square foot for assemblage.

d. Subtract $1.00/square foot for demolition and grading to street level and surfacing.

e. Value $4.00/square foot or $118,260.

f. Present net income under 4% potential of graded parking, so disregard.

2. Armacost Property.

a. Two hundred feet on east side of Wyandotte between 15th and 16th; 142 feet deep; 28,400 square feet.

b. Base price $4.00/square foot.

c. Add $1.00 for assemblage.

d. Demolition $2,000.

e. Value $5.00/square foot or $140,000 after demolition.

f. Net rent of $6,000/yr. under 4%, so disregard.

3. Hutchings Property.

a. Seventy-three feet, two inches, on west side of Wyandotte 16th to 17th; 171.75 feet deep; 12,572 square feet.

b. Base price, $3.75.

c. Assemblage, add 50¢.

d. Demolition and grading, subtract $2,000.

e. Value of land, $51,431.

f. Net rental, $4,000 (after taxes, insurance, maintenance).

g. Subtract 4% value of parking, leaving rental value of improvements at approximately $1,943.

h. Capitalize at 12% for $16,185.

i. Add to land value for total of $67,616.

4. Asa Brown Property.

a. Old house facing 16th off Central 52.75 × 85; 4,483 square feet.

b. Base price, $4.

c. Demolition, grading, surfacing, $800.

d. Net rent under 4%, so disregard.

e. Value, $17,132.

5. Holland Apartments.
   a. West side of Central between 16th and 17th, 98 ×168; 16,464 square feet.
   b. Base price, $3.75.
   c. Add 50¢ for assemblage.
   d. Subtract $6,000 for demolition, grading, surfacing.
   e. Net rent under 4%, so disregard.
   f. Value, $63,972.

EXHIBIT VI: URBAN REDEVELOPMENT PROSPECTUS

Stage I (Prior to Any Construction)

A. Urban Redevelopment Corporation formed with 600,000 shares @ $5 for capitalization of $3 million.

B. Four hundred thousand square feet in Renewal Area; 100,000 square feet in surrounding area.

C. Initially:

1. People in Renewal Area put 220,000 square feet in corporation @ $5/square foot subject to $300,000 in mortgages for paid in capital of $800,000.
2. People in surrounding area put in 50,000 square feet at $6 subject to $100,000 in mortgages for additional capital of $200,000.
3. People who have financial interest in neighborhood put in $400,000 cash (80,000 shares @ $5).

D. Total paid in capital in land and cash $1,400,000.

E. Options now acquired on 100,000 more square feet in Renewal Area and 50,000 more in surrounding area at average price of $5.50/square foot (cost of options $50,000).

BALANCE SHEET

	Assets	*Liabilities*
Cash	350,000	
220,000 sq. ft. Renewal Area	1,100,000	
50,000 sq. ft. surrounding area	300,000	
Options on 150,000 sq. ft.	50,000	
	$1,800,000	
Mortgages on Renewal Area		300,000
Mortgages on surrounding area		100,000
Issued 280,000 shares @ $5		1,400,000
		$1,800,000

INCOME WITHOUT DEVELOPMENT "AS IS"

	Expenses	*Income*
Apartment & rooming houses, 400 units (30% vacancy)		150,000
Business leases (10)		50,000
500 parking spaces $80/yr.		40,000
		$240,000
Taxes and insurance	50,000	
Maintenance	30,000	
Utilities	50,000	
Miscellaneous and interest	30,000	
	$160,000	
Net income before depreciation		$ 80,000

Stage II

A. Non-Kansas City capital brought in for 200,000 more shares @ $5 for $1 million.

B. Funds used to pick up land now under option 100,000 square feet in area and 50,000 more in surrounding to pay off $200,000 of mortgages.

C. Now with or without Urban Renewal the following is done:

1. Ninety per cent of existing structures demolished.
2. Two hundred-unit motel with landscaping, pool, etc., put up at $11,000/room for $2,200,000.
3. One hundred-unit FHA apartment at $14,000/unit average for $1,400,000.
4. Four-unit service store shopping area at $250,000.
5. Six landscaped scattered public parking lots with 80-car capacities for total of 480 car spaces at cost of $200,000.
6. Landscaping, tennis courts and temporary use of sites for future expansion, $50,000.

D. It is believed that FHA financing can be obtained at 5½% with a 30-year or longer amortization schedule. Conventional mortgages will run 6% on 20 years. For all of these calculations we are going to use an average of 25 years at 5½% which gives a constant of 7.38%. In later stages the FHA financing will greatly increase relative to any conventional financing. For initial calculations, therefore, we will subtract 5½% representing the interest from 7.38%, the constant, giving an amortization factor of 1.88% for determining cash flow.

Using 1.88 initial amortization to make up 7.38% constant gives a cash throw-off of $51,100.

BALANCE SHEET

	Assets	Liabilities
Cash	300,000	
320,000 sq. ft. Renewal Area	1,600,000	
100,000 sq. ft. surrounding area	600,000	
Motel	2,200,000	
100-unit apartment	1,400,000	
Service stores	250,000	
6 parking lots	200,000	
Non-used site beautification	50,000	
Miscellaneous	50,000	
	$6,650,000	
Old mortgages		100,000
Conventional mtg., motel and land		1,800,000
FHA on apartments and land		1,400,000
Conventional on parking lots		450,000
Conventional on surrounding area		300,000
Conventional on service stores and land		200,000
480,000 shares @ $5		2,400,000
		$6,650,000

INCOME (NET AFTER REAL ESTATE TAXES)

	Expenses	Income
Old structures		20,000
Surrounding area		30,000
Motel @ $1,000/unit/yr. (net)		200,000
Apartments @ $1,200/unit/yr. (net)		120,000
Stores		30,000
480 parking spaces @ $150/yr.		72,000
		$472,000
Using 5½% int. on $4,250,000 mortgages	233,000	
Without Urban Renewal real estate taxes		
30% of $6,000,000 at 4% or approx.	80,000	
Insurance (motel on net lease)	18,000	
Miscellaneous	10,000	
	$341,000	
Net income before depreciation and mortgage amortization		$131,000

Without Urban Renewal straight line depreciation gives $160,000 depreciation and offsets profit.

With Urban Renewal, taxes get reduced $60,000 and this becomes tax-free cash throw-off with double declining balance depreciation if desired.

Stage III

A. One hundred thousand square feet of surrounding land sold off for worthwhile developments @ $8/square foot and tax-free profit of $200,000 (tax loss carry-forward from depreciation).

B. Funds applied against conventional mortgages.

C. Additional 100-unit FHA built at $1,400,000.

BALANCE SHEET

	Assets	*Liabilities*
Cash	300,000	
320,000 land	1,600,000	
Motel	2,200,000	
200 apartments	2,800,000	
Stores	250,000	
Parking lots	200,000	
Miscellaneous	100,000	
	$7,450,000	
FHA mortgages		2,800,000
Conventional mortgages		2,050,000
Capital		2,400,000
Surplus		200,000
		$7,450,000

INCOME (NET AFTER REAL ESTATE TAXES)

	Expenses	*Income*
Old structures		20,000
Motel @ $1,000/unit/yr. (net)		200,000
200 apartments @ $1,200/unit/yr. (net)		240,000
Stores		30,000
480 parking spaces @ $150/yr.		72,000
		$562,000
Using 5½% interest on $4,450,000 mortgages	244,750	
Without Urban Renewal, taxes—real estate	100,000	
Insurance	20,000	
Miscellaneous	25,000	
	$389,750	
Net income before depreciation and mortgage amortization ($200,000 profit on resale of surrounding area not considered)		$172,250

Without Urban Renewal tax abatement and after 1.88% amortization you have approximately a cash throw-off of $98,590.

With Urban Renewal and tax abatement this cash throw-off figure is increased by $80,000 to make cash throw-off $178,590.

Double declining balance depreciation would continue to make this last figure tax free.

Stage IV

A. Remaining old structures demolished.

B. Thirty thousand square feet more land acquired @ $7 square foot (previously optional) (?).

C. Two hundred more FHA apartments.

D. Fifty additional units added to motel.

BALANCE SHEET

	Assets	*Liabilities*
Cash	300,000	
320,000 land	1,600,000	
30,000 sq. ft. more land @ $7/sq. ft.	210,000	
Motel–additional 50 units	2,750,000	
400 apartments	5,600,000	
Stores	250,000	
Parking lots	200,000	
Miscellaneous	100,000	
	$11,010,000	
FHA mortgages		5,600,000
Conventional mortgages for increase in additions		760,000
Old Conventional mortgages		2,050,000
Capital		2,400,000
Surplus		200,000
		$11,010,000

INCOME (NET AFTER REAL ESTATE TAXES)

	Expenses	*Income*
Motel @ $1,200/unit/yr. 250 units (net)		300,000
400 apartments @ $1,400/unit/yr. (net)		560,000
Stores		40,000
Parking lot–550 cars at $200/yr.		110,000
		$1,010,000
Using 5½% interest on $8,410,000 mortgages	426,550	
Without Urban Renewal, taxes–real estate	140,000	
Insurance	30,000	
Miscellaneous	30,000	
	$626,550	
Net income before depreciation and mortgage amortization		$ 383,450

Without Urban Renewal tax abatement and after 1.88% amortization you have an approximate cash throw-off of $225,342.

With Urban Renewal and tax abatement this cash throw-off figure is increased by $120,000 to make a cash throw-off of $345,342.

Double declining balance depreciation continues to make this last figure tax free.

Chapter XV

Comparative Analysis: Urban vs. Rural Real Estate

For the purpose of this chapter, we will limit ourselves to income properties and exclude "development land" both urban and rural. We will define "development land" as that type of property which doesn't produce enough net income to pay real estate taxes. This could be an obsolete building in New York whose underlying land was being held for urban renewal or 100 acres on the edge of Los Angeles being held for residential construction.

To prevent this from becoming a Ph.D. thesis, we will arbitrarily limit ourselves to the following six examples, three urban and three rural:

Example A: 100-unit apartment building, five years old, being sold for $2 million; 90% average occupancy; $400,000 gross rentals; $150,000 utilities, maintenance and labor; $50,000 real estate taxes; $200,000 net before debt service. Potential loan $1,500,000, 8% interest, 21 years amortization, 10% constant. Cash flow on $500,000 equity: $50,000 per year.

Example B: 100,000-square foot office building, 15 years old, selling for $2 million. Gross rents with 90% occupancy; $500,000 per year; utilities, maintenance, labor $250,000; real estate taxes $100,000; net before debt service $150,000. Potential loan $1 million at 7% with 18 years amortization, 10% constant. Cash flow $50,000 on $1 million equity.

Example C: 150,000-square foot department store in new shopping center on lease to national tenant, top credit, for 30 more years on net lease. Sales price $2 million; net rent 9% or $180,000 per year. Potential loan $1,600,000; 6½% interest, 17 years amortization, 10% constant. Cash flow $20,000 on $400,000 equity.

Example D: 10,000-acre ranch, all deeded, at $200 per acre for $2 million with 600-cow capacity, 100 miles from major city. Anticipated gross rent at $40 per cow or $24,000 per year. Real estate taxes and landlord type expenses $10,000 for net of $14,000. Potential loan $500,000; 7% interest, 4% amortization; 11% initial debt service of $55,000 per year. Cash deficit $41,000 per year.

Example E: 20,000-acre ranch at $100 per acre; 300 miles from major city; all deeded; sales price $2 million; carrying capacity 1,200 cows at $60 per cow for gross rent of $72,000 per year. Real estate taxes and landlord expenses $12,000 for net of $60,000. Potential loan $800,000, 6% interest, 4% amortization or $80,000 debt service with annual cash deficit of $20,000.

Example F: 15,000 deeded acres and 40,000 acres government lease for $2 million sales price. Carrying capacity 3,000 cows at $65 per head or $195,000 gross rent per year. Taxes, government rentals, and all expenses $35,000 for net of $160,000. Potential loan $1,400,000 at 7% interest, 4% amortization with $145,000 debt service and $15,000 per year positive cash flow. Property 800 miles from major city.

The following are facts that should be ground into an equation:

1. Commercial properties will get a 3% depreciation for tax purposes, but must be prepared to sustain a real 2% obsolescence and depreciation factor.

2. Every year maintenance will increase and occupancy will go down.

3. In areas where competing new construction can be anticipated, rental increases may or may not keep pace with inflation.

4. In any period of political crisis, rent ceilings can be anticipated on apartment buildings, putting landlords in a squeeze. (Examples: post-WW II France; New York City; and Phase 2 of the current Nixon Program.)

5. "Tenant revolts" can be anticipated on cheaper apartments, but probably not on more expensive ones.

6. Rent ceilings on commercial properties possible, but unlikely.

7. Four per cent per year historical growth on remote land areas. Six per cent per year growth can be anticipated in areas where non-agricultural absorption may occur.

8. Major impact of tremendous per head labor and equipment savings on larger operations now being felt in grazing lands. In examples, note that the 600-head ranch gets a $40 per cow rent; the 1,200-head ranch, $60 per cow; and the 3,000-head operation can demand $65 per cow. While this trend has only become established in the last year, it still doesn't fully reflect the economics of larger size.

With the inevitability of the unionization of farm labor, this will become more extreme. Smaller operations only employing two or three people will still have to raise wage rates to the union scale to hold their people. The biggest problem is not the base rates, but the 40-hour-week with time-and-a-half or double time for overtime. Cows don't know that it is Saturday or Sunday.

9. The main depreciable entity on large western ranches is fencing and water facilities. On new fencing, you get 10% depreciation; on "used fencing" you can take 20%. The fencing on the government lease

belongs to the tenant and you can depreciate this too. In some instances, you get the 7% investment credit. For the first five years of ranch ownership, an appreciation factor of 5% is realistic.

10. Insofar as agricultural land is itself the instrument of production, there is no vacancy factor. For any given season, the level of the market on beef or grain adjusted by the fertility of the soil and various operational factors can be translated into instant rental value. On large holdings, there is currently a mad scramble of potential tenants for leases.

11. At least in this country, there has never been a ceiling imposed on agricultural rents.

12. Commercial buildings and apartments are forever restricted to their "neighborhood." Historically, in U.S. cities, most neighborhoods deteriorate and become less fashionable with time. This is an obsolescence factor unrelated to the construction itself.

13. How many 30-year-old structures in the U.S. does the reader know which are competitive with new offices, hotels, or apartments?

14. New apartments and commercial buildings can be erected without limitation. Competitive buildings with no economic sense may go up for political purposes, such as the 2 million square feet of the New York Port Authority buildings along the Hudson.

15. Historically, a lending agency looked at the following on a real estate loan:

a. Sufficient collateral value to cover unpaid balance in the event foreclosure became necessary.

b. Sufficient cash income to support debt service.

c. An evaluation of future trends to determine how long the preceding will continue to exist.

16. For emotional and public image, the lending agency wanted to avoid foreclosure, so current cash flow from rents was given paramount importance. Little recognition was given to cash flow generated by tax consequences on other sources of owner's income nor, for that matter, was adequate attention paid to future rentals and expenses. Consequently, items, such as a sudden increase in real estate taxes, a big jump in janitorial salaries, or an extra 10% in apartment vacancies, were often as dismaying to the lender as to the owner.

17. Inflation or no inflation, a lending agency should recognize that every year a building will become 2% less desirable and a neighborhood a minimum of 1% worse for a total factor of 3%.

18. On the other hand, a large working ranch historically becomes 5% more valuable each year. A 20,000-acre ranch is its own neighborhood. Contrary to an urban investment, increased population and "con-

gestion" can only help values. Unless the "neighbors" were three-headed monsters from Mars, a rise of population from two to a square mile to five to a square mile would probably be beneficial to surrounding land values.

19. In summary, if the urban properties become less valuable at the rate of 3% per year and rural properties become more valuable at the rate of 5% per year, the difference is 8%. In an excessively simplistic manner, one might say one could have 8% per year less rent in rural land and still come out even with an office or apartment building. However, it is not that easy, particularly with income tax consequences.

The following chart is a rough draft for concept purposes only. All figures are rounded off. The "standing forage deduction" is the cured grass and feed on a western ranch. This is covered in previous chapters. In general, it takes two or three years for a clump of forage in arid country to reach edible size and the value of such growth ranges from $2 to $3 per acre. This amount is always an item of controversy as it is deductible to the buyer and ordinary income to the seller and should be agreed on in writing. The amount of deduction as a percentage of cash outlay was not included because of the effect of purchase money mortgages with prepaid interest which would be customary on the three ranches. For the purpose of this chart, this type of tax leverage was ignored.

COMPARATIVE ANALYSIS FROM A LENDER'S VIEW

1. The amounts under "loan" for each of the six properties are what can be borrowed at the present time from conventional lending agencies such as insurance companies or the Federal Land Bank. The reasons for the varying amounts may not necessarily make sense, but this is the situation as it exists. No consideration in this chart is given to additional amounts or more exotic terms that could be picked up from purchase money mortgages from sellers.

2. The extremely high proportion of the loan, 80% on the department store, reflects the credit of the tenant on a 30-year lease.

3. The extremely low percent, 25% on ranch D, reflects the fact that the high price, proximity to a city, and low rent percentage almost make this a "raw land" investment on which most lending agencies refuse to loan at all.

4. The substantially higher percentage of loan on the apartment building over the office may be just a fashion of the moment due to some psychological combination of the following:

1st Year's Investment	*Example A: Apartments*	*Example B: Office Bldg.*	*Example C: Dept. Store (30-yr. lease net)*	*Example D: 600-Head Ranch (all deeded)*	*Example E: 1,200-Head Ranch (all deeded)*	*Example F: 3,000-Head Ranch (¼ deeded, ¾ leased)*
Cost/cow unit	—	—	—	$ 3,330	$ 1,660	$ 660
Gross sales price	$2,000,000	$2,000,000	2,000,000	2,000,000	2,000,000	2,000,000
Gross income	400,000	500,000	180,000	24,000	72,000	195,000
Expenses	200,000	350,000	-0-	10,000	12,000	35,000
Net income	200,000	150,000	180,000	14,000	60,000	160,000
Loan	1,500,000	1,000,000	1,600,000	500,000	800,000	1,400,000
Equity	500,000	1,000,000	400,000	1,500,000	1,200,000	600,000
Debt service	150,000	100,000	160,000	55,000	80,000	145,000
Cash flow	50,000	50,000	20,000	(41,000)	(20,000)	15,000
Depreciation taxwise	(80,000) (4%)	(60,000) (3%)	(60,000) (3%)	(100,000)[1]	(150,000)[1]	(200,000)[1]
Depreciation or accretion actual	(60,000) (3%)	(60,000) (3%)	(60,000) (3%)	100,000 (5%)	100,000 (5%)	40,000 (2%)
Cash flow as % of equity	10%	5%	1.3%	(2.7%)	(1.7%)	2½%
Percent of deductibility of income	40%	40%	37.5%	700%	250%	125%
Growth in value of investment	$ 140,000[2]	$ 90,000[2]	$ 120,000[2]	$ 114,000[2]	$ 160,000[2]	$ 200,000[2]

[1] Includes standing forage.
[2] Accretion plus net income (as if free and clear).

a. The mammoth publicity of how much "pent-up demand" there is for housing.

b. The competition of FHA and other government agencies with conventional financing.

c. The possibly false security from having multiple tenants in small units over a few larger commercial tenants who might leave.

d. A smaller percentage of labor and material cost in expenses with less future hazards of increase in total expense.

e. A greater historical stability of tenants (this may have been true in the past, but not with the greater population mobility of today).

5. The large percentage of government lease in Ranch F is a very definite hazard and should enter into a lender's thinking more than it does. While most Bureau of Land Management land, forest permits, or state leases have gone with certain deeded tracts for over 50 years, there is no legal prevention for cancellation without compensation. This is the reason the land accretion factor is only 2% of the sales value, as opposed to 5% on the "all-deeded" properties. The large rental value of the overall ranch is, of course, conditioned on the retention of the government land. Despite the very real risks of the situation, the lending agencies, particularly the Federal Land Bank, will still go substantially higher, as a matter of tradition, on this type of property.

COMPARATIVE ANALYSIS FROM THE STANDPOINT OF TAX CONSEQUENCES

1. Under the 1969 Tax Bill, apartment buildings get a better depreciation rate than commercial construction. If the property is tied in with some type of government subsidy like FHA guarantees or urban renewal tax abatement, it can get 200% declining balance if "new in use."

2. With the exception of properties involving an FHA guarantee, a major part of the equity might be financed with purchase money second mortgages. These frequently involve 10% downpayments and a year's interest in advance. Normally, 12 months' interest in advance is deductible. This has the following effects:

a. Non-deductible equity "hard" dollars are greatly reduced.

b. After first year, cash input for interest and amortization is increased.

c. There may be a substantial negative cash flow.

d. Percent of deductibility; if depreciation equals mortgage amortization, may get to 100% on urban properties and possibly 110% on rural the first couple of years.

e. To an individual in a combined federal-state tax bracket of over 70%, the after-tax investment may be quite low.

3. In large western ranches in arid country, the fencing on deeded plus government leased land might be as high as 15% of the total value. (As a custom, the fencing on both BLM and state leased land is considered property of the tenant.) On a five-year write-off, this can be a significant amount. In addition, most of the facilities for the "containment, storage, and care" of the cattle are entitled to the 7% investment credit. In general, for the first few years, deductions are proportionately greater on rural properties. After that, you have "shot your wad" and urban properties will get more depreciation.

4. While not part of the previous chart, in its attempt to encourage agriculture and U.S. soil improvement, the government has a substantial array of soil improvement, pond construction, water conservation, and "restoration" measures that would have to be capitalized in urban areas but are permitted to be deducted in rural land as a "tax incentive." They are generally of a nature that would improve the rental potential. In some cases, you can get various government agencies to participate on the cost with direct cash subsidies. Particularly is this the case if you have some Bureau of Land Management property on the ranch. Much of this money is allocated annually on a per county basis. Strange to say, in counties of partial urbanization, more money may be available for the farms that remain than in real rural counties. If you own a farm in such a county it will pay to investigate.

5. Urban properties held for long periods of time may avoid the problem of "depreciation recapture" on improvements. This may not be true on many of the ranch improvements that might be classified as "personal property."

6. In general, because of the absence of the obsolescence factor and the general expectation of a 5%-per-year increase in rural land values, you can get better purchase money mortgage terms on a ranch than on a city building. The seller knows it will probably be worth more if he has to take it back in a few years and this wouldn't be true of a city building.

In the event the seller can get the buyer to put in some deductible soil improvements and restrict him against overgrazing or soil abuse, he has total security on a ranch or farm. Frequently, these types of requirements are inserted into the mortgage document. (See Chapter IX on "Buying a Ranch.")

7. In summary, for the first four or five years, rural properties

make a better tax shelter than urban. Subsequent to the fifth year, urban properties are superior.

COMPARATIVE ANALYSIS FROM THE STANDPOINT OF RISK

1. Risk of excessive depreciation, obsolescence, and neighborhood deterioration: This is substantial in urban properties and practically nonexistent on agricultural properties.

2. Risk of increased vacancies and lower rentals: substantial in urban; unlikely in rural. Large usable tracts of productive rural land can always be rented. In commercial properties, cost of moving and costs of operation may be such that property couldn't be rented at any price.

3. Risk of increased operational expense: Substantial in urban; in rural properties, the only big hazard is increased real estate taxes.

4. Risk of adverse government action: In this country, only apartment buildings are historically exposed to rent ceilings; commercial and agricultural properties are not. In many foreign countries, the situation is reversed. Large agricultural holdings are highly exposed to confiscation, particularly those owned by foreigners.

5. Risk of unlawful actions, e.g., "tenant revolts," "rent strikes," vandalism by tenants: This is generally limited to apartment buildings, particularly to the government subsidized types.

PART V

LAND PROCESSING AND MISCELLANEOUS

Chapter XVI

Land Classification for Development and Marketing

This chapter is going to avoid urban land in established communities. Here properties for commercial, industrial, and residential use have been the subject of hundreds of books, thousands of studies, and the core of the real estate industry over the last 100 years. We will limit ourselves to the more outlying properties which are associated with the automobile, the new superhighways, and the ever more common use of the airplane and eventually the helicopter.

The most important characteristic of land in relationship to development and marketing for other than agriculture, mining, or timber use is proximity to metropolitan centers. For this purpose, we will use a Roman numeral designation:

I. *Within 30-minute automobile drive of major source of employment.* This generally puts property inside of city limits with all utilities and public facilities available. This makes land suitable for permanent residences, associated shopping centers, schools, and commercial services.

II. *Within one-hour radius of source of employment.* Here all utilities and roads may not be available and some may have to be put in, but it is still suitable for permanent residences and associated activities.

III. *Within three-hour automobile radius of major metropolitan area.* Satisfactory for middle income recreational or vacation home complexes. Usually only electricity and telephones available. Normally a county or state all-weather road to property line.

IV. *Beyond three-hour car radius of major city but within 30 minutes of airport that has scheduled commercial service.*

V. *Beyond 30-minute range of scheduled aircraft.*

The next classification relates to topography, climate, and land use, and will be designated by capital letters:

A. Highly productive for row crops or suitable for irrigation with cost of water economically feasible. Lifting from well deeper than 900 feet or purchasing from aqueduct at prices in excess of $40 per acre foot is not feasible except for certain specialty crops.

B. Proximity to ocean or large lake, or in an area of sufficient available waterflow that a lake can be built.

C. Proximity to mountains and skiing country.

D. Equitable mild climate (Southern California, Florida).

E. Scenery, hunting or fishing.

F. Barren waste land, dense brush, or swamp.

Example: Rolling mountainous arid country 40 miles south of Rawlins, Wyoming, would be designated V, F. Carrizo Plain 90 miles north of Los Angeles would be designated II, DE. Winston area 50 miles north of Kansas City could be designated II, B.

The processing and marketing of land could fall into the following, not necessarily exclusive, groupings:

1. Economically feasible self-sufficient agricultural properties. For cattle operations, it should be large enough to handle 1,000 cows. For grain, cotton, or other crops, it should be big enough to produce in excess of $100,000 per year gross. Properties of this capacity would ordinarily range in excess of a $500,000 price and would be sold as working ranches or farms by brokers for a 5% real estate commission.

2. Economically feasible agricultural properties, too small for self-contained modern operation, that can be leased out to neighboring ranches or farms on agricultural net cash lease or share cropping arrangement. Price $100,000 to $500,000. Marketed by ranch broker at 5%.

3. Semi-recreational type ranch or farm, just big enough to avoid "hobby" classification, $50,000 to $100,000, sufficient agricultural production to avoid "raw land" classification and get tax and other subsidies. Marketed by broker at 7 to 10% commission.

4. Raw land tracts in excess of 100 acres. Marketed by broker at 10% commission.

5. Forty- to 100-acre raw land tracts. Marketed by "developer," who furnishes nothing but survey and platted roads. Developer takes 100% mark-up on cost and pays out half of his gross profit in advertising and sales commissions, and takes 20% discount when he cashes in his finance paper.

Example: John Doe buys 4,000-acre tract at $200 an acre or $800,000 with $100,000 down payment and release clauses in mortgage. He markets in tracts of 40 acres average at $400 per acre, 10% down. He does nothing but furnish survey, plats in and dedicates roads to individual tracts, and puts in gravel road to development entrance. Sales completed in 18 months.

Outgo		*Ingo*	
Down payment	$ 100,000	Down payment on lots	$ 160,000
Platting & survey	30,000		
Road to area	10,000		
Sales office on site	20,000	Interest over the 18 months	60,000
Sales office in town	10,000		
2 sales mgrs. & 4 men for 1½ years	100,000	100 notes of $14,400 discounted 20% are cashed in at $1,152.00	1,152,000
Travel & telephone	30,000		
Advertising & other expense	20,000		
Interest, taxes, & carrying charges	100,000		
Mortgage amortization	700,000		$1,372,000
	$1,120,000		1,120,000
		Net profit in 18 mos.	$ 252,000

6. Raw land marketed in 5-acre "estates" registered with HUD. Same purchase terms as the preceding. One thousand acres retained for joint facilities (golf course, lake, club house, shops). Water, electricity, telephones, concrete road brought to property line (not sewer, gas, security guard). Sale of 600 lots completed in three years, priced at $2,000 per acre or $10,000 per tract.

Example:

Outgo		*Ingo*	
Down payment	$ 100,000	Down payment on lots, $1,000 on 600	$ 600,000
Platting & survey	50,000		
Registration with HUD, legal, etc.	100,000	Interest on lots sold over 3-year period	500,000
Roads	200,000		
Utilities	300,000		
Joint facilities	1,100,000		
Sales offices	50,000	600 notes of $9,000, each cashed in at 20% discount (higher discount if they are subordinated to house construction mortgage)	4,320,000
4 sales mgrs. 20 salesmen in 4 cities for 3 years	1,000,000		
Travel & telephone	300,000		
Advertising & other expense	500,000		
Interest, taxes & carrying charges	400,000		
Mortgage amortization	700,000		
	$4,800,000		$5,420,000
			4,800,000
		Net profit in 3 yrs.	$ 620,000

7. In states where it is still permitted by state and county law, the 4,000 acres is platted for one-acre raw land sales with 1,000 acres held out for platted roads and golf course that doesn't go in, minor joint facilities and exhibition houses. Sales accomplished on the high pressure mail order basis of two years ago. Three thousand-acre lots

marketed at $2,000 per acre, 5% down. One-year crash advertising campaign after 6 months of getting it through HUD.

Outgo		*Ingo*	
Down payment	$ 100,000	Down payment on lots, $100 on 3,000	$ 300,000
Platting & survey	200,000		
Registration with HUD, (6 mos. of legal wrangling if it could be registered and also state blue sky trouble)	300,000	Interest	200,000
10 sales mgrs. & 50 salesmen	1,000,000	3,000 notes of $1,900 discounted 40%[1]	3,420,000
Travel & telephones	300,000		
Free dinner & trips	100,000		
Joint facilities	100,000		
Advertising & miscellaneous	700,000		
Interest, taxes & carrying charges	150,000		
Mortgage amortization	700,000		
	$3,650,000		$3,920,000
			3,650,000
		Net profit in 18 mos.	$ 270,000

In making a comparative analysis of the three techniques of raw land sales that John Doe could have gone into as indicated in Nos. 5, 6, and 7, we see that his before tax return on his activities averaged out around $200,000 per year, or $100,000 after taxes, as everything would have been subject to either individual or corporate ordinary income taxes. This is a high return but no bonanza for an extremely risky business.

Reviewing the hazards:

1. The tracts wouldn't sell within the estimated time limits or at the anticipated prices.
2. County, state, or federal authorities would throw up unexpected road blocks after construction had started.
3. Labor strikes on Nos. 6 and 7.
4. Difficulty in discounting the notes at the anticipated rates.

Let us look at the $1,900 note of No. 7. The title work of foreclosure might be prohibitive, the cost of collection and administration would certainly average 3%, and without the mass advertising program there would be minimum resale activity. Some of the tract salesmen

[1] In California, by statute, there can be no deficiency judgement on real estate purchase-money mortgages. Hence, discount would be greater than 40%. At present time, this type of sales promotion is prohibited in almost every county in California.

have been selling with no interest on the mortgages. These have to be discounted 60% after they are "seasoned." Seasoning refers to somebody who has made three or four consecutive payments. Deficiencies run 50% the first year, but go down to 10% after the first year with those who have kept their payments up.

If John Doe had taken his 4,000-acre purchase at $200 per acre or $800,000 with $100,000 down and had been able to market it in four 1,000-acre recreational horse ranches at $270 per acre in eight months or $1,080,000, paid a 5% real estate commission, and $10,000 for platting and roads, he would be equally as well off, with little risk and minimal cash outlay. Under some circumstances, his profit might even qualify as capital gain. If he took mortgages back, they would be large enough to be saleable at minimal discounts, if they were secured by useable properties.

Certain facts become self-evident on analysis:

1. There is no dearth of John Does. "Developing" and marketing five-acre estates or one-acre mail order lots is an advertising game. It has nothing to do with agriculture and very little to do with real estate. In other words, anybody could buy 4,000 acres at $200 per acre and go through one of the various gyrations just described.

2. There is no dearth of 4,000-acre tracts over the United States, particularly west of the Mississippi.

3. The fact that one owns 4,000 acres or 20,000 acres is no incentive to go into John Doe's raw land business. It is a different and unrelated business, and not necessarily a profitable one.

4. There may be merit in selling and financing property for the John Does. There may even be merit in joint venturing with John Does, if they furnish the risk capital for developing and marketing.

5. There is no relationship between raising cattle, running a packing house, and operating a retail grocery store. The retail grocer does not have to buy his meat from you. Neither does the John Doe just described, who operates an advertising and marketing organization, have to buy his land from you. Neither do you have to sell your land to a particular John Doe, nor can you necessarily net more on your land by getting into his mail order business on one-acre tracts, even if these sales are still legal.

6. Mark-up on sales is not significant. It is the net profit you have left when the deal is wound up that counts. Also important is the level of risk that you took winding it up as well as the time and effort that were required.

7. There are lots of bright "financial wizards" in the United

States; there are lots of high pressure salesmen, sophisticated in all of the advertising media; there is a lot of raw land in 4,000-acre tracts; there are lots of misguided people who will buy anything if they only have to make a $50 down payment. Subject to the new protective regulations, these can be put together in all kinds of volume combinations. However, there has rarely been a sales gimmick, a new "financial concept," or anything that has had a monetary success that isn't immediately flooded by equally bright people getting on the bandwagon. They all go the way of the "Dutch Tulip Craze" of the 1800s, the miniature golf courses of the 1930s, or the hula hoop of the 1960s.

8. The only way to have reasonable stability is to have control of a product that isn't easily duplicated or access to a market that competitors will have trouble reaching. Within the land field, an example on the selling side would be "assemblage." Control of 200,000 contiguous square feet around 57th and Madison in New York would be unique. There would be no comparables. In the rural West, 4,000-acre tracts are not uncommon, but 100,000 acre-assemblages are. There are very few anywhere in the United States. Without the power of eminent domain, they are impossible to put together. You control your own environment. A potential user must come to you.

On the buying side, an example of a limited market would be 45-year-old executives, with teen-aged boys, who are in 60% tax brackets, who want to raise their sons in a rural atmosphere, and who can plunk down $100,000 cash in down payment and prepaid interest. If you have special access to such a market, you are unlikely to have much trouble from mass media competition.

The winds of change blow slowly in basic industries and are accompanied by lots of creaking and groaning. Two such basic industries are meat and land. Amplifying an analogy used earlier, there is a long gap between the gleam in a bull's eye and steak on the table. This is also true between a 2,000-acre farm and a lot with a house on it in a suburban development.

The owner of a cow herd who is getting 30¢ per pound for a yearling steer on the hoof is dismayed when he pays $8 for a 1-pound sirloin at a New York restaurant. He threatens boycotts, stands up and shouts at the Cattlemen's conventions, and demands a senate investigation. Likewise the farmer who sold his farm at $300 per acre is chagrined when he finds his cousin who moved to town has just paid $8,000 for the half-acre lot on which his contractor is building a home. Both are convinced that the "damned middle-men" are becoming millionaires at their expense and that the whole thing is somehow "immoral."

In competitive basic industries this is probably not so. The price gap between the basic raw material and the retail product is largely due to the following:

1. Processing costs.
2. Wastage during processing.
3. Marketing expense.
4. Interest charges during all of above stages.

Let us start with a 1,000-pound choice slaughter steer at 30¢ per pound in the hands of the feeder. He is sold, moved to a packing plant and comes out a 550-pound carcass at 70¢. Head, feet and hide are lucky to have brought 2¢ per pound. The grocery chain buys the carcass, butchers it, packages the better cuts, displays it, hires salesmen, pays rent, and sells the better cuts for $1.50 per pound. The restaurant hires waiters, pays rent, pays cooks, hires musicians, advertises in the paper, and charges you $8. There are farmers, feedlots, packers, grocery stores, and restaurants who, from time to time, manage to go broke at these mark-ups.

Other than the fact that all of these people pay interest on their capital and are capable of going broke, there is very little similarity between the five separate businesses involved in the processing and marketing of beef. The fact that you are great at gathering calves in a blizzard does not qualify you to run a packing plant. The fact that you are an expert in handling the packing house worker's union does not mean that you know how to arrange display cases in a grocery store. None of these people necessarily know anything about a restaurant, and, when they attempt to run one, it is usually a disaster.

Margins of profit relate to processing and merchandising costs, and, in competitive basic industries, they level out. The rancher who can produce a steer for 28¢ and sell it for 30¢ may very well be netting a lot more than the restaurant operator who buys a steak for $1.50 and sells it for $8.

While various segments of the industry or public may from time to time get irritated at farmers, packers, grocers, or restaurateurs, they have gotten used to them. Modern land development is a bit different. Traditionally, as cities grew, farm land on the edge was bought by users, and houses were put up on an individual basis. By griping, complaining and "knowing somebody" the owner might get water, sewers, streets moved to his door. Modern tract development and "new suburbs" are a little different.

The unattractive names associated with the activities give an idea of the public view. A "speculator" buys the 2,000 acres from the farmer at $300 per acre. He may put in a road, pay interest on a mortgage, hire attorneys to get the area zoned properly. Next a "promoter" buys 200 acres of the more usable, close in, flat ground at $500 per acre. He sets up a sewer district, works with the utility companies, gets electricity and water, hires planners, architects, plats roads, sidewalks, etc. When he is through, he has 160 acres in 40-acre tracts and 40 acres in dedicated roads and a plot that he gives to the school district.

He sells a 40-acre tract to a "developer" at $2,000 per acre. The developer puts in the internal streets, utilities, files building restrictions, sets up a sales office, and proceeds to sell half-acre lots in groups of four or five to "builders" at $6,000 per lot. Approximately 40% of the tract goes for streets, sidewalks, playyard, and common area. The builder puts on $25,000 homes and sells the package for $40,000. Of this amount, $2,000 goes for salesmen, advertising and sales office. During each of these processes described, somebody was paying 8% interest on all funds tied up. In addition there were loan fees, placement charges, discount points, filing fees, lawyers, accountants, FHA fees, appraisal fees, brokers fees, assessments, hook-on charges, and taxes every step of the way.

Along these "land processing" steps, the margins of profit also relate to the risks. The builder, who bought the lot at $6,000, puts on the $25,000 investment in a house, and hopes to sell it for $40,000 gross or $38,000 after sales expenses, is expecting to net $7,000 per lot. However, he is also bearing the risk of delays for strikes, material shortages, or failure to sell the house when completed. During these periods, interest charges go merrily along.

Again, as in the beef industry, competition and history determine the profit margins. If great, sure quantities of money could be made with little risk by buying land from farmers at $300, putting in a road and selling it at $500, competition would flock in and cause one of these things to happen:

1. The farmer would want more than $300.
2. The buyer would not pay $500.
3. The "speculator" would have to put in more than a road to sell it.

As the rancher who gets up before dawn may not be any good as the restaurateur who goes to bed at that time, so might the buyer and merchandiser of 500-acre tracts be no good at selling a one-acre lot with a scenic view from the living room window to a housewife. These are different games, different businesses, different margins of profit, and different markets. Further, it does not relate to how much comparative net either will have in his bank account at the end of the year.

In summary, there is no magic to the acquisition, processing, and merchandising of land. It is much like any other commodity:

1. You can buy it in quantity wholesale and market it in smaller increments retail.

2. You can "process it" by putting in roads, sewers, utilities, and joint facilities. All of these have price tags which can be determined within reasonable accuracy by engineer's or construction manuals or the monthly Dodge Reports.

3. Different size tracts and different levels of improvements have appeal to different types of markets.

4. The class of market determines the appropriate method of selling, whether by mail order, newspaper, television, high-priced salesmen, low-priced salesmen, or shares distributed by a public underwriter. In other words, it would not be particularly intelligent to attempt to market a $1,000,000 ranch by commercial television. Nor would an investment banking house be interested in selling a single $5,000 lot.

5. As in any other commodity, interest charges and other carrying costs associated with the maintenance of an "inventory" will vary with the level at which the inventory is "processed," and this would be a top management decision based upon the anticipated sales targets.

6. On the completion of the sales, the decision on the financing terms, the level of finance paper to be carried back, and the amount of the finance paper needed to be discounted in order to maintain a proper cash flow balance – all of these are decisions made daily by every major American industrial entity from automobile manufacturers to the proprietors of dancing schools.

Obviously, the ideal situation would be to purchase land for $100 per acre, put in improvements costing $1 per acre, incur sales expenses costing $2 per acre; sell one-acre lots for $1,000 per acre and immediately discount the finance paper with no administrative expense at 100 cents on the dollar. In the harsher world of reality this situation is "possible but unlikely."

Chapter XVII

New Public Land Policy

PAST HISTORY

The United States now has an area of some 2.3 billion acres of land, almost 766 million acres of which are owned by the federal government. If we exclude Alaska (which is heavily laced with extensive public lands) federally owned lands in the remaining 49 states comprise about one-fifth of the total area—and those federally owned lands belong to each and every taxpayer in the country. The resources of these lands produce revenue for the federal government and create work or play for many of our people. On the other hand, the federal government, acting as proprietor, annually spends terrific sums of money for their protection and development.

Some of the biggest problems concerning public lands stem from the fact that this one-fifth of our area is not proportionately distributed over all 50 states. Uncle Sam owns almost 50% of the total land area in the 11 contiguous westernmost states—ranging from a little over 29% in Washington to more than 86% in Nevada. Public lands in New Mexico alone exceed the total area of the states of Maryland and Pennsylvania combined, while in Colorado the public land acreage exceeds the area of the entire state of Indiana—and these comparisons *exclude* Indian reservations. As indicated in previous chapters, much of this land is operationally integrated with private land, and the two taken together affect rental potential and resale value.

By the time of our Revolution, all of our colonies owned some land within their respective borders, and several even had large external land claims. As time went on, and those colonies came to statehood, they turned much of their land over to the common government—primarily as a collective protection measure against the larger landed states. By this type of cession, our new national government got title to all land outside the original 13 colonies. At one time, three-fourths of our whole nation was in federal ownership . . . and, over our years of national expansion, 29 of our 50 states have been created from that "public domain."

From the time of President Jefferson, various territories have been added to the United States, and all acquired territories became the

HIGHLIGHTS IN THE HISTORY OF THE PUBLIC DOMAIN

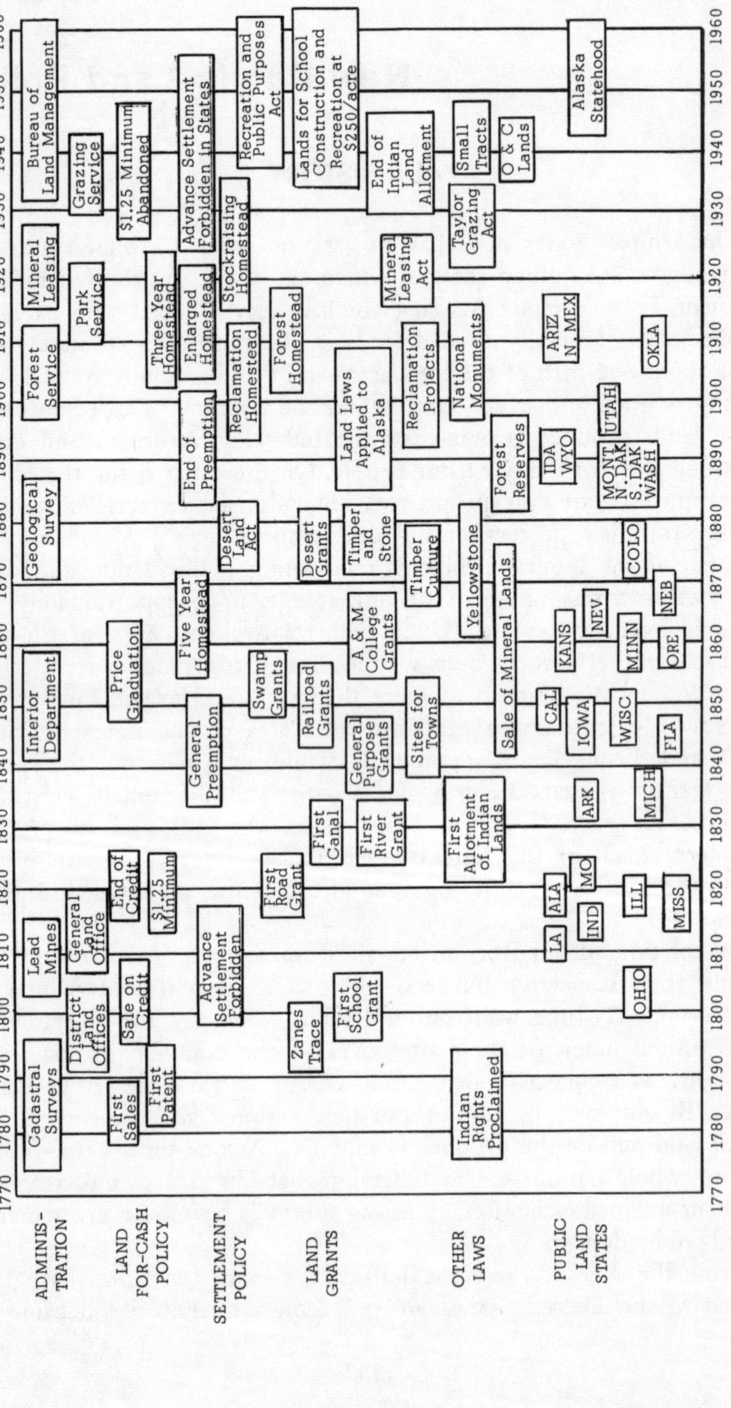

Source: Bureau of Land Management, Department of Interior

property of the American people. The federal government owned them, was responsible for taking care of them, and called them "public domain."

The disposal of public lands came to be a matter of concern to Congress after seven of the original states had passed to our central government their claims to certain western lands as part of the agreement on which the United States was founded. The old Northwest area, lying west of Pennsylvania and north of the Ohio River, became our first public domain.

Congress did not have any really firm ground on which to legislate for the public domain, because there were foreign titles to worry about, plus the hard fact that American Indians firmly and physically held a large amount of this soil. And until *their* prior rights were taken care of, a new title was not worth a great deal to any settler.

During the early years, four basic policies were adopted concerning the disposal of public lands. These had to do with a rectangular system of surveys, public land auctions, issuance of federal patents as a confirmation of ownership, and the provision for free school lands. All of these, with possible exception of the money-making auction procedures, have been justified as having been wise moves.

Faced with the sizable Revolutionary War debt on the one hand and with an abundance of land on the other, the government's most obvious course of action was the sale of its land on a large scale. So, a General Land Office (now the Bureau of Land Management) was set up in 1812, primarily to sell those public lands to defray the war debt. A great demand was growing for western land. Selling slowly at first, it picked up such volume after the turn of the 19th Century that the proceeds from land sales reached a point of accounting for over a third of the overall total government income. Along with this sale of land, the federal government made large grants of public lands to the states, providing them the wherewithal for public school facilities. This early land grant assistance to the public school system has been of unquestioned benefit to our country up through the present time.

Whatever may have been its failings, the early land grant policy served to accelerate national and personal energies, creating the greatest construction and colonization project ever undertaken up to then. The West changed from a wilderness to a civilization, and the country became unified.

Disposal of public lands dominated the politics of the 1800's as, in fact, it did the entire economy. Problems of settlers and frontiersmen at times became major political issues. Shortly after the Revolution, the central government had acquired ownership of about 150 million acres of land. However, by the 1850's, that amount of federally owned land had grown tenfold, with the area of public domain constituting three-fourths of the total land area (1.9 billion acres) of the entire nation. A monstrous landholding!

During that early period, land had been granted to various recipients for the growing common good of the country. Since the Revolution, it had been passed along in varying amounts to military personnel—as inducement to serve as fighting men, as well as rewards for their actions and past performance. Over 50 million acres were so awarded. Additionally, land grants to railroads constituted a major program—a necessary one through which to induce the westward growth of our transportation system. The land grants did not, of course, build these railroads but provided a basis for credit and sound private investment in their construction. With this aid, the railroads could hurry up the economic development of those outlying areas, carry government freight and traffic at reduced rates, and then raise the market value of other western lands. Although more than 130 million acres were patented to the railroads, this really only related to the construction of some 18,000 miles of line—less than 8% of the total railroad mileage built, up to that time, in the United States.

A sample pattern of land grant aid to a railroad would amount to alternate sections of land, extending for specified distances on either side of the proposed railroad line. Such an arrangement provided benefits to both the railroads and the government (through the concessions on freight rates) and constituted another important aspect of our early land disposal. Some of these checkerboarded areas out west are still owned by the railroads, bringing in a minor amount of revenue through grazing leases.

Almost all of our land grant programs quickly opened the door to a new burst of land speculation, and our settlers found themselves faced with the same basic problem that we have today—high prices for decent and productive land. Some means of federal sponsorship had to be found to provide lands for the honest settler out in the West.

The Homestead Act of 1862, a good stride forward in that direction, was one of the more important laws enacted in the history of our country. The principle of free homesteads for settlers had long been the goal for which the West had struggled, and as each succeeding land law, more liberal than its predecessors, was passed, that goal was attained in the 1862 Act. It was the culmination of an increasingly liberal land policy, and to it has been attributed the rapid settlement of the West and the large percentage of farm owners in the

United States. It also has been regarded as a prime solution for providing an outlet for the surplus and discontented labor of the East. The 1862 Act permitted unrestricted settlement on public lands for all settlers, requiring only residence, cultivation, and some improvement of a tract of 160 acres. Anyone who was a citizen and was 21 years old, or the head of a family, was eligible for this homesteading, so long as he did not already own as much as 160 acres. After living on the land for six months, he could buy the homestead for $1.25 an acre or, if he preferred, after five continuous years of occupancy, the settler could apply for and receive title to the 160 acres for a straight filing fee of $15.

Even with the 1862 Homestead Law, land speculation and monopolization continued. As before, it was still possible for foresighted speculators to rush out to the frontier ahead of the settlers, purchase the best lands, and then hold them for the increase in value which the oncoming throngs of settlers would automatically create. The speculators were able to secure the most desirable lands—those close to water, timber, markets, and communication routes. (So you can see that land speculation remains pretty much the same, from century to century.) The arriving settler had the choice of buying at the speculator's prices from the land-grant railroads which kept their checkerboarded lands also at pretty high prices, from the states (whose land policies were tighter than those of the federal government), or of going farther out on the trails in order to be able to exercise his homestead privilege—where facilities for community life were limited.

An 1891 amendment to the Homestead Act of 1862 permitted settlers to commute their claims by a money payment after 14 months of nominal or 8 months of actual residence. In the 20 years following, over 100,000 settlers commuted homesteads, comprising some 20 million acres. This abuse was particularly prevalent in the case of timberlands, where a settler would get quick possession and then sell out. A large proportion of these "quick turnover" settlers, in fact, were women—schoolteachers and the like—who used this method of supplementing their salaries during the vacation months.

In 1906, a Forest Homestead Act was passed, authorizing limited homesteading on as much as 160 acres of public lands, classified for agriculture but located within a national forest. In 1909, an enlarged Homestead Act increased area limitation in western states to 320 acres of public lands, when classified as dry-farming lands and not susceptible to irrigation. In 1916, a Stock Raising Homestead Act increased area limitations for homesteading up to 640 acres when public lands were suitable only for grazing livestock. This Act, involving no cultivation of lands but requiring certain range improvement, was repealed at the time of the Taylor Grazing Act of 1934.

Speaking of grazing, let's back down a few years and look at our public domain as seen through the eyes of a stockman or rancher.

Grazing by livestock on our western rangeland really started in earnest with the big Texas trail herds that brought a flood of cattle into the Great Plains area during the several decades immediately following our Civil War. Soon after that war, the larger cattle ranches were established, and before the end of the century most of our open range that was worth anything at all had livestock on it.

The early 1880's saw not only the peak of the expansion of the railroads into the West but the beginning of the real problem of settler versus large rancher with respect to the use of land. Growth of the settler population and all the new homesteading activity involved wide use of fencing by those newcomers, and the previously open spaces all but disappeared during that era. The homesteader, of course, protected his interests with a fence, while the cattlemen protected their waterholes and grazing lands by any means at their disposal—including gunpowder.

This situation soon bubbled to the surface at the federal government level, where various remedies developed. The Public Land Commission in 1880 proposed that good grazing lands be disposed of in chunks large enough to make their management effective—2,560 acres. Later, after the turn of the century, that same Commission came up with the idea of federal grazing districts, which was subsequently disapproved . . . for the time being. As a substitute measure, however, many important range areas were established as national forest areas in which grazing administration and control could be carried out. Still later, but prior to World War II, the several special homestead acts earlier mentioned were passed, bringing some 100 million acres of grazable public lands under private ownership.

Most of the public domain remaining by 1934 was suited only for livestock grazing, and its potential even for this wasn't much in many cases. All of it that could produce enough forage to support livestock already was being grazed. Moreover, many of the livestock owners grazing their animals on public lands lacked a clear legal right to do so, but that didn't bother them—they continued with it anyhow. These lands generally had been overstocked and were being improperly used, and their productivity had dropped way below the original level, which was low to start with. This situation became further compounded by extensive droughts occurring throughout the country in the 1930's.

By now, inter-departmental rivalry had sprung up between the Departments of Agriculture and Interior as to just which department would have jurisdiction over public lands. . . . Settlement of that question came to a head in the Taylor Grazing Act, passed in June, 1934, which, in addition to creating livestock grazing districts, assigned to the Department of the Interior the responsibility for administrative control of the public domain.

The Taylor Grazing Act provided a permanent system of management for the western grazing lands and introduced one of the most comprehensive conservation programs ever attempted for our public lands and resources. It established specific authority for the classification of lands in order to assure proper usage—something previously lacking in federal land legislation—and for the prohibition of disposal except when the land could be classified as suitable for the purpose sought. Its primary purpose was to stop continuing injury to public rangelands through overgrazing, soil deterioration, and other misuse. All remaining unreserved and unappropriated public lands—chiefly in 10 western states, and excluding Alaska—were closed to indiscriminate settlement and use. Although reserved from transfer to private ownership, the lands remained open for staked mining claims as well as for public hunting, fishing, camping, and other outdoor recreation.

For the first time in our history, real authority had been given for the classification of land according to its best use and for the rejection of applications for other uses. Provision was made in the Taylor Act for the exchange of land of equivalent value with states or with private individuals, as well as the sale of odd chunks of land, the object in either case being better consolidation of federal lands—or "blocking up" —into more compact parcels. Conservation and propagation of wildlife within the grazing districts was provided for, as well as were the rights to hunt and fish there. Lands could be transferred from grazing districts to national forests, and vice versa, when better administrative boundaries would result from the transfer. Finally, provisions were made for erosion and flood control programs, water development, and general improvement of the lands. This was indeed a multiple-use Act.

Aside from the main feature of this legislation, which was the establishment of grazing districts, it presented a system for the licensing of livestock grazing, plus a firm program of land management. Provision initially was made for 32 grazing districts, involving an aggregate acreage of about 80 million acres, plus separate authority for the issuance of leases for grazing in certain of those areas not otherwise suitable for district administration. Grazing permits, running for as long as 10 years, are issued within each district. For the lease of isolated tracts not within a grazing district, preference is given to adjacent or nearby landowners who are in the stock raising business. Because of its reserved and preferential property status during the years since the time of the Taylor Grazing Act, this vast area of public lands became known as the National Land Reserve.

HOW WE LOOK AT THEM TODAY

By the middle of this century, the pattern of events and the many changing circumstances moved the average citizen toward a closer relationship with the open spaces and, thus, with our country's public lands. World War II had operated to expose our more countrified youth to the growing mainstream of metropolitan America—for better or for worse—and the media of TV and other instant communications had made all family groups conscious of the benefits they could begin to expect from the areas of our public domain. Recreation grew to be one of the top occupations, and everyone suddenly became interested in grabbing hold of a few acres of land to call his own—be it seashore, mountain, desert, what have you. The entrepreneurs and the land developers continued on with their respective dance steps, and by the time of this writing, the average citizen had become thoroughly aware of the rewards, as a taxpayer, which he came to expect from our extensive public land holdings.

By the 1950's and 1960's, the growing number of problems connected with the administration of our public lands—and the constantly increasing complex of laws connected with it—became very unwieldy. We had surplus landholdings in practically all departments of our federal government, and each department had a different way to handle them. We had no workable system of exchanging public lands between the federal government and any given state government. The fee levels and procedures connected with livestock grazing on public lands were antiquated. No uniform land appraisal system was in use or recognized. In short, in our modern-minded country, whose people were rapidly becoming land-oriented, we needed to take a long overall look at the entire public lands picture. This increased demand for the proper use of public lands generated a corresponding need for new management procedures on the part of the federal government. The Interior and Insular Affairs Committees of both the Senate and the House, recognizing that this would have to be a bipartisan effort, suggested that a Commission be set up to study the broad aspects of the problem, reporting back to Congress as required. This project finally became law in 1964, as P.L. 88-606.

Form 4115–6
(July 1964)
(formerly 4–1096)

UNITED STATES
DEPARTMENT OF THE INTERIOR
BUREAU OF LAND MANAGEMENT

TERM GRAZING PERMIT
Act of June 28, 1934 (48 Stat. 1269), as amended

PERMIT CONDITIONS ON REVERSE

State	
Grazing District	
Date	
TERM OF PERMIT	
From	To

Name of Permittee	Address *(Include zip code)*

YOU ARE HEREBY AUTHORIZED to graze on the Federal range in the *(allotment or unit)* in the above State and Grazing District, the number and class of livestock indicated herein for the periods and within the area described below, which is the equivalent of animal-unit months of feed. All livestock, six months of age or over, will be counted as a part of the total number of livestock allowed under this permit and fees will be charged accordingly.

BLM GRAZING PERMIT FORM, COVERING LIVESTOCK GRAZING WITHIN FEDERAL GRAZING DISTRICTS

THIS PERMIT IS SUBJECT TO THE CONDITIONS PRINTED ON THE REVERSE HEREOF

ACCEPTED:

(Signature of Permittee)

(Signature of District Manager)

PERMIT CONDITIONS

1. This permit is subject to temporary adjustment, if the necessity arises, to protect or conserve the public lands affected.

2. This permit will cease to be effective as to any of the lands described herein immediately upon the termination of administration of said lands by the Bureau of Land Management. Furthermore, this permit is subject to termination, in whole or in part, at any time because of:
   a. Noncompliance of the permittee with rules and regulations now or hereafter approved by the Secretary of the Interior;
   b. Loss of control by the permittee of all or a part of the property upon which it is based;
   c. Failure of the permittee to demonstrate that the actual commensurate rating of the base property upon which it is based is equal to the estimated rating of such property at the time of the issuance of this permit.

3. If the permittee desires any use of the Federal range different, either as to time or numbers, from that provided for in this permit, he must notify the District Manager in writing of the change desired at least 10 days prior to the beginning of each grazing period described in the permit. Failure on the part of the permittee to so notify the District Manager will result in the permittee's being liable for the full grazing fee even though he makes no use or only partial use of the range, *provided* the range is available and usable. If the requested change in use is approved the District Manager will issue an adjusted fee notice or authorize the change by letter if total use remains the same.

4. Each year during the term of this permit and before the beginning of each grazing period provided for in the permit, the permittee will be furnished a notice of the fees, fixed or determined by the Director of the Bureau of Land Management, chargeable for that period. Fee payments *must* be made to the District Manager in the manner and within the time specified in the notice.

5. Use of the Federal range for grazing purposes is forbidden during any period of delinquency in the payment of fees.

6. This permit is subject to the Taylor Grazing Act, *as amended*, and the rules and regulations promulgated thereunder by the Secretary of the Interior.

7. This permit applies to all Federal range within the the area described, including the surface of unpatented mining locations or claims not needed by locator for mining purposes or in extracting and removing the mineral deposits therein. It is understood that the permittee will exercise due care not to disturb or damage any mining improvements thereon.

8. This permit is subject to the provisions of Executive Order No. 10925 of March 6, 1961, *as amended*, which sets forth the nondiscrimination clauses. A copy of which may be obtained from the Signing Officer.

9. It is further understood and agreed that no Member of, or Delegate to, Congress, or Resident Commissioner, after his election or appointment, or either before or after he has qualified, and during his continuance in office, and no officer, agent, or employee of the Department of the Interior, other than members of the District Advisory Boards appointed in accordance with Section 18 of the Taylor Grazing Act (53 Stat. 1002; 43 U.S.C. 3150-1) shall be admitted to any share or part in this permit, or to derive any benefit to arise therefrom; and the provisions of Section 3741 Revised Statutes (41 U.S.C. 22; 18 U.S.C. Sections 431-433, and 43 CFR, Part 7), enter into and form a part of this permit, so far as the same may be applicable.

Form 4120–2
(September 1968)

UNITED STATES
DEPARTMENT OF THE INTERIOR
BUREAU OF LAND MANAGEMENT

GRAZING LEASE

Issuing Office

Number

THE UNITED STATES OF AMERICA, acting by and through the Bureau of Land Management, Department of the Interior, for and in consideration of the representations made in the application for lease and subject to all terms and conditions herein, by these presents grants for grazing purposes to:

embracing the following lands:

BLM GRAZING LEASE FORM, COVERING LIVESTOCK GRAZING ON LANDS OUTSIDE FEDERAL GRAZING DISTRICTS

subject to future adjustments by the authorized officer; the annual grazing use of the lands is specified as follows:

This lease is issued subject to all rules and regulations of the Secretary of the Interior now or hereafter in force: Said rules and regulations are incorporated by reference herein and are made a part hereof. The general terms and conditions are set forth on the reverse hereof. The special terms and conditions are as follows:

I HEREBY accept this lease for grazing livestock and agree to the stipulations outlined herein.

____________________ (Date)

____________________ (Signature of Lessee)

THE UNITED STATES OF AMERICA

Lease effective *(date)*____________________

By____________________ (Authorized Officer)

for a period of______ years.

____________________ (Title)

____________________ (Date)

(Lease terms on reverse)

LEASE TERMS
(See 43 CFR 4120)

Sec. 1 – In consideration of the foregoing, the lessee hereby agrees to:

(a) Pay the required grazing fee in conformance with the billing. Annual grazing fee payments are due the United States upon issuance of the billing notice and are payable in advance of the first grazing period for the full amount as indicated on the fee notice. The lease may be cancelled for failure to pay the grazing fee in accordance with the fee notice.

(b) Use the lands in conformance with the management stipulations set forth in the lease.

(c) Observe all Federal, state, and local laws and regulations relating to the conservation or protection of game and other birds and animals.

(d) Take all reasonable and necessary actions to prevent, suppress, and control fires.

(e) Use the leased lands for grazing purposes only.

(f) Comply with local laws and ordinances with respect to fences.

(g) Maintain in good repair any range improvements on the leased lands, now or hereafter constructed.

(h) Comply with all Federal, state, and local livestock sanitary laws.

(i) Allow authorized representatives of the Department of the Interior, Federal agents, or game wardens to enter the leased lands at any time for the purpose of inspection and official business.

Sec. 2 – The lessor expressly reserves the right to:

(a) Permit, under applicable laws and regulations, the use and disposal of the mineral, timber, or other resources on or in the leased lands.

(b) Close portions of the leased area to grazing or other use whenever, because of depletion of the vegetal cover due to drought, epidemic, fire, or other cause, such action is deemed necessary to restore or preserve the range. A temporary closing of an area does not exclude or reduce such area from the lease.

(c) Reduce the leased area, if it is determined to be excessive for the number of stock grazed thereon by the lessee or if it is determined that such action is required for the protection of: sources of water for communities; camping places; stock driveways; roads, or trails, inhabited areas; community growth or development; or feeding grounds near communities for the use of domestic livestock; or, because of proximity to slaughtering or shipping points, for use of stock to be marketed; or multiple use management, including, but not limited to recreation, wildlife, mineral development, timber regeneration or reforestation and other purposes.

(d) Adjust the authorized grazing use to conform to changes in grazing capacity.

(e) When modification in the lease area occurs, adjust the grazing fee for the lease year following the modification.

(f) Classify and dispose of any or all the leased lands, under applicable laws and regulations and adjust the lease accordingly.

Sec. 3 – It is further understood and agreed that:

(a) Nothing herein contained shall restrict the acquisition, granting, or use of permits or rights-of-way under applicable law. The leased lands are managed for multiple use purposes. The lands shall at all times be open to use by others for prospecting, mineral leasing and mining purposes, access to and egress from other Federal lands, hunting, fishing, recreation, and for all other lawful purposes, without hindrance or interference by the lessee.

(b) The lessee shall not use, sell, or remove any vegetative resource or any timber growing on the leased lands except as authorized by this lease or by permit.

(c) No range improvements may be constructed on the leased lands without the prior written consent of the lessor.

(d) Upon the expiration or earlier termination of this lease, and upon written application filed by the lessee within thirty (30) days of its expiration or termination, the authorized officer, in his discretion, may require a subsequent grazing user to agree to compensate the lessee for any grazing improvements of a permanent nature. The lessee will be allowed three months from the date of expiration or termination of the lease within which to remove his improvements. If not removed the improvements may become the property of the United States.

(e) The authorized officer may terminate and cancel this lease upon the lessee's default in the performance or observance of any terms, convenants, and stipulations hereof, or of the regulations of the Department of the Interior now or hereafter in force, or of any cooperative agreement entered into with the Bureau of Land Management. No improvements may be removed when the lessee is in default.

(f) Assignment of this lease will not be recognized by the United States without proper application and written consent of the authorized officer.

(g) The lessee may relinquish this lease at any time. The lessee may be released from liability under this lease only if he has complied with all terms and conditions of this lease.

(h) This lease may be terminated or adjusted because of loss of control by the lessee of all or a part of his preference right lands, or if this lease was issued improperly through error with respect to any material fact.

(i) This lease applies to all public land described herein, including that portion of the surface of unpatented mining locations or claims not needed by the locator for mining purposes. The lessee will not disturb or damage any mining improvements and will avoid damage or injury to his livestock because of mining operations.

(j) No Member of, or Delegate to, Congress, or Resident Commissioner, after his election or appointment, or either before or after he has qualified, and during his continuance in office, and no officer, agent, or employee of the Department of the Interior, other than members of the district advisory boards appointed in accordance with Section 18 of the Taylor Grazing Act (53 Stat. 1002; 43 U.S.C. 315c-1) shall be admitted to any share or part in this lease, or derive any benefit that may arise therefrom. See 41 U.S.C. 22; 18 U.S.C. 431-433, and 43 CFR 7.

(k) This lease is subject to the provisions of Executive Order No. 11246 of September 24, 1965, which sets forth the nondiscrimination clauses. A copy of this order may be obtained from the authorized officer.

It is further convenanted and agreed that all additional conditions or stipulations attached hereto are made a part hereof.

Administration of Federal Lands by Agency, 1968

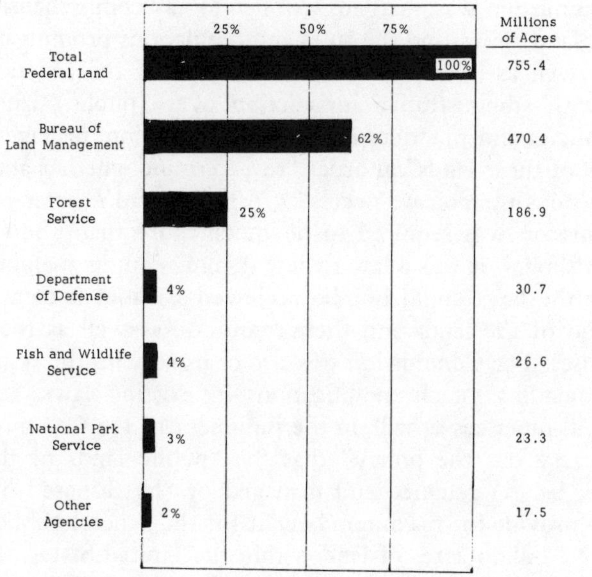

Source: PLLRC Study, Inventory Information of Public Lands, Table A2a, 1969

The bulk of the federal lands are administered by the Bureau of Land Management and the Forest Service.

As the result of this legislation, the Public Land Law Review Commission (PLLRC) was created. It called for a membership of 19 persons . . . 6 from U.S. Senate appointment, 6 from House of Representatives appointment, 6 from presidential appointment, plus a chairman. To condense a long story, the PLLRC staff was headed up by a director, Mr. Milton Pearl, who did an outstanding job with it through the completion of its work in June, 1970. Unfortunately, his untimely death shortly thereafter precluded his being able to witness the many follow-on actions which are being taken to implement the recommendations of the PLLRC.

The PLLRC held its organizational meeting in Washington, D.C. on July 14, 1965, at which time it elected unanimously Representative Wayne N. Aspinall (D-Colo.) as chairman, and Milton A. Pearl as director. The director was charged with the responsibility of assembling a staff and formulating a program that would produce all the information and data necessary as a foundation for the Commission's deliberations, conclusions, and recommendations. The Act creating the Commission declared that the nation's public lands should be retained and managed or, disposed of, all in a manner to provide the maximum benefit for the general public. This goal was the Commission's objective.

The Commission was charged with making a "comprehensive review of (public land) laws, and the rules and regulations promulgated thereunder" as well as "the policies and practices of the federal agencies charged with administrative jurisdiction over (public) lands insofar as such policies and practices relate to the retention, management, and disposition of those lands" in order "to determine whether and to what extent revisions thereof are necessary." This broad charter meant that the Commission was required to do much more than codify existing statutes. Although it was a law review commission, its members recognized that the laws could not be reviewed without a comprehensive examination of the lands and their resources, as well as the uses and potential uses. The Commission was also charged with the responsibility of recommending "such modifications in existing laws, regulations, policies, and practices as will, in the judgment of the Commission, best serve to carry out the policy" that the "public lands of the United States shall be (a) retained and managed or (b) disposed of, all in a manner to provide the maximum benefit for the general public."

Of the 2.2 billion acres of land within the United States, the federal government owns 755.3 million acres, of which 724.4 million acres were specifically within the definition of lands concerning which the PLLRC was charged with the responsibility of making recommendations. Recognizing that there are both known and unknown values in those lands, the Commission never lost sight of the potential significance that its recommendations might have because of these values.

For the purposes of its report, the PLLRC considered all the resources and uses of the public lands to be commodities. Accordingly, in addition to the traditional resources of minerals, timber, forage, intensive agriculture, water, and fish wildlife, there were included outdoor recreation and the various spatial uses, such as for residential, commercial, and industrial purposes.

The comprehensive research program examined each and every public land law as well as the regulations, practices, and procedures involved in their administration. However, throughout its work, the Commission took a broad approach to matters of policy and did *not* consider any subject before it in a law by law review. Nor did they attempt to identify in their recommendations all of the inconsistent laws that should be repealed or possibly modified upon adoption of the recommendations.

Deliberations of the PLLRC went on for five years, with the effort subdivided into several functional areas of interest or concern. In each such functional area, separate studies were made to whatever extent was necessary, either by the PLLRC itself, or—more frequently—by contract research activities whose specialty related to a given problem area.

By the time the report was being put in final rough form, there were 18 areas of interest for which specific recommendations were being made and 137 specific recommendations for approval and implementation.

In the early summer of 1970, the final report of the Public Land Law Review Commission was delivered to the President, concurrent with its delivery to the two houses of Congress. It was entitled *One Third of the Nation's Land*, is available from the Government Printing Office for a modest fee, and is the reference text to which much of the material hereafter used in this chapter is attributed. The variety and number of chapters in that report reflect the depth to which this Public Lands Study was conducted, and a listing of them at this point is considered timely.

For each principal subtopic of study, the PLLRC came up with several relevant recommendations. Due to their diversity, it would be pointless to tabulate them all here.

Instead, we will show the spread of chapter titles concerned, and a *first recommendation* (generally the most significant) made by the PLLRC concerning that subject.

Planning Future Public Land Use

Goals should be established by statute for a continuing, dynamic program of land use planning. These should include:

Use of all public lands in a manner that will result in the maximum net public benefit.

Disposal of those lands identified in land use plans as being able to maximize net public benefit only if they are transferred to private or state or local government ownership, as specified in other Commission recommendations.

Management of primary use lands for secondary uses where they are compatible with the primary purpose for which the lands were designated.

Management of all lands not having a statutory primary use for such uses as they are capable of sustaining.

Disposition or retention and management of public lands in a manner that complements uses and patterns of use on other ownership in the locality and the region.

Public Land Policy and the Environment

Environmental quality should be recognized by law as an important objective of public land management, and public land policy should be designed to enhance and maintain a high quality environment both on and off the public lands.

Timber Resources

There should be a statutory requirement that those public lands that are highly productive for timber be classified for commercial timber production as the dominant use, consistent with the Commission's concept of how multiple use should be applied in practice.

Range Resources

Public land forage policies should be flexible, designed to attain maximum economic efficiency in the production and use of forage from the public land, and to support regional economic growth.

Mineral Resources

Congress should continue to exclude some classes of public lands from future mineral development.

Water Resources

The implied reservation doctrine of water rights for federally reserved lands should be clarified and limited by Congress in at least four ways: (1) amounts of water claimed, both surface and underground, should be formally established; (2) procedures for contesting each claim should be provided; (3) water requirements for future reservations should be expressly reserved; and (4) compensation should be awarded where interference results with claims valid under state law before the decision in *Arizona* v. *California*.

Fish and Wildlife Resources

Federal officials should be given clear statutory authority for final land use decisions that affect fish and wildlife habitat or populations on the public lands. But they should not take action inconsistent with state harvesting regulations, except upon a finding of overriding national need after adequate notice to, and full consultation with, the states.

Intensive Agriculture

The homestead laws and the Desert Land Act should be repealed and replaced with statutory authority for the sale of public lands for intensive agriculture when that is the highest and best use of the land.

The Outer Continental Shelf

Complete authority over all activities on the Outer Continental Shelf should continue to be vested by statute in the Federal Government. Moreover, all Federal functions pertaining to that authority, including navigational safety, safety on or about structures and islands used for mineral activities, pollution control and supervision, mapping and charting, oceanographic and other scientific research, preservation and protection of the living resources of the sea, and occupancy uses of the Outer Continental Shelf, should be consolidated within the Government to the greatest possible degree.

Outdoor Recreation

An immediate effort should be undertaken to identify and protect those unique areas of national significance that exist on the public lands.

Occupancy Uses

Congress should consolidate and clarify in a single statute the policies relating to the occupancy purposes for which public lands may be made available.

Tax Immunity

If the national interest dictates that lands should be retained in Federal ownership, it is the obligation of the United States to make certain that the burden of that policy is spread among all the people of the United States and is not borne only by those states and governments in whose area the lands are located.

Land Grants to States

No additional grants should be made to any of the 50 states.

Administrative Procedures

Congress should require public land management agencies to utilize rule-making to the fullest extent possible in interpreting statutes and exercising delegated discretion, and should provide legislative restrictions to insure compliance with this goal.

Trespass and Disputed Title

Statutes and administrative practices defining unauthorized use of public lands should be clarified, and remedies available to the Federal Government should be uniform among land management agencies. Where necessary, statutory authority for policing by Federal agencies should be provided.

Disposals, Acquisitions, and Exchanges

Statutory eligibility qualifications of applicants for public lands subject to disposal should generally avoid artificial restraints and promote maximum competition for such lands. Preferences for certain classes of applicants should be used sparingly.

Federal Legislative Jurisdiction

Exclusive Federal legislative jurisdiction should be obtained or retained only in those uncommon instances where it is absolutely necessary to the Federal Government, and in such instances the United States should provide a statutory or regulatory code to govern the areas.

Organization, Administration, and Budgeting Policy

The Forest Service should be merged with the Department of the Interior into a new department of natural resources.

The recommendations of the PLLRC (just sampled) have to be put into action by various parts of the federal hierarchy—Interior, Agriculture, HUD, etc. The larger or more general recommendations will be—or already have been—the subject of legislation introduced into our Congress. For instance, the "Public Land Policy Act of 1971" (HR 7211) was introduced into the House of Representatives by Representative Aspinall, embracing many of the broad findings and conclusions of the PLLRC. Another bill (HR 10049) which reflected the Commission's proposals was introduced in July, 1971, cited as the "National Resource Land Management Act of 1971." Other legislation is pending in this general field.

An example of departmental action stemming from the PLLRC report can be seen in the recent rate increases for livestock grazing on public lands. Relative to recommendations of the report, the Bureau of Land Management has twice raised (1971, then 1972) those fees which earlier had been at unreasonably low rates.

"With about one-third of the country's land in its ownership, the federal government is a giant landowner. To a substantial extent, federal ownership of the public lands is a coincidence of history. Most of these lands were obtained as our national territory expanded. Although some were dedicated to meeting specific needs, the remaining unreserved public domain lands are mostly those for which there was neither a federal need nor demand under federal laws providing for transfer into non-federal control. Consideration of policies for these lands must generally start from the premise that they are not in federal ownership because of some direct tie to federal sovereign objectives.[1]

In its role as proprietor, the federal government has much the same interest as other landowners. It wants at least the same degree of freedom as other landowners to manage and use its resources.

[1] *One Third of the Nation's Land*, Public Land Law Commission, Government Printing Office, Washington, D.C. 20402.

As a proprietor, the federal government wants to maximize the net economic return from sales of land and resources.

The government, in the role of proprietor, has an interest in assuring the availability of sufficient funds to finance programs at a level that will result in a net monetary gain. It is also interested in the furtherance of research to achieve better use of the land.

The federal proprietor, in addition, has an interest in controlling users of the land in order to maintain the resource base and minimize damage or adverse environmental impacts. In performing these and other functions, every owner seeks maximum freedom of action, and the federal government is no exception. As owner of the public lands, the government wants to be free from control by state or local government and to pay no more for the support of local government than other landowners.

Before giving consideration to the noneconomic elements of the public interest that may require retention of land, the federal government, strictly from the standpoint of a proprietor, is interested in the relationship between the cost of administering lands and the income received.

State and local governments that will be affected by land use decisions expect, as a minimum, that they will be consulted and have a voice in the federal decision making process. They expect the United States in that way to give consideration to relevant state and local programs and also to consider the impact of public land actions on state and local governments. These units of government want the United States to share with other landowners in bearing the costs of providing services, not only for the public lands but for the community as a whole.

The public lands have played a vital, though changing, role in the development of the nation. Historically, they served as an inducement for the development of the frontier and, before the Civil War, as a major source of revenue. Today, the public lands must serve more complex and rapidly changing needs. Even though other aspects of national policy may overshadow public land policy, the public lands are, indeed, still important to all the people of the country.

Chapter XVIII

Land Development

For the purposes of this chapter "land development" will refer to grading, processing, improving, or constructing in such a manner as to increase the value of land for agricultural, commercial, or residential use. Associated with these processes are acquisition, financing, remarketing, or holding for increased rental value. Such development or upgrading might include bringing in irrigation water to change land from grazing to row crop cultivation; bringing electricity, roads, and sewers to make it suitable for residential use; and putting in rails, heavy utilities, and warehouses to make it attractive to industry.

Traditionally, a "land developer" has differed from a "builder" or "contractor" in that he puts in the roads and utilities, sets up zoning and restrictions, does the general planning and layout of the area, but leaves the actual construction of houses or plants to others. In the last 25 years, large firms have entered the field which furnish complete packages of planners, land acquisition, architects, financing entities, contractors, and sales agencies.

Until the American Institute of Certified Public Accountants started throwing cold water in the fall of 1968, the term "land development" had a special meaning to the go-go funds of the security world. Essentially, it meant a corporation that bought land at $100 per acre for nothing down with a release clause in the mortgage; plotted it into one-acre lots, engaged in a razzle-dazzle promotion campaign; and sold the lots at $2000, $50 down and $10 per month to retired post office employees.

Stage 2 involved creation of "fantastic earnings" from the gross income of the "sales." Stage 3 involved selling the stock of the development corporation to the public on some multiple of "price-earnings" ratio.

Certain patterns and formulas evolved:

1. A common ratio has been one-third to land cost; one-third to advertising; and one-third to the salesman.
2. Most of the "development" involved no improvements or utilities, but the following would be in the ball park as per half-acre lot costs for rural north Missouri within 5 mile radius of a town of 20,000:
   a. Gravel road............................$ 200

b. Asphalt road	300
c. Concrete road	500
d. Water	1,000
e. Electricity	200
f. Telephone	100
g. Gas	400
h. Sewers	1,000

3. The above are costs to property line, not hook up charges. It is assumed there will be 100 homes and that main utility lines have to be run 5 miles to city source at the developer's expense.

4. Where recourse finance paper and tough collection agencies are used, payment records are fairly good. However, where such paper is to be cashed in, the current market is a 60% discount. The principal problem is the cost of foreclosure and the administrative cost of payment collection.

The following has taken the bloom off the rose:

1. The lot owners found no resale opportunity. Because of the false promises of developers and/or salesmen, they flooded all government agencies with complaints.

2. Federal, state, and, particularly, county authorities clamped down all along the way. Many counties now require utilities to be in *before* a single lot is sold.

3. Sales organizations came under the scrutiny of the Federal Interstate Land Sales Act.

4. The market became saturated as thousands of "developers" got on the bandwagon.

5. The public itself became sophisticated and thoroughly unimpressed with free airplane trips, dinners, and elaborate colored brochures on what was "going to happen." They became aware that the golf course was not going in; that only 5% of the lots were being built on, and these were shacks; and that they were not going to be able to resell their $2,000 "investment" at a profit or even sell it at a loss to get out from under the collection agency that had bought their mortgage and was threatening to report them to the local retail credit association.

However, despite the dismal picture just painted, there are many legitimate developments and legitimate firms in the business. It has been a substantial burden on them to overcome the aroma left by their less ethical competitors, both in the minds of the public that buys their products and the Wall Street fraternity that markets their securities.

With the beginning of grain cultivation about 5000 B.C., man began

The answer to all of the four questions is yes. This is a new and growing market. Most of the American traditional and historical living patterns are in a state of flux. It is highly questionable whether they will be valid over the next 10 years. Even today we see the following:

1. Thirty-thousand-dollar homes being built on ½-acre $40,000 lots to get into a particular neighborhood.
2. Apartment rents in central cities being worth 40% more if 24-hour guards are maintained at all entrances.
3. Fifty-mile commuting to get into smog free area.
4. Lots being worth three times as much if inside of walled compounds with armed sentries at gate and 24-hour patrols.
5. Automatic elevators being replaced with male operators and alarm systems because of muggings in many new hotels.
6. Difficulty in getting burglary insurance on most rural homes, even in expensive neighborhoods.

It is quite possible that the single most important event in the United States real estate field in this decade was the "Sharon Tate" murders in the fashionable section of Beverly Hills. The second most significant event has yet to occur but is inevitable. This is when the weather conditions will be such that Los Angeles or New York will have a killer smog that will cause a hundred plus deaths and will send thousands to the hospital.

Turning from the permanent residence field of "land development," let us move to the new one of the coming decade – the recreational, retirement, or second-home complex. They are usually related to one or more of the following:

1. Proximity to sea.
2. Proximity to a lake.
3. Hunting and fishing.
4. Horse activities.
5. Skiing.
6. Mountains and scenery.
7. Clean dry air.
8. Quiet and open spaces.
9. Golf courses.
10. Forests and hiking trails.
11. Total removal from all urban problems.
12. Joint facilities of club houses, tennis courts, swimming pools.
13. Restrictions to compatible people of similar interests.
14. *Total security* of property and furnishings when not occupied.

The usual pattern seems to be 500 to 1,000 half-acre lots with $10,000 to $25,000 homes, with 2,000 to 3,000 acres of golf courses, lakes, bridle trails, and common facilities on which dues are paid. An additional 1,000 acres are sold to "investors" in 20 or 40 acre-lots who want to hold land for speculative increase as well as recreation. The overall complex is 3,000 to 5,000 acres.

Normally, macadam roads, water, and electricity are furnished to the property line. Butane gas tank service is available. In the past, septic tanks were used but many counties have suddenly required sewers and a treatment plant, which have created a traumatic experience for a large number of major developers. In counties where this is required before lot sales can be commenced, it has effectively stopped all small tract development.

In mountainous or rocky country, sewers and a treatment plant for 500 half-acre lots could well run $500,000 or $1,000 per lot. On 1,000 lots it might go $600,000 or $600 per lot. The laterals are much less expensive once the main trunks, pumping stations, and treatment plant are in. Septic tanks for the average weekend home should not cost over $300 and would be put in by the owner at the time of construction of the house, and not in advance.

Water consumption runs 80 gallons per day per individual in a modern home with indoor plumbing or 400 gallons per house. This breaks down to 1% car washing, 1% laundry, 3% lawn, 48% flushing toilets, 30% bathing, and 17% cooking. A well and pump with a 25-gallon per minute capacity and a 20,000-gallon storage tank facility could handle 100 homes. Any irrigation would have to be confined to the middle of the week when the majority of the homes were unoccupied.

From a 600-foot well depth the total facility might cost $130,000. Using two miles of 6-inch pipe at $7,000 per mile, three miles of two-inch pipe at $4,000 per mile, the total cost might run $156,000 or $1,560 per lot. A shallower well or a source of larger capacity closer in, spread over more homes, could cut this in half.

Studies of all of these figures bring certain truths home to roost. Starting from scratch in a new area, a developer of 100 lots might have a cost of $4,000 per lot in bringing water, sewers, electricity, telephone, and a hard surface road to the property line. By being in an existing municipality or in an area serviced by existing utility companies with these available at the edge of the development line, he can afford to pay considerably more for his land. Because of high road and utility costs, there is a lot of financial pressure to establish higher dwelling densities in order to spread these costs over more units.

A compromise that is showing increased recognition of these skyrocketing utility costs plus the new demand for living space and open areas is the concept of grouping the living units but having joint ownership of open areas belonging to all of the lot holders, or having the open space tied up by restrictions for limited joint use in a private park complex. The same pressures for grouping and sharing of expenses exist in the security requirement. A grouped area with a single road entrance, with or without a wall, can be watched by a single guard. Running three eight-hour watches or five men, including staggered Sundays, would run $3,000 per month. Split over 100 homes, this would only cost $30 per month. In a more isolated rural area, with limited in and out traffic but a single road entrance, a single armed caretaker and his family would probably be adequate against normal thieves and vandals.

A characteristic of some adherents of the new "anti-establishment culture" is a desire for rural living. Any non-protected, non-occupied home is fair game, either for thievery to support the "habit" or, more commonly, vandalism tied in with some complex form of "protest." Any home, no matter how remote, known to contain food, liquor, and a saleable television set, with its occupants gone for two weeks, is a dead duck. The situation is not unique to history or to the United States. What is probably unique is that for 50 years we have had a law-abiding citizenry that would make such a place relatively safe. We are merely reverting to the "normal situation" existing over most of the world's history where rural dwellers had to group in fortified villages. Depending on one's time and place, the brigands could be wandering bands of Saxons, Bedouins, Indians, or Hippies.

Going back to the middle-income individual who wants a recreational second-home and actually plans to build, the large companies in the business have evolved a proximity formula for a volume market. The site must not be over a three-hour automobile ride from a metropolitan area in excess of 1,000,000 people. This puts it within the range of the pocketbook for a three-day weekend. Obviously, some people will drive further and some can afford an airplane and some potential buyers live in towns of 200,000 – but there is no volume market. We are referring to people who will pay $5,000 for lots with all utilities in and who will erect $15,000 vacation homes on such lots. This does not refer to the now illegal $2,000-per-acre tract that the owner might occasionally camp on, if he can find it on the "developers" map.

We have covered the following markets:

1. The individual who would rather live in a close-in apartment to save the $300 per month expense of a second car.

2. The one who would build a $40,000 home on a $45,000 lot to live in a certain urban neighborhood.

3. The $30,000 home on a ⅓-acre suburban lot costing $8,000.

4. The $50,000 home on a 4-acre "suburban farm" at $3,000 per acre 20 miles out.

5. The part time farmer 50 miles out.

6. The trailer court 20 miles out.

7. The $15,000 vacation home on a $5,000 lot within a three-hour driving range of metropolitan area.

8. The $2,000 one-acre "investment" lot in the middle of no-where.

In respect to the vacation home complex several things become evident:

1. There is plenty of competition.

2. It is a market that can become saturated. It is estimated that California can only absorb 50,000 lot sales per year.

3. It is under severe scrutiny by federal, state, and county authorities.

4. Contractors and construction workers require immediate payment in cash. If $2,000-per-lot development money has to go in for roads and utilities, the "$5 down and $1 when you can catch me" technique of sales will not work unless the developer is prepared to tie up enormous amounts of capital.

5. The volume market falls into two categories: (a) within daily commuting distance to one's job, and (b) within a three-hour car drive for weekend recreation.

Let us now explore a limited but relatively untapped market. This is the $50,000-per-year 45-year-old executive with growing children with the following wishes or objectives:

1. A desire to make a long range land speculation of a sizable nature.

2. The need to qualify the property as a "working ranch" in order to qualify for the tax benefits under the law.

3. The need, in California, to have a property big enough to get in the agricultural preserve to save real estate taxes.

4. An outdoor-oriented family who will derive recreational benefits from the property.

In most areas, a property in excess of 40 acres is exempt from all zoning and governmental sales restrictions. In California 20-acre-tracts are generally exempt in most counties if a tract plan is filed and every lot has access to a public platted road.

To qualify with the U.S. Treasury the owner has a greater burden of proof and must show that the farm or ranch is large enough to be "economically feasible" and not just a hobby. A 300-acre minimum is a good safe number unless it's a highly concentrated citrus or nut grove. These same elements must be considered in qualifying for the agricultural preserve.

The buyer of these large tracts of land picks up these advantages:

1. The property is large enough that it can have agricultural use or be leased out to neighboring farmers or ranchers.

2. The U.S. Treasury can be convinced that it's not a hobby.

3. It is big enough to be of future resale value to a developer if the owner does not want to develop himself.

4. It is big enough to justify employing accounting, legal, and farm management advisors.

5. The anticipated speculative advantages and tax write-offs might justify a caretaker or farmhand's salary. This is an unsatisfactory but partial answer to the all-important security question (too expensive).

6. Under the 1969 tax bill, if the owner is married and files a joint return, he is given a $25,000-per-year permitted loss without getting into the complex problems of the Excess Deductions Account.

7. Under the hobby section (Section 183) of the IRS Code, he must have two years of profit out of five or appear before a special review board. It is believed that for this purpose interest and real estate taxes will be excluded from "expense" and that increases in land value will be counted as "income."

8. Expenses connected with personal use of home, swimming pool, etc., must be segregated. If total property is rented occasionally, these items can be pro-rated.

The developer picks up certain advantages from the 40-acre-and-up tract developments:

1. He is exempt from the zoning and sales restrictions.

2. The mortgages are large enough to justify title work, title insurance, foreclosure proceedings in event of default, reasonable collection, and administrative costs. Hence they are negotiable and can be sold with normal discounts, *e.g.*, 15% discount on an 8% mortgage with a responsible signer.

3. Septic tanks are perfectly satisfactory on 20-acre tracts and would be exempt from any county sewer requirements. Federal Housing Administrations or Farmers Home Administration loans would accept this level of low density for sewer exemptions.

4. Rectangular 40-acre tracts on both sides of existing public road or constructed laterals would hold road expense to reasonable proportions in a fairly large development.

5. Five- to 10-gallon-per-minute capacity shallow wells with large capacity storage would be adequate to supply 10 to 15 houses of low density (weekend) occupancy without exhausting the local water table. In many areas individual well systems and storage could be put in for $3,000 per house without contamination from septic tanks.

As one moves from the recreational second-home of the $15,000-per-year salary level to the tax-sheltered investment ranch of the $50,000-per-year executive, one breaks the restrictive collar of the three-hour driving radius. The latter owner can take commercial air to a nearby town and hire a rental car or have a jeep parked at the airport. On larger ranches these expenses would be deductible.

Certain compromises can be effected between the large completely-staffed working ranch and a marginal 40-acre property. For example:

1. For a partnership to buy a large ranch and put up individual houses for partners.
2. Own individual homes or condominiums and have large open acreage and facilities in common.
3. Have individual ranches extending out pie-shaped from central compound with individually owned houses. The latter could have:
    a. Walled enclosure and single caretaker for security and to take care of joint maintenance.
    b. Single water facility, swimming pool, tennis court, and joint-irrigated horse paddock.
    c. Government lease land held in common for joint tenants.

Land development for recreation purposes in the last quarter century has passed through three historical phases: (1) prior to 1962, (2) 1962 to 1968, and (3) post 1968.

Prior to 1962, tracts were largely sold after a dam had been built, some roads put in, and with 20 to 30% down payments required. Most buyers commenced construction immediately or within six months. There was little expectation to purchase for resale. Electricity, roads, telephones, and water were either present or under imminent construction. Other than a lake, joint facilities, such as swimming pool, club house, golf course, and bridle trails, were relatively rare. Sales and marketing were low key with an on-the-spot office, two or three salesmen, and some newspaper advertising. The marketing was directed exclusively at the nearest urban centers, rarely more than 50 miles distant.

Areas like Jackson Hole, Wyoming, Rancho Santa Fe, California, Palm Beach, Florida grew by word of mouth and were limited to the very wealthy who could take two- and three-month vacations, and were not restricted by transportation costs. In these areas no attempt was made to solicit the middle-income mass market, and, in fact, everything possible was done to keep them out.

The period 1962-1968 saw the advent of the "Dog and Pony Act"–large land auctions, heavily advertised on television and every news media; free dinners; massive sales forces operating on 40% commissions; telephone campaigns; and fancy offices on Wilshire Boulevard. Half-acre lots were sold in the middle of the Nevada desert for $1,000, with no roads, incomplete surveys, no water or any prospect of ever getting any, totally false brochures, and irresponsible salesmen. Innocent people signed contracts for deeds which were promptly discounted by the promoters, before the lending agencies got wise.

The purchasers then had the alternative of keeping up the payments or having their credit reputation jeopardized. The amounts of money were not great enough to justify the employment of attorneys to file damage suits for fraudulent statements.

Buyers, caught in the frenzy, purchased with the intent to resell at a profit, making 100% in their 10% equity. Very few sales were made locally where people knew the property, but most were made in New York, Chicago, or Los Angeles.

As everybody got in the act, the public got more sophisticated. Better Business Bureaus, Chambers of Commerce, and Real Estate Boards issued warnings. Prosecutions for using the mails to defraud were given publicity. People began to look, at least, at the property before they bought. Developers now had to put in a few facilities and an exhibition home or two before launching the campaign.

After 1968, the Federal SEC, the Department of Housing & Urban Development, various state legislatures, and most local counties stepped into the act, and the balloon burst. The action by the American Institute of C.P.A.'s to refuse to recognize the fictitious earnings cut off most of the companies from the capital equity markets. This, in turn, denied them the funds to put in the pre-sale capital requirements demanded by the new county and state regulations. The stock market collapse of 1969 completed the fiasco.

While these actions finished off the high pressure spurious market, certain other events in 1969 and 1970 gave an added boost to the legitimate developers. Among them were:

1. Renewed interest in ecological improvement.

2. Real fear of smog.

3. Desire to get children away from the "drug culture" and urban violence.

4. Thorough disgust with garbage strikes, traffic, noise, minorities, dirt, and congestion.

5. Complete awareness that the Tate murders got the publicity, but that the frequency of beatings, rapes, kidnappings, burglaries, and knifings are assuming massive proportions, with most newspapers entering into a tacit agreement to downplay them or not report them for fear of accelerating the incidents.

In this post 1970 period, what skills are required in a rural land development organization?

1. Ability to achieve control of large assembled tracts by purchase, option, or joint venture agreements at reasonable prices.

2. Skill in handling relationships with the Bureau of Land Management, Army Corps of Engineers, Bureau of Sport, Fisheries and Wildlife, U.S. Forest Service, state Land Boards, state legislatures, rural county zoning boards, county courts, irrigation and water districts, environmental control boards, county and state Rural Planning Commissions, Farmers Home Administration, Federal Land Banks, Productions Credit Associations, FHA, FNMA, HUD, SEC, and state security commissions.

3. Knowledge of hydrology, water engineering, well construction reservoirs, pumps, water litigation, and priority of water rights.

4. Road and utility construction.

5. Formation of water districts, irrigation districts, sewer districts, and marketing of their bonds.

6. Land use allocation, water allocation, lot and road platting, and joint use agreements and easements.

7. Financing of utility construction, FHA commitments, interim financing for construction, release clauses for partial developments, joint venture agreements, and joint marketing agreements.

8. Construction contracts and architects' agreements and responsibilities.

9. Marketing and sales organizations and advertising campaigns.

10. Financing house and lot sales.

11. Marketing and discounting purchase money mortgage paper derived from such sales.

12. Technical expertise in agricultural management for interim use of land inventories.

13. Experience in rural tax shelter presentations for selling "working ranches" as part of complex.

14. Access to high bracket rurally-oriented investors for tax-sheltered rural land sales.

15. Ability and experience in structuring packages to avoid "hobby farm" regulations and to qualify properties for "agricultural preserve."

16. Contacts and experience with local rural regulatory bodies or agencies to get participation on roads, REA Cooperatives, irrigation ditches, telephones, etc.

17. Game and fish management with controlled recreational hunting.

18. Security watches, patrols, burglarism and vandalism control.

19. Bridle trail, horse jumping, polo, and associated horse facility management.

20. Knowledge of sailing, power boats, water skiing, docks, boat ramps, maintenance facilities, etc.

21. Abilities in mountain climbing, skiing, camping, skeet shooting, archery, etc.

Summarizing the changes of the last two years, this is what has happened to the land development industry.

1. HUD registration and local governmental controls have eliminated high pressure sales of small tracts without utilities.

2. Pre-sale construction and capital requirements have eliminated lot sales with nominal down payments for all but the most well-financed developers.

3. Major corporations, formerly in this field, are exploring 40-acre-and-up sales and admit it is a new market in which they have no background but wish to enter.

4. For strong, well-financed corporations who can meet the pre-sale capital inputs of the new regulations, the market has opened up – there is substantially less competition.

5. The large tract sales are not necessarily less profitable. Developer A buys a 10,000-acre ranch at $100 per acre for $1,000,000, puts in roads, water and electricity for $500,000 and sells 100 farms of 100 acres each for $20,000 for a total of $2,000,000, netting $400,000 after $100,000 in brokerage commissions. All mortgages are negotiable at par.

Developer B buys 2,000 acres at $500 per acre for $1,000,000, puts in utilities, facilities, and interest coming to $9,000,000 and sells for $12,000,000 in 2,000-half-acre lots plus 1,000 acres of joint use property.

He spends $800,000 in advertising and overhead and $600,000 in sales commissions, netting $600,000, much of which is in paper that has to be heavily discounted if sold.

6. For apartments near the downtown, housing developments in the suburbs, and recreational homes in the country – the name of the game is *security* – walled compounds, 24-hour guards, and roving patrols.

Chapter XIX

Bibliographical Analysis of Tax Laws

Back in the mid-19th century, "Cowboy Justice" was swift and informal. "A railroad man, a newcomer in the community and, therefore, excusable for his audacity, was charged with a grave crime. He had hired a lawyer from San Antonio to defend him.

"The lawyer introduced himself at the outset by objecting to the whole court procedure. 'You have no authority in this case!,' he cried. Judge Roy Bean squinted his cold blue eyes. He thumped one of his guns against the top of the table. 'Set down,' he commanded.

" 'You have no jurisdiction in this case, and I demand constitutional rights and protection for my client.'

"The law west of the Pecos glared at the young lawyer. 'Oscar,' he called over to his assistant who acted as barkeeper and constable during rush hours, 'Come over here. In about eight minutes I expect to find this here prisoner guilty and order you and the boys to take him out and hang him. What'er you intend to do?'

" 'Take 'im out and hang 'im of course,' Oscar answered without hesitation.

" 'Supposin'," Judge Bean went on, 'I decide you better hang his lawyer along with him. Then what would you do?'

" 'Why, hang 'im Judge. It ain't no more trouble to hang two than one.'

"Bean turned his attention back to the young lawyer, 'Ain't that enough jurisdiction for you? Now, young jack-leg, you set down. I'm the law west of the Pecos. I run my court the way I see fit, an' that's my rulin'.' "[1]

Contrary to the opinion of some individual taxpayers, Income Tax Law today is a bit more complicated. The final decision is usually left to a judge (juries are fairly rare), but he is influenced by some combination of the following:

[1] Vinegarroon, *The Saga of Judge Roy Bean,* Ruel McDaniel, Southern Publishers, Kingsport, Tenn., 1936, p. 80.

1. The amended Internal Revenue Code.

2. The Treasury's own interpretations and policies of the code as published from time to time in its *Regulations*.

3. The Treasury's answers to variously posed questions as published in its *Rulings*.

4. The opinions and decisions of various tax courts and federal district courts.

5. Appellate court decisions such as the Circuit Court of Appeals or the U.S. Supreme Court.

Insofar as no two cases are ever exactly alike and usually contradictory decisions can be found, there is no such thing as a dead cinch. Times and circumstances change; geographic areas vary; and judges are only human. The fact that a reasonably high frequency of decisions get reversed on appeal may be partly due to this but partly due to the fact that an appeal is expensive and you don't usually try it unless you think you have a reasonable chance of winning. The decision of whether to take an appeal, unfortunately in many instances, is contolled by the economics—whether the benefits to be gained from a successful appeal are worth the costs.

The Tax Reform Act of 1969 generally played havoc with the so-called "gentlemen-farmers" or "non-farmers." The purpose of the act was to tighten so-called "loopholes" that were available to a farmer who was not dependent upon farm income for his livelihood. The pressure on Congress to pass something which would limit the outside investor was tremendous. Congress, in its enthusiasm, over-reacted in certain areas and severely limited all the tax benefits which were inherently available to all farmers. The law continues to contain several items which make it beneficial for an outside investor to invest in agricultural enterprises and, particularly, in livestock. The purpose of this chapter is to set forth the changes brought about by the Tax Reform Act of 1969 and The Revenue Act of 1971 and to discuss in more detail some of the areas of the tax law which have been the subject of objection and litigation and upon which the success of a successful tax shelter depends.

The areas of the Tax Reform Act of 1969 which had bearing upon the farmer-rancher and which are discussed herein are:

1. Recapture of farm losses through the establishment of an excess deduction account (EDA).

2. Total or partial recapture of soil and water conservation expense and land-clearing expense deductions.

3. Capitalization of citrus grove development cost.

4. Casualty loss treatment.

5. Recapture of depreciation taken after 1969 on livestock held for dairy, draft, breeding or sporting purposes.

6. Extension of livestock holding period for capital gain treatment.

7. The elimination of the male and female animals or "like kind" for purposes of a tax-free exchange.

8. Presumption of "engaged in for profit" for hobby loss purposes.

9. Depreciation in limitation on real property.

10. Interest limitations.

11. Limitations of deductions for charitable contributions of raised products such as livestock and crops and, to a certain extent, on contributions of capital assets.

12. Gradual elimination of the alternative capital gains tax on long-term capital gains in excess of $50,000.

The Revenue Act of 1971 tightened some of the "loopholes" left by the Tax Reform Act of 1969 but also gave the livestock farmer and rancher some tax boosts. The provisions of primary importance are:

1. Restored investment credit on equipment and added livestock (except horses) for the first time.

2. Established the year in which the hobby loss presumption commences.

3. Liberalized depreciation rates by establishment of Asset Depreciation in Range System (ADR).

4. Closed Excess Deduction Account loophole for Subchapter S corporations.

Despite the 1969 and 1971 tax law changes, the law still contains some inherent benefits for the cash-basis farmer-rancher taxpayer. The areas of discussion set out in this chapter are:

1. Recent legislation.
2. Prepaid expenses.
3. Development expenses.
4. "Farming" and "Farmer."
5. Depreciation and investment credit.
6. Tax treatment of gains.

PREPAID EXPENSES

The prepayment of feed costs by a taxpayer utilizing the cash method of tax accounting is an excellent method of lowering income for the particular tax year. It is a common practice in the cattle business (breeding herds and cattle fattening programs) to prepay the feed and maintenance costs in the fall of the year for all or a portion of the next year. The prepaid expenses are advantageous for the two primary reasons: (1) an economic inducement to a rancher to run tenant cattle as the rancher receives his feed and expense money on the front end, and (2) a distinct tax advantage to the cattle owner for, by making the year-end payment, he can deduct the costs of the feed and a portion of the miscellaneous expenses as an operating expense for the particular tax year in which the payment is made.

Additionally, a taxpayer, defined as a "farmer" by the Internal Revenue Code, is entitled to deduct the farm expense as an operating business expense, and any resulting loss can be used to offset non-farm income. Then, in a particular year, the farm loss may be used to tax shelter the non-farm income.

The historical and necessary ingredient in the operation of a tenant cattle business is the prepayment of feed costs. The Internal Revenue Service, on the other hand, has historically foot dragged in approving year-end feed deductions by cash-basis taxpayers. The IRS attacks on the disallowance normally fall in the following categories:

1. The payments or expenditures are advance payments and, in actuality, deposits against future purchases.

2. The expenditures are not ordinary or necessary business expense in the year of payment.

3. The expenditure materially distorts income.

4. The expenditures create an asset having a useful life beyond the year of payment which would require allocation over the period to which it is related—which means an allocation of the deductions in relation to the tax years in which the feed is fed to the cattle.

Case decisions make up the law on prepaid expense deductions. The statutes, regulations and rulings are silent on guidelines establishing when a deduction is allowable. The significant cases concerning deduction of advanced purchases of feed are listed and discussed in the accompanying bibliography. The *Lillie* case summarizes the earlier case decisions involving advance purchases of feed. The *Ernest* and *Cravens* cases laid down the guidelines for approving year-end deduction. The *Shippey* case distinguished *Ernest* and *Cravens* on the facts and disallowed the deduction.

Lilley also distinguished the cases allowing the prepayment on the facts and by implication reaffirming the *Ernest* and *Cravens* guidelines by distinguishing them. More recently the *Estate of Cohen* case involving Oppenheimer feeder contracts has approved the prepaid deductions of feed where the requisite guidelines are met. A summary of the case law involving prepaid feed deductions would indicate that the following criteria must be met before the deduction is allowable:

1. The purchase of feed must be final without the possibility of refund.

2. The feed must be physically delivered to or set aside for the purchaser.

3. A price differential for quantity purchases must be present.

4. Either a shortage of feed must exist or a necessity to insure future supply.

5. Feed and labor costs must be segregated.

The historical and economic reason for requiring advance purchases of feed differs between a range operation and a commercial feeding operation. However, many of the purposes overlap. Primarily, the basis for allowance of an advance purchase of feed at the year end is:

1. To insure the availability of feed for the forthcoming year.

2. To obtain a price break on large purchases.

3. To induce a rancher or feeder to enter into an overall favorable deal by providing cash in advance which can be used in his business.

The government has taken the position that only feed purchases can be prepaid. Therefore, it is important that maintenance and labor costs are segregated and not lumped in with advance purchases of feed. If the costs are not separated an argument can be advanced that a portion of or all of the prepayment must be allocated to the tax year reflecting consumption and services rendered.

A payment for pasturage or forage which includes standing crops, legumes or grass should be classified as feed. This classification is opposed to an advance rental payment which would be required to be proratably distributed between the tax years. Pasturage is considered feed on the basis that it is available and in the field for consumption, somewhat analogous to corn stalks purchased after corn picking for purposes of gleaning by livestock.

RECENT LEGISLATION

The Tax Reform Act of 1969 covers a broad spectrum of the tax law. Certain provisions of the act aim at farming and ranching. The strictly non-agriculture provisions are interlocking and, thus, must be considered to prevent the overall effect on the taxpayer's tax position. This section will specifically discuss the provisions relating to agriculture and, to a certain extent, will tie in the non-agricultural pro-

AVERAGE PRICE RECEIVED BY FARMERS FOR ALL HAY (BALED) ON THE 15th OF MONTH
IN DOLLARS PER TON

Crop Year	July	Aug.	Sept.	Oct.	Nov.	Dec.	Jan.	Feb.	Mar.	April	May	June	Average[1]
1952	22.00	24.10	25.00	25.60	26.00	26.40	26.40	25.60	24.40	23.60	22.70	20.80	26.90
1953	20.20	20.60	20.90	21.20	22.00	23.00	23.80	23.70	23.10	22.80	21.80	20.40	21.90
1954	19.90	21.30	22.00	22.30	22.90	23.30	23.50	23.30	23.00	22.40	22.20	21.10	21.90
1955	20.10	20.10	20.40	20.60	20.90	21.40	21.50	21.30	21.00	21.10	21.00	19.90	22.50
1956	19.70	20.10	20.70	21.50	21.90	22.70	22.90	22.50	21.60	21.10	20.10	18.60	22.20
1957	17.60	18.00	18.20	18.50	18.90	19.20	19.00	18.70	18.50	18.20	17.70	17.10	19.30
1958	17.10	17.20	17.60	18.00	18.20	18.80	19.30	19.30	18.80	18.80	18.40	17.90	18.80
1959	18.40	19.40	19.90	20.50	21.00	21.90	22.20	22.50	22.90	22.50	21.60	20.20	22.20
1960	19.20	19.40	19.60	20.20	20.60	21.00	21.30	21.20	20.60	20.00	19.80	19.10	21.70
1961	19.30	19.50	19.70	20.20	20.50	20.70	21.60	21.40	21.80	21.40	21.40	19.70	20.60
1962	19.10	19.60	20.20	20.30	21.00	21.60	22.30	23.20	23.20	22.50	21.80	20.90	21.60
1963	21.30	21.90	22.60	23.00	23.90	24.70	25.00	24.70	24.00	23.50	22.30	20.90	24.60
1964	20.80	21.70	22.60	22.90	23.50	24.40	25.40	25.70	25.70				
1965													

[1] Weighted average by sales. *Source: Department of Agriculture*

Note that hay moves up an average of 2% per month in most years from the time it is put up through January. The chart does not reflect the additional $4/ton you might have to pay in transportation if you miscalculate and run out during the winter and have to haul hay through the snow from a neighbor's barn. You are really gambling in snow country if you have not bought your feed by December.

visions to complete the total tax picture. The 1971 Revenue Act changes are brought in where applicable.

FARM LOSSES

Under the Tax Reform Act, a Farm Loss Section, Section 1251, was added to limit losses for cash basis taxpayers (IRC). Unless the taxpayer has $50,000 of non-farm adjusted gross income, there is no difficulty and no restriction on his farm losses (except for the Hobby Loss Provision which will be discussed later). Even if the taxpayer has a $50,000 non-farm adjusted gross income, he can still deduct $25,000 per year loss. He can also deduct amounts in excess of $25,000 per year; however, the farm loss in excess of $25,000 is entered in an "excess deduction account" (EDA). The account balance in subsequent years is reduced to the extent of farm net income and added to by any losses in excess of $25,000.

On eventual disposition of certain "farm recapture property," gains which would otherwise be entitled to capital-gain treatment are taxed as ordinary income. The gains to be treated as ordinary income include those from the sale or other disposition of farm property (but not buildings) used in the business of farming, including livestock and harvested crops.

The law was effective commencing with 1970. Example: In 1971 you have non-farm income of $100,000 and incur a net farm loss of $45,000. Your farm loss deduction of 1971 is still $45,000. Twenty thousand dollars of the loss is added to the excess deductions account (EDA). In 1972 the farm operations show a $5,000 profit; in addition, you realize $10,000 capital gain on the sale of livestock held for breeding purposes. Result: The $5,000 operating income reduces the EDA by $5,000 to $15,000. On the $10,000 capital gain on the sale of the livestock, only $5,000 (which would normally be subject to tax, due to the capital gains deduction) is treated as ordinary income and further reduces the account to $5,000, which is a dollar for dollar offset to the extent of the entire $10,000.

Farm losses will be recaptured upon the disposition of the following types of property:

1. Depreciable personal property held for more than six months.
2. Cattle or horses held for two years or more and other livestock held for one year or more for draft, breeding, dairy or sporting purposes.
3. Land held for more than six months.

4. Unharvested crops growing on land which has been held for more than six months.

There would be no farm loss recapture on disposition of improvements to real property although such property would be subject to recapture under the provisions of Sec. 1250.

The farm loss recapture is not applicable to transfers at death or by gift (unless the potential gain on the farm property is more than 80% of the unrealized gain on the farm property held by the donor at the beginning of the year).

An individual will be subject to the farm recapture rules only if he is a cash basis taxpayer and in any taxable year his non-farm adjusted gross income exceeds $50,000 and his farm net loss is over $25,000 (the amounts are $25,000 and $12,000 for a married person filing separately, whose spouse also has farm income or deductions).

A corporation or a trust is not entitled to the benefit of the dollar exemptions. It must establish an EDA (or add to it for any farm loss without regard to the amount of non-farm income.)

The 1970 Revenue Act clarified the law in regard to a Subchapter S corporation. The stockholder with the greatest non-farm income is added to the corporation's non-farm income. If the total exceeds $50,000, all losses in excess of $25,000 must be maintained in an EDA. The exemption is not available if any shareholder is a shareholder in another Subchapter S corporation.

LAND EXPENDITURES

Code Sec. 1252 provides for recapture of certain land improvement and clearing expenditures. Sec. 1252 is aimed at those expenditures taken within the limitation provisions of soil and water conservation expenditures under Sec. 179 and land clearing under Sec. 182. Sec. 179 provides for a limitation of 25% of gross income from farming in any particular year where Sec. 182 is limited to 25% of net income from farming.

Under Code Sec. 1252, if farm land is held for less than 10 years and is disposed of in 1970 or later, a percentage of the total post-1969 deductions for soil and water conservation expenditures and land clearance expenditures will be recaptured as ordinary income. Result is that the gain on the sale will be taxed as ordinary income to the extent of the recapture—the recapture cannot exceed the gain.

If the land is held for five years or less, the recapture percentage is 100%. The recapture percentage is reduced by 20% for each year the land is held in excess of five years. Consequently, there is no recapture after the tenth year. The recapture is applicable to expenditures made after January 1, 1970; however, the holding period can relate to before the enactment of the law. EXAMPLE: A ranch is acquired on January 15, 1963. On October 1 of 1970, the ranch is sold for a $40,000 gain. Fifteen thousand dollars is expended for soil and water conservation expenditures in 1970. The recapture percentage would be 40% since the land was sold within the eight years after purchase. Therefore, $6,000 of the $40,000 gain is treated as ordinary income under Sec. 1252 (40% of $15,000).

If the taxpayer had pre-1969 soil and water conservation expense carry-over (above the 25% gross income from farming) such carry-over expenses would not be subject to recapture.

CITRUS GROVE EXPENSES

Expenses for developing citrus groves are no longer an elective deductible item but must be capitalized under new Code Sec. 278. The capitalization rule applies to all trees planted after date of the enactment. An exception is in the case of replanting required because of casualty losses, such as from freezing, disease, drought, pests, etc.

CASUALTY LOSSES

Code Sec. 1231 (a) was amended to provide for the netting of casualty losses with other Sec. 1231 gains and losses. Any uninsured casualty loss must first be used to offset other Sec. 1231 gains. If the net result is a loss after netting all Sec. 1231 gains and losses, the net losses are deductible from ordinary income.

For example, if a purchase cow should die, any deduction up to the extent of the cow's adjusted tax basis would depend upon other Sec. 1231 gains and losses. If there are Sec. 1231 gains, then the aggregate death losses would first offset these gains. The net gain would be a Sec. 1231 gain and the net loss would be an ordinary loss.

LIVESTOCK RECAPTURE

IRC Sec. 1245 as amended calls for recapture of post-1969 depreciation as ordinary income on the sale of livestock. This is a departure from the old law in that livestock was specifically exempted.

The effect is that, on purchased breeding and dairy cattle, all or a portion of the gain on culls from the herd (sales price in excess of adjusted tax basis) is treated as ordinary income rather than under Sec. 1231 as under the old law.

For example, a cow is purchased for $250, depreciated to $100, and later sold from the herd for $150; the $50 gain (difference between the $100 adjusted tax basis and $150 sale price) would be ordinary income to the extent of the depreciation taken since 1969. Assume the cow had been depreciated $25 in 1970–$25 would be treated as ordinary income and $25 as Sec. 1231 income.

LIVESTOCK HOLDING PERIOD

The holding period (time owned) for eligibility of cattle and horses for long-term capital gain was extended from 12 months to 2 years (Sec. 1231 (b) (3)). The extended period is effective for cattle and horses acquired after 1969. Other livestock such as swine and sheep still are governed by the 12-month rule.

The primary effect of the extension of the holding period would be tax treatment of the heifers which are held for the breeding herd and culled before actually being placed in the herd. The entire sale proceeds on raised heifers under 24 months of age would now be treated as ordinary rather than as capital gains. See Treas. Regs. Sec. 1. 1231-2.

LIVESTOCK EXCHANGES

Under amended Code Sec. 1031, livestock of different sexes are not property of a "like kind" which would qualify for a tax-free exchange. This hits at the practice of exchanging male calves for female calves on a tax-free exchange basis.

The exchange of heifers for bulls at an early age could still be accomplished with minimal tax assessment. For example, if bulls were exchanged for heifers at birth and $40 a head assigned as a value on the animals, then the taxpayer would have $40 of ordinary income. However, this, from a tax standpoint, would be more advantageous than waiting until the calves were weaned, which could have a value of $120–taxable as ordinary income.

HOBBY LOSSES

The old hobby loss provision, IRC Sec. 270, was repealed and a new code, Sec. 183, added. The Code Sec. 270 covered any type of business loss and eliminated losses in excess of $50,000 in cases where the losses exceeded $50,000 in at least five consecutive years.

Sec. 183 denies a deduction of losses for an activity "not engaged in for profit." However, if the taxpayer can show a profit (income exceeds deductions) in two out of five years of operation, it is presumed that he is engaged in a profit-making activity. For the breeding and raising of horses, the profit test is expanded to two out of seven years. There was no statutory law governing hobby loss prior to the enactment of Sec. 183. The courts looked at the individual factual situation and made a determination regarding profit or profit motive based upon the particular operation. Sec. 183 statutorily sets a period of profit years which presumes the taxpayer is engaged in the activity for profit.

The hobby loss provision is completely separate from the EDA, and, thus, a taxpayer could have losses below $25,000 for a period of years and still run afoul of the hobby loss provision.

The commencement of the presumptive period is clarified by the Revenue Act of 1971. A new section 183(e) provides that for taxable years commencing after December 31, 1969, a taxpayer may elect to delay a determination as to whether the presumption applies until the close of the fourth (sixth in the case of horses) taxable year after the taxable year in which he first engages in the activity. Taxable years beginning before January 1, 1970, do not count to commence the five- or seven-year periods—which means the presumption would not be applied until the end of 1974.

In order to make this election, the taxpayer must execute a waiver of the statute of limitations (ordinary statute of limitations is three years), so if it is later determined that the activity was a hobby, an adjustment can be made. A taxpayer should still be able to show that he was engaged in an activity for profit even though he did not show a profit for two out of five or seven years. The statute is an affirmative presumption he is engaged in the activity for profit if there is a profit for two out of five or seven years. Thus, there should not be a negative presumption with the taxpayer having the burden of showing he was engaged in the activity for profit if the two out of five year test were not met as if Sec. 183 did not exist.

Sec. 183 also provides for the establishment of advisory groups drawn from the cattle and horse industries to establish and assist IRS in establishing standards for application of the rules.

REAL PROPERTY

The depreciation methods applicable to real estate have been severely curtailed. Fast depreciation on buildings or other real estate bought or constructed after July 24, 1969, is no longer available. On used real estate acquired after July 24, 1969, only straight-line depreciation may be utilized. On new property acquired after that date, 150% declining balance method may be utilized; however, on eventual disposition, the accelerated depreciation in excess of the allowable straight-line depreciation is subject to being recaptured as ordinary income to the extent of the gain on a sale.

There are special rules which are applicable to certain urban and rehabilitated housing which provide for more liberal depreciation methods. However, for farm and ranch property, the straight line and 150% depreciation would be applicable. Fences, corrals and other depreciable farm property would fall in the same category as buildings and, thus, be limited to straight line or 150% depending upon whether they are new or used.

INTEREST LIMITATIONS

Code Sec. 163 (d) was added to limit investment interest. For 1970 and 1971, investment interest is a tax preference item and, therefore, would be subject within the tax preference exemption to the 10% minimum tax. The first item of determination on the limitation is whether or not the interest is an investment interest. The limitation is for non-corporate taxpayers. As long as a rental operation is not a net lease, then interest paid on rental property would not be investment interest, and, thus, there would be no limitation on the interest deduction, nor would it be considered as a tax preference item.

A net lease is defined as (1) a business expense deduction allowed in respect to the property by Code Sec. 162 total less the 15% of rental income, or (2) the lessor's being either guaranteed a specified rate or guaranteed against loss. The limitation commences in 1972. However, the overall effect of the limitation will be to hit only the giant interest deductions. Real estate people should be hit very little. The Revenue Act of 1971 refined the depreciation of net lease.

Here's how the limitation works: Interest paid for borrowed funds that create investment income –interest, dividends, rents, royalties and new short-term capital gains–will be disallowed only to the extent it exceeds: (1) $25,000 ($12,500 on a separate return of married persons), plus (2) your net investment income, that is, your investment income (interest, dividends, rents, etc.), less your investment expenses (disease, bad debts, depreciation, etc.), plus (3) your net long-term capital gains, plus (4) 50% of any investment in excess of the sum of the first three items.

Additionally, there is an indefinite carry-over, meaning that what you can't deduct in the year you pay can be paid over indefinitely and offset against your net investment income, plus $25,000 in later years.

In appreciated real estate deals, the result is that eventually all interest will be deductible. EXAMPLE: In January, 1972, you buy a piece of land for $500,000. The entire $500,000 purchase price is financed with a 10% interest and, thus, a $50,000 interest payment. Assuming you have no investment income and no long-term capital gains, the result is that in 1972 you could deduct $37,500 ($25,000 plus one-half of the excess above $25,000). The other $12,500 is not deductible.

Assume further that in the next year you sell the property for $750,000 and have a $50,000 interest payment in 1973. You could be permitted to deduct the 1973 $50,000, plus the $12,500 carry-over from 1972.

The reason is that in 1973 you have $250,000 of net long-term capital gains; added to this is the automatic $25,000 exclusion, which gives a total of $275,000, which more than offsets the $50,000 plus the $12,500 carry-over.

CHARITABLE CONTRIBUTIONS

The Tax Reform Act made various changes involving the deductibility of contributions of property to charitable organizations. The farmer and rancher up until the change in the tax law could contribute raised products (animals and crops) to a charity and deduct the full price (market value) of the items contributed. For a cash basis taxpayer, this was particularly advantageous in that he had a "zero" tax basis, having deducted the cost of raising the product; he could deduct the full market value and not have the market value treated as income.

The Tax Reform Act hits at this in two areas, at least as it affects farmers and ranchers: (1) gifts of ordinary income property which would have the deduction limited to tax basis (not value), and (2) appreciated capital gain property. Examples of the appreciated capital gain property would be breeding cows which have been depreciated to a tax basis below the market value, and in such cases the extent of the deduction would be limited to the tax basis of the cows.

CAPITAL GAINS

The alternative 25% capital gains tax is to be gradually phased out. For 1970, the rate is 29½%; for 1971, the rate will be 32½%. For 1972 and thereafter, the combined effect of the 50% capital gains deduction and the maximum 70% rate on the ordinary income of individuals creates a maximum 35% rate on capital gains.

The alternative 25% capital gains rate is not completely eliminated. It continues to apply to aggregate long-term capital gains which do not exceed $50,000.

DEVELOPMENT EXPENSES

Capital expenditures are not deductible as a business expense. Such costs must be recovered through an allowance for depreciation and obsolescence. Not all capital expenditures are depreciable. Expenditures for ditching, terracing, land clearing, damming, etc., have no determinable useful life and, therefore, are not subject to depreciation. Congress recognized the position of the farmer of not being entitled to a business deduction or a depreciation deduction and in 1954 added Section 175 to the Code.

Soil and Water Conservation Expenses

IRC Sec. 175 provides for soil and water conservation expense deduction up to 25% of the gross income from farming in any one year. Soil and water conservation expenses are defined broadly. See Treas. Regs. Sec. 1.175-2 for kinds of expenditures. The language of the Statute is specific and limiting. In the wording of the Code the key words are "engaged in the business of farming," "soil and water conservation," and "land used in farming."

The business of farming aspect is defined in the same manner

Bibliography

AUTHORITY	FACTS OR QUOTE	HOLDING OR APPLICATION
1. IRC § 162 (a)	"162 (a). In General. There shall be allowed as a deduction all the ordinary and necessary expenses paid or incurred during the taxable year in carrying on any trade or business . . ."	Permits a deduction of all ordinary and necessary expenses.
2. Treas. Reg. § 1.162-1 (a)	"1, 162-1. Business expenses—In General. Business expenses deductible from gross income include the ordinary and necessary expenditures directly connected with or pertaining to the taxpayer's trade or business. . ."	Elaboration of ordinary and necessary business expenses.
3. Treas. Reg. 1.461-1 (a) (1)	"1. 461-1. Taxpayer using cash receipts and disbursements method. Under the cash receipts and disbursements method of accounting amounts representing allowable deductions shall, as a general rule, be taken into account for the taxable year in which paid."	Establishes general rule that a cash-basis taxpayer can take deduction in taxable year in which paid.
4. *Lillie*, 45 T.C. 54 (1965), Aff'd. 320 F.2d 562 (CA-9, 1966)	The Lillies fed cattle through cattle feeding companies which charged a lump sum and included feed and service. Customarily large payments were made at the year's end for feed and service to be rendered over the following year. The payments were not broken down between feed and yardage. A refund would be paid if the advance payment exceeded the ultimate cost.	The Tax Court denied a deduction for year-end purchase of feed for the following reasons: 1. Distinguished and cited *Cravens*, *Ernst* and *Shippy* cases. 2. No shortage of feed. 3. No preferential treatment resulting from the purchases. 4. No predetermined price for feed. 5. Cost of feed included charges for valuable and significant services rendered by the cattle feeding companies. 6. Payment considered a deposit. 7. Refund was made on value of unconsumed feed. 8. Court of Appeals 9th Circuit affirmed Tax Court decision.

AUTHORITY	FACTS OR QUOTE	HOLDING OR APPLICATION
5. *Estate of Frank Cohen,* TC Memo, 1970-272	Cohen's authorized a management agent, Atlas Management Corporation, to secure a cattle feeder. Atlas Management Corporation purchased feed in advance from the cattle feeder. In one instance the prepayment was denied, and in the other it was approved. The disapproval was on the basis of the same objections raised by the *Lillie* case. On the approval side the Court distinguished from the *Lillie* case and discussed such items as clear purchase of feed, etc.	The Court denied a deduction in one contract and approved it in another. The deduction was allowed on the basis that the quality and quantity of feed was specified in the contract and the amount charged did not include performance of any service. There was no provision for a refund, and the feed was clearly purchased. The Court seemed to rely heavily on the fact that there was a separate provision in the contract providing for the payment of handling and services.
6. *Gaddis* vs. *U.S.,* U.S. Dist. Ct., Miss., June 18, 1971	Chicken farmer made large year-end purchase of feed with delivery in the next tax year.	Court allowed the purchase, as: 1. Purchase price was actually paid under contractual obligation. 2. No refund. 3. No service to be rendered for amount paid.

as for other purposes in the Code such as for methods of accounting. This area does not normally give any real problems and applies to a landlord or a tenant. However, a landlord who receives a "fixed rental" is not in the business of farming unless he participates to a material extent in the operation or management of the farm. The participation is tied to the "material participation" concept as provided in social security taxes on self-employment income.

The land used in farming means land that is currently being used in farming and under certain conditions would permit land that had been used in the past. It would appear that a farm can be looked at as a unit in determining whether land is currently being used in farming. There are no reliable guidelines to determine how much of the farm can be out of production or whether the land can be physically separated and still have the unit considered together for "land used in farming."

Gross income from farming would be more likely to apply to widely separated land. It would appear that a taxpayer could have land even in separate states and still have the income considered as a unit against which you could apply the 25% limitation. The 25% limitation can be carried over to future years.

Land Clearing Expenses

The 1962 Code added Section 182 providing for land clearing expense deductions. The section was added to fill the gap left by soil and water conservation expense to permit deductions on new land expenses. Section 182 has severe deduction limitations of $5,000 or 25% of taxable income derived from farming in any one year. Taxable income from farming is defined as gross income reduced by the proper deductions except the land clearing expenses. However, you can add to this taxable amount gains on livestock. Thus, in effect, taxable income is net farm income plus the taxable amount of capital gains on livestock. There is no carry-over as with soil and water conservation expenses.

The taxpayer must be in the *business of farming* and the land must be for suitable use in farming. The deduction is allowable for clearing of land which includes removal of rocks, stones, trees, stumps, brush, movement of land, building of water courses, etc.

Fertilizer and lime expenses are currently deductible as provided in IRC Sec. 180 even though the residue may result in a carry-over to future years.

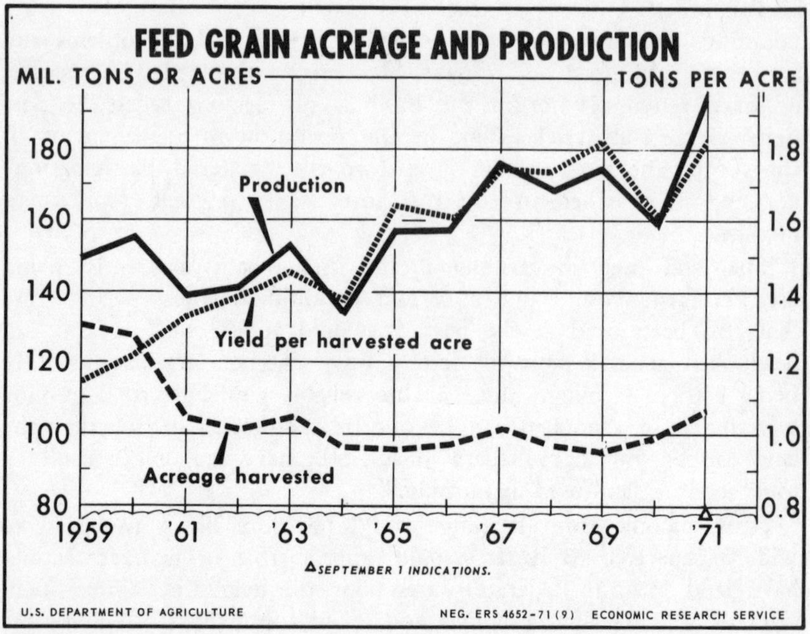

One really first-rate, rip-snorting drought or crop failure would completely wipe out the "crop surplus problem." In any case, the trend has been dramatically reversed. (Courtesy U.S. Department of Agriculture)

Recapture of Land Expenditures

The Tax Reform Act of 1969 added IRC Sec. 1252 providing that, if farm land is held less than 10 years and disposed of after 1969, a percentage of the land expenditures are recaptured as ordinary income —depending on how long the property was held. See Sec. 1252 on land expenditures for more complete discussion.

Bibliography

AUTHORITY	FACTS OR QUOTE	HOLDING OR APPLICATION
1. IRC Sec. 175 (a)	In General. A taxpayer engaged in the business of farming may treat expenditures which are paid or incurred by him during the taxable year for the purpose of soil or water conservation in respect of land used in farming, or for the prevention of erosion of land used in farming, as expenses which are not chargeable to capital account. The expenditures so treated shall be allowed as a deduction.	
2. Treas. Regs. Sec. 1.175-1	Soil and water conservation expenditures—In General. Under section 175, a farmer may deduct his soil or water conservation expenditures which do not give rise to a deduction for depreciation and which are not otherwise deductible. The amount of the deduction is limited annually to 25 percent of the taxpayer's gross income from farming. Any excess may be carried over and deducted in succeeding taxable years. As a general rule, once a farmer has adopted this method of treating soil and water conservation expenditures, he must deduct all such expenditures (subject to the 25-percent limitation) for the current and subsequent taxable years. If a farmer does not adopt this method, such expenditures increase the basis of the property to which they relate.	
3. Treas. Regs. Sec. 1.175-2	Definition of soil and water conservation expenditures—(a) Expenditures treated as a deduction. (1) The method described in section 175 applies to expenditures paid or incurred for the purpose of soil or water conservation in	

AUTHORITY	FACTS OR QUOTE	HOLDING OR APPLICATION
	respect of land used in farming, or for the prevention of erosion of land used in farming, but only if such expenditures are made in the furtherance of the business of farming. More specifically, a farmer may deduct expenditures made for these purposes which are for (i) the treatment or moving of earth; (ii) the construction, control, and protection of diversion channels, drainage ditches, irrigation ditches, earthen dams, watercourses, outlets, and ponds; (iii) the eradication of brush; and (iv) the planting of windbreaks. Expenditures for the treatment or moving of earth include but are not limited to expenditures for leveling, conditioning, grading, terracing, contour furrowing, and restoration of soil fertility. (2) The following are examples of soil and water conservation: (i) constructing terraces, or the like, to detain or control the flow of water, to check soil erosion or sloping land, to intercept run-off, and to divert excess water to protected outlets; (ii) constructing water detention or sediment retention dams to prevent or fill gullies, to retard or reduce run-off of water, or to collect stock water; and (iii) constructing earthen floodways, levees, or dikes, to prevent flood damage to farmland.	
4. Treas. Regs. Sec. 1.175-3	Definition of "the business of farming." The method described in section 175 is available only to a taxpayer engaged in "the business of farming." A taxpayer is engaged in the business of farming if he cultivates, operates, or man-	

AUTHORITY	FACTS OR QUOTE	HOLDING OR APPLICATION
	ages a farm for gain or profit, either as owner or tenant. For the purpose of section 175, a taxpayer who receives a rental (either in cash or in kind) which is based upon farm production is engaged in the business of farming. However, a taxpayer who receives a fixed rental (without reference to production) is engaged in the business of farming only if he participates to a material extent in the operation or management of the farm. A taxpayer engaged in forestry or the growing of timber is not thereby engaged in the business of farming. A person cultivating or operating a farm for recreation or pleasure rather than a profit is not engaged in the business of farming. For the purpose of this section, the term "farm" is used in its ordinary, accepted sense and includes stock, dairy, poultry, fish, fruit, and truck farms, and also plantations, ranches, ranges, and orchards . . . A taxpayer is engaged in "the business of farming" if he is a member of a partnership engaged in the business of farming.	
5. Treas. Regs. Sec. 1.175-4	*Regulations*—Definition of "land used in farming." (a) For the purpose of section 175, the term "land used in farming" means land which is used in the business of farming and which meets both of the following requirements: (1) The land must be used for the production of crops, fruits, or other agricultural products, including fish, or for the sustenance of livestock. The term "livestock" includes cattle,	

AUTHORITY	FACTS OR QUOTE	HOLDING OR APPLICATION
	hogs, horses, mules, donkeys, sheep, goats, captive fur-bearing animals, chickens, turkeys, pigeons, and other poultry.	
	Land used for the sustenance of livestock includes land used for grazing such livestock.	
	(2) The land must be or have been so used either by the taxpayer or his tenant at some time before, or at the same time as, the taxpayer makes the expenditures for soil or water conservation or for the prevention of the erosion of land. The taxpayer will be considered to have used the land in farming before making such expenditures if he or his tenant has employed the land in a farming use in the past. If the expenditures are made by the taxpayer in respect of land newly acquired from one who immediately prior to the acquisition was using it in farming, the taxpayer will be considered to be using the land in farming at the time that such expenditures are made, if the use which is made by the taxpayer of the land from the time of acquisition by him is substantially a continuation of the use which was made of the land immediately prior to its acquisition. On the other hand, if the land is being initially prepared by the taxpayer in order to make it suitable for a particular farming use other than the one to which the land was devoted prior to its acquisition by the taxpayer, such land is not considered to be "land used in farming" at the time of its preparation.	

AUTHORITY	FACTS OR QUOTE	HOLDING OR APPLICATION
6. IRC Sec. 182	(a) In General. A taxpayer engaged in the business of farming may elect to treat expenditures which are paid or incurred by him during the taxable year in the clearing of land for the purpose of making such land suitable for use in farming as expenses which are not chargeable to capital account. The expenditures so treated shall be allowed as a deduction. (b) Limitation. The amount deductible under subsection (a) for any taxable year shall not exceed whichever of the following amounts is the lesser: (1) $5,000 or (2) 25 percent of the taxable income derived from farming during the taxable year. For purposes of paragraph (2), the term "taxable income derived from farming" means the gross income derived from farming reduced by the deductions allowed by this chapter (other than by this section) which are attributable to the business of farming. (c) Definitions. For the purposes of subsection (a)— (1) The term "clearing of land" includes (but is not limited to) the eradication of trees, stumps, and brush, the treatment or moving of earth, and the diversion of streams and watercourses. (2) The term "land suitable for use in farming" means land which as a result of the activities described in paragraph	

AUTHORITY	FACTS OR QUOTE	HOLDING OR APPLICATION
	(1) is suitable for use by the taxpayer or his tenant for the production of crops, fruits, or other agricultural products or for the sustenance of livestock.	
7. Treas. Regs. Sec. 1.182-3 (a)	(a) "Clearing of land." (1) For purposes of section 182, the term "clearing of land" includes (but is not limited to)— (i) The removal of rocks, stones, trees, stumps, brush or other natural impediments to the use of the land in farming through blasting, cutting, burning, bulldozing, plowing, or in any other way; (ii) The treatment or moving of earth, including the construction, repair or removal of nondepreciable earthen structures, such as dikes or levies, if the purpose of such treatment or moving of earth is to protect, level, contour, terrace, or condition the land so as to make it available for use as farming land; and (iii) The diversion of streams and watercourses, including the construction of nondepreciable drainage facilities, provided that the purpose is to remove or divert water from the land so as to make it available for use in farming. (2) The following are examples of land clearing activities: (i) The cutting of trees, the blasting of the resulting stumps, and the burning of the residual undergrowth.	

AUTHORITY	FACTS OR QUOTE	HOLDING OR APPLICATION
	(ii) The leveling of land so as to permit irrigation or planting. (iii) The removal of salt or other minerals which might inhibit cultivation of the soil. (iv) The draining and filling in of a swamp or marsh. (v) The diversion of a stream from one watercourse to another.	
8. Rev. Rul. 59-42, 1959-1 C.B. 47	Expenditures for brush control on productive land are not soil and conservation expenses but are deductible as an ordinary business expense without limitation.	
9. *Coffin*, 41 T.C. 83 (1963)	Question here was what made up the gross income from farming. Taxpayer had received government payments.	Court held that government payments were part of gross income from farming.
10. *Behring*, 32 T.C. 1256 (1959)	A portion of the farm was under cultivation and the remaining of the farm was not under cultivation at the time it was being prepared for irrigation.	The court looked at the farm as a unit for purposes in determining "used in farming" for purposes of soil and water conservation and expenses.
11. IRC Sec. 1252	Gain on sale or disposition of land is treated as ordinary income up to the amount of deductions previously taken as soil or water conservation or land clearing expenditures made after 1969, where the land was held five years or less. Gain is partially ordinary income to the extent of previous deductions where held less than 10 years and more than 5 years. The recapture diminished at the rate of 20% per year between 5 and 10 years.	

"FARMING" AND "FARMER"

"Farming" and "Farmer" take on a specific meaning within the Internal Revenue Code and Regulations. The definition of "farming" is used by the Code and Regulations in the generic sense relating to all activities of ranching and cultivating of the soil. A "farmer" can be a sole proprietorship, partnership, corporation, and a land owner or tenant.

Farming is defined in Treas. Regs. Sec. 1. 61-4(d) and 1.175-3. Note the definition set out in the Bibliography.

A business considered as being in the business of "farming" can utilize the cash receipts and disbursements method of accounting. Otherwise, since inventories are involved, an inventory or accrual method of accounting needs to be used.

This discussion is not concerned with the profit motive and economic motive problem relating to hobby farms.

IRS agents have attacked the absentee owners "farmer" status. Most challenges are raised where the taxpayer earns substantial off-farm or ranch income and in showing farm or ranch losses for a particular year or over a period of years. Though the concept is similar to the "hobby farm" challenge a distinction exists in that the disallowance or challenge relates to capitalization of expenses. In hobby farm situation the expenses are considered personal and thus not deductible nor can they be capitalized.

By denying the "farmer" status IRS would propose to carry raising or feeding expenses over to the year of sale with the effect of offsetting profit in the year of sale. (See Rev. Rul. 64-148 for the government's position.)

IRS has not been successful in most instances in contending an operation is not "farming" primarily due to the broad categorical definition of farming in the Code.

BIBLIOGRAPHY

AUTHORITY	FACTS OR QUOTE	HOLDING OR APPLICATION
1. Tres. Regs. § 1.61-4(d)	"Definition of 'farm' as used in this section—the term 'farm' embraces the farm in an ordinarily accepted sense, and includes stock, dairy, poultry, fruit, and truck farms; also plantations, ranches, and all land used for farming operations. All individuals, partnerships, or corporations that cultivate, operate, or manage farms for gain or profit, either as owners or tenants, are designated as farmers . . ."	
2. Treas. Regs. § 1.175-3	"Definition of 'the business of farming'—A taxpayer is engaged in the business of farming if he cultivates, operates, or manages a farm for gain or profit, either as owner or tenant . . . The term 'farm' is used in the ordinary, accepted sense and includes stock, dairy, poultry, fish, fruit, and truck farms, and also plantations, ranches, ranges, and orchards."	
3. Treas. Regs. § 1.147 1-6	Inventories of livestock raisers and other farmers—(a) A farmer may make his return upon an inventory method instead of the cash receipts and disbursements method. It is optional with the taxpayer which of these methods of accounting is used but, having elected one method, the option so exercised will be binding upon the taxpayer for one year for which the option is exercised and for subsequent years unless another method is authorized by the Commissioner as provided in paragraph (e) of § 1.446-1.	

AUTHORITY	FACTS OR QUOTE	HOLDING OR APPLICATION
4. Rev. Rul. 64-148, IRB 1964-20	The ruling relates to a grower, processer, packager and marketer of fruit. The ruling states the operation is a merchandising process and thus the costs must be capitalized by including in costs of goods sold.	Not analogous to ranching in that the ruling applied to an integrated operation from initial growing to actual marketing. A rancher, on the other hand, is involved only with one phase of production—the growing and preparing for market. The ruling should not be applied nor should an attempt be made to relate to ranching.
5. *Lillie*, 45 T.C. 54 (1965), Aff'd. 320 F.2d 562 (CA-9, 1966)	Dr. Lillie was an absentee cattle feeder. The court said in relation to "farmer" status, "The parties are in agreement that petitioners are engaged in the business of raising cattle for profit and are therefore entitled to deduct the cost of feed as an ordinary and necessary business expense under the provisions of Section 162(a) . . ."	The court was concerned with the question of prepaid expenses. However, it is significant that the parties agreed Dr. Lillie was in the "business of farming" wherein the feeding of cattle was contracted through a commercial "custom" feedlot with no personal effort on the part of Dr. Lillie.

DEPRECIATION AND INVESTMENT CREDIT

Regular Depreciation

Breeding livestock is a depreciable asset when used in the farming or ranching business. As such it is eligible for application of the various depreciation methods which are: (1) straight line, (2) sum-of-the-years-digits, (3) 200% declining balance, and (4) 150% declining balance method. The sum-of-the-years-digits and 200% declining balance methods can be applied only to property where the original use commences with the taxpayer.

"Original use" or "new in use" are technical words somewhat difficult to define as they relate to breeding cattle. For example, is a cow used when bred or does she become used only after dropping a calf? Is a bull used after he is tested to determine progeny or is he still new? A case can be built for the position that a cow is used *only* after she has calved, and that a bull is still new after testing and becomes used after placement as a herd bull.

The "fast" methods of depreciation require the animals to have a projected useful life of three (3) years or more.

In most instances the accelerated methods of depreciation are advantageous as they provide a rapid recoupment of capital committed. The 200% declining balance (if eligible) is generally the better method as salvage value need not be deducted before commencing depreciation. The limiting factor is that depreciation must cease when salvage is reached.

The 150% or 1½ the straight line rate can be applied to used livestock. The 150% gives you a faster recovery of capital than the straight line.

Some controversy centers around the requirement that depreciation commences *when placed in service*. A question sometimes raised on audit is whether an immature heifer or bull is placed in service when acquired for the herd—not bred or used to breed. Unfortunately, the law is not clear as to whether an immature animal can be depreciated. One argument against depreciating an immature animal is it is an appreciating asset and not a wasting asset. On the other hand, there is not authority for delaying depreciation until maturity when clearly the animal is otherwise eligible for depreciation. Therefore, the liberal approach would be to depreciate the animal when placed in the herd regardless of the state of maturity.

Extra First Year Depreciation

Breeding animals (cows and bulls) are eligible for the 20% additional first year depreciation subject to certain requirements. The animal can be new or used but must have an estimated useful life of at least six (6) years.

The 20% additional depreciation comes off the top and establishes a new basis for regular depreciation. The amount of depreciation is not prorated. The entire 20% is a depreciation deduction if the animal is placed in service during the year.

Auditing agents have on occasion questioned the taking of 20% additional depreciation on immature heifers. The law is not clear as to whether heifers are eligible for 20% depreciation. Whether or not the 20% can be applied to immature animals is dependent on eligibility for regular depreciation.

Some agents have permitted the 20% depreciation on heifers in the year purchased. Other agents have required the depreciation be delayed until the year the animal reaches maturity. In either event the depreciation can be taken—the matter in controversy is in what year.

The amount of 20% depreciation in any one year is limited to property cost of $10,000 for an individual and $20,000 for a joint return. The amount of actual deduction is thus limited to $2,000 and $4,000.

Recapture of Depreciation

Livestock became subject to the recapture of depreciation rules via the Tax Reform Act of 1969. The Amended Sec. 1245 (a) (2) (c) recaptures post-1969 depreciation or ordinary income to the extent of any gain on disposition. The amount of depreciation recapture will be insignificant in most grade cows as the adjusted tax basis will normally approximate the cull price.

Investment Credit

Livestock (except horses) held for breeding and dairy purposes are eligible for investment credit for the first time in the Revenue Act of 1971; the 7% credit against taxes is a good tax savings. On a $250 cow held for seven or more years, the credit would be $17.50. See upcoming section for more complete discussion.

Acceleration Depreciation Range (ADR)

The ADR added by Revenue Act of 1971 is intended to minimize disputes over the extent of depreciation. On assets placed in service after 1970, a taxpayer can continue to use estimated useful lives based on facts and circumstances or he can use a new class life system. The ADR permits a 20% variance from the established guideline class life for each class of assets as established by Rev. Proc. 62-21.

The guideline lives can be decreased or increased by 20% without justification. For example, a farmer could use 8 to 12 years useful life for equipment and 5½ to 8½ years for cattle.

Buildings can be included or excluded from ADR at the option of the taxpayer. If ADR is elected for the year, all other assets must be covered.

New IRC Section 1.67(m) permits use of the half-year convention on new purchases of individual items. Generally, under the half-year convention, a half year's depreciation is taken on all assets placed in service during the year. You can use variations of the half-year convention but no depreciation allowances are permitted which would *generally* provide larger depreciation allowances during the first year of service than would be permitted if all assets were placed in service ratably throughout the year.

If you elect to use the half-year convention, you can handle the depreciation in two ways: (1) Assets placed in service in the first half of the year are considered as being held the entire year and assets placed in service the last half of the year are considered as being placed in service at the end of the year with depreciation commencing the first of the next year; or (2) all assets can be considered as being placed in service at the midpoint of the year. For calendar year taxpayers, that means July 1.

Bibliography

AUTHORITY	FACTS OR QUOTE	HOLDING OR APPLICATION
1. IRC § 167 (a)	(a) General Rule. There shall be allowed as a depreciation deduction a reasonable allowance for the exhaustion, wear and tear (including a reasonable allowance for obsolescence)— (1) of property used in the trade or business or (2) of property held for the production of income.	
2. IRC § 167 (b)	(b) Use of Certain Methods and Rates. For taxable years ending after December 31, 1953, the term "reasonable allowance" as used in subsection (a) shall include (but shall not be limited to) an allowance computed in accordance with regulations prescribed by the Secretary or his delegate, under any of the following methods: (1) the straight line method, (2) the declining balance method, using a rate which would have been used had the annual allowance been computed under the method described in paragraph (1), (3) the sum of the years-digits method, and (4) any other consistent method productive of an annual allowance which, when added to all allowances for the period commencing with the taxpayer's use of the property and including the taxable year, does not, during the first two-thirds of the useful life of the property, exceed	

AUTHORITY	FACTS OR QUOTE	HOLDING OR APPLICATION
	the total of such allowances which would have been used had such allowances been computed under the method described in paragraph (2). Nothing in this subsection shall be construed to limit or reduce an allowance otherwise allowable under subsection (a).	
3. IRC § 167 (c)	(c) Limitations on Use of Certain Methods and Rates. Paragraphs (2), (3), and (4) of subsection (b) shall apply only in the case of property (other than intangible property) described in subsection (a) with a useful life of 3 years or more.	
4. IRC § 179 (a)	(a) General Rule. In the case of section 179 property, the term "reasonable allowance" as used in section 167(a) may, at the election of the taxpayer, include an allowance, for the first taxable year for which a deduction is allowable under section 167 to the taxpayer with respect to such property, of 20 percent of the cost of such property.	
5. IRC § 179 (b)	(b) Dollar Limitation. If in any one taxable year the cost of section 179 property with respect to which the taxpayer may elect an allowance under subsection (a) for such taxable year exceeds $10,000, then subsection (a) shall apply with respect to those items selected by the taxpayer, but only to the extent of an aggregate cost of $10,000. In the case of a husband and wife who file a joint return under section 6013 for the taxable year, the limitation under the preceding sentence shall be $20,000	

AUTHORITY	FACTS OR QUOTE	HOLDING OR APPLICATION
	in lieu of $10,000.	
6. IRC § 179 (d) (1)	(d) Definitions and Special Rules— (1) Section 179 Property. For purposes of this section, the term "section 179 property" means tangible personal property— (A) of a character subject to the allowance for depreciation under section 167.	
7. IRC Sec. 1245 (a) (2) (c)	Placed livestock under recapture of depreciation.	
8. IRC Reg. § 1.179-1 (a)	. . . a taxpayer (other than a trust) may elect for the first taxable year for which a deduction with respect to such property is allowable under section 167 to the taxpayer to include as part of the "reasonable allowance" allowable under section 167(a) an additional allowance of 20 percent of the cost or of a portion of the cost of such property. A trust is not eligible for the additional depreciation allowance under section 179. The allowance under section 179 is in addition to the depreciation allowable under section 167 computed on the balance of the unrecovered cost of the property after adjustment for the allowance under this section.	
9. IRC Reg. § 1.179-1 (b)	(b) Proration not required. The allowance under section 179 is determined without any proration based on the period of time the section 179 property has been in service during the taxable year.	

TAX TREATMENT OF GAINS

Internal Revenue Code Sec. 1231 provides for special treatment of the proceeds from sale of livestock held for breeding purposes. The advantage of being classified as a "Sec. 1231" asset is that all of gains and losses are added together. If losses exceed the gains, the gains and losses are treated as ordinary income and ordinary losses—the net losses are fully deductible. On the other hand, if the gains exceed the losses, the gains in excess of the losses are treated as a capital gain. The obvious advantage of a capital gain is that only 1/2 the gain is subject to tax further limited to the maximum tax on the first $50,000 and being no more than 25% of the gain.

To qualify for §1231 treatment, cattle and horses must be held (owned) for 24 months or more and must be held for breeding purposes. The key phrases that determine qualification are "held for 24 months" and "held for draft, dairy or breeding purposes."

The 24 months holding requirement commences with the date of acquisition which is the date of purchase, birth or death of decedent in the event of inherited property. Therefore, the primary prerequisite is that the animal must be owned for 24 months (stocks and real estate on the other hand need be held only six months) to qualify.

The "held for breeding purposes" are technical words relating to the purpose for which the animals are held. A cow is not necessarily eligible because it is a cow. For example, if the rancher is in the business of raising cows for sale, such cows would not qualify for § 1231 treatment.

Since § 1231 treatment is so advantageous, intensified effort should be made to qualify maximum numbers. The situations creating maximum capital gains treatment are:

1. Replacement heifers for the breeding herd.
2. Culling or "churning" the herd of undesirable animals.
3. Dispersal sale or herd liquidation.

Herd Replacements

Herd replacement by raised heifers should follow a set pattern for maximum qualification. For example, at roundup, heifers intended for the breeding herd could be cut from the herd and segregated if possible. As the animals mature, they should be continually surveyed and cut from the breeding herd for such reasons as not meeting herd standards, conformation, color, or failure to breed. These culled heifers intended to be held for the breeding herd should be considered § 1231 animals on sale. Of course, it could be considered unreasonable to keep all heifers for the breeding herd and, for example, eventually cut out half for the herd. Such cut animals need to be at least 12 months of age to qualify when sold.

Culling

Culling or "churning" the herd produces tax advantages for the cash-basis taxpayer, particularly for raised animals. The proceeds from the sale of the breeding livestock (assuming the taxpayer is on the cash method of accounting) are treated as a capital gain On the other hand, the cost of raising the animal has been written off as a current business expense. The older animals are culled out and new ones added in—the procedure has the effect of converting ordinary income to capital gain.

The amount of culling for any given herd should be commensurate with herd management. Tax implications should be considered a result of herd management as opposed to tax management dictating herd management. Ten percent of the herd per year is sometimes used as a culling rate rule of thumb. But the extent of culling according to good herd management will ultimately be dictated by range, cattle and weather conditions and capital considerations.

Liquidation

Herd liquidation or dispersal sale should qualify all breeding animals in excess of 24 months of age. Treas. Regs. Sec. 1.1231-2 (b)(2) sets out an example of when the entire breeding herd would qualify. The Treas. Regs. concede the earlier case decisions are outstanding examples of guidelines upon which the taxpayer can hang his hat and have a basis for planning. Sec. 1231 provides the animals must be 24 months old before being eligible for treatment as a § 1231 asset. Therefore, it reasonably follows that an animal on dispersal must be 24 months old to have the proceeds treated as a § 1231 asset.

The *Malat* v. *Riddell* case cited in the Bibliography may be cited in establishing the intent to hold for capital gains. This case defined "primarily" as meaning "of first importance." The question frequently arises in dispersal sale as to how many of the animals are eligible for capital gain. The statute interjects the subjective "intent to hold" element. As a consequence, objective actions are looked at to determine subjective intent—all of which is very confusing but vital to the taxpayer.

Recapture

The Tax Reform Act of 1969 attempted to recover as ordinary income previously taken deductions such as depreciation and losses. See the new legislation section for a discussion of recapture of land expenditures, depreciation on livestock and real property and Excess Deductions Account. All of these provisions can offset the Section 1231 advantages.

Bibliography

AUTHORITY	FACTS OR QUOTE	HOLDING OR APPLICATION
1. IRC § 1231(a)	(a) General Rule. If, during the taxable year, the recognized gains on sales or exchanges of property used in the trade or business, plus the recognized gains from the compulsory or involuntary conversion (as a result of destruction in whole or part, theft or seizure, or an exercise of the power of requisition or condemnation or the threat or imminence thereof) of property used in the trade or business and capital assets held for more than six months into other property or money, exceed the recognized losses from such sales, exchanges, and conversions, such gains and losses shall be considered as gains and losses from sales or exchanges of capital assets held for more than six months. If such gains do not exceed such losses, such gains and losses shall not be considered as gains and losses from sales or exchanges of capital assets . . .	
2. IRC § 1231(b)	(b) Definition of Property Used in the Trade or Business. For purposes of this section— (1) General Rule. The term "property used in the trade or business" means property used in the trade or business, of a character which is subject to the allowance for depreciation provided in section 167 . . .	
3. IRC § 1231(b)(3)	(3) Livestock.—Such term includes— (A) cattle and horses, regardless of age, held by the taxpayer for draft, breeding, dairy, or sporting purposes, and held by him for 24 months or more from the date of acquisition, and	

Bibliography

AUTHORITY	FACTS OR QUOTE	HOLDING OR APPLICATION
	(B) other livestock, regardless of age, held by the taxpayer for draft, breeding, dairy, or sporting purposes, and held by him for 12 months or more from the date of acquisition.	
4. Treas. Regs. § 1.1231-2 (a) (1)-(2)	Livestock held for draft, breeding, or dairy purposes. (a) (1) In the case of cattle, horses, or other livestock acquired by the taxpayer after December 31, 1969, section 1231 applies to the sale, exchange, or involuntary conversion of such cattle, horses, or other livestock, regardless of age, held by the taxpayer for draft, breeding, dairy, or sporting purposes, and held by him— (i) For 24 months or more from the date of acquisition in the case of cattle or horses, or (ii) For 12 months or more from the date of acquisition in the case of such other livestock. (2) In the case of livestock (including cattle or horses) acquired by the taxpayer on or before December 31, 1969, section 1231 applies to the sale, exchange, or involuntary conversion of such livestock, regardless of age, held by the taxpayer for draft, breeding, or dairy purposes, and held by him for 12 months or more from the date of acquisition.	

AUTHORITY	FACTS OR QUOTE	HOLDING OR APPLICATION
	(b) (1) Whether or not livestock is held by the taxpayer for draft, breeding, or dairy purposes depends upon all of the facts and circumstances in each case. The purpose for which the animal is held is ordinarily shown by the taxpayer's actual use of the animal. However, a draft, breeding, or dairy purpose may be present if an animal is disposed of within a reasonable time after its intended use for such purpose is prevented or made undesirable by reason of accident, disease, drought, unfitness of the animal for such purpose, or a similar factual circumstance. Under certain circumstances, an animal held for ultimate sale to customers in the ordinary course of the taxpayer's trade or business may be considered as held for draft, breeding, or dairy purposes. However, an animal is not held by the taxpayer for draft, breeding, or dairy purposes merely because it is suitable for such purposes or merely because it is held by the taxpayer for sale to other persons for use by them for such purposes. Futhermore, an animal held by the taxpayer for other purposes is not considered as held for draft, breeding, or dairy purposes merely because of a negligible use of the animal for such purposes or merely because of the use of the animal for such purposes as an ordinary or necessary incident to the other purposes for which the animal is held.	

AUTHORITY	FACTS OR QUOTE	HOLDING OR APPLICATION
	(c) These principles may be illustrated by the following examples: Example (1). An animal intended by the taxpayer for use by him for breeding purposes is discovered to be sterile or unfit for the breeding purposes for which it was held, and is disposed of within a reasonable time thereafter. This animal is considered as held for breeding purposes. Example (2). The taxpayer retires from the breeding or dairy business and sells his entire herd, including young animals which would have been used by him for breeding or dairy purposes if he had remained in business. These animals are considered as held for breeding or dairy purposes. The same would be true with respect to young animals which would have been used by the taxpayer for breeding or dairy purposes but which are sold by him in reduction of his breeding or dairy herd, because of, for example, drought. Example (5). The taxpayer is in the business of raising registered cattle for sale to others for use by them as breeding cattle. It is the business practice of this particular taxpayer to breed the offspring of his herd which he is holding for sale to others prior to sale in order to establish their fitness for sale as registered breeding cattle. In such case, the taxpayer's breeding of such offspring is an ordinary and necessary incident to his holding them for	

AUTHORITY	FACTS OR QUOTE	HOLDING OR APPLICATION
	breeding purposes. However, those cattle held by the taxpayer as additions or replacements to his own breeding herd to produce calves are considered to be held for breeding purposes, even though they may not actually have produced calves. Example (6). A taxpayer, engaged in the business of buying cattle and fattening them for slaughter, purchased cows with calf. The calves were born while the cows were held by the taxpayer. These cows are not considered as held for breeding purposes.	
5. *McDonald* v. *Comm.*, 214 F. 2d 341 (CA-2, 1954)	Breeding animals were sold before the animal reached maturity. The animals were held for the herd and would have been placed in the herd if they would have met all requirements.	Overturned the maturity requirement set up by IRS. Established the principle that immature animals culled from the herd would qualify as § 1231 assets.
6. *Estate of Smith*, 23 T.C. 690 (1955)	Rancher physically segregated breeding and sale herds. Sales were only occasionally made from breeding herd and the herd received preferential treatment.	Provide a basis for maximum herd qualification of §1231 treatment on sale of immature animals held for the breeding herd. The animals were culled from the herd and interjected the taxpayer's intent to "hold" for the herd.
7. *Hancock*, 31 T.C. 752 (1959)	Rancher was building a new herd and claimed all heifers were a part of the breeding herd. Only culls were sold–the bulk of the animals were placed in the breeding herd.	Court held that efforts were directed toward the breeding of the herd. The culls were thus eligible for § 1231 treatment.
8. *Cluck* v. *Comm.*, 29 T.C. 7 (1957), aff'd. 261 F. 2d 267 (CA-5, 1958)	Taxpayer conditioned culled breeding animals in the feedlot several months prior to sale as fattened cattle.	Held that animals continued to be breeding animals for purposes of § 1231 even if fattened. The fattening process did not convert from breeding to "held for sale."
9. *O'Neil* v. *U.S.*, 211 F. 2d 701 (CA-9, 1954)	The taxpayer had retained two-year-old heifers to be bred and eventually placed in the herd.	Further established the intent of the taxpayer in regard to the placing of young animals in

AUTHORITY	FACTS OR QUOTE	HOLDING OR APPLICATION
	However, due to drought conditions the heifers were sold before being bred. The taxpayer was permitted to treat the proceeds as capital gains.	the breeding herd. Section 1231 reads in terms of "held" for breeding purposes. An intervening cause such as a drought forced a sale and since the heifers were over 12 months of age they were then considered a § 1231 asset.
10. *Moore* v. *U.S.*, 246 F. Supp. 19 (N.D., Miss., 1965)	Taxpayer established sale herd, replacement herd and a breeding herd. Heifers were continually weeded out at approximately 12 to 14 months of age and were transferred to the replacement herd. The heifers were bred and remained in the replacement herd and were continually culled. Culling was also made from the breeding herd.	Followed *MacDonald* case. Gives a good rundown of the law eliminating the maturity test for culled animals. Reaffirms earlier decision and the practice of segregating sale and breeding herds.
11. *Malat* v. *Riddell*, 86 Sup. Ct. 1030 (1966)	This case involved the definition of IRC Sec. 1221 and the statutory language "held by the taxpayer primarily for sale to customers in the ordinary course of trade or business." The case involved real estate sales and whether the taxpayer had acquired the property for investment or whether the property was acquired for sale to customers. If held for investment then the gain on sale would be a capital gain.	The court defined "primarily" as "of first importance" or "principally." The decision refutes to a certain extent the government argument of dual purpose and permits the subjective intent of the taxpayer to be considered. Thus, if a taxpayer acquires property for investment and later deems it is to his best advantage to dispose of the property, then the capital gains would still be applicable. The case could have application in the culling of breeding animals or liquidating of a herd in that it could permit introduction of the taxpayer's intent to hold the animals for investment purposes, though the Treas. Regs. § 1231-2(a) recognizes the dispersal of a herd and culling from a herd. The regulations are primarily a result of litigation attacking sale of brood sows farrowing one year and sold the next.

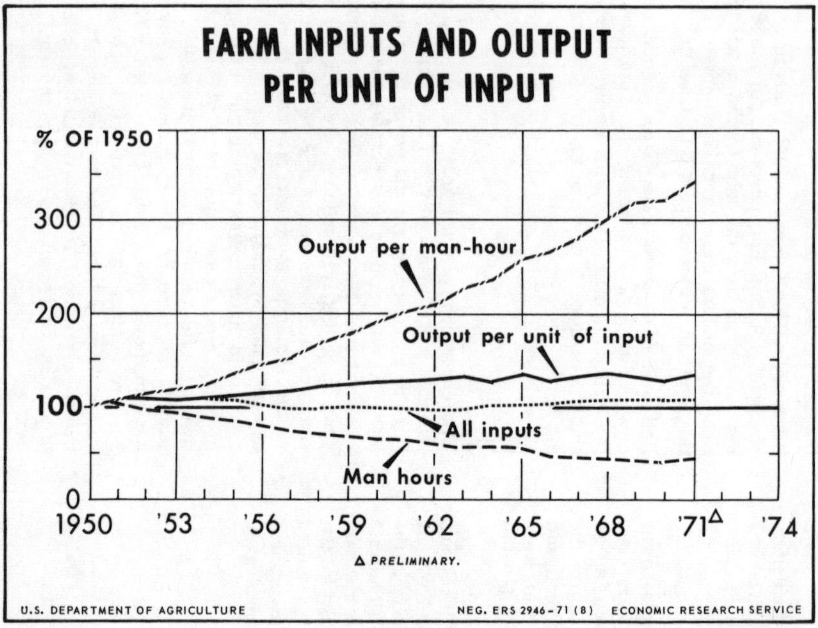

Never have such lines on a simple 20-year chart portrayed such a complete and cataclysmic revolution. All bets off! All preconceived formulas are obsolete. Nothing like this has ever happened before. Conventional agricultural economists can turn in their suits. Nobody knows where we're heading. (Courtesy U.S. Department of Agriculture)

Index

M